38.476234
WIL

D1351599

1933385

OF WALES, NEWPORT
LIBRARY
AND
INFORMATION
SERVICES
CAERLEON

STUDIES IN WELSH HISTORY

Editors

RALPH A. GRIFFITHS   CHRIS WILLIAMS
ERYN M. WHITE

19

A FORGOTTEN ARMY

FEMALE MUNITIONS WORKERS OF SOUTH WALES,
1939–1945

A FORGOTTEN ARMY

FEMALE MUNITIONS WORKERS OF SOUTH WALES, 1939–1945

by

MARI A. WILLIAMS

UNIVERSITY OF WALES, NEWPORT
LIBRARY
AND
INFORMATION
SERVICES
CAERLEON

Published on behalf of the
History and Law Committee
of the Board of Celtic Studies

CARDIFF
UNIVERSITY OF WALES PRESS
2002

© Mari A. Williams, 2002

British Library Cataloguing-in-Publication Data
A catalogue record for this book is available from the British Library.

ISBN 0-7083-1726-X

All rights reserved. No part of this book may be reproduced, stored in a retrieval system, or transmitted, in any form or by any means, electronic, mechanical, photocopying, recording or otherwise, without clearance from the University of Wales Press, 6 Gwennyth Street, Cardiff, CF2 4YD.
www.wales.ac.uk/press

The right of Mari A. Williams to be identified as the author of this work has been asserted by her in accordance with the Copyright, Designs and Patents Act 1988.

Every effort has been made to trace the copyright holders of the illustrative material in this volume, but in case of query please contact the publishers.

Jacket design by Jane Parry
Typeset at the University of Wales Press
Printed in Great Britain by Dinefwr Press, Llandybïe, Carmarthenshire

EDITORS' FOREWORD

Since the Second World War, Welsh history has attracted considerable scholarly attention and enjoyed a vigorous popularity. Not only have the approaches, both traditional and new, to the study of history in general been successfully applied to Wales's past, but the number of scholars engaged in this enterprise has multiplied during these years. These advances have been especially marked in the University of Wales.

In order to make more widely available the conclusions of recent research, much of it of limited accessibility in postgraduate dissertations and theses, in 1977 the History and Law Committee of the Board of Celtic Studies inaugurated a new series of monographs, *Studies in Welsh History*. It was anticipated that many of the volumes would originate in research conducted in the University of Wales or under the auspices of the Board of Celtic Studies. But the series does not exclude significant contributions made by researchers in other universities and elsewhere. Its primary aim is to serve historical scholarship and to encourage the study of Welsh history. Each volume so far published has fulfilled that aim in ample measure, and it is a pleasure to welcome the most recent addition to the list.

CONTENTS

ACKNOWLEDGEMENTS

This study is based on my thesis entitled ' "A Forgotten Army":
The Female Munitions Workers of South Wales, 1939–1945',
which was undertaken at the University of Wales, Cardiff, and
awarded the degree of Ph.D. in 1999. During the research
period and the preparation of this manuscript I received
invaluable assistance from a number of individuals and
institutions. I owe a great debt to the twenty-two former war
workers who welcomed me into their homes and so generously
shared their personal experiences and memories of wartime life.
Thanks are also due to the librarians and archivists at the
following institutions: Aberdare Public Library; Cardiff Central
Reference Library; Salisbury Library and the Arts and Social
Studies Library, University of Wales, Cardiff; Glamorgan
Record Office; Gwent Record Office; Mass-Observation
Archive, University of Sussex; Merthyr Tydfil Town Public
Library; Modern Records Centre, University of Warwick;
National Library of Wales, Aberystwyth; Pontypridd Public
Library; Public Record Office, Kew; South Wales Miners'
Library, Swansea; South Wales Coalfield Archive, University of
Wales, Swansea; Treorchy Public Library; and West Glamorgan
Record Office. Material from the Mass-Observation Archive is
reproduced with permission of Curtis Brown Ltd, London, on
behalf of the Trustees of the Mass-Observation Archive Copy-
right Trustees of the Mass-Observation Archive. I am also
extremely grateful for the financial assistance provided by the
Llewelyn Williams Postgraduate Studentship of the University of
Wales.

    My friends and colleagues at the University of Wales, Cardiff,
and at the University of Wales Centre for Advanced Welsh and
Celtic Studies, Aberystwyth, have been a constant source of
encouragement throughout the years and I thank them all for
their support and companionship. I am particularly indebted to

Professor Geraint H. Jenkins, Dr Bill Jones, Dot Jones and Professor Chris Williams for their assistance and good advice. Thanks are also due to Professor Dai Smith for providing the inspiration and creating the opportunities which first led me to pursue this study. I am grateful to the editors of the Studies in Welsh History Series for their helpful comments and advice on the original manuscript, and to Ruth Dennis-Jones and other staff at the University of Wales Press for their help in preparing the manuscript for publication. The last word and big thank-you must go to my family and particularly my father, Gwilym Alltwen Williams, for their support, encouragement and, above all, patience! *Diolch o galon.*

Mari A. Williams

LIST OF TABLES

LIST OF ILLUSTRATIONS

Between pages 156 and 157

ABBREVIATIONS

AEU	Amalgamated Engineering Union
CB	County Borough
DR	Directive Reply
FR	File Report
GRO	Glamorgan Record Office
GwRO	Gwent Record Office
MB	Municipal Borough
MFGB	Mineworkers' Federation of Great Britain
M-O A	Mass-Observation Archive
NLW	National Library of Wales
NUGMW	National Union of General and Municipal Workers
PP	Parliamentary Papers
PRO	Public Record Office
RD(C)	Rural District (Council)
ROF	Royal Ordnance Factory
SWCA	South Wales Coalfield Archive
SWMF	South Wales Miners' Federation
SWML	South Wales Miners' Library
TC	Topic Collection
TGWU	Transport and General Workers' Union
TLC	Trades and Labour Council
TNT	Trinitrotoluene
TUC	Trades Union Congress
UD(C)	Urban District (Council)
YMCA	Young Men's Christian Association
YWCA	Young Women's Christian Association

INTRODUCTION

Mr Hall, addressing a meeting of women industrial war workers at Aberaman on Sunday, described the occasion as 'unique'. It was. It marked very plainly the revolution which has taken place in the lives of thousands of women of this valley since war began. Their everyday lives are no longer bound by their homes, the street, and perhaps the unemployed club. All this large audience of women and girls (and many more in the valley) travel miles every day to work in great war factories and handle the most modern type of machine, pouring out the shells and the weapons which are enabling us to withstand, and eventually defeat, the dark challenge of the panzers and the Luftwaffe . . . War has opened the way for these women to enter Industry . . . Our MP says that the war factories now established in South Wales 'will play a big part in post-war reconstruction'. What will be women's role in all this? The question is full of possibilities. Women's life in South Wales may be transformed.[1]

In the eyes of the newspaper reporter who witnessed this historic meeting in July 1942 between the female war workers of Aberaman and George Hall, their local MP, the impact of the Second World War on the lives of the women of south Wales was undoubtedly remarkable.[2] By the summer of 1942 tens of thousands of local women had been drawn into the great industrial army which produced essential armaments for members of the British forces. The establishment of five Royal Ordnance Factories (ROFs) in the counties of Glamorgan and Monmouth – the largest of which, Bridgend ROF, employed *c.*35,000 workers at its peak – had played a crucial role in the creation of this predominantly female workforce.[3] Between 1939

---

[1] *Aberdare Leader*, 11 July 1942.
[2] 'South Wales' in the context of this study refers to the two counties of Glamorgan and Monmouth.
[3] D. A. Thomas, 'War and the economy: the south Wales experience', in Colin Baber and L. J. Williams (eds.), *Modern South Wales: Essays in Economic History* (Cardiff, 1986), pp. 251–77. The five Royal Ordnance Factories (ROFs) were situated at Bridgend, Hirwaun and Llanishen in Glamorgan, and Glascoed and Newport in Monmouthshire. A further three ROFs were established in Wales at the site of the old Nobel works at Pembrey in Carmarthenshire, at Marchwiel in Denbighshire and at Rhyd-y-mwyn, near Mold in Flintshire.

and 1945 the number of insured female workers in Wales
increased by 134 per cent, compared with an average increase of
just 30 per cent throughout the whole of Britain.[4] At the end of
the war it was reported that Wales had been one of the first
wartime 'regions' of Britain to employ more females than males
in the engineering industry and allied trades. Indeed, when wartime production reached its peak in 1943, 55 per cent of all
Welsh war workers were females compared with 52 per cent in
the north-west of England and under 50 per cent in all other
English regions.[5] In the industrial communities of south Wales,
where female employment opportunities had previously been
extremely limited, the scale and speed of the changes which
wartime conditions initiated in the lives of the female population
were quite astonishing. Small wonder, therefore, that writers and
historians would argue in later years that the wartime employment experience brought about a revolution in the lives of the
women of south Wales.[6]

Yet, despite the remarkable expansion in female work opportunities, it is surprising how little is known about the experiences
of the women who were employed in the large munitions
factories of south Wales during the Second World War. To those
who had witnessed this wartime revolution, the lack of attention
paid to Welsh female war workers by future historians would
have been difficult to comprehend. In 1943 Elizabeth Andrews,
the Labour Party's women's organizer in Wales, challenged
Welsh historians to take account of the experiences of Welsh
women when writing their histories of Wales. In her opinion, the
valuable contribution which the women of Wales were making
towards the war effort deserved to be acknowledged and documented by future writers: 'In these days of war for freedom and
democracy, when women are doing such noble work, to ignore
them is a grave injustice.'[7] Several decades later the historians of
Wales finally rose to the challenge and the work experiences of
Welsh women have in recent years received due attention and

---

[4] Brinley Thomas (ed.), *The Welsh Economy: Studies in Expansion* (Cardiff, 1962), p. 38.
[5] *Western Mail*, 9 May 1945.
[6] See E. D. Lewis, *The Rhondda Valleys* (London, 1959), p. 274; J. W. England, 'The
Merthyr of the twentieth century: a postscript', in Glanmor Williams (ed.), *Merthyr Politics:
The Making of a Working-Class Tradition* (Cardiff, 1966), pp. 82–101; Gareth Alban Davies,
'The fur coat', in Meic Stephens (ed.), *A Rhondda Anthology* (Bridgend, 1993), pp. 150–7.
[7] *Western Mail*, 9 January 1943.

recognition.[8] Regrettably, however, Elizabeth Andrews's calls for a detailed investigation of the effects of the Second World War upon the lives of the women of Wales – 'the most submerged of all groups'[9] – remain as yet to be answered. This examination of the experiences of the 'forgotten army'[10] of female munitions workers, who performed dangerous but vital work in the filling of shells and detonators, is one response to that appeal.

Since the 1970s historians and sociologists have debated at length the extent to which the wartime employment experience affected the lives of women across the world.[11] The impact of the war upon the lives of British women has featured prominently in the historiography, with discussion being focused on the apparent improvements which were initiated in the social and economic status of the female population. Writing in 1974, Arthur Marwick argued that the war 'meant a new economic and social freedom for women, the experience of which could never be entirely lost'.[12] In recent years, however, closer scrutiny of many aspects of the working lives of British women in the years before, during and after the war has exposed the need for a more cautious reading of events. While there can be little doubt that the new experiences of wartime employment brought about far-reaching changes in the everyday lives of British women, the assumption that war work initiated a greater equality between the sexes has been challenged. Historians such as Harold Smith and Penny Summerfield have drawn attention to the means by which pre-war gender divisions at the workplace and in the home were maintained throughout the war years, and were enshrined both in government policy and in the work and wage

---

[8] See, in particular, Angela V. John (ed.), *Our Mothers' Land: Chapters in Welsh Women's History, 1830–1939* (Cardiff, 1991); Jane Aaron et al. (eds.), *Our Sisters' Land: The Changing Identities of Women in Wales* (Cardiff, 1994); R. Merfyn Jones, *Cymru 2000: Hanes Cymru yn yr Ugeinfed Ganrif* (Caerdydd, 1999), ch. 9, pp. 137–51; Deirdre Beddoe, *Out of the Shadows: A History of Women in Twentieth-Century Wales* (Cardiff, 2000).

[9] David Smith, 'The future of coalfield history in south Wales', *Morgannwg*, XIX (1975), 57–70.

[10] The words of 'Respondent 16', a former employee of Bridgend ROF, interviewed by the author, 4 November 1991.

[11] For some of the more recent contributions to the debate, see Ruth Roach Pierson, *'They're Still Women After All': The Second World War and Canadian Womanhood* (Toronto, 1986); Nancy Baker Wise, *A Mouthful of Rivets: Women at Work in World War II* (San Francisco, 1994); Joy Damousi and Marilyn Lake (eds.), *Gender and War: Australians at War in the Twentieth Century* (Cambridge, 1995).

[12] Arthur Marwick, *War and Social Change in the Twentieth Century: A Comparative Study of Britain, France, Germany, Russia and the United States* (London, 1974), p. 160.

agreements signed by employers and trade unionists.[13] The visual and literary images constructed by government propagandists and advertisers also played an important function in this process,[14] for they placed their own limitations upon the roles expected of women both during and after the conflict.[15]

The female munitions workers of south Wales were subject to all these wider social, economic and cultural constraints, and their experiences of wartime employment should be evaluated accordingly. However, in order to assess accurately the impact which the war had on the general social and economic condition of the female workers of south Wales, it is vital that the discussion is located firmly in its Welsh economic, social and cultural context. Few works on the British wartime experience have paid due attention to the distinctive nature of the Welsh situation,[16] and Welsh historians have also failed to make any serious attempt to examine the impact of the Second World War upon the social and cultural life of Wales. Such studies are long overdue. In this examination of the experiences of the industrial communities of south Wales it will be seen that the wartime employment of thousands of local women initiated a rapid transformation in the social, economic and cultural life of the region. Since the mid-1920s the inhabitants of these communities had lived under the shadow of a deep and prolonged economic depression which brought the coal industry to its knees. Thousands were forced to leave south Wales in search of work,

[13]   See, in particular, Harold L. Smith, 'The effect of the war on the status of women', in idem (ed.), *War and Social Change: British Society in the Second World War* (Manchester, 1986), pp. 208–29; idem (ed.), *Britain in the Second World War* (Manchester, 1996), pp. 61–74; Gail Braybon and Penny Summerfield, *Out of the Cage: Women's Experiences in Two World Wars* (London, 1987); Penny Summerfield, 'Women, war and social change: women in Britain in World War II', in Arthur Marwick (ed.), *Total War and Social Change* (London, 1988), pp. 95–118; eadem, *Women Workers in the Second World War: Production and Patriarchy in Conflict* (London, 1989 edn); eadem, 'Approaches to women and social change in the Second World War', in Brian Brivati and Harriet Jones (eds.), *What Difference Did the War Make?* (London, 1993), pp. 63–79; eadem, ' "The girl that makes the thing that drills the hole that holds the spring . . .": discourses of women and work in the Second World War', in Christine Gledhill and Gillian Swanson (eds.), *Nationalising Femininity: Culture, Sexuality and British Cinema in the Second World War* (Manchester, 1996), pp. 35–52.
[14]   See J. D. Cartwell, *Images of War: British Posters, 1939–45* (London, 1989).
[15]   For a fuller discussion of this theme, see the following: Ruth Roach Pierson, 'Embattled femininity: Canadian womanhood and the Second World War', in T. G. Fraser and Keith Jeffery (eds.), *Men, Women and War* (Dublin, 1993), pp. 195–210; Deborah Montgomerie, 'Reassessing Rosie: World War II, New Zealand women and the iconography of femininity', *Gender and History*, 8, no. 1 (1996), 108–32.
[16]   Works which refer to the neutral stance taken by Plaid Genedlaethol Cymru (the Welsh Nationalist Party) during the war are the exceptions to the rule.

while the friends and families they left behind fought a long and bitter struggle against unemployment, poverty and ill-health. In many respects, therefore, the demands of wartime production brought immediate social and economic salvation to the area as thousands of new jobs were created in the purpose-built munitions factories. As W. H. Mainwaring, the Rhondda East MP, declared in 1946, 'this last terrible catastrophe in the world's history was actually a relief to South Wales, because the ghastly thing relieved us of unemployment.'[17]

Few could have anticipated that the vast majority of the workers who would gain employment in the new industrial establishments would be women. In 1931 females accounted for less than 20 per cent of the occupied population in the two counties of Glamorgan and Monmouth.[18] Moreover, female job opportunities were not only scarce, but were confined to a very narrow range of occupations associated predominantly with the service sector. Local reaction towards the mass wartime employment of females as industrial workers was likely, therefore, to be quite different from that recorded in districts where women had previously performed industrial work and had been employed in far greater numbers. In spite of the radical political tradition of the South Wales Coalfield, the opinions which many of its inhabitants, both male and female, expressed at the sight of a new female industrial workforce proved to be extremely conservative. It would appear that this society's long history of dependence upon unwaged female labour in the home made it difficult for some to accept the possibility that women could be more than just 'maids and mams'. In the industrial communities of south Wales, where the working lives of men and women had been strictly segregated, almost every aspect of the social culture had been shaped by the sexual division of labour. Life revolved around the fortunes of the male-dominated heavy industries, and as such the interests and concerns of the female population had always remained of secondary importance. For example, the lack of attention paid to 'women's issues' in the political life of the coalfield communities was a reflection of the lower cultural status afforded to their concerns. As Chris Williams has argued in his

---

[17] *Parliamentary Debates* (Hansard) (5th series), vol. 428, 390 (28 October 1946).
[18] *Census of England and Wales, 1931, Occupation Tables* (London, 1934), pp. 395, 410.

history of the politics and society of the Rhondda, 'considerations of occupational and class interest so dominated the ethos of the local Labour movement as to exclude almost completely any sense of gender.'[19]

In many ways, therefore, the war experience seemed to threaten the very premise on which the work and social culture of this industrial society had been based. As thousands of women entered the unfamiliar territory of the war factories, taking on the traditionally masculine and culturally superior role of industrial worker and wage-earner, conventional gender roles and identities were immediately challenged. The complex relationship between wars and the construction and reconstruction of gender has been the subject of much discussion and debate in recent years as historians have explored the means by which wartime conditions 'either alter or reinforce existing notions of gender'.[20] As Joy Damousi and Marilyn Lake have argued in their study of the Australian wartime experience, wars may have 'contradictory effects' on gender roles and relations, 'entrenching traditional stereotypes and expectations while at the same time providing the conditions in which those old patterns may be disrupted and dissolved'.[21] In view of the gendered nature of the social and economic changes which the Second World War brought to the lives of the people of south Wales, this concept has particular relevance to the Welsh experience. Although wartime conditions enforced a need to redefine and reinterpret some of the roles traditionally assigned to Welsh men and women, it was also the case that the war experience reinforced conventional expectations and gender values. Continual reference to the novelty and unfamiliarity of the wartime employment pattern also served to reinforce the notion that this was a temporary situation, established purely as an 'emergency' measure. For many contemporaries, the wartime entry of thousands of females into

---

[19] Chris Williams, *Democratic Rhondda: Politics and Society, 1885–1951* (Cardiff, 1996), p. 17.

[20] Margaret Randolph Higonnet et al. (eds.), *Behind the Lines: Gender and the Two World Wars* (New Haven, 1987), p. 5. See also Ruth Roach Pierson, 'Beautiful soul or just warrior: gender and war', *Gender and History*, 1, no. 1 (1989), 77–86; Miriam Cooke and Angela Woollacott (eds.), *Gendering War Talk* (Princeton, 1993); Penny Summerfield, *'My Dress for an Army Uniform': Gender Instabilities in the Two World Wars* (Lancaster, 1997); eadem, 'Gender and war in the twentieth century', *The International History Review*, XIX, no. 1 (1997), 3–15.

[21] Damousi and Lake (eds.), *Gender and War*, p. 5.

industrial employment in south Wales was interpreted as a social and economic anomaly. Although such disorder might be tolerated during wartime, it was hoped that at the end of the war the restoration of 'normal' employment patterns, with men as the chief breadwinners, would be assured.

Women's own responses to the changes which the war initiated in their working lives must also be considered carefully, for their personal testimonies may provide fresh insight into the diversity of experience, emotion and meaning which they attached to their wartime roles.[22] The dangers inherent in a history which is overly dependent upon the subjective evidence of the individual are all too clear, but there is little doubt that few other sources enable the historian to tap directly into the wide range of 'ambivalent memories' which wartime experiences evoked.[23] Commenting on her own experiences as a historian who collected and used autobiographical sources, Penny Summerfield noted that 'decisions about whether to work or not were by no means the only things that women remembered about their wartime experiences':

> It is possible to list others, many of which had both positive and negative sides to them. Such a list would include going into different work settings away from home, mixing with new people and coping with separation; learning different types of work and finding satisfaction or boredom in it; enjoying new opportunities for sociability and courtship as well as experiencing sexual harassment; dealing with fatigue and work-related health problems; coping with wartime shortages of food and clothing and with readjustments at the end of the war; feeling the exhilaration of contributing to the war effort as well as doubt about producing instruments of death.[24]

[22] For a discussion on the importance and value of subjective, individual testimonies in historical writing, see Raphael Samuel and Paul Thompson (eds.), *The Myths We Live By* (London, 1990), pp. 2–22.

[23] See, for example, Dorothy Sheridan, 'Ambivalent memories: women and the 1939–45 war in Britain', *Oral History*, 18, no. 1 (1990), 32–40; Bridget Macey, 'Social dynamics of oral history making: women's experiences of wartime', ibid., 19, no. 2 (1991), 42–8; Mavis Nicholson, *What Did You Do in the War, Mummy? Women in World War II* (London, 1995).

[24] Summerfield, 'Approaches to women and social change in the Second World War', p. 72. For an incisive study of the interaction between popular discourse and women's personal accounts of their wartime experiences, see eadem, *Reconstructing Women's Wartime Lives: Discourse and Subjectivity in Oral Histories of the Second World War* (Manchester, 1998).

Regrettably, very little autobiographical material relating to
women's war work is available to the Welsh historian. Although
the recollections of some of the female munitions workers of
south Wales have been voiced publicly in recent years,[25] only one
collection of written accounts of the wartime memories of Welsh
women has so far appeared in print.[26] Surprisingly few references
are made to factory employment in British women's wartime
fiction and none relates to the Welsh experience; moreover,
attempts to trace unpublished memoirs by Welsh women war
workers have so far proved fruitless.[27] In a bid to redress this
situation and to recover the lost voices of the 'forgotten army' of
Welsh female munitions workers, this study incorporates the oral
evidence of twenty-two former war workers who were interviewed by the author between 1991 and 1993.[28] The varied and,
at times, conflicting personal recollections of these women serve
as an important complement to the body of documentary
evidence which does not always succeed in telling their story. In
their reminiscences, former war workers frequently expressed the
opinion that their wartime contribution was not adequately
recognized.[29] Munitions workers did not feature prominently in
post-war Victory marches nor on war memorials, and until
recently they remained conspicuously absent from the history
books. This volume seeks to redress that situation by highlighting
the vital role played by the Welsh 'munitionettes' in the Second
World War. In addition to contributing to the poorly documented field of Welsh women's history, it offers an excellent
opportunity to examine several other much-neglected aspects of
Welsh history. The role played by Wales and its people in

---

[25] BBC Radio Wales broadcast, 'The girls who made the thing-ummy-bobs',
7 November 1989; Fay Swain, *Wales and the Second World War: Women* (Bridgend, 1989),
pp. 12–19; Philip Tapper and Susan Hawthorne, *Wales and the Second World War*
(Bridgend, 1991), pp. 41–7; Mark Davies (ed.), *The Valleys Autobiography: A People's History of
the Garw, Llynfi and Ogmore Valleys* (Blaengarw, 1992), pp. 73–4; Hilda H. Price,
'Experiences in World War II', *Llafur*, 6, no. 1 (1992), 110–13.
[26] Leigh Verrill-Rhys and Deirdre Beddoe (eds.), *Parachutes and Petticoats: Welsh Women
Writing on the Second World War* (Dinas Powys, 1992).
[27] See Jenny Hartley, *Millions Like Us: British Women's Fiction of the Second World War*
(London, 1997).
[28] Transcripts of the recordings have been deposited at the South Wales Miners'
Library (SWML), Swansea, and the Museum of Welsh Life, Cardiff.
[29] Evidence of Respondents 3, 4, 5 and 16; BBC Radio Wales broadcast, 'The girls
who made the thing-ummy-bobs', 7 November 1989; evidence of Edna Gorshkov in
Verrill-Rhys and Beddoe (eds.), *Parachutes and Petticoats*, pp. 83–4.

the war effort has received scant attention in the past, and this examination of the experiences of the female munitions workers may be seen as an important contribution to the wider historiographical debate on the impact of the Second World War on Welsh society.

In this study of the experiences of the female munitions workers of south Wales, full consideration will be given to the themes outlined above. Beginning with an examination of the working lives of the women of south Wales before the war, chapter 1 provides essential background to the wartime experience. The limitations of the working experiences of Welsh women during the inter-war years contrasted sharply with the opportunities which became available as a result of wartime production demands. Chapter 2 traces the steps which led to the creation of the new Welsh female industrial workforce and examines the reaction of the women themselves, as well as their employers, trade union representatives and members of the local community, towards their role as munitions workers. Although many contemporary observers were of the opinion that the lives of the local female population had been transformed by their experiences of wartime employment, the evidence presented in chapter 3 reveals that conventional expectations regarding their responsibilities towards their homes and families were firmly maintained. On a personal level, however, there can be no doubt that the Second World War had a profound impact on the lives of the female war workers of south Wales. When production began at the large munitions factories located in the region and further afield, thousands of women suddenly found themselves working in new and unfamiliar surroundings, earning wages which provided opportunities for an equally unfamiliar measure of social and economic independence. Chapter 4 looks at the ways in which the war broadened the personal experiences and outlook of the female population, and examines local reaction to the wartime change in the economic and social profile of the Welsh munitions workers. The wider social and economic implications of the war are examined in chapter 5, where attention is focused on the patterns of female employment in south Wales in the years immediately following the war. The study concludes with an assessment of the legacy of the wartime experience for the women of the industrial communities of south Wales.

I

'MAIDS AND MAMS': WOMEN'S WORK BEFORE THE SECOND WORLD WAR

In its *Industrial Survey of South Wales*, which was published in 1932, the Board of Trade concluded that 'one of the outstanding characteristics of the industrial life of the region' was the extremely small proportion of female to male workers.[1] The 1921 census had revealed that females accounted for only 17.4 per cent of the total occupied population in the survey district, while in England and Wales they comprised almost 30 per cent.[2] At this time the economy of south Wales was almost wholly dependent on the heavy industries of coal, iron and steel, and few employment opportunities existed for women. From the early 1920s onwards, however, the fortunes of the south Wales coal industry spiralled downwards and between 1921 and 1936, when 241 pits were closed, the associated male workforce was almost halved.[3] In the aftermath of the General Strike and miners' lockout of 1926 the region was plunged into a deep and prolonged economic depression, and the following decade was dominated by high unemployment rates and a consequent increase in poverty and ill-health.[4] By 1931 the percentage of insured persons who were unemployed in the counties of Glamorgan and Monmouth stood at 35.3 per cent and remained at over 30 per cent for the next six years. The problem was at its most severe in the coalfield, and on different occasions during the 1930s over 80 per cent of all insured males were registered as unemployed at black spots such as Ferndale, Merthyr Tydfil and Blaina.[5]

For the female inhabitants of these coalfield communities, this about-turn in the fortunes of the coal industry presented many new and difficult challenges as established employment practices

[1] Board of Trade, *An Industrial Survey of South Wales* (London, 1932), p. 7.
[2] Ibid.
[3] Hywel Francis and David Smith, *The Fed: A History of the South Wales Miners in the Twentieth Century* (London, 1980), p. 33.
[4] See Mari A. Williams, '"In the wars": Wales 1914–1945', in Gareth Elwyn Jones and Dai Smith (eds.), *The People of Wales* (Llandysul, 1999), pp. 188–98.
[5] Ministry of Labour, *Local Unemployment Index* (London, 1931–9).

were slowly transformed, enforcing a re-evaluation of the region's traditional economic dependence upon male labour. When male members of the household found themselves unable to find work, many of their daughters and wives became the sole wage-earners in their families, eking out a living through serving others in shops and homes. Between 1923 and 1930 the number of insured females in south Wales increased by 13 per cent, whereas the number of insured males fell by 7 per cent.[6] Members of the unemployed male population regarded this state of affairs as unacceptable and, as the depression wore on, calls for a solution to the economic problems of south Wales became clamant. Yet few unemployed men could take comfort from the proposals which were mooted in the early 1930s by government planners and economic advisers. Plans to restructure the industrial and economic base of south Wales suggested making greater use of the large reservoir of untapped female labour, while no effective solution to the problem of long-term male unemployment seems to have been identified.

Given the complete dominance of the coal industry in the region, it is perhaps not surprising that the fears and aspirations of the male workforce were to overshadow those of the female population in the history of south Wales during this period. Indeed, the prevailing image of the unemployed miner has proved something of an obstacle for historians who have attempted to address the experiences of the women who were also members of this 'unemployed' society. As Andrew J. Chandler has argued in his study of unemployment in the South Wales Coalfield during the inter-war years:

> The myth of the 'unemployed man' is just one more encumbrance to the historian of inter-war Wales. Not only does it exclude the experience of women, in the more real sense of 'the unemployed family' (i.e. the un-waged family), but it is also an image linked to the idea of the uniform operation of the processes of immiseration and demoralisation on and throughout coalfield society during the period.[7]

---

[6]   Board of Trade, *An Industrial Survey of South Wales*, p. 18.
[7]   Andrew J. Chandler, 'The re-making of a working class: migration from the South Wales Coalfield to the new industry areas of the Midlands *c.*1920–1940' (unpublished Ph.D. thesis, University of Wales, 1988), p. 52.

Recent studies of the lives of Welsh women during the inter-war period have shown a greater awareness of the wide range of living and working conditions experienced by women of different ages, marital and occupational status.[8] In the world of work, in particular, the opportunities made available to single and married females could be starkly different, and it is important to recognize the dangers of generalizing the female experience of employment during this period. Moreover, the concept and nature of the 'work' which females performed must be placed firmly within its context and evaluated accordingly.[9] Although only a minority of the female population of south Wales was enumerated as being engaged in full-time employment, the reality was that the vast majority of women undertook 'work' of some kind, albeit casual, part-time or even unwaged work which was often performed within the informal setting of the home.[10]

In view of the fact that official employment statistics collated by various government departments and offices took no account of such work and enumerated only those females who were engaged in full-time paid employment, it was hardly surprising that south Wales returned one of the lowest female participation rates in Britain.[11] Indeed, during the first half of the twentieth century, the activity rate of the Welsh female population remained consistently lower than that of females in all other parts of England and Wales.[12]

As table 1.1 shows, less than 20 per cent of females in the working age groups were recorded as being gainfully occupied in Glamorgan and Monmouthshire during 1921 and 1931. Although the percentage of occupied females increased from 32.3 to 34.2 per cent in England and Wales between 1921 and

[8] See Deirdre Beddoe, 'Women between the wars', in Trevor Herbert and Gareth Elwyn Jones (eds.), *Wales between the Wars* (Cardiff, 1988), pp. 128–60; eadem, 'Munitionettes, maids and mams: Women in Wales, 1914–1939', in John (ed.), *Our Mothers' Land*, pp. 189–209.

[9] See John (ed.), *Our Mothers' Land*, pp. 1–2; R. E. Pahl (ed.), *On Work: Historical, Comparative and Theoretical Approaches* (Oxford, 1988).

[10] See Mari A. Williams, 'Aspects of women's working lives in the mining communities of south Wales, *c*.1891–1939', *Folk Life*, 38 (2000), 56–70.

[11] The participation (or activity) rate is the number per 1,000 women with jobs.

[12] See E. James, 'Women at work in twentieth century Britain', *Manchester School of Economic and Social Studies*, XXX (1960), 283–99; L. J. Williams and Dot Jones, 'Women at work in nineteenth century Wales', *Llafur*, 3, no. 3 (1982), 20–32; Dot Jones, 'Serfdom and slavery: women's work in Wales, 1890–1930', in Deian R. Hopkin and Gregory S. Kealey (eds.), *Class, Community and the Labour Movement: Wales and Canada, 1850–1930* (Aberystwyth, 1989), pp. 86–100.

Table 1.1: Number of females occupied and percentage as total in age group,[1] 1911–1931

Area[2]	1911		1921		1931	
	Number	%	Number	%	Number	%
Glamorgan	81409	20.2	89227	19.6	89529	19.8
Monmouthshire	27134	19.4	28367	17.7	27731	17.9
Wales	215681	23.6	213149	21.2	206139	21.0
England and Wales	4830734	32.5	5065332	32.3	5606043	34.2

[1] 1911: aged 10 and over; 1921: aged 12 and over; 1931: aged 14 and over.
[2] In this table, and all that follow, Glamorgan and Monmouthshire = administrative counties of Glamorgan and Monmouthshire (with associated County Boroughs).
Source: 1911, 1921 and 1931 Census Occupation Tables.

Table 1.2: Number of occupied males and females and percentage as total in age group,[1] 1921–1931

Area	1921				1931			
	Males		Females		Males		Females	
	Number	%	Number	%	Number	%	Number	%
Glamorgan	**421097**	**88.5**	**89227**	**19.6**	**415371**	**90.8**	**89529**	**19.8**
Cardiff CB	69357	89.4	22921	29.1	72622	90.0	27700	30.9
Merthyr Tydfil CB	27239	88.3	4713	16.4	24932	91.7	3913	15.3
Swansea CB	52629	88.7	14374	23.5	55195	90.8	15103	23.5
Aberdare UD	18699	89.2	2802	14.2	17597	92.0	2470	13.8
Bridgend UD	2969	83.5	968	26.9	3209	88.2	1109	27.7
Maesteg UD	9625	88.8	1332	13.6	8723	91.3	1041	12.1
Mountain Ash UD	14392	88.6	1840	12.5	13390	91.9	1516	11.8
Neath MB	6327	87.9	1600	22.4	11528	91.6	2565	20.3
Ogmore and Garw UD	10204	88.9	1193	12.0	9766	93.3	944	10.8
Pontypridd UD	15752	88.9	2943	17.9	14004	89.5	2593	17.3
Rhondda UD	55889	89.8	6831	12.5	50461	92.4	5484	11.4
Monmouthshire	**153456**	**88.9**	**28367**	**17.7**	**149475**	**91.3**	**27731**	**17.9**
Newport CB	31096	88.5	8823	25.0	30013	91.4	9079	26.2
Abertillery UD	13180	89.6	1521	11.9	11450	93.7	1221	11.6
Blaenavon UD	4591	91.2	555	12.7	4049	92.1	461	12.1
Ebbw Vale UD	12273	90.3	1593	13.4	11164	92.4	1316	12.5
Nantyglo & Blaina UD	5568	89.1	614	11.1	4466	89.8	481	10.7
Pontypool UD	2339	91.0	565	22.7	2337	94.1	472	19.8
Tredegar UD	8668	90.0	1214	14.4	8108	91.2	1000	12.9

[1] 1921: aged 12 and over; 1931: aged 14 and over.
Source: 1921 and 1931 Census Occupation Tables.

1931, largely as a result of the employment opportunities which were created in the new industry areas of London, the south-east and the English Midlands,[13] in south Wales the few jobs that were available to members of the female population remained extremely limited.[14] There were also considerable variations in the number and proportion of females who were occupied in the two counties of Glamorgan and Monmouth, with larger commercial centres such as Cardiff, Swansea, Bridgend and Newport offering far greater opportunities for employment than the smaller coal-mining settlements (table 1.2). As the authors of the *Second Industrial Survey of South Wales* reported in 1937:

> it must be remembered that the customs of family life in large towns permit girls greater freedom in seeking paid work than do those of mining valleys: domestic work is not so heavy, the average age at which marriage takes place is probably higher, and the prejudice against the taking of paid employment by married women is certainly less in the towns than in the valleys.[15]

An examination of the 1921 and 1931 census occupation tables reveals that, although female work opportunities in retail, clerical and professional occupations increased in the administrative districts of Glamorgan and Monmouthshire during that decade, the vast majority of occupied females, both in the larger towns and in the smaller mining settlements, continued to be employed in the service industry. In the Cardiff CB, where 30.9 per cent of the 89,740 females aged fourteen years and over were occupied in 1931, 11,128 (40.2 per cent) were employed in the personal service sector. Although only 10.8 per cent of the 8,773 females aged fourteen years and over were returned as occupied in the Ogmore and Garw UD in 1931, the proportion employed in the personal service sector was also extremely high and had

---

[13] See Neal A. Ferguson, 'Women's work: employment opportunities and economic roles, 1918–1939', *Albion*, 7, no. 1 (1975), 55–68; Sylvia Anthony, *Women's Place in Industry and Home* (London, 1932), p. 20.

[14] Even in districts such as Swansea and Neath, where women had once been employed in great numbers in the tinplate industry, opportunities had contracted as a result of both the wider economic depression and the increased mechanization of work processes. PP 1929–30 (XVII, Cmd. 3508), *A Study of the Factors which have Operated in the Past and those which are Operating now to Determine the Distribution of Women in Industry*, pp. 17–18.

[15] *Second Industrial Survey of South Wales* (3 vols., Cardiff, 1937), II, pp. 82–3.

increased from 39.1 per cent in 1921 to 43.2 per cent.[16] As was the situation in many other mining districts, female work opportunities in the Ogmore and Garw UD were limited to an extremely narrow range of occupations and, aside from domestic service, shop work or a position in the teaching profession, little else was available for the female population.

It should be stressed, however, that census figures did not provide a true picture of the numbers of females who were involved in paid work during this period.[17] For example, females who worked on a part-time or casual basis were simply not counted and their economic contribution passed unrecognized. Similarly, statistics compiled by the Ministry of Labour showing the unemployment rates at local employment exchanges within the region were also poor indicators of the true number of females who were 'out of work'. In the first instance, all those registered as unemployed at employment exchanges would have to be insured, a criterion which immediately excluded the majority of both occupied and unoccupied females.[18] In its report on the industrial condition of 'South Wales and Monmouthshire' (an area which included Glamorgan, Monmouthshire and part of Carmarthenshire) which was published in 1934, the Ministry of Labour recorded that the total number of insured females in the whole region was around 14,000 – a figure which accounted for only 10.7 per cent of the total number of females who were registered as occupied in the area in 1931.[19]

The majority of females who lived in Glamorgan and Monmouthshire were classed, therefore, neither as 'gainfully occupied' nor as 'unemployed' but as 'unoccupied'. In the Rhondda UD in 1931, 88.6 per cent of the 47,906 females aged fourteen years and over were returned as 'unoccupied', while in the Nantyglo and Blaina UD in Monmouthshire the proportion was as high as 89.3 per cent. Even in the commercial centres of Cardiff and Swansea almost 70 per cent of females over the age

[16]   *Census of England and Wales, 1931, Occupation Tables*, pp. 395, 576.

[17]   See Bridget Hill, 'Women, work and the census: a problem for historians of women', *History Workshop Journal*, no. 35 (1993), 78–94.

[18]   See W. R. Garside, *The Measurement of Unemployment: Methods and Sources in Great Britain, 1850–1979* (Oxford, 1980).

[19]   PP 1933–4 (XIII, Cmd. 4728), *Ministry of Labour, Reports of Investigations into the Industrial Conditions in Certain Depressed Areas. Vol. III, South Wales and Monmouthshire*, p. 140.

of fourteen were similarly enumerated.[20] It is clear that the
official statistics provided by both the census and the Ministry of
Labour failed to give an accurate picture of the working experiences of the female population. No account was taken of the
contribution which women made to the family and the local
economy through casual, part-time work, while the vital but
unwaged work which 'unoccupied' females performed in their
homes was simply not acknowledged.

The vast majority of the 'unoccupied' female population of
south Wales were married women whose experiences of work
were located firmly in the domestic sphere. Between 1911 and
the outbreak of the Second World War, married women formed
only about 10 per cent of the labour force of England and
Wales.[21] The marriage bars which were applied in many of the
professions, including the civil service, the banking profession
and retail sector, served as a powerful practical and ideological
barrier against the employment of married women. Local education authorities in the counties of Glamorgan and Monmouth
also forcefully applied a marriage bar in the teaching profession
throughout the inter-war years.[22] For the majority of women in
south Wales, therefore, the act of getting married signalled the
end of their careers as full-time paid workers. In an area
dominated by heavy industry, marriage was an important stage
in the female life-cycle, and in the county of Glamorgan in 1931
nearly 70 per cent of all women aged between twenty and fifty-
nine were married – a proportion which rose to over 75 per cent
in the mining communities.[23] Very few married women held full-
time occupations outside their homes, and this fact was deeply
entrenched in the employment culture of the region. As stated by
Gwynne Meara, there was a 'stronger feeling in favour of women
staying home than in other parts of the country', and this was
also noted by D. G. R. Belshaw.[24]

---

[20] *Census of England and Wales, 1931, Occupation Tables*, pp. 395, 410, 579.
[21] Jane Lewis, *Women in England, 1870–1950: Sexual Divisions and Social Change* (Hemel
Hempstead, 1984), p. 55.
[22] See Alison M. Oram, 'Serving two masters? The introduction of a marriage bar in
teaching in the 1920s', in London Feminist History Group (ed.), *The Sexual Dynamics of
History* (London, 1983), pp. 134–48.
[23] *Census of England and Wales, 1931, County of Glamorgan* (London, 1932), pp. 30–3.
[24] Gwynne Meara, *Juvenile Unemployment in South Wales* (Cardiff, 1936), p. 44; D. G. R.
Belshaw, *The Changing Economic Geography of Merthyr Tydfil* (Merthyr Tydfil, 1955), p. 27.

Table 1.3: Marital status of the occupied female workforce (aged twelve and over), shown as percentage occupied in marital group, 1921

Area	Marital status as % occupied			Total occupied females	Occupied as % in marital group		
	S	M	W/D		S	M	W/D
Glamorgan	83.2	8.9	7.9	19.6	42.2	3.3	18.0
Cardiff CB	83.0	8.7	8.3	29.2	58.7	5.2	24.4
Merthyr Tydfil CB	81.3	9.1	9.6	16.4	35.7	2.8	17.1
Swansea CB	84.3	7.4	8.2	23.5	49.5	3.5	8.2
Aberdare UD	83.8	8.2	8.1	14.2	31.8	2.2	12.8
Rhondda UD	82.1	10.9	7.0	12.5	28.6	2.4	11.3
Monmouthshire	83.1	9.3	7.6	17.7	39.2	3.0	17.1
Newport CB	85.1	7.5	7.4	25.0	53.4	3.6	20.8
South Wales[1]	83.3	8.9	7.8	18.9	41.0	3.2	17.7
England and Wales	77.9	13.7	8.4	32.7	60.9	9.1	26.1

S: Single; M: Married; W/D: Widowed/Divorced
[1] The 'South Wales Region' comprised part of Monmouthshire, part of Breconshire, part of Carmarthenshire and the whole of the administrative county of Glamorgan (with associated County Boroughs).
Source: 1921 Census Occupation Tables.

Married women comprised a small percentage of the occupied female workforce of south Wales, and the actual number of married women who worked accounted for only a tiny percentage of the total number of married women. As table 1.3 shows, in 1921 when 9.1 per cent of all married women in England and Wales were occupied, only 3.2 per cent of married women were returned as occupied in the 'South Wales Region',[25] and 3.3 per cent and 3 per cent in the counties of Glamorgan and Monmouth respectively. In the mining areas the number of married women who were engaged in full-time employment was particularly low. In the Aberdare and Rhondda UDs, where married women accounted for 8.2 per cent and 10.9

[25] See footnote to Table 1.3 above

per cent of the occupied female workforce respectively, their participation rate in the two areas stood at only 2.2 per cent and 2.4 per cent.[26] Between 1921 and 1931 the proportion of married women in the occupied female workforce of England and Wales increased from 13.7 per cent to 16 per cent. Unfortunately, the 1931 census does not provide a detailed breakdown of the marital status of occupied females at a local level. However, even if a slight increase in the proportion of occupied married women was also recorded in the counties of Glamorgan and Monmouth, the participation rate of the married women of south Wales would still have remained extremely low.

The vast majority of the married women of south Wales were preoccupied with domestic responsibilities and, in the mining districts, women provided a vital service to their menfolk and to the coal industry by carrying out a daily round of heavy domestic chores, often at great cost to their own health and welfare.[27] In homes which lacked piped water, electricity and labour-saving appliances, the lot of the miner's wife involved a great deal of heavy and labour-intensive work.[28] It is clear that many women regarded their role within the home as a full-time occupation and undertook their domestic chores in a strict and orderly fashion. Indeed, an official from the Porth (Rhondda) branch of the Co-operative Women's Guild maintained in 1936 that 'domesticity' was 'the main occupation and the basis of existence for most women' in the area.[29] The oral evidence collected by Rosemary Crook in the Rhondda suggests that the uniformity of

[26] *Census of England and Wales, 1921, County of Glamorgan* (London, 1923), pp. 71–2.

[27] See Dot Jones, 'Counting the cost of coal: women's lives in the Rhondda, 1881–1911', in John (ed.), *Our Mothers' Land*, pp. 109–33; Mari A. Williams, 'Yr ymgyrch i "achub y mamau" yng nghymoedd diwydiannol de Cymru, 1918–1939', in Geraint H. Jenkins (ed.), *Cof Cenedl XI: Ysgrifau ar Hanes Cymru* (Llandysul, 1996), pp. 117–46.

[28] For first-hand evidence of the domestic work performed by women in the mining households of south Wales, see Rosemary Crook, ' "Tidy women": women in the Rhondda between the wars', *Oral History*, 10, no. 12 (1982), 40–6; Bill Jones and Beth Thomas, *Teyrnas y Glo: Golwg Hanesyddol ar Fywyd ym Meysydd Glo Cymru/Coal's Domain: Historical Glimpses of Life in the Welsh Coalfields* (Cardiff, 1993), pp. 21–4; Dei Treanor et al. (eds.), *Green, Black and Back: The Story of Blaenllechau* (Treorchy, 1994); S. Minwel Tibbott and Beth Thomas, *O'r Gwaith i'r Gwely: Cadw tŷ, 1890–1960/A Woman's Work: Housework, 1890–1960* (Cardiff, 1994); Carol White and Sian Rhiannon Williams (eds.), *Struggle or Starve: Women's Lives in the South Wales Valleys between the Two World Wars* (Dinas Powys, 1998). For a male perspective, see the following works by two south Wales miners: B. L. Coombes, *These Poor Hands: The Autobiography of a Miner Working in South Wales* (London, 1939), pp. 40–1; and Wil Jon Edwards, *From the Valley I Came* (London, 1956), pp. 11–12.

[29] *The Rhondda Clarion*, no. 5, February 1936.

the women's experiences, replicating those of their menfolk underground, led to the creation of a separate female work culture which centred on their domestic experiences.[30] Research undertaken by Elizabeth Roberts and Joanna Bourke reveals that this was characteristic of female behaviour in other close-knit working-class communities in Britain, where women developed their own sets of neighbourhood values and moral codes which were often directly linked to domestic achievements.[31] Several of the commentators who visited the working-class homes of south Wales during the inter-war years were full of admiration for the high standards of housekeeping maintained by their female occupants. Observers remarked that even during periods of extreme economic hardship, the wives of the unemployed men of south Wales took great pride in ensuring that their children looked neat and presentable and strove 'to maintain a cheerful demeanour in a family that has little cause for cheerfulness, and keep house when the circumstances that made housework orderly cease to exist'.[32] Gwynne Meara, who visited several homes in south Wales during the course of his inquiry into juvenile unemployment in the early 1930s, was clearly impressed by what he saw:

> Generally, housewives in South Wales are house-proud, and the gleaming brass and shining steel are a measure of that pride. Perhaps nothing is more eloquent of the strength and pride of these people, in the face of dire hardship, than the common saying that it does not cost anything to be clean.[33]

In recent years this emphasis upon cleanliness and order within the home has been interpreted as an expression of women's power or control over this dominant aspect of their lives. Success in the home could be translated as a triumph over adverse conditions or, as Angela V. John has suggested, 'an

---

[30]   Crook, 'Tidy women', 41.

[31]   Joanna Bourke, *Working-Class Cultures in Britain, 1890–1960: Gender, Class and Ethnicity* (London, 1994), pp. 67–71; Elizabeth Roberts, *A Woman's Place: An Oral History of Working-Class Women, 1890–1940* (Oxford, 1995 edn), pp. 192–4; eadem, *Women and Families: An Oral History, 1940–1970* (Oxford, 1995), pp. 210–11.

[32]   *Annual Report of the Aberdare Medical Officer of Health, 1928* (Aberdare, 1929), p. 10; PP 1934–5 (X, Cmd. 4957), *First Report of the Commissioner for the Special Areas (England and Wales)*, p. 136.

[33]   Meara, *Juvenile Unemployment in South Wales*, p. 97.

assertion of control . . . which, implicitly, if not openly, acknowledged a workplace and one which was their own, under their control'.[34] There is much evidence to suggest that in the mining communities of south Wales, as in other working-class districts, it was the women who were regarded as the 'bosses' of their homes.[35] In reality, however, the level of authority or 'power' which they actually wielded, both in their homes and in their wider communities, was extremely limited.[36] As Jane Elliott maintains, the ideology which lay behind the creation of the Welsh Mam, was based firmly on maintaining the strict sexual division of labour both within and outside the home:

> the image conveys a set of dominant values regarding women's role in society . . . whatever the *reality* may have been, the *idea* that the woman's principal responsibility was in the home, whilst her husband was the primary breadwinner, represented dominant thinking both inside and outside South Wales.[37]

This powerful ideal also served to reinforce the notion that women should be solely responsible for managing domestic tasks. Consequently, in many of the mining districts of south Wales the suggestion that men should assist their womenfolk around the house was often seen as demeaning and emasculating.[38] There is even some evidence to suggest that males who carried out domestic chores were mocked. The unusual sight of men washing doorsteps and windows in the Garw valley while their wives had taken leave from their homes to go hop-picking (another

[34] Angela V. John, 'A miner struggle? Women's protests in Welsh mining history', *Llafur*, 4, no. 1 (1984), 86.

[35] Crook, 'Tidy women', 43; evidence of Will Trigg in Davies (ed.), *The Valleys Autobiography*, p. 66. In her study of working-class families in Lancashire, Elizabeth Roberts concluded that 'the majority of both men and women firmly believed that women were the "bosses" in the home and family'. Roberts, *Women and Families*, p. 83.

[36] See Deirdre Beddoe, 'Images of Welsh women', in Tony Curtis (ed.), *Wales: The Imagined Nation* (Bridgend, 1986), pp. 227–38; Diana Bianchi, 'The creation of a myth: the Welsh Mam', *Radical Wales*, no. 17 (1988), 11–13.

[37] Jane Elliott, 'The Welsh Mam', in Rob Humphreys and Anna-Marie Taylor (eds.), *Opening up 'The Keep' by Gwyn Thomas* (Swansea, 1996), p. 42.

[38] Oral evidence suggests that if a man did help out around the house, his assistance was given 'behind closed doors' and 'covertly in order to avoid embarrassment, and what might be interpreted as an affront to his manhood'. Evidence of Sarah Bowen in Jeffrey Grenfell-Hill (ed.), *Growing Up in Wales: Collected Memories of Childhood in Wales, 1895–1939* (Llandysul, 1996), p.16; Jaclyn J. Gier, 'Miners' wives: gender, culture and society in the south Wales coalfields, 1919–1939' (unpublished Ph.D. thesis, Northwestern University (US), 1993), p. 182.

LIB

example of women's economic activity which went unrecorded in the census returns) was described as 'comical' by one local observer in September 1934.[39] In an interview with Rosemary Crook, a female respondent from the Rhondda (b. 1908) remarked somewhat disparagingly that her brother was 'like a girl, he would do anything to help in the house'.[40]

However, as the economic problems of the coalfield worsened and an increasing number of men found themselves placed on the unemployment register, the foundation upon which this sexual division of labour had been constructed appeared to be collapsing. With husbands and sons out of work the sharp divisions which separated the working experiences of the male and female populations were increasingly blurred. In mining households there was less work for women to perform around the house as some of the chores directly associated with serving the returning miner – the carrying and heating of water for bathing and the washing of dirty clothing – disappeared for the time being. Some unemployed men began openly assisting their wives and mothers with household chores – an act which may have provided them with the sense of purpose and authority which they had been denied as a result of their inability to support their families.[41] In 1937 the authors of the *Second Industrial Survey* observed that, in many households, 'older unemployed men' were at hand to help their wives with domestic tasks.[42] Similarly, in his study of juvenile unemployment in the district, Gwynne Meara remarked that it was:

> quite usual for lads to tell you that they have spent part of the morning 'cleaning up at home', and a considerable part of their time is spent in this way – in minding younger children, and generally, in helping their mothers about the house.[43]

[39]   *Glamorgan Gazette*, 14 September 1934.
[40]   Crook, 'Tidy women', 42.
[41]   In the novel, *Times Like These* by Gwyn Jones, which focuses upon the experiences of a south Wales mining family during the inter-war period, Luke Biesty, the unemployed son, is seen assisting his mother with many of the household chores and expresses his astonishment at the arduous nature of her daily labours. Gwyn Jones, *Times Like These* (London, 1936), pp. 25–8.
[42]   *Second Industrial Survey of South Wales*, II, pp. 81–2.
[43]   Meara, *Juvenile Unemployment in South Wales*, p. 97.

Such commentaries seem to indicate that during periods of male unemployment the load of the housewife could be lightened as the volume of domestic work was reduced and male members of the household readily came to her assistance. In reality, however, this shift in responsibilities and authority may well have led to tension between many couples as male members of the household found it difficult to come to terms with their loss of status as breadwinners.[44] Furthermore, when male members of the family became unemployed, the need for married women to take up paid work to support their families became greater. For most married women, the only employment available was low-paid, casual or part-time work, such as charring, taking in washing, or selling food and drink. One woman from Llangynwyd (b. 1918), whose husband was incapacitated by illness, found that there were very few job opportunities for married women like herself in her locality:

> I had two girls to bring up . . . and I thought, if only I could have a little job. I tried Woolworths and that was five shillings a week, but no, I was married – it couldn't be done. So I was asking everyone where I could go and they said, 'Go to the bank in the morning and scrub the steps!' Well, I thought, I can't do that. I thought I was a cut above that! . . . so I took up knitting in those days, had to sit up half the night to get money.[45]

Since the type of work which was available for married women was of a casual or temporary nature and was usually related to the domestic sphere, many women did not regard such employment as being 'proper' work. In an interview with Diana Gittins, a woman from the Rhondda gave the following response when asked whether or not she had worked after getting married: 'No, never worked no more. Oh – I went out working in *houses* to earn a few shillings, yes, I worked with a family, my mother's and my sister's, and took in washing – to friends.'[46]

[44] See J. M. Keane, 'The impact of unemployment: a study of the social effects of unemployment in a working-class district of Cardiff in the depression years, 1930–1935' (unpublished M.Sc. (Econ.) thesis, University of Wales, 1983), pp. 59–61.

[45] Evidence of Respondent 16.

[46] Diana Gittins, *Fair Sex: Family Size and Structure, 1900–39* (London, 1982), p. 115. Similar comments were made by respondents in the following articles: Crook, 'Tidy women', 42; Graham Goode and Sara Delamont, 'Opportunity denied: the voices of the lost grammar school girls of the inter-war years', in Sandra Betts (ed.), *Our Daughters' Land: Past and Present* (Cardiff, 1996), pp. 103–24.

In spite of the general disapproval of the employment of married women, it was accepted that in dire economic circumstances many had little choice but to seek work which would provide the family with a few extra shillings.[47] Even so, such women were usually pitied, for the mere fact that they had to work was seen as a poor reflection on the ability of their husband to provide for his family. Married women who worked did not choose to do so but were 'compelled' to because of the 'pressure of a reduction of family incomes'.[48]

The notion that the unemployment of male members of the family could somehow empower females does not seem to hold true, therefore, for even if the volume of 'home work' decreased, there were other physical and psychological burdens to carry and little opportunity for relief. As the annual report of the South Wales and Monmouthshire Council of Social Service noted in 1937, male unemployment did not necessarily initiate a more equal partnership between husband and wife:

> Unemployment seems to transfer to the women the headship of the home. The whole burden of home management, the feeding and clothing of the children, the cheering of a despondent man, the careful eking out of unemployment allowance – these are the major tasks of an unemployed home, and it is to the women they fall.[49]

Emma Noble who, along with her husband William, had established the Maes-yr-haf Educational Settlement in the Rhondda, had seen little evidence of greater co-operation between married couples in the area. At a conference held at Maes-yr-haf in 1933, she 'urged husbands to realize the needs of their wives for something to take them out of themselves and widen their minds', while subsequent discussion brought out the necessity for 'change in both men and women – in men to understand that

---

[47] In her study of family size and structure, Diana Gittins noted that female respondents from the south-east of England were more likely to disapprove of the employment of married women than respondents from south Wales who accepted that during times of economic hardship, married women had little choice but to take up paid employment. Gittins, *Fair Sex*, pp. 114–15.

[48] Board of Trade, *An Industrial Survey of South Wales*, p.157; PP 1933–4 (XIII, Cmd. 4728), p. 140.

[49] South Wales and Monmouthshire Council of Social Service, *3rd Annual Report, 1936–37: Life in South Wales Today* (Cardiff, 1937), p. 22.

their wives need more outside interests, and in women to give their husbands a share in the management of the home'.[50]

For many wives of the unemployed, the extra work and worry came at a great cost to their personal welfare, as they sacrificed their own health for the sake of that of their husbands and children.[51] An Interim Report into the relationship between unemployment and health published by the Pilgrim Trust in 1937 concluded that 'it is the unemployed man's wife that has to bear the brunt of poverty due to unemployment'.[52] In the Trust's completed inquiry into unemployment, *Men Without Work* (1938), much evidence of female suffering and ill-health in south Wales was put forward:

> It was a matter of daily experience to observe the obvious signs of mal-nutrition in the appearance of the wives of unemployed men with families. They obviously did without things for the sake of their husbands and children, and it was by no means certain that they keep for their own use the 'extra nourishment' provided expressly for them in a large number of cases by the Unemployment Assistance Board. Undernourishment, combined with the strain of 'managing' on very limited resources and dealing with the domestic crises which almost inevitably crop up from time to time during a long spell of unemployment make heavy demands on the physical and psychic resources of mothers of families.[53]

One of the main indicators of poor health among the female population of the mining areas was the high incidence of maternal deaths recorded during this period of economic hardship. In 1934, when the maternal mortality rate of England and Wales stood at 4.41 deaths per 1,000 live births, a maternal mortality rate of 10.7 was recorded in the Ogmore and Garw

[50] Barrie Naylor, *Quakers in the Rhondda, 1926–1986* (Brockweir, Chepstow, 1986), p. 48.
[51] See Margaret Llewellyn Davies (ed.), *Life as We Have Known It*, 1st edn 1931 (London, 1977); Margery Spring-Rice, *Working Class Wives: Their Health and Conditions* (Harmondsworth, 1939).
[52] The Pilgrim Trust, *Interim Reports of Unemployment Inquiry*, no. IV, H. W. Singer, 'Unemployment and health' (London, 1937), p. 13.
[53] The Pilgrim Trust, *Men Without Work* (Cambridge, 1938), p. 139.

UD, and 11.99 in the Rhondda UD.[54] There is little doubt that the health problems of miners' wives were exacerbated by their poor living conditions and their continued heavy domestic workload. As the miner and author, B. L. Coombes (1894–1974), noted, many women paid a heavy price for their unending labour: 'The women work very hard – too hard – trying to cheat the greyness that is outside by a clean and cheerful show within. They age before they should because of this continual cleaning and polishing.'[55] In the opinion of a correspondent who wrote to the *Aberdare Leader* in 1937, the women in many homes in the area were nothing more than 'household slaves' who washed 'over and over again the same dirty clothes, dirty dishes', and undertook 'an endless round of drudgery'.[56] The Monmouthshire-born writer, Gwyn Jones (1907–99), painted a similarly dark picture in his novel *Times Like These* (1936), where Polly Biesty, a miner's wife and mother, reflected on the experiences of women in her community whose lives seemed inevitably bound to the same unhappy cycle:

> It was like destiny. Every month you saw it: a young girl marrying strong and happy, then breaking, breaking; all the cares of the kitchen, the family, the pay-ticker, the never-ending round of washing, scrubbing, cooking, clearing away, polishing; the constant inflow of dirt; the child-bearing in agony after conception without desire and gestation without longing; brats at the heels, brats at the apron-strings, a daunting procession of life-drainers. At the best a life of denial and poverty, at the worst degradation.[57]

This very gloomy picture, though fictional, no doubt embodied strong elements of the truth. However, there were glimmers of hope on the horizon with the introduction of new facilities to aid the miner's wife. By the 1930s the campaign to establish pithead

---

[54] *Annual Report of the Rhondda Medical Officer of Health, 1934* (Ferndale, 1935); *Annual Report of the Ogmore and Garw Medical Officer of Health, 1934* (Cardiff, 1935). Continuing concern for the high maternal mortality rates recorded in Welsh districts eventually prompted the government to conduct an official inquiry into the matter; see PP 1936–7 (XI, Cmd. 5423), *Ministry of Health, Report on Maternal Mortality in Wales*. For an examination of the steps taken to improve maternal welfare in the south Wales valleys during the inter-war years, see Williams, 'Yr ymgyrch i "achub y mamau" '.

[55] Coombes, *These Poor Hands*, p. 21.

[56] *Aberdare Leader*, 20 February 1937.

[57] Jones, *Times Like These*, p. 135.

baths had gathered some momentum in the South Wales Coalfield, and their arrival was heralded as a 'blessing' to both the miners and their wives.[58] Speaking at a miners' meeting at Treherbert in June 1931, David Lewis, the local miners' agent, urged the colliers to think of their womenfolk when voting on the proposed scheme to establish pithead baths at Fernhill: 'It would be a big boon to the women of the valleys if all their men were able to bath at the pit head and leave all the dirt of the colliery there.'[59] However, the miners of Fernhill remained unconvinced of the advantages to their wives and daughters, and the following month they voted against the establishment of baths at the colliery.[60] The impact which pithead baths had upon the workload of miners' wives should not be exaggerated, however, and it is important to remember that the wives of miners remained preoccupied with many other domestic responsibilities, including the washing and drying of pit clothes, long after the establishment of colliery baths.[61] As Neil Evans and Dot Jones have suggested in their examination of pithead bath provision in south Wales, 'when one burden placed upon women was reduced so others . . . were piled on.'[62] For example, in his annual report for the year 1937–8, the medical officer of health for the Neath RDC maintained that the opening of pithead baths at Seven Sisters and Cefn Coed, Creunant, had not only given mothers in the area 'a greater chance of enjoying better health', but had also enabled them to devote more time to their young children – the implication being that these children had not received sufficient attention in the past.[63] When the issue of pithead baths was discussed by the Mountain Ash Education Committee in June 1935, a female member raised a similar point, noting that the majority of the women in the district 'who had to perform heavy duties and were unable to attend to their children as they might desire', would benefit greatly from the introduction of this service.[64]

[58]   See Neil Evans and Dot Jones, ' "A blessing for the miner's wife": the campaign for pithead baths in the South Wales Coalfield, 1908–1950', *Llafur*, 6, no. 3 (1994), 5–28.
[59]   *The Rhondda Gazette*, 6 June 1931.
[60]   Ibid., 11 July 1931.
[61]   Mrs F. H. Smith, 'In a mining village', in Davies (ed.), *Life as We Have Known It*, pp. 67–72; James Hanley, *Grey Children: A Study in Humbug and Misery in South Wales* (London, 1937), pp. 54–5; Winifred Griffiths, *One Woman's Story* (Rhondda, 1979), p. 109.
[62]   Evans and Jones, 'A blessing for the miner's wife', 22.
[63]   *Aberdare Leader*, 3 September 1938.
[64]   Ibid., 8 June 1935.

A similar attitude was revealed when efforts were made to establish nurseries in the area during the same period. These were not facilities established to assist mothers to go out to work; rather, they were to help make them 'better' mothers by teaching them how best to care for their children. Educationalists and politicians alike were agreed that nursery schools could reinforce the dominant ideal of 'motherhood' by educating mothers in the art of 'mothercraft'. Speaking at the annual conference of Education Associations (Nursery School Section) in January 1938, W. Morris Jones, director of education for the Rhondda, declared that it was the children in the area who were now 'bringing up' their mothers, for the Rhondda nursery school was 'teaching the mothers, through the older children, the importance of an adequate, all-round diet'.[65] As Jane Lewis has argued, female members of the Labour Party who promoted nursery education during the 1930s were also more interested in 'equalizing educational opportunity' than with 'providing assistance to working women'.[66] Members of the women's section of the Caerphilly Labour Party seemed particularly sceptical about the real contribution such institutions could make in their area. During a discussion on the establishment of nurseries in November 1937, one member voiced her fear that nurseries would simply 'give mothers more time to gossip'.[67] The firm belief that the married woman's primary responsibility rested in the home with her family thus remained unaltered by these developments in child-care and miners' welfare.

As for the young girl who may have aspired to lead a different life from that of her mother, there was little to suggest that her dreams could be realized. After all, daughters were destined to become wives and mothers and their lives usually followed the pattern set by their elders. Full-time employment, if it could be found, was merely one temporary stage in that life-cycle, to be undertaken only until marriage and children intervened. In 1921 single females formed over 80 per cent of the female workforce in all parts of Glamorgan and Monmouthshire. Employment

[65] *Western Mail*, 4 January 1938.
[66] Jane Lewis, 'In search of a real equality: women between the wars', in Frank Gloversmith (ed.), *Class, Culture and Social Change: A New View of the 1930s* (Brighton, 1980), pp. 208–39.
[67] South Wales Coalfield Archive (SWCA), Caerphilly Labour Party, Women's Section minutes, 30 November 1937.

opportunities varied considerably between the large commercial centres and the mining districts: nearly 60 per cent of all single women were engaged in full-time work in the Cardiff CB, while less than 30 per cent were occupied in the Rhondda UD.[68] A breakdown of the marital status of occupied females in these localities is not provided in the 1931 census occupation tables. However, by comparing the proportions of female juveniles (aged between fourteen and twenty) who were engaged in full-time work in the two districts, it is evident that the working experiences of the young female population in the two areas remained starkly different. In the Cardiff CB, over two-thirds of the 14,709 female juveniles were recorded as gainfully employed. Conversely, 76.8 per cent of the 7,403 female juveniles enumerated in the Rhondda UD were classed as 'unoccupied'.[69]

Given the scarcity of employment opportunities in the mining districts, many young women found that they had little choice but to stay at home and assist with domestic chores and with the care of their younger siblings.[70] Writing in 1933, Walter Haydn Davies noted that in many large families, the education of older female children suffered as a consequence, for 'when they should be improving themselves physically and mentally they have to take care of the younger children whilst the mother has to attend to some pressing household duty.'[71] Conversely, the daughters of unemployed miners, or those who had been brought up in smaller families where there was less demand for their domestic assistance, found themselves having to stay on at school long after the legal school-leaving age. In 1937 the *Second Industrial Survey of South Wales* estimated that 40 per cent of girls aged between fourteen and eighteen had either remained at school beyond the legal school-leaving age or were assisting their

---

[68] *Census of England and Wales, 1921, County of Glamorgan*, pp. 67–72; *Census of England and Wales, 1921, County of Monmouth* (London, 1923), pp. 49–50.

[69] *Census of England and Wales, 1931, Occupation Tables*, pp. 652–3.

[70] Madeline Rooff, *Youth and Leisure: A Survey of Girls' Organisations in England and Wales* (Edinburgh, 1935), p. 227; Meara, *Juvenile Unemployment in South Wales*, pp. 43–4.

[71] Walter Haydn Davies, 'The influence of recent changes in the social environment on the outlook and habits of individuals, with special reference to mining communities in south Wales' (unpublished MA thesis, University of Wales, 1933), p. 32. Although some young females were fortunate enough to go on to higher education, usually to train for the teaching profession, it was the daughters of mining families, rather than the sons, who were likely to be denied such educational opportunities during periods of economic hardship. See Goode and Delamont, 'Opportunity denied', pp. 114–21.

families at home.[72] A minimum legal school-leaving age of fourteen had been instituted by the Education Act of 1918 and was not raised until 1936, when exemptions up to the age of fifteen could be granted by the local education authorities. In his 1934 survey of south Wales girls aged between fourteen and sixteen, Gwynne Meara found that 42.2 per cent of the 7,073 who were eligible to leave school at the end of the summer had returned to enrol for another term in September – the incidence of this practice being particularly high in Pontypridd, Aberdare, Merthyr Tydfil, Ebbw Vale, Mountain Ash and the Rhondda.[73] Local juvenile advisory committees also reported that the lack of work available in these areas had led a considerable number of young females to remain at school.[74] Indeed, some schools faced difficulties in accommodating the growing number of pupils who filled their classrooms. In March 1935 the headmaster of the Tredegar County School reported an excess of 148 pupils in attendance, a fact which he attributed to the lack of employment available for young girls in the district.[75]

As conditions in the coal industry deteriorated and it became impossible for families to support their unoccupied children, a growing number of young females were forced to leave their home districts to take up work wherever it could be found. As the Board of Education reported in 1931:

> In the days of prosperity in South Wales, the problem of finding occupation for girls in the mining valleys was not as acute as it is to-day; then, the percentage of girls who married very young was exceptionally high, and before marriage they were needed at home to help to attend to the needs of the family and of the lodgers who generally formed part of the household. Now, however, changed conditions are compelling the girls to seek remunerative occupations outside their home area.[76]

For the majority of young girls who found themselves looking for work, there were but two choices available to them – either to

---

[72]   *Second Industrial Survey of South Wales*, III, p. 17.

[73]   Meara, *Juvenile Unemployment in South Wales*, p. 31.

[74]   *Aberdare Leader*, 11 and 18 April 1936;   *Second Industrial Survey of South Wales*, III, pp. 137, 157.

[75]   *Western Mail*, 5 March 1935.

[76]   Board of Education, Pamphlet no. 86, *Educational Problems of the South Wales Coalfield* (London, 1931), p. 63.

enter domestic service, or find employment as shop assistants. During the inter-war years the number of occupied females aged between sixteen and eighteen increased substantially in many parts of south Wales. In the Pontypridd and Rhondda area the number of girls insured rose by 28 per cent between 1923 and 1930, while the number of insured boys fell by 18 per cent. A great many of the young females who now entered the labour force were employed in the distributive and retail trades. In south Wales the number of insured workers occupied in these trades increased by 46 per cent between 1923 and 1930.[77]   In many of the mining towns, between 60 and 70 per cent of all insured women, and between 70 and 80 per cent of all insured girls were employed in those trades.[78] Gwynne Meara noted that in some areas the distributive industries, including the millinery and tailoring trades and manufacturers of food and drink, provided employment for 'a fairly considerable number' of girls in the region.[79] In Merthyr and the Rhondda many young females were said to be employed at the co-operative stores and in other shops and offices.[80]

This expansion in the employment opportunities for young girls was not to be applauded, however, for when work was found it was usually in 'blind alley' occupations, where wages were kept low and the opportunities for training and promotion were non-existent. The Board of Trade's *Industrial Survey* of 1932 found that juveniles aged between sixteen and eighteen formed one-eighth of the total number of insured workers in the distributive trades, while youngsters aged between fourteen and sixteen, who were not insurable, numbered at least as many. The survey investigators concluded that 'the rapid increase in juvenile entry into such services as distribution and catering – unorganised trades in which "blind alley" occupations are all too frequent – must be viewed with some misgiving'.[81] Working conditions were generally unsatisfactory and much anxiety was voiced at the long hours which shop assistants were forced to work, usually for very low wages. Although the Shops Act of 1934 had made provisions

[77] John Gollan, *Youth in British Industry: A Survey of Labour Conditions To-day* (London, 1937), p. 126; Meara, *Juvenile Unemployment in South Wales*, p. 23.
[78] *Second Industrial Survey of South Wales*, I, p. 188.
[79] Meara, *Juvenile Unemployment in South Wales*, p. 33.
[80] *Second Industrial Survey of South Wales*, III, pp. 135, 151.
[81] Board of Trade, *An Industrial Survey of South Wales*, p. 148.

for regulating the hours worked by juveniles – reducing their normal maximum hours to fifty-two hours a week, and from December 1937 to forty-eight hours a week – many problems remained. Few shop assistants were members of trade unions, and allegations of exploitation were common.[82] The Board of Trade's *Industrial Survey* of 1932 found that many employers substituted juveniles for adult labour during times of bad trade.[83] Moreover, as Hilda Jennings discovered at Bryn-mawr, young workers who were employed at wages varying from 3*s*. to 10*s*. a week were often dismissed as soon as they reached insurable age.[84] Systematic inquiries carried out by shops inspectors on behalf of the Pontypool UDC greatly disturbed members when it was revealed that some young girls worked over ninety hours per week.[85] At the annual conference of the National Amalgamated Union of Shop Assistants, Warehousemen and Clerks at Leeds in April 1938, a delegate from the Rhondda condemned the practice prevailing in his area whereby shop assistants were forced to work behind closed doors when the premises were shut, by employers who 'professed to be Christians'.[86] Similarly, in December 1938 the attention of members of the Aberdare UDC was drawn to the poor employment conditions of female shop assistants in the town, many of whom, it was claimed, worked between sixty and seventy hours a week.[87]

However, for the thousands of young Welsh women who found employment as domestic servants during this period, long hours of service behind closed doors were an accepted part of their working lives. In common with many other areas of Britain the number of females employed as domestic servants in south Wales increased significantly in the decade 1921–31.[88] Gwynne Meara noted that the proportion of occupied juvenile females (aged between fourteen and eighteen) who were employed in

---

[82] Modern Records Centre, Warwick, MSS 292/79C/56; MSS 292/79M/29; MSS 292/79R/12; MSS 292/79R/13; Pontypridd Public Library, Pontypridd Trades Council and Labour Party minutes, 10 December 1934.

[83] Board of Trade, *An Industrial Survey of South Wales*, p. 22.

[84] Hilda Jennings, *Brynmawr: A Study of a Distressed Area* (London, 1934), p. 109.

[85] *Free Press of Monmouthshire*, 4 March 1938.

[86] *Western Mail*, 18 April 1938.

[87] Glamorgan Record Office (GRO), Aberdare UDC minutes, 8 December 1938.

[88] Neal A. Ferguson notes that the personal service industry was 'the numerically largest and third fastest growing category of female employment during the inter-war years' in England and Wales. Ferguson, 'Women's work', 58.

personal and institutional service in the region had increased from 42.6 per cent in 1921 to 53.6 per cent in 1931. This was, he concluded, 'the only occupation open to them on any large scale'.[89] By 1931, 44 per cent of the total occupied female work-force of the two counties of Glamorgan and Monmouth were employed in the range of occupations listed in the census occupation tables under the 'personal service' class, a category which included domestic servants, lodging and boarding-house keepers, inn-keepers, barmaids, waitresses, laundry workers and charwomen. As table 1.4 shows, the vast majority of females employed in this sector in 1931 were occupied as domestic servants. Indeed, in some parts of south Wales, notably in Mountain Ash, Merthyr Tydfil and Breconshire, over 80 per cent of girls entered domestic service on leaving school.[90]

The daughters of unemployed miners had little choice but to enter domestic service as a means to an end and, from the early 1920s, their entry to this occupation was assisted by the establish-ment of government-run training centres which unemployed females were instructed to attend. From 1921 onwards the Ministry of Labour's Central Committee on Women's Training and Employment provided the females of south Wales with domestic instruction at 'Homecraft Centres' which had been established at Bryn-mawr, Cardiff, Merthyr Tydfil, Neath, Newport, Port Talbot, Swansea and Llanelli by 1923.[91] In 1928, the year which saw the passing of the Industrial Transference Act, a further three 'Domestic' or 'Home Training Centres' were set up in south Wales, where unemployed females between the ages of fifteen and forty enrolled for courses of thirteen or seventeen weeks' duration, and were instructed in the basics of 'cooking, laundry-work, needlework, house-wifery, physical exercises and simple hygiene'.[92] By 1930, centres had been established at Aberdare, Abertillery, Bargoed, Cardiff, Neath, Maesteg, Merthyr Tydfil, Pontypridd and Tonypandy, and between January 1925 and June 1930, 3,045 females had been trained, 73.5 per cent of whom were placed in domestic

---

[89] Meara, *Juvenile Unemployment in South Wales*, p. 40.
[90] Ibid., p. 33.
[91] *The Second Interim Report of the General Committee on Women's Training and Employment for the period ending 31st December 1922* (London, 1923), p. 34.
[92] E. C. Owen, 'Domestic Training Schemes for unemployed women and girls', *Cambria*, no. 3 (1930), 38.

Table 1.4: Number and percentage of females (aged fourteen and over) occupied as domestic servants and in other occupations within 'personal service' group, 1931

| Area | Females occupied in 'personal service' occupation group | | | | | |
| | Domestic servants | | Others | | Total | |
	Number	%	Number	%	Number	%
Glamorgan	**28074**	**72.8**	**10494**	**27.2**	**38568**	**100.0**
Cardiff CB	7012	63.0	4116	37.0	11128	100.0
Merthyr Tydfil CB	1302	73.3	475	26.7	1777	100.0
Swansea CB	4514	69.2	2005	30.8	6519	100.0
Aberdare UD	842	77.3	247	22.7	1089	100.0
Bridgend UD	378	71.5	151	28.5	529	100.0
Maesteg UD	350	79.5	90	20.5	440	100.0
Mountain Ash UD	543	82.8	113	17.2	656	100.0
Neath MB	718	74.2	250	25.8	968	100.0
Ogmore & Garw UD	325	79.7	83	20.3	408	100.0
Pontypridd UD	768	72.1	297	27.9	1065	100.0
Rhondda UD	1908	80.8	453	19.2	2361	100.0
Monmouthshire	**9956**	**76.7**	**3025**	**23.3**	**12981**	**100.0**
Newport CB	2909	69.5	1279	30.5	4188	100.0
Abertillery UD	409	76.3	127	23.7	536	100.0
Blaenavon UD	176	76.9	53	23.1	229	100.0
Ebbw Vale UD	443	76.5	136	23.5	579	100.0
Nantyglo & Blaina UD	155	80.7	37	19.3	192	100.0
Pontypool UD	155	72.1	60	27.9	215	100.0
Tredegar UD	339	76.4	105	23.6	444	100.0

Source: 1931 Census Occupation Tables.

service.[93] A similar function was filled by the Juvenile Instruction Centres (known as Juvenile Unemployment Centres before 1929), which catered for those aged between fourteen and eighteen. By 1930 there were nineteen such centres in south Wales offering young females similar courses of instruction to those provided at the Home Training Centres. Some un-employed girls from the South Wales Coalfield were sent further afield to attend residential courses at institutions such as Lapeswood in Sydenham Hill and Newbold Beeches in

[93] Ibid.

Leamington Spa, where they too could 'fit themselves to take up domestic work'.[94] Failure to comply with orders to attend Home Training or Instruction Centres could incur a fine, as one fifteen-year-old girl from Aberaman was to find out in July 1937 when she refused to attend a course of instruction at the Robertstown Juvenile Instruction Centre.[95]

The emphasis placed upon providing young girls with a sound education in domestic subjects had both a practical and an ideological purpose. The daughters of miners were expected to become the wives of miners in the future, and 'training' for their prospective 'careers' could now be acquired not only within their own homes, but at the state-run centres. When the manager of the Port Talbot employment exchange called a meeting at the town in November 1934 to outline a scheme for the training of unemployed women and girls, he declared that the object of the Ministry of Labour was not only to give those girls a 'thorough training in domestic arts to enable them to take their places as domestic helps', but also, 'to make good wives and mothers'.[96] A few weeks later, in an address delivered at the Young Men's Christian Association (YMCA) hall in the town, Eirene Lloyd Jones, publicity officer for the ministry's Central Committee on Women's Training and Employment, gave high praise to the training centres and instruction courses which had provided local girls with 'a splendid opportunity of receiving the right kind of training to enable them to become good helpers in the homes, good wives and good mothers'.[97] Her sentiments were echoed in 1937 by the Revd Colin M. Gibb of Aberdare, who believed such training to be 'an invalu-able education for young women' which went a long way 'to fit them to run their homes in subsequent years with skill and knowledge'.[98]

In her study of working-class communities, Joanna Bourke found evidence that women themselves were eager to acquire such training, for they regarded the experience as an opportunity to

[94] Claudia Owen, 'Hyfforddiant i ferched allan o waith', *Y Gymraes*, XXXVI, no. 2 (1932), 37; Eirene Lloyd Jones, 'The work of the Central Committee on Women's Training', in Welsh School of Social Service (ed.), *Wales and the New Leisure* (Llandysul, 1935), pp. 22–3; *The Rhondda Gazette*, 22 February 1930; *Glamorgan Gazette*, 7 December 1934.

[95] *Aberdare Leader*, 3 July 1937.

[96] *Glamorgan Gazette*, 2 November 1934.

[97] Ibid., 7 December 1934.

[98] *Aberdare Leader*, 25 September 1937.

improve their status within the home by reducing the 'menial' elements of housework and emphasizing the more specialized and skilled forms of domestic labour. Improving the quality of goods and services produced by the housewife seemed to be the key to raising the status of women.[99]

The women of south Wales appeared to share such ideas. In 1931 it was claimed that most of the women who attended evening classes in domestic education in the South Wales Coalfield did so because they were eager to 'acquire greater skills and aptitude as home-makers, rather than to gain commercial advantage'.[100] The Pilgrim Trust recorded that women who had been domestics before their marriage 'seemed to look back on that period as having opened up to them new worlds of interest and provided training and experience which was of use to them in their present lives'.[101]

However, the vast majority of girls who were trained at these new establishments were destined for work away from their homes and their localities as the Home Training Centres began to feed the more affluent areas of Britain with a steady stream of domestic servants. As Eirwen Owen, chief woman officer for the Ministry of Labour in Wales, explained in 1930: 'The main object of the scheme was to relieve the industrial market by inducing women and girls between the ages of 16 and 40 years who were unemployed and inexperienced in household duties, to enter domestic service after training.'[102] A training scheme inaugurated in 1928 and supported by the Lord Mayor's Fund was established specifically to transfer juveniles from the mining areas of England and Wales to the more prosperous parts of the country. By the end of 1930 approximately 50 per cent of all the juveniles transferred through this scheme had come from Wales.[103] Between February 1928 and February 1931 the Home Training Centres of south Wales placed 1,409 girls in domestic employment outside Wales, while only 351 found work in other parts of Wales.[104] By 1931 it was estimated that over 10,000 girls

[99] Bourke, *Working-Class Cultures in Britain*, p. 69.
[100] Board of Education, *Educational Problems of the South Wales Coalfield*, p. 58.
[101] The Pilgrim Trust, *Men Without Work*, p. 264.
[102] Owen, 'Domestic Training Schemes for unemployed women and girls', 38.
[103] Ministry of Labour, *Report on the Work of Local Advisory Committees for Juvenile Employment, 1930* (London, 1931), p. 13.
[104] Board of Education, *Educational Problems of the South Wales Coalfield*, p. 65.

from south Wales worked as domestic servants in London alone.[105]

It soon became apparent that female migration from the colliery districts of south Wales was proceeding more rapidly than male migration, and the Ministry of Labour confirmed that twice as many girls as boys, between the ages of fourteen and eighteen, had left for England between 1930 and 1934.[106] With no improvement recorded in local employment opportunities, the Ministry of Labour reported in 1934 that 'the solution to the problem of unemployment amongst women in Wales' remained in their transfer to more prosperous areas of the country.[107] The transference policy was executed with even greater vigour from the mid-1930s onwards and, between 1934 and the end of June 1937, 7,277 women and 5,198 girls (aged between fourteen and eighteen) had been transferred by the Ministry of Labour from south Wales to employment in other districts.[108] However, a great many young females made private arrangements to look for work away from their homes, and it can only be estimated that the actual number who left south Wales considerably exceeded the figures quoted by the Ministry of Labour.[109] The detrimental social and cultural consequences of this movement of young people soon became evident. The Ministry of Health reported in 1938 that 39 per cent of the female population present in Merthyr Tydfil in 1921, and who might have been expected to have formed the population aged between fifteen and twenty-four in 1931, had left the area.[110] In the Rhondda in June 1935 a 'dearth of suitable mates' for local men was reported, due to 'the great exodus of young women who have obtained employment in London and elsewhere'.[111]

---

[105] *Second Industrial Survey of South Wales*, II, p. 81.

[106] *Parliamentary Debates* (Hansard) (5th series), vol. 320, 2213 (25 February 1937); Goronwy H. Daniel, 'Labour migration and age-composition', *Sociological Review*, XXXI, no. 3 (1939), 281–308.

[107] PP 1933–4 (XIII, Cmd. 4728), p. 141.

[108] *Parliamentary Debates* (Hansard) (5th series), vol. 328, 223 (28 October 1937).

[109] *Second Industrial Survey of South Wales*, III, p. 121. This point is also made by Andy Chandler, 'The Black Death on wheels: unemployment and migration – the experience of inter-war south Wales', *Papers in Modern Welsh History 1* [1982], 1–15.

[110] Ministry of Health, *Reports on Public Health and Medical Subjects*, no. 86, E. Lewis-Faning, 'A study of the trend of mortality rates in urban communities of England and Wales, with special reference to "Depressed Areas"' (London, 1938), p. 20.

[111] *The Rhondda Gazette*, 22 June 1935.

It could be argued that, by providing unemployed females with the opportunity of employment and regular wages, the transference policy proved to be beneficial to many unemployed girls and their families. After all, as Gwynne Meara remarked in 1936, despite being 'an occupation which is overworked and underpaid', domestic service did 'offer girls the chance of permanence and a large measure of stability'.[112] Furthermore, part of the wages earned by many of these transferred females could be sent back home to their families.[113] The mother of a mining family from the Rhondda, whom the writer H. V. Morton visited in 1931, explained how daughters were now of greater economic value to local households than sons:

> Girls are better than boys for South Wales now! Did you see the boys standing at the street corner on 'the dole'? That's where my boys would be if I'd had sons . . . What we should do without the girls I don't know. My three eldest are all in service in London – a place called Putney – and they're good to us when the pit's not working.[114]

One former domestic servant who was interviewed during the 1970s explained that she sent a parcel home from London to her family in south Wales every month and pooled her wages with those of her sisters to send extra contributions home.[115] Occasionally, the employers themselves provided help for the families of their young servants. In an interview held in 1991, a native of Nantyffyllon (b. 1912), who went to London to work as a domestic when she was fourteen years of age, recalled the kindness shown by her employers towards her family back home:

> They sort of maintained my family as a sort of distressed family, if you understand . . . every Christmas there used to come, by rail, a big tea-chest full of goodies, you know – everything! Oh marvellous! Well, you can imagine. On top, a present for the three of them, my sister and two brothers, and even a box of crackers were here! My mother used to get a

---

[112] Meara, *Juvenile Unemployment in South Wales*, p. 36.

[113] The Pilgrim Trust, *Interim Reports of Unemployment Inquiry*, no. III, H. W. Singer, 'Transference and the age structure of the population in the Special Areas' (London, 1937).

[114] H. V. Morton, *In Search of Wales* (London, 1932), pp. 260–1.

[115] Pam Taylor, 'Daughters and mothers – maids and mistresses: domestic service between the wars', in John Clarke et al. (eds.), *Working-Class Culture: Studies in History and Theory* (London, 1979), pp. 121–39.

pound of tea and a very, very rich Christmas pudding with money in the pudding as well![116]

However, such benevolent employers were the exceptions to the rule. Most domestic servants received extremely low wages, and any contributions sent home to families in Wales would have involved great sacrifices on the part of the young servant.[117] Wages could vary from as little as 4s. a week to a maximum of around 10s. and, although accommodation and food were usually provided – often of a very poor standard – the payments received were extremely low for the long hours put in. Juveniles under the age of eighteen were invariably paid at lower rates. Sylvia Anthony noted that many of the young girls who came from the distressed mining areas of south Wales and Durham to the south of England to work as domestics in the early 1930s accepted resident wages of around 7s. a week.[118] Following the introduction of the means test regulations implemented under the Unemployment Act of 1934, girls who resided at home could be held liable for the support of other household members and an increasing number were forced to leave the South Wales Coalfield in order that their unemployed parents did not lose their entitlement to benefits. In the words of S. O. Davies, the Merthyr Tydfil MP, these regulations were quite simply 'breaking up homes' and 'driving children away'.[119]

As a steady stream of young girls continued to leave south Wales in the direction of English towns and cities, concern soon focused on ensuring their social and moral welfare in their new and unfamiliar surroundings. The National Vigilance Association, based in London, reported in 1926 that:

Large numbers of Welsh girls do come, but experienced workers hold that the majority should never have been allowed to come. They are untrained, inexperienced, and quite unsuited to life in London. There is a demand

---

[116] Evidence of Respondent 13.

[117] In her study based on the oral evidence of Welsh women who worked as domestic servants between 1921 and 1939, Rosemary Scadden found that only eight out of seventeen women sent any money home. Rosemary Scadden, ' "Be good sweet maid, and let who will be clever": a study of Welsh girls in domestic service during the inter-war period' (unpublished M.Sc. (Econ.) thesis, University of Wales, 1996); p. 53.

[118] Anthony, *Women's Place in Industry and Home*, p. 36.

[119] *Parliamentary Debates* (Hansard) (5th series), vol. 313, 1530 (22 June 1936).

here, in clearly defined areas, for a poor type of servant at poor wages, and in practice the Welsh girls fit that demand.[120]

It became clear that the severity of the economic situation in the coalfield was driving many families to send young and inexperienced girls away, often to take up employment positions with unscrupulous employers.[121] The Rhondda Juvenile Advisory Committee reported in 1931 that several local families had been forced to 'disregard, to some extent, the evil effects of the wrong choice of work on the girl's future'.[122] Indeed, some parents were prosecuted for placing girls of school age in domestic service away from their homes. In a case which was heard at Bargoed magistrates' court in 1929, a father from Ystradmynach was fined for sending his thirteen-year-old daughter to work in London.[123] Tales of young, vulnerable Welsh girls who found themselves working for uncharitable employers in unacceptable living conditions were not uncommon.[124] And as Beatrice Watts Morgan, wife of David Watts Morgan, the Rhondda East MP, pointed out in 1928, the problems facing such girls were aggravated by the 'absurdly ridiculous anomaly' in the unemployment insurance scheme which denied domestic servants any rights to unemployment relief if they left their positions of employment.[125] The case of one Welsh girl who arrived at the Shepherd's Bush employment exchange in 1926, 'penniless and hungry, having run away from her place', highlighted the plight of domestics who found themselves in straitened circumstances far away from their families and friends.[126] As a weekly Rhondda newspaper explained in 1928, many Welsh girls were 'forced to submit to servility and hardship until such time as they can save sufficient money out of their wages to return home or find employment elsewhere'.[127]

---

[120] NLW, MS 15450C, letter from the secretaries of the National Vigilance Association, London, which appeared in the *Cardiff Times*, 20 November 1926.

[121] See Deirdre Beddoe, *Back to Home and Duty: Women between the Wars, 1918–1939* (London, 1989), p. 64.

[122] *Glamorgan Free Press and Rhondda Leader*, 16 May 1931.

[123] *Western Mail*, 21 December 1929.

[124] See the evidence of Lettice Maud Argust (b. 1912) in Grenfell-Hill (ed.), *Growing Up in Wales*, pp. 37–9; *Y Cymro*, 27 May 1933, 11 January 1936; Beddoe, 'Women between the wars', pp. 135, 143–4.

[125] *Rhondda Fach Gazette*, 3 March 1928.

[126] Ministry of Labour, *Report on the Work of Advisory Committees for Juvenile Employment, 1926*, p. 27.

[127] *Rhondda Fach Gazette*, 3 March 1928.

By the early 1930s it had become evident that urgent action needed to be taken in order to halt the flow of young people out of south Wales and bring hope to communities which had been decimated by the effects of long-term unemployment. Somewhat belatedly, therefore, the government took the first steps towards addressing the 'problem of South Wales' and commissioned several surveys and reports of the area, each of which presented its own ideas as to the best means to restructure the shattered economy of the region.[128] In effect, however, the majority of these surveys were nothing more than sounding-boards which offered only patchwork solutions to the people of south Wales. Yet, some of the proposals which they put forward were translated into action and, from 1934 onwards, a series of Special Areas Acts were passed in a bid to bring new investment into the depressed regions of England and Wales, including the Special Area of South Wales. The means by which these new measures would restructure the economy of south Wales provoked a great deal of discussion at the time for it was evident that the process of 'changing the face of south Wales' would involve a drastic transformation in the nature of the industrial workforce.[129]

In several of the industrial surveys and reports which were undertaken during this period, economists and planners drew attention to the large body of unoccupied females in the region which could be regarded as a potential supply of labour for any new industrial undertakings. Writing in 1936, Hilary Marquand estimated that there were 'some thousands now assisting in domestic work at home who would be ready to take work in industry if it were available'.[130] He concluded that about 60,000 female juveniles could 'form an almost inexhaustible reservoir of

---

[128] See Board of Trade, *An Industrial Survey of South Wales*; PP 1933–4 (XIII, Cmd. 4728); PP 1934–5 (X, Cmd. 4957); PP 1935–6 (XIV, Cmd. 5039), *Report of the Royal Commission on Merthyr Tydfil; Second Industrial Survey of South Wales*. A wide range of unofficial surveys were also undertaken during this period and contributed greatly to the body of literature which documented the 'problem' of south Wales. See, for example, Gwynne Meara, *Unemployment in Merthyr Tydfil: A Survey made at the request of the Merthyr Settlement* (Newtown, [c.1933]); idem, *Juvenile Unemployment in South Wales*; H. A. Marquand, *South Wales Needs a Plan* (London, 1936); Labour Party, *South Wales: Report of Labour Party's Commission of Enquiry into the Distressed Areas* (London, 1937); Political and Economic Planning [PEP], Broadsheet no. 94, *The Problem of South Wales*, 9 March 1937.

[129] See Brinley Thomas, 'The changing face of south Wales', *The Listener*, 23 March 1938; Lord Portal, 'The industrial future of south Wales', *Transactions of the Honourable Society of Cymmrodorion* (1938), 19–32.

[130] Marquand, *South Wales Needs a Plan*, p. 200.

labour for the maximum development likely to take place in the Region during the next five years in industries employing female labour'.[131] Such views were echoed in the *Second Industrial Survey* which put forward the slightly more conservative estimate that '35,000 girls and young women would be available for industrial employment in South Wales if the development of industry should prove sufficient to absorb them'.[132] Hilda Jennings, one of the Survey investigators, expanded:

> It may be assumed that in the event of suitable light industries being introduced into the region, the supply of young women and girls would far exceed the numbers of wholly unemployed women and girls at present registered at the Employment Exchange (5,622); in addition to existing potential supplies, a considerable proportion of the 37,500 girls (approximately) who will be free to leave the Elementary Schools in Monmouthshire and Glamorgan during the next three years might be reckoned as likely to be available for local industry, should the demand arise.[133]

In May 1939 the Industrial Development Council of Wales and Monmouthshire estimated that there were, in addition, some hundreds of thousands of women over the age of twenty, the majority of whom were married, who could become available for work 'if it were reasonably attractive and offered to them'.[134]

However, given the unfamiliarity of female industrial employment in the region, it was no easy task to convince the local population that their womenfolk should become involved in this type of work. As the *Western Mail*'s 'Woman Correspondent' remarked in July 1935:

> It is true that the Welsh girl is not factory-minded, and it is, therefore, not surprising that of the 5,000 who have left the district only 500 have entered industries . . . How can Welsh girls be expected to take kindly to factory conditions when nothing in the traditions of their home or social life has prepared them for this kind of work? There is no factory experience in South Wales worth talking about in which girls may find preparation.[135]

[131] Ibid., p. 68.
[132] *Second Industrial Survey of South Wales*, II, p. 83.
[133] Ibid., III, p. 17.
[134] GRO, Industrial Development Council of Wales and Monmouthshire Papers, 'Is unemployment ending? Part I', 22 May 1939.
[135] *Western Mail*, 6 July 1935.

The parents of many young girls seemed particularly opposed to the idea of sending their daughters to work in factories,[136] and the local juvenile advisory committees frequently remarked on their reluctance to allow their daughters to take up industrial work, particularly in far-away towns and cities.[137] Of the sixty-seven girls placed in employment by the Mountain Ash Juvenile Advisory Committee during the year 1935–6, only seven were occupied in work other than domestic service.[138] In the Rhondda, the Juvenile Advisory Committee reported in 1935 that only four girls had been placed in factory work outside the district during the past year, despite the fact that several positions had been offered to local unemployed females. In the opinion of the committee, there was

> a marked parental objection to the transfer of girls to factory work in other districts . . . The chief objection voiced by parents was that when girls were engaged on such work their evenings were free for recreational facilities and that it was practically an impossibility for welfare workers to exercise the necessary degree of supervision over the girls during their leisure hours.[139]

This comment provides an interesting gloss on contemporary attitudes towards the social aspect of female employment, for parents clearly did not favour placing their daughters in work which allowed greater opportunities for social independence. In addition to the general concern that factory work would not equip young women with the skills required to make them good wives and mothers,[140] it was feared that the social and moral character of Welsh girls would be affected by their experiences of

[136] A native of Bridgend who worked as a domestic servant in England during the inter-war period, recalled that her mother was strongly opposed to factory employment: 'My mother thought that was awful . . . She had a bit of silly pride; the girls all swore and were rather common, she had that idea. "You mustn't go in a factory, it's not nice." ' Quoted in Samuel Mullins and Gareth Griffiths, *Cap and Apron: An Oral History of Domestic Service in the Shires, 1880–1950* (Leicestershire Museums, 1986), p. 1.

[137] *Glamorgan Free Press and Rhondda Leader*, 6 May 1933; *Rhondda Fach Gazette*, 4 May 1935; *Aberdare Leader*, 18 April 1936.

[138] *Aberdare Leader*, 11 April 1936.

[139] *Rhondda Fach Gazette*, 4 May 1935.

[140] See the account of the heated discussions which took place at a domestic service exhibition held at the Royal Agricultural Hall, London, in January 1938, when a Miss Eva Bristow alleged that female factory workers lacked a basic knowledge of domestic skills and accused them of being 'dance mad'. *Western Mail*, 20 January 1938.

industrial employment. The claim made in 1936 by T. A. Jones, the manager of the Rhondda labour exchange, that the idea of placing her daughter in factory employment was 'anathema to the average Rhondda mother', received much publicity in the pages of *Y Ddraig Goch*, the monthly publication of Plaid Genedlaethol Cymru (the Welsh Nationalist Party), where it formed part of a wider debate regarding the potentially harmful influence of the English industrial lifestyle on the traditional social and cultural loyalties of Welsh girls.[141] Despite the evidence that girls who were employed as domestic servants could just as easily be 'led astray' when placed under poor employers in undesirable surroundings, it was widely believed that one of the benefits of service in private homes – as opposed to employment in large factories – was that the employers would take some interest in the well-being of their young servants. In 1926 the Ebbw Vale Juvenile Advisory Committee reported that local girls who took up positions as domestic servants away from their localities and 'expected, once free from the supervision of their parents, that they would have a "good time"', were often disappointed to find themselves placed in homes where similar restrictions on their free time were in force.[142] There were no such guarantees of supervision and care when girls were placed in industrial work and lodged with people who had no reason to take an interest in their welfare. Members of the Nantyglo and Blaina UDC called for 'greater protection' of young females who were drafted from south Wales to work in the new industry areas, after hearing that two girls from the district who had been sent by the Ministry of Labour to work in factories in Birmingham had simply been taken to their hostel and left to find their own way to the factory.[143] The parents of Welsh girls who had been placed in factory employment in Slough would no doubt have supported such demands that better provision be made for their daughters. In a story which appeared in the London-Welsh press in January 1938, it was claimed that many of the Welsh factory girls were leading a 'wild life' in the city and were frittering away their

---

[141] *Y Ddraig Goch*, 10, no. 8 (1936), 6. See also Elizabeth Williams, 'Diwydiannau i ferched Cymru: awgrym i'r Blaid Genedlaethol', ibid., 4, no. 8 (1931), 5.
[142] Ministry of Labour, *Report on the Work of Advisory Committees for Juvenile Employment, 1926*, p. 15.
[143] *Western Mail*, 25 February 1936.

earnings on cosmetics and other luxuries in London's West End.[144]

However, for many of the young women of south Wales, this shift towards industrial employment may not have been so unappealing. The authors of the *Industrial Survey* of 1932 pointed out that a growing number of Welsh women were entering factory employment in many parts of Britain and claimed that the prejudice against industrial work had been 'virtually destroyed' as young women welcomed the work opportunities offered to them in the new industries.[145] It was clear that many females relished the prospect of factory employment as an alternative to domestic service or shop-work. Since the early 1920s the growing disinclination of young women towards domestic work had become evident and, by the latter half of the 1930s, a shortage of domestic servants was reported in some parts of Britain. In the opinion of Eirene Lloyd Jones of the Ministry of Labour's Central Committee on Women's Training and Employment, the two main factors which had led to the decline in the number of female servants were the ineligibility of domestic workers for unemployment insurance, and the lack of social opportunities available to them in such employment.[146] As Madeline Rooff noted in her 1935 survey of female youth groups, factory employment offered young women 'greater opportunities for social life, in the give and take of gossip, the constant activity and even the noise of factory life'.[147]

For those who had personal knowledge or experience of domestic service, the reasons behind the 'servant shortage' were altogether clearer. Sylvia Anthony estimated that 'ten hours a day, sixty-four a week', would be 'a moderate computation of the average amount of time of a domestic servant's duty'.[148] A former domestic servant from Cardiff claimed in 1939 that the work had become 'repugnant' to many young women because 'it is a matter of chance whether it might be slavery to them. A good mistress is as rare as the finding of a precious stone in a scrap-heap.'[149] By the late 1930s the 'sophisticated town girls' of

---

[144] Ibid., 20 January 1938.
[145] Board of Trade, *An Industrial Survey of South Wales*, p. 157.
[146] *The Times*, 17 April 1937.
[147] Rooff, *Youth and Leisure*, p. 78.
[148] Anthony, *Women's Place in Industry and Home*, pp. 28–9.
[149] *South Wales Echo*, 8 August 1939.

Cardiff and Newport were reported to be increasingly reluctant to undertake domestic work.[150] Young women in these towns were aware of the new work opportunities being created in both offices and light industries in their areas, where working conditions allowed for greater companionship at the workplace and fewer restrictions on their leisure time. For Mary Biesty, the miner's daughter portrayed in Gwyn Jones's novel *Times Like These*, life as an office worker in the busy town of Newport had opened new doors and opportunities which contrasted sharply with the experiences of her contemporaries back home in the mining village of Jenkinstown:

> In Newport she had girl friends with interests like her own, she had variety, an ever-widening horizon; but in Jenkinstown there was nothing but the coal and perpetual talk about it . . . How could she possibly keep her former sympathies and interests? She was free, earning her own living, making her way in the world, dressing differently, speaking differently, mannered differently, from the rest of them. It puzzled her that her family seemed never to suspect that she was finding ambitions to be more than a miner's wife and drudge.[151]

There was certainly plenty of evidence to suggest that expectations were changing as the young women of south Wales began to seek a more varied working and social life than that experienced by their mothers. In previous decades, the leisure activities of males and females in the mining communities in particular had always closely mirrored their strictly segregated roles in the workplace. In the words of the Rhondda-born writer, Rhys Davies (1901–78): 'the colliers trod their exclusive world, its main province the underground labyrinths, and pubs and clubs above almost as private.'[152] Gradually, however, as economic conditions enforced changes in the employment structure of these communities, new social and cultural patterns were also very much in evidence. The pressing social and economic problems facing the industrial communities of south Wales prompted many women to take an increasingly prominent and active role in

---

[150] *Western Mail*, 10 July 1936, 12 September 1936, 23 and 25 January 1937, 26 April 1937, 4 June 1938, 8 July 1938.
[151] Jones, *Times Like These*, p. 78.
[152] Rhys Davies, *Print of a Hare's Foot* (London, 1969), p. 88.

political, philanthropic and recreational activities in their communities.[153] Moreover, the great expansion in more commercial
forms of public entertainment during the inter-war years gave
many women the opportunity of socializing in institutions other
than just the chapels. As Stephen Ridgwell has noted, the cinema
was a place of particular importance to the females of south Wales,
having 'a sufficient air of "respectability" about it – denied to such
institutions as the pub – to make it reasonably acceptable for
women, even unaccompanied, to attend'.[154] But even though the
cinema was gradually accepted as a suitable venue for female
audiences, the growing popularity of other venues for public entertainment, most notably the dance-halls, was regarded with disdain
by some commentators.[155] In the opinion of social leaders and
moralists, such as D. Lleufer Thomas, stipendiary magistrate for
Pontypridd and the Rhondda, and Enoch Davies, chairman of the
Pontypridd Licensing Sessions, 'dancing and its concomitants'
were the 'curse of the district'.[156] Both men maintained that they
were familiar with the negative social consequences of the dance-
halls, for many women had appeared before them at the local
courts, usually to bring affiliation orders against men in respect of
illegitimate children allegedly conceived after an evening of
dancing. However, as many women left their homes to take up
work in towns and cities away from their localities, thus adopting
new social customs and values, it was inevitable that these more
unwelcome forms of leisure activities would make an appearance

[153] For first-hand information on the work of the women's branches of the Labour
Party in the South Wales Coalfield, see the autobiography of Elizabeth Andrews, (the
Labour Party's women's organizer in Wales, 1919–1948), *A Woman's Work is Never Done*
(Ystrad Rhondda, 1956). Details on the establishment of women's sections of the Labour
Party and Women's Co-operative Guilds in the Rhondda are provided in Williams,
Democratic Rhondda, pp. 106–7, and Neil Evans and Dot Jones, '"To help forward the
great work of humanity": women in the Labour Party', in Duncan Tanner, Chris
Williams and Deian Hopkin (eds.), *The Labour Party in Wales, 1900–2000* (Cardiff, 2000),
pp. 215–40. See also Ada L. Wright, 'Clubs and centres for women', in Welsh School of
Social Service (ed.), *Wales and the New Leisure*, pp. 54–5; Alun Burge, 'A "subtle danger"?
The voluntary sector and coalfield society in south Wales, 1926–1939', *Llafur*, 7, nos. 3
and 4 (1998–99), 127–41.

[154] Stephen Ridgwell, 'South Wales and the cinema in the 1930s', *Welsh History Review*,
17, no. 4 (1995), 595.

[155] Mrs Coombe-Tennant JP, 'The adolescent and the home', *The Welsh Outlook*, XV,
no. 9 (1928), 278–9; *Rhondda Fach Gazette*, 20 August 1932; *Y Darian*, 23 December 1926,
11 October 1934.

[156] Royal Commission on Licensing (England and Wales), *Minutes of Evidence, 16th Public
Session, 21 January 1930* (London, 1930), q. 6994; *Glamorgan Free Press and Rhondda Leader*, 8
February 1930.

back home. The unfamiliar sight of 'young ladies walking openly into public houses' was particularly frowned upon by the local Rhondda press in 1938, as returnees who were home for the Christmas period threw constraint to the wind.[157]

Soon, however, a more obvious challenge to local conventions would become evident as the establishment of new industries in south Wales threatened to transform the traditional industrial and economic base of the region. In the wake of the Special Areas Acts, state-funded trading estates were established at Treforest, Dowlais and Port Talbot, where new industries moved in, tempted by financial incentives and by the large body of unoccupied female labour in the districts.[158] The fact that few women in south Wales had any experience of factory work did not appear to present problems for these new companies. In fact, the presence of this 'green' and inexperienced workforce appeared to be one of the main attractions for the firms who decided to settle in the area. Industrialists were full of praise for the female workers of south Wales who could not only 'be quickly trained' but demonstrated an 'adaptability and willingness to work'.[159] However, as Miriam Glucksmann has argued, it is likely that the employers' preference for such inexperienced female workers was nothing more than 'a search for the cheapest available source of labour'.[160]

It was not long, however, before the initial enthusiasm shown for such projects faded. Many onlookers became disappointed and disillusioned with the new industrial undertakings as it became clear that a growing number of females were being employed in the new factories, leaving the problem of long-term male unemployment unsolved.[161] When announcements were made that two large clothing factories were to be established at Bridgend and at either Aberdare or Merthyr, it was also made

---

[157] *The Rhondda Gazette*, 1 January 1938.

[158] For example, in a letter sent to Lord Greenwood in May 1936, Thomas Jones CH explained that he was trying to persuade Montague Burton Ltd to establish a factory in south Wales, 'where there is a large supply of potential female labour'. Thomas Jones, *A Diary with Letters, 1931–1950* (Oxford, 1954), p. 212.

[159] *Second Industrial Survey of South Wales*, II, p. 84; III, p. 229.

[160] Miriam Glucksmann, 'In a class of their own? Women workers in the new industries in inter-war Britain', *Feminist Review*, no. 24 (1986), 7–37. See also eadem, *Women Assemble: Women Workers and the New Industries in Inter-War Britain* (London, 1990).

[161] Philip Massey, *Industrial South Wales: A Social and Political Survey* (London, 1940), p. 176.

clear that the 1,400 jobs which they would create were for females only.[162] Factory owners and managers soon found themselves having to justify their recruitment policies to angry and disappointed male audiences. Speaking in June 1936, the managing director of the Port Talbot trading estate argued that people should accept the fact that both the men and the women of south Wales deserved to find work in their own communities, and he criticized those who believed that the trading estates employed too many females. In his opinion, 'this should not be an argument against the estate because the problem of finding work for women and girls is possibly as acute as the male employment problem.'[163] However, few seemed convinced by his arguments and the unhappy voices were not to be quelled easily.

The Treforest trading estate, which largely served the Pontypridd and Rhondda area, also became the focus of criticism as growing numbers of females, juveniles in particular, found ready employment on the site.[164] By October 1938, 227 females were employed at Treforest, 127 (55.9 per cent) of whom were under eighteen years of age.[165] Although males made up the majority of the workforce at the estate (numbering 455 in total), a fear that the true objective of the enterprise (to bring work to unemployed men), was not being met, continued to dominate public opinion. One correspondent who wrote to the *Western Mail* in January 1939 questioned the motives behind the recruitment of so many young females:

> Am I right in my belief that this estate was largely financed by the state in an endeavour to assist unemployment among the men of South Wales? If it is to be used to deflect girls from domestic service to provide cheap labour for trading concerns then, I imagine, it fails in its object, and most housewives will agree.[166]

Resentment at the increased use of female labour was particularly strong in the surrounding mining communities. A report published in 1939 revealed that there was a marked

---

[162] *Western Mail*, 27 March 1936, 12 March 1938.
[163] Ibid., 5 June 1936.
[164] Massey, *Industrial South Wales*, p. 176.
[165] *The Rhondda Gazette*, 15 October 1938.
[166] *Western Mail*, 30 January 1939.

'prejudice in the Rhondda' against the employment of females in factories.[167] Given that the male unemployment rate stood at 41.5 per cent at Ferndale, 39.7 per cent at Tonypandy and 35.5 per cent at nearby Porth in March 1939, it is not surprising that many residents felt this way.[168] During the first week of that month, as the roof was being placed on the new Rowton factory at Dinas, the editorial of one local newspaper voiced their concerns publicly:

> We are afraid that the vast majority of the workers at that factory will be young women and girls. While we do not despise any sort of work openings in these valleys, it is works that will give employment to our men that we so badly need in the Rhondda. These valleys have always depended for their sustenance upon what their men have earned. The day may come when the remnant of the population will be dependent upon neither what their own men or women earn. We may, if a suspended state of crisis continues, become a sort of Rowton House of the Kingdom. We are told that the teachers who recently canvassed the valleys for accommodation for people in case of war brought in most remarkable reports. People who are keeping children on 3s. a week on Public Assistance welcome the idea of keeping a couple extra if they can get 18s. instead of 6s. for doing it. But imagine us Rhondda Valley people becoming boarding house-keepers and dependent upon factory girls.[169]

These developments were not a good augury for the future. One Rhondda resident decried the fact that parts of the valley could soon 'resound to the voices of factory lasses, as well as the ring of the colliers' boots on the metalled roads'.[170]

In the opinion of many local men, the efforts of the government to revitalize the economy of the region through the establishment of new industries had been a disappointing failure. By June 1939 a total of only 3,043 new jobs had been created in all the factories established in the region since the inception of the 'Special Area of South Wales and Monmouthshire'.[171] The fact that many of those positions had been taken up by local females made the situation all the more intolerable. In 1942 Eli

---

[167] PEP, *Report on the Location of Industry* (London, 1939), p. 64.
[168] Ministry of Labour, *Local Unemployment Index*, March 1939, p. 4.
[169] *The Rhondda Gazette*, 4 March 1939.
[170] *The Rhondda Leader*, 25 March 1939.
[171] *The Times* (Special Areas Number), 27 June 1939.

Ginzberg estimated that females comprised over 40 per cent of the workforce employed in the new firms and concluded that 'the subsidized expansion tended more to bring women into the labor [*sic*] market than to reduce the number of unemployed men'.[172] Yet, although the women of south Wales were considered to have gained industrial positions at the expense of the unemployed male population, the scale of these developments should not be exaggerated. Up until the outbreak of the Second World War, south Wales remained very much a 'barren region' in terms of the employment opportunities it offered its female population.[173] Indeed, of all the Development Areas in Britain, the South Wales Area employed the lowest proportion of females. In 1939, only 15 women were employed in the region for every 100 men, compared with an average of 38 for every 100 in England and Wales.[174] Only a small proportion of local women had obtained employment in the new factories in the region and the majority continued to be engaged in the narrow range of occupations which had dominated their working experiences for several decades. The working lives of married women in the district were barely affected by the new industrial developments, for the strong opposition against their full-time employment ensured that the majority remained preoccupied with domestic responsibilities.

In the event, it was the waging of war which brought the greatest transformation in female employment opportunities in south Wales as the demands of wartime production brought new investment and thousands of new jobs to the region. The rearmament programme pursued by the British government from the mid-1930s onwards resulted in an expansion in iron and steel production and in new building activity with the erection of military establishments such as storage depots and aerodromes.[175] But by far the most important of these developments was the proposal to site several large war factories in south Wales, where bombs, shells and detonators were to be manufactured. The large body of unemployed men and women who

---

[172] Eli Ginzberg, *A World without Work: The Story of the Welsh Miners* (New Jersey, 1991), p. 144 (originally published in 1942 by Harper & Brothers, as *Grass on the Slag Heaps*).
[173] Philip Massey, 'Portrait of a mining town', *Fact*, no. 8 (1937), 66.
[174] J. H. Dunning, 'Employment for women in the Development Areas 1939/51', *Manchester School of Economic and Social Studies*, XXI, no. 3 (1953), 271–7.
[175] Thomas, 'War and the economy', p. 253.

were immediately available to take up work in the region had been a determining factor in the decision to site new plants in south Wales.[176] Yet, as news of the government's plans reached the area, local reaction was not altogether favourable. Many were unhappy that the proposal to build arsenals and military sites in south Wales was the only solution which the government could offer to alleviate unemployment in the region. In August 1934 a councillor from Maesteg argued that local people would 'rather starve than be employed in making instruments to kill others'.[177] Other people were angered by the fact that the government could find vast amounts of money to invest in a rearmament programme in south Wales at a time when a large proportion of the local population was suffering as a consequence of mass unemployment and poverty. At a demonstration against the means test at Aberafan in October 1937, protesters brandished banners carrying the slogan 'Millions for War – Starvation for the Unemployed'.[178]

Other local residents reacted rather more pragmatically to the developments. After all, if new industrial establishments were to be built in the district, their construction would create employment for several hundred men long before production at the factories commenced. Responding to the news that an estimated £2,650,000 was to be spent on the construction of a new ordnance factory at Glascoed, a local ex-serviceman expressed his delight on behalf of friends living in the area and members of the younger generation.[179] In the Bridgend area, where local officials had made concerted efforts to persuade the government to locate a new munitions works, the announcement in 1936 that a new filling factory was to be built at a cost of over £4,500,000 on a site of 121 acres at Waterton Court farm, on the outskirts of the town, was reported to have been the cause of great 'jubilation'.[180] By 1938 when the new plant was under construction, nearly 900 men worked on the site and practically all the available unemployed labour at Bridgend town and in the nearby Ogmore, Garw and Llynfi valleys had been absorbed.[181]

---

[176] P. Inman, *Labour in the Munitions Industries* (London, 1957), p. 215.
[177] *Glamorgan Gazette*, 10 August 1934.
[178] Ibid., 5 November 1937.
[179] *Free Press of Monmouthshire*, 14 January 1938.
[180] *Glamorgan Gazette*, 14 September 1934, 22 May 1936; *Western Mail*, 4 March 1938.
[181] *Western Mail*, 4 March 1938; *Parliamentary Debates* (Hansard) (5th series), vol. 336, 871 (23 May 1938).

It was not long before representatives from neighbouring local authorities, particularly from the mining districts, began calling on the government to bring similar plants to their areas. In the Rhondda, where long-term male unemployment remained a serious problem, frequent demands were made for a new factory to be built in the locality.[182] In October 1936 a columnist writing in *The Rhondda Gazette* argued that the new works should be brought to the depressed Valleys 'rather than spoiling the amenities of the Vale of Glamorgan . . . that arsenal ought to be in the Rhondda or Dowlais'.[183] The residents of Merthyr Tydfil voiced similar opinions on the matter but were disappointed by the reply received from the secretary of state for war, who argued that local conditions were unsuitable for the erection of a large filling factory which needed to be located on a 'large and fairly level area at some distance from habitation'.[184]

Eventually, however, as the demands of wartime production increased, thousands of men and women from areas such as the Rhondda and Merthyr Tydfil were given the opportunity of sharing the economic benefits of the war economy. In the months preceding the war, several German, Czech and Austrian refugee industrialists arrived in south Wales to establish new factories at sites which had failed to attract investors from closer to home.[185] Many of these new enterprises settled in the vacant premises at the Treforest trading estate, while others, such as A. Polikoff Ltd, Mendle Brothers and Flex Fasteners (owned by R. E. Benidict Bernstiel), opened factories at Ynys-wen and Dinas in the Rhondda. In March 1938, when the government assumed powers to direct industries to manufacture products which were essential for rearmament, production demands and output at many of these firms increased, so creating hundreds of

---

[182] *The Rhondda Gazette*, 30 January 1937, 20 March 1937, 6 November 1937.

[183] Ibid., 3 October 1936. The decision to site Bridgend ROF in the heart of the countryside was also condemned in verse in 1938. See Eliot Crawshay-Williams, 'Munition Works, Vale of Glamorgan', in idem, *No One Wants Poetry* (Newtown, 1938), p. 49. I am grateful to Dr Robert Smith for this reference. Concerns regarding the environmental impact of the war factories were also voiced in Monmouthshire. During a debate on the siting of Glascoed ROF, Alderman Arthur Jenkins, MP for Pontypool, made a plea to locate the factory elsewhere in order to 'preserve the beauty of Glascoed'. *Free Press of Monmouthshire*, 14 January 1938.

[184] *Parliamentary Debates* (Hansard) (5th series), vol. 328, 265 (28 October 1937).

[185] C. C. Salway, *Refugees and Industry* (London, 1942); Anthony Glaser, 'Jewish refugees and Jewish refugee industries', in Ursula R. Q. Henriques (ed.), *The Jews of South Wales: Historical Studies* (Cardiff, 1993), pp. 177–205.

new jobs. At the Treforest trading estate twenty-four factories
were requisitioned for wartime production by the Ministry of
Aircraft Production. The first factory to be established at the
Dowlais trading estate in 1938 also began work on a precision
engineering contract for the Ministry, while the following year
ICI opened an agency factory on the estate to produce
ammonia.[186] Iron and steel manufacturers, such as the Curran
Works at Cardiff and the Blaenavon Works at Monmouthshire,
negotiated contracts with the Ministry of Supply and the
Ministry of Aircraft Production respectively, and began producing cartridge cases and light alloy forgings.[187] Elsewhere,
clothing and luxury goods manufacturers, such as the Goblenz
plastic-jewellery works at Treforest and Polikoffs of Ynys-wen,
switched to produce plastic badges and military clothing for the
armed services.[188]

This expansion in production at the new factories of the
region had an immediate effect upon local employment opportunities. Yet, it was evident once more that it was the female
population that was benefiting most of all from the creation of
the new jobs. At Treorci, for example, following the opening of
Polikoffs clothing factory in March 1939, the female unemployment rate fell from 21.2 per cent in February 1939 to 9.4 per
cent by May. Although the male unemployment rate had also
fallen from 31.1 per cent to 20.3 per cent during the same
period, the opening of the new factory had clearly not had the
same impact on the lives of local men as it had on those of
the young women of the district.[189] Members of the Rhondda
Education Committee remarked that during the school year
1939–40 almost all the girls in the district had left school at the
age of fourteen to take up employment at the factory whereas
previously, due to the shortage of work opportunities in the area,
the vast majority would have remained at school until they were

[186] J. R. Castree, 'An economic investigation of industrial estates in Wales' (unpublished MA thesis, University of Wales, 1966), p. 35; Thomas, 'War and the economy',
pp. 255–6.
[187] GRO, Industrial Development Council of Wales and Monmouthshire Papers, 'List
of south Wales firms available for and wishing to undertake government work and orders'
(1939); The War Effort at the Curran Works, Cardiff (Cardiff, 1945); Gwent Record Office
(GWRO), Records of the Blaenavon Co. Ltd.
[188] Isobel Wylie Hutchinson, 'Wales in wartime', National Geographic Magazine, LXXXV
(1944), 751–68.
[189] Ministry of Labour, Local Unemployment Index, February–May 1939.

fifteen or sixteen years of age.[190] Growing numbers of girls from the Merthyr Tydfil area were also attracted to factory work. The annual report of the Merthyr Tydfil Juvenile Employment Committee for 1939 noted that there had been 'a decided change-over from domestic employment to factory employment' among the young females of the district. Whereas twenty-one girls had been placed in domestic work during October 1938, only three domestic 'placings' were recorded during November 1939, while thirty-one girls had been taken on at local factories.[191]

It was not until 1940–1, when the large munitions factories which had been established in south Wales began to recruit their new workforces, that the full impact of wartime conditions on the employment prospects of local women became apparent. In total, nine new factories – including the five ROFs at Bridgend, Glascoed, Hirwaun, Llanishen and Newport – were erected in south Wales by or on behalf of the government in connection with the rearmament programme, and it was not long before tens of thousands of local women were employed at these works.[192] By 1943 Bridgend and Glascoed ROFs, two of the largest shell-filling factories in the area, employed a total work-force of around 50,000 people, over 70 per cent of whom were females.[193] Females also dominated the 14,000-strong workforce employed at Hirwaun ROF, a factory which specialized in the manufacture of small arms, whilst at the Treforest trading estate near Pontypridd a total of 16,300 men and women were engaged on essential wartime work by April 1944.[194]

In an extremely short period of time, the working experiences of the female population of south Wales had undergone a bewildering transformation. Only two years before the outbreak of the war, south Wales returned one of the lowest proportions of occupied females in Britain and was described as a 'region in which there is normally little industrial employment for female

<hr>

[190] *The Rhondda Gazette*, 15 June 1940.
[191] Merthyr Tydfil Town Public Library, Merthyr Tydfil Education Committee minutes, Juvenile Employment Committee Report, 21 November 1939.
[192] *Parliamentary Debates* (Hansard) (5th series), vol. 329, 395 (17 November 1937); ibid., vol. 334, 1281 (14 April 1938); Ernest Street, 'Royal Ordnance Factory, Glascoed', *Gwent Local History*, no. 60 (1986), 15–18.
[193] Ian Hay, *R.O.F.: The Story of the Royal Ordnance Factories, 1939–1948* (London, 1949), p. 68; Street, 'Royal Ordnance Factory, Glascoed', 15.
[194] Thomas, 'War and the economy', p. 255.

labour'.[195] As an area dominated by heavy industries, the opportunities for full-time paid employment had always been extremely scarce for members of the female population. In the mining districts, married women and many of their daughters were preoccupied with heavy domestic chores directly associated with the employment of their menfolk in the coal industry. The economic crisis which brought about the collapse of the coal industry, and forced thousands of mining families to survive on public assistance, brought immediate changes to the lives of the female members of those households. Young women who had previously accounted for a large proportion of the 'unoccupied' female population left their homes in search of work, often supplementing their families' meagre income. Invariably, however, the only work which was available to them was low-paid employment in the service and retail sectors, where the long hours and poor working conditions offered little opportunity for social or economic independence, and virtually no protection by trade unions. Economic pressures also forced many married women to take part-time work in addition to their usual domestic chores. Since the majority of the women of south Wales had little experience of full-time employment, let alone industrial work, the nature and scale of the economic and social revolution which wartime conditions initiated had a dramatic effect on both the lives of the women of south Wales and the life of the wider community.

---

[195] *Second Industrial Survey of South Wales*, II, p. 80.

II

THE WOMEN OF SOUTH WALES 'GO TO IT'

In September 1944, Councillor Iorwerth Thomas of Cwm-parc, Rhondda, provided the readers of a local newspaper with his observations on the 'magic effect' of the war on the local community. His reflections captured the mood and feelings of the period as the people of the mining valleys contemplated with awe the changes which had taken place in their lives since the outbreak of the war:

> The whole economic and social status of the community has been transformed by the entry of its surplus population into war factories. We have now what can be termed as the 'new rich'. Rhondda's human derelicts – the Flotsams and Jetsams of the valleys – are now conveyed daily on the tide of war prosperity. The former underfed women of all ages, whose husbands have been totally incapacitated owing to ill-health or injuries are now engaged in feeding the war machine . . . The war has been responsible for the creation of a new social problem in these valleys. The revolutionary change of attitude on the part of thousands of married and single women is a definite break with the past industrial traditions of the community.[1]

It is not surprising that Iorwerth Thomas chose to dwell on the effects of the war on the female population of the Rhondda. In the field of employment, wartime conditions had brought new responsibilities and opportunities and the lives of many local women appeared to have been completely transformed. Since the outbreak of the war, thousands of Welsh women had been drawn into wartime industries and a new female workforce had been created. Between July 1939 and July 1943 – the peak year of British wartime production – the number of insured female workers in Wales had increased by 139 per cent.[2] In south Wales, where munitions manufacture was conducted on a grand scale in several newly established war factories, the mass

[1] *The Porth Gazette and Rhondda Leader*, 16 September 1944.
[2] PEP, *Manpower: A Series of Studies of the Composition and Distribution of Britain's Labour-Force* (London, 1951), p. 42.

employment of the female population was a dramatic departure from past industrial and social traditions.

The creation of this new, predominantly female body of industrial workers had an immediate impact on the social and economic life of south Wales. Not only was the traditional economic base of south Wales rapidly transformed by wartime conditions, but the new workforce was acquiring skills and work practices which could have far-reaching implications for future industrial developments in the region. Those who witnessed the female munitions workers at their workbenches were astounded by the competence and efficiency of the new industrial recruits. A newspaper reporter who visited a south Wales factory in August 1941 gave the following account of the scene inside one of the factory workshops where local women were employed:

> Here, they do the bulk of the lighter mechanical work on shells, bombs, detonators, trench mortar charges, fuses and hand grenades. Many of them are examiners. They come by train and bus from cities, towns and villages within a 30 mile radius. They are of all ages. One shell-filling gang includes a grandmother and a girl just turned 18. I saw a red-headed girl not 5 feet in height, filling cordite charges for anti-aircraft shells with a rapid rhythm that would give Nazi airmen a headache, and a woman of 65 who spends three hours a day travelling to and from work, weighing strands of cordite to a minute fraction of a gramme.[3]

The female munitions workers employed at this factory were described as an accomplished and highly skilled team, which was making a valuable contribution to the war effort. Yet, in this commentary, and many others like it, little consideration was given to the significance which the female war workers themselves might attach to their experiences of factory employment.[4] The vast majority of the female war workers of south Wales found themselves sitting at factory benches, performing tasks which were a far cry from their previous working experiences. Apart from learning new working skills and techniques, the war workers forged new friendships and social networks which

---

[3] *Free Press of Monmouthshire*, 15 August 1941.
[4] For a detailed discussion of the disparity between collective expressions of wartime life, as depicted in wartime films, and the personal disquiet and anxiety felt by the individual, see Nick Hayes and Jeff Hill (eds.), *'Millions Like Us'? British Culture in the Second World War* (Liverpool, 1999).

provided access to a wider and more varied social life, while the economic benefits of wartime employment brought welcome relief to their personal and family situations. Munitions work also gave the women of south Wales the opportunity to participate directly in the war effort. After all, the munitions workers produced armaments – the basic tools of every military campaign. In many ways, therefore, war work proved to be both psychologically, economically and socially rewarding to many of those who were engaged in it. Yet, closer examination of the daily experiences of munitions workers at the workplace, their relationships with other workers and their feelings towards their roles as producers of armaments, reveals that, for some women, war work brought little satisfaction. The majority of munitions workers were 'directed' and conscripted to serve in the war factories and, although life within the factory walls proved to be thoroughly enjoyable for some, other workers began their shifts with fear and dread.

In order to comprehend fully how the women of south Wales reacted to their new roles as industrial workers, it is vital to examine the processes which led to their entry to the factories. It was not until the early summer of 1940, following Churchill's appointment as prime minister, that measures were first taken to formulate the policies and administration which would control manpower and industry throughout the conflict. In June 1940 a new Factory and Welfare Department and Advisory Board was created under the leadership of Ernest Bevin, the Minister of Labour and National Service. Local welfare officers were appointed to oversee the manpower and labour demands of factories in each of Britain's twelve 'districts', and in Wales, Ivor Thomas, who had previously been engaged as warden of the Pontypool Educational Settlement, took up his position at Cardiff under R. J. Humphreys, district controller of Wales (renamed regional controller in 1941).[5] One of the first tasks set

---

[5] *Western Mail*, 15 August 1940. Two of the welfare officers who were appointed to assist Ivor Thomas at the Ministry of Labour offices at Cardiff had a similar background in social and welfare work: Alice Huws Davies (widow of T. Huws Davies, editor of *The Welsh Outlook*, 1920–5) had represented Wales on the Ministry of Labour's Central Committee on Women's Training and Employment and had worked at Coleg Harlech, while Eirene Lloyd Jones, daughter of Thomas Jones CH, had been employed by the Central Committee on Women's Training and Employment. For fuller details on the wartime organization and administration of the Ministry of Labour and National Service in Wales, see Public Record Office (PRO), Lab 12/137.

before these officers was to establish the extent and nature of the available and potential supply of labour in their area. In the summer of 1940 a manpower survey was commissioned by William Beveridge, chairman of the Manpower Requirements Committee of the Production Council, with the aim of securing detailed information as to the exact numbers of men and women who could be employed in work of 'national importance'. Only after collating this important information would the local Ministry of Labour officers be able to plan their mobilization schemes and target the available labour in their respective areas.

In south Wales, the manpower survey was conducted by J. Frederick Rees, principal of the University College of South Wales, Cardiff, with the assistance of Hilda Jennings, D. E. Evans and L. N. Hopper.[6] Their investigations into the supply of labour in the region focused on a wide range of potential sources – including unemployed persons, part-time workers and juveniles – in six sample areas: Merthyr Tydfil, the Rhondda, Pontypridd, Pontypool, Newport and Cardiff. In the main, however, the survey investigators concentrated on assessing the potential reserves of female labour, and detailed reports on the situation prevailing in the six sample areas were furnished to the Manpower Requirements Committee. From all six areas the reporters heard evidence that many females employed in 'non-essential' occupations, such as domestic servants or shop assistants, could be drawn into the munitions factories. Moreover, it was noted that a considerable number of domestic servants currently occupied outside the region would return home to take up war work in their localities when such opportunities became available. Returns made to a questionnaire circulated among several of the women's clubs organized by the Welsh Council of Social Service in the Rhondda suggested that these exiled young women would come home at once 'if good pay and conditions of work, as well as close proximity to their homes were ensured'.[7] Earlier reports from the office of the Ministry of Labour's district controller in Wales had also indicated that a potential supply of

---

[6] GRO, Sir J. Frederick Rees Papers, 'Papers of a survey of manpower in south Wales, made by Principal J. F. Rees, assisted by Hilda Jennings, D. E. Evans and L. N. Hopper, as part of the national survey by Sir William Beveridge, July–August 1940' (hereafter *Beveridge Manpower Survey*, 1940).
[7] Ibid.

'several thousands of women and girls', most of whom were returnee domestic servants, could be employed in wartime production.[8]

In addition to investigating the number of women who could be drawn from non-essential occupations, the researchers examined the potential supply of 'unoccupied' females in each area. At Merthyr Tydfil the local Assistance Board officer told the investigators that a 'considerable number' of dependent women could become available for wartime work. He added that new factories in the area were not experiencing any difficulties in recruiting female labour locally, a sign that there was a large unregistered potential supply of workers which would reveal itself when demand arose. Street samples and returns made to the questionnaire circulated among the local women's clubs indicated that there was a 'considerable reserve' of female labour in the Rhondda valleys also. Door-to-door inquiries at Ferndale and Maerdy in the Rhondda Fach had revealed that many dependent females could be regarded as being immediately available for work. Over one hundred girls in the five hundred households visited had stated that they would be willing to take up full-time work. At Pontypridd the manager of the employment exchange intimated that the introduction of short-time working in the coal mines, and the consequent reduction in family incomes, might also persuade many miners' wives and daughters to enter the war factories. Indeed, the replies received from the women's clubs in the area confirmed that work was 'desired by many women' precisely because of this loss of income.[9]

The results of the manpower survey were very encouraging, for the women of south Wales seemed only too eager to come forward and play their part in the war effort. Given that the state's appeal for female war workers retained its voluntary principle until 1941, propaganda became a powerful tool in the campaign to recruit their services at war factories. The women of south Wales were frequently targeted in the radio broadcasts

[8] PRO, Lab 12/82. Similar evidence was put forward in GRO, Industrial Development Council of Wales and Monmouthshire Papers, 'Is unemployment ending? Part II', 5 June 1939; and Percy Watkins, *Educational Settlements in South Wales and Monmouthshire* (Cardiff, 1940), p. 9.

[9] *Beveridge Manpower Survey*, 1940.

produced for the Ministry of Information by the BBC. Jack Jones
(1884–1970), the Merthyr-born writer who was employed by the
ministry as an itinerant speaker during the war, was also commissioned to write several of these radio broadcasts. Jones knew
his people well and produced scripts which would appeal directly
to the men and women of the south Wales valleys. In a moving
tribute to the women of south Wales entitled 'Women in
adversity', he pointed to the courage and determination which
they had shown in the face of mining disasters throughout the
years, qualities which would give them the strength to carry on
through the current conflict:

> the regal courage of the women of our mining communities shines like a
> beacon light through the gathering darkness of despair. Dozens of times
> the women-folk of the Welsh miners have had to face up to such blows, the
> heaviest of which have practically wiped out the working populations of
> little townships.[10]

The same powerful images were presented in two other 'radio
pictures' which Jones wrote in the early years of the war, namely,
'Keep the home fires burning' (1939) and 'Wales marches on'
(1941),[11] both produced in collaboration with T. Rowland
Hughes.[12] Both the wives and daughters of miners were portrayed as stoic characters, well-equipped to cope with the
imminent challenge of war, and always unstinting in their efforts
to support the actions of their menfolk. In the short piece, 'Wales
marches on', Gwen, a miner's daughter, returns home from her
position as a domestic servant in London to announce that she
intends to enlist for war work. Her father's reaction captured the
feelings of many other parents from the mining communities
who were now seeing their sons and daughters being given the
opportunity to take up paid employment locally:

> This war, bad as it is in many ways, has been the making as well as
> the breaking of many. Young chaps that nobody had much use for in

---

[10] Jack Jones, 'Women in adversity', in Patrick Hannan (ed.), *Wales on the Wireless: A Broadcasting Anthology* (Llandysul, 1988), p. 103.

[11] NLW, Jack Jones MSS 88 and 144.

[12] T. Rowland Hughes (1903–49), a celebrated Welsh-language novelist and poet, had been employed as a producer with the BBC at Cardiff since 1935.

peacetime have helped to save this country from Hitler's gang. Now our
Gwen, instead of looking after those well able to look after themselves, is
going to serve her country. What is there wrong in that?[13]

The actual effect such broadcasts had upon the radio audience
of south Wales is impossible to measure. Yet, it would appear
that these carefully crafted works did make quite an impression
on their intended targets, for thousands of women entered the
munitions factories of south Wales long before any measures to
'direct' them had been applied. As William Hornby, the official
war historian, remarked, the ROF at Bridgend, 'where unemployment persisted even in 1940, had the least difficulty in
recruiting labour'.[14] In fact, the main problem facing Ministry of
Labour officials in the region was not a shortage of labour, but a
shortage of jobs in which to place the available workforce.[15] In
April 1940, George Hall MP complained that no action had
been taken to find work for females in his constituency of
Aberdare. Unemployed women were still being transferred away
from their home districts to take up domestic work and he
demanded their immediate return to war work in their locality.[16]

The first steps to recruit labour for the ROFs at Bridgend and
Glascoed got under way in January 1940, when it was reported
that 350 female applicants had been interviewed for positions at
Bridgend and sixty men and women had applied for clerical and
maintenance work at Glascoed.[17] Patriotic motives certainly
played their part, and many of these volunteers must have welcomed the opportunity to make such a direct contribution to the
war effort. Britain's entry into the war had stirred strong anti-
German sentiments and, for those who had lost loved ones
during the Great War, munitions work gave them the chance to
seek their revenge. Not all the new recruits were driven by such
motives, however, and it became increasingly evident that many
were attracted by the social and economic benefits of factory
employment. In January 1940, the Merthyr Tydfil Juvenile
Employment Committee reported that 90 per cent of the young

[13] NLW, Jack Jones MS 144.
[14] William Hornby, *Factories and Plant* (London, 1958), p. 101.
[15] H. M. D. Parker, *Manpower: A Study of War-time Policy and Administration* (London,
1957), p. 282.
[16] *Parliamentary Debates* (Hansard) (5th series), vol. 359, 847 (16 April 1940).
[17] PRO, Lab 12/82.

women on their registers preferred factory employment to domestic work because 'the prospect of having a night off' appealed to them.[18] For women who had experienced un-employment, or had been occupied in low-paid 'blind alley' jobs, the wages which could be earned at munitions factories were another important attraction.[19] In January 1941 a shortage of waitresses was reported at Swansea as young girls left their lower-paid jobs in the cafés and entered the munitions factories. At Cardiff, the headmistress of a local girls' school complained that the high wages paid at the war factories were tempting some of the older pupils to leave school earlier than they should, while the voluntary evacuation scheme run by the local authority ran into difficulties in 1941 when many of the female volunteers rushed to join the city's growing industrial army.[20] The govern-ment was evidently fully aware of the fact that high wages would attract new workers to its factories. In autumn 1941, when increased production demands led to a great recruitment drive in the war factories of south Wales, the Ministry of Labour's cam-paigns to target unoccupied married women in the area made explicit references to the high wages which could be earned 'on munitions'. A poster which appeared in the south Wales press in November 1941 declared in bold print that an average weekly wage of £3 was currently being paid to female munitions workers in the area. Faced with such a lucrative proposition, thousands of women eagerly came forward.

By 1941 labour shortages had become a serious problem in many of the war factories of Britain and it was clear that the state would have to apply compulsory measures to 'direct' the female population to wartime service if production needs were to be met. The body responsible for advising the Ministry of Labour on matters relating to the registration and mobilization of women was the Women's Consultative Committee whose mem-bers included MPs, trade unionists and Ministry of Labour representatives. The committee, which met for the first time in March 1941, played a key role in formulating the mobilization

[18] *Merthyr Express*, 20 January 1940.
[19] See the evidence of Megan Jones (b. 1915), who immediately left her job as an assistant at a chemist shop when she realized how much money could be earned at Bridgend ROF. Grenfell-Hill (ed.), *Growing Up in Wales*, p. 41.
[20] *South Wales Evening Post*, 8 January 1941; *Western Mail*, 23 June 1943; GRO, Cardiff RDC minutes, 13 June 1941.

programme, for it decided which groups of women were to be drawn into wartime service and in which order, and which groups were to be protected from compulsion. Until March 1941 the Ministry of Labour pursued a voluntary appeal for female war workers, resisting the introduction of any measures which could threaten or disrupt the family unit. However, following the passing of the Registration of Employment Order in March 1941, all women aged between eighteen and forty-five were called on to register at their local employment exchanges, giving notice of their work situation and the nature of their domestic or parental responsibilities. The registration process began on 19 April 1941, when all those born in the year 1910 were called forward. Subsequently, every few weeks, women from a different age group were registered. In south Wales, reaction to the actions of the government appeared favourable. In March 1941 the chief conciliation and industrial relations officer of the Ministry of Labour in the region reported that

> the news that the Government has decided to register women for war work has been well received and the local press has done much to prompt enthusiasm for the scheme. The general opinion even among women is that the scheme should have been introduced much earlier.[21]

Although the registration orders called on both married and single women to register for war service, not all these women would eventually be 'directed' to war work. It was decided that certain categories of women would be exempt from compulsion, namely, pregnant women, mothers of children under fourteen years of age, and women who had specific 'domestic responsibilities' which, according to the criteria of the Women's Consultative Committee, rendered them unavailable for work.[22] In granting such exemptions, the government not only made clear its desire to protect the family as an institution, but also reinforced a traditional view of the role of women as wives, mothers and carers within the home and family unit. In her examination of the wartime policy of the United States government, Sonya Michel has argued that the country's leaders upheld

[21] PRO, Lab 10/367.
[22] For a detailed discussion on the nature of the 'domestic responsibilities' which secured exemption from compulsory war work, see ch. 3.

similar ideals regarding the role of women as defenders of the
family and the nation:

> Official recognition of the significance of home and family reassured the
> American public that the society had not lost its grip on the essential values
> of civilization. Women *as mothers* were charged with perpetuating the
> culture that men were fighting for; abandoning this role in wartime would
> not only upset the gender balance but undermine the very core of
> American society.[23]

Even though the British state eventually went further than any
of the other warring nations in its conscription of female labour,
this ideology remained central to the mobilization policies which
it pursued throughout the war, and formed the basis of its
classification of female labour into the two categories of 'mobile'
and 'immobile' workers. Only single, childless women aged
between twenty and thirty were to be regarded as mobile
workers who could be transferred to work in areas of the country
where a labour shortage had been reported. All married women,
regardless of their domestic circumstances, were regarded as
immobile and would not be called upon to take up war work in
factories away from their homes. With the passing of the
National Service (No.2) Act in December 1941, the first step to
conscript female workers was taken. The call-up of single women
aged between twenty and thirty began in January 1942, and,
following the passing of the Employment of Women (Control of
Engagement) Order in February, eligible women within this age
group could only take up work through their local employment
exchange or Ministry of Labour agency.[24] These measures gave
the state considerable powers to place women either in the
services or in wartime industries and, in the months which
followed, its powers of conscription were gradually extended as
the criteria which secured exemption were changed to meet the
growing demands of wartime production. By 1943 the Ministry
of Labour had extended its registration order to include women

---

[23] Sonya Michel, 'American women and the discourse of the democratic family in
World War II', in Higonnet et al. (eds.), *Behind the Lines*, pp. 154–67.
[24] These regulations and those that followed evidently called for some explanation, as
the following publications indicate: Dr Edith Summerskill, *Women Fall In: A Guide to
Women's Work in War-Time* (London, 1941); Labour Research Department, *A Complete
Guide to the Call Up of Women* (London, [c.1943]).

up to the age of fifty, while those who had not been deemed available for full-time employment were found part-time jobs. As the official historian M. M. Postan noted, these changes to the employment orders directed an ever-increasing number of women into wartime service:

> What brought women in was the growing vigour with which the Orders were applied, the wider use of official powers, and, above all, the gradual paring down of the definitions of 'immobility' and 'domestic responsibilities' by which a large group of women had originally been shielded from mobilisation.[25]

The effect of these measures became immediately evident in the munitions factories of Wales, as thousands more women workers were drawn into their workforces. By January 1942 it was reported that more than a third of all Welsh war workers were female. Two months later, the proportion had increased to more than half, a figure which the *Western Mail* declared as being 'particularly gratifying in view of the fact that the women of Wales are by no means factory-minded'.[26] In the shell-filling factories, where the demand for unskilled labour was particularly acute, females were employed in great numbers. As table 2.1 shows, the workforce at both Bridgend and Glascoed ROFs quickly swelled in the early months of production, and by the end of 1941 the two factories employed over 44,000 workers, nearly 70 per cent of whom were female. By 1942 it was reported that only 3 per cent of all those employed at British ROFs were skilled men, while females made up 57 per cent of all employees by the following year.[27] At the ROFs of Bridgend and Glascoed, women were estimated to comprise between 70 and 80 per cent of the total workforce by this period.[28]

The employment of such large numbers of men and women brought new life to communities where mass unemployment and poverty had reigned in recent years. The new prosperity which wartime employment suddenly generated in the mining valleys

[25] M. M. Postan, *British War Production* (London, 1952), pp. 221–2.
[26] *Western Mail*, 23 January 1942, 23 March 1942.
[27] Inman, *Labour in the Munitions Industries*, p. 181; Ministry of Information, *British Women at War* (London, 1944), p. 48.
[28] J. M. Hooks, [United States Department of Labor, Bulletin of the Women's Bureau] *British Policies and Methods in Employing Women in Wartime* (Washington, 1944), p. 26.

Table 2.1: *Number of males and females employed at Bridgend and Glascoed Royal Ordnance factories, 1940–1941*

Date	Bridgend ROF			Glascoed ROF		
	Males	Females	Total	Males	Females	Total
15 April 1940	700	250	950	170	–	170
20 May 1940	1200	1150	2350	1200	–	1200
17 June 1940	1471	2071	3542	1389	214	1603
16 September 1940	2064	3884	5948	3083	1270	4353
14 October 1940	2418	4946	7364	2407	1501	3908
11 November 1940	2835	6005	8840	3077	2190	5267
9 December 1940	3327	6810	10137	3715	2618	6333
13 January 1941	3999	7374	11373	*	*	*
10 February 1941	4614	8559	13173	4651	3386	8037
17 March 1941	5225	10613	15838	4843	3879	8722
21 April 1941	7283	15913	23196	5301	4471	9772
12 May 1941	7642	16432	24074	5353	4665	10018
16 June 1941	8265	17569	25834	5721	5489	11210
14 July 1941	8338	18792	27130	5768	5446	11214
11 August 1941	8384	19943	28327	5729	5479	11208
17 November 1941	8581	23465	32046	5804	6640	12444

* No figures available.

Source: PRO, Lab 12/82.

was immediately visible to Thomas Jones CH, the south Wales and Monmouthshire divisional food officer, who wrote in 1942: 'The waging of war has filled the valleys with work and wages. Boys swagger in the streets with pocketfuls of money. Omnibuses crowded with women and girls rumble to and fro between the scattered mining villages and the concentrated munition factories.'[29] The men and women who were employed at Bridgend ROF were drawn from a wide geographical area, stretching from Merthyr Tydfil on the northern rim of the coalfield to the Aman and Swansea valleys in the west. The workforce employed at Glascoed ROF, near Pontypool, came mainly from the industrial towns and villages of Monmouthshire, although some travelled from as far north as Crickhowell and

[29] Thomas Jones, 'Foreword', in Ginzberg, *A World without Work*, p. xxvi.

from Cardiff in the south.[30] Even the Curran Works at Cardiff attracted workers from as far afield as Rhymney, Merthyr and Aberdare.[31]

The arrival and departure of convoys of buses and trains carrying hundreds of women of all ages to and from the war factories were an unusual sight in the towns and villages of south Wales and remained something of a novelty throughout the war, as revealed in this detailed description of female munitions workers penned by a reporter from the *Aberdare Leader* in October 1943:

> Women and girls of all ages, married and unmarried, wearing turbans and 'slacks', smoking, laughing, haversacks slung on their shoulders, or little attaché cases in their hands – contrasting rather incongruously with 'permed' hair and lipstick – hurrying in large numbers to the bus and railway station, or, at the end of the day, pouring out of them in a swarm, tired, work-stained, but still laughing and cracking a joke. An unfamiliar sight surely in Wales, where women's place was always regarded as being in the home.[32]

This portrayal of a merry band of war workers, tired but happy and united in a common cause, was a recurring image in the wartime descriptions of female munitions workers.[33] In the opinion of Margaret Goldsmith, the war factories of Britain became great social melting-pots, as women of all ages, marital status, social classes, and backgrounds forgot their differences and joined together in wartime service.[34] The women who formed new workforces in the war factories of south Wales were also drawn from a wide range of age groups. Mollie Tarrant, the Mass-Observation investigator who undertook a wartime study of the coal mining town of Blaina in Monmouthshire, remarked upon the 'wide age-span' of the local female war workers: 'A large number of the war workers are married, most are young . . . and many women in their forties and fifties are among the crowds

[30] PRO, Lab 26/90 and 26/91; *Beveridge Manpower Survey*, 1940.
[31] *The War Effort at the Curran Works, Cardiff.*
[32] *Aberdare Leader*, 9 October 1943.
[33] See Vera Douie, *Daughters of Britain: An Account of the Work of British Women during the Second World War* (London, 1949), p. 95.
[34] Margaret Goldsmith, *Women at War* (London, 1943), p. 193.

which come from the munition workers' trains.'[35] However, the vast majority of the Welsh workers shared the same social and economic background: most of the women who were employed at Bridgend ROF, for example, came from the surrounding mining communities. Residents of the same street, or even members of the same family, travelled together to the factory and sometimes worked next to one another on the factory benches. And, although many women became friends with workers from towns and villages many miles away from their own homes, their new associations rarely cut across class barriers.

In many ways, therefore, the factories of south Wales were places which reinforced existing class and cultural identities, fostering a real sense of community and comradeship among the workforce. Lasting friendships were formed between the workers, many of whom worked alongside each other throughout the war. Even though the majority of the tasks performed at the work-benches were extremely tedious and potentially dangerous, the friendly banter and impromptu sing-alongs in the workshops – often to the accompaniment of *Music While you Work* – lightened the atmosphere.[36] Indeed, the camaraderie among the workers was likened by one former ROF employee to the bond between the local colliers who laboured underground in the pits.[37] The communal feeling was often carried through to the social life of the factories. For example, workers from the various depart-ments or sections within Bridgend ROF established their own singing and dance groups and organized lunchtime concerts for the entertainment of their fellow workers.[38] Jennie Lee, MP for Cannock and wife of Aneurin Bevan, was immediately struck by the community spirit fostered among workers at the wartime factories which she visited:

> The factory canteen for instance was a happy place to go into. It was a club, a concert hall, a debating society as well as a place to eat . . . Especially where women were employed, those breaks for tea were a great

[35] Mass-Observation Archive (M-O A), File Report (FR) 1498, 'Blaina: a study of a coal mining town', November 1942, p. 88. For a detailed discussion of the objectives, contents and conclusions of this unique wartime study, see Brian Roberts, 'A mining town in wartime: the fears for the future', *Llafur*, 6, no. 1 (1992), 82–95.

[36] Evidence of Respondents 1, 3, 5, 6, 12 and 15.

[37] Evidence of Respondent 4.

[38] A photograph of 'The Pelleteers', a concert troupe formed by workers from the pellet section at Bridgend ROF, is reproduced in Hay, *R.O.F.*, p. 84.

feature of the working day, life was strenuous, life was earnest, but there was also drama, excitement, a heightened sense of living in those wartime factories. The men and women in them were earning their living. But they were doing a great deal more than that and were very conscious that they were. This was their way of fighting Hitler. They were answering back in the one way they knew.[39]

To all those involved in the manufacture of munitions, the knowledge that they were making a direct contribution to the war effort was never far from their minds. Although some workers might not wish to dwell on the consequences of their war work and the havoc wreaked by the shells and bullets which they had handled with such care, others drew great strength from the fact that their efforts could help save the lives of their loved ones who were fighting at the front. Workers strove to meet production targets, thus ensuring a steady supply of armaments. Frustrated by the amount of time they wasted sitting in the factory's air-raid shelters, one group of workers from Bridgend ROF even asked for special permission to continue working during air raids:

> We'd sit there [in the shelters], tired to the world, and you knew what a lovely warm shop you had up there and then, I don't know who said it, but 'That's what the bugger [Hitler] wants us to do – not fill any bombs, come on girls, let's get cracking!' And that's how it started.[40]

Great care was also taken to ensure that the munitions being produced met the high standards of the inspectors. As one ex-munitions worker explained: 'We put a lot into it and it was such accurate work, you couldn't send nothing out that wasn't right, because you knew somebody's life depended on it.'[41] Morale at the factory was boosted when news was received of a successful military campaign using munitions produced by the workers. At Bridgend ROF, for example, pictures of German battleships sunk by shells produced at the factory were displayed alongside the wall-charts which recorded the daily production output of

[39] Jennie Lee, *This Great Journey: A Volume of Autobiography, 1904–45* (London, 1963), pp. 200–1.
[40] Evidence of Respondent 16.
[41] Evidence of Respondent 3.

each workshop.[42] 'Victory shows' and exhibitions were also organized at some south Wales factories in a bid to 'educate the workers to the importance of the part they filled' and to 'make them conscious of their responsibilities' to the war effort.[43] Sometimes, the factory workers came in direct contact with servicemen who had used munitions which had been produced at the factory. Women who had written messages of encouragement to the soldiers on the shell-cases occasionally received letters of thanks in reply,[44] while members of the armed forces sometimes visited the factories to express their appreciation in person.[45]

Yet, despite such displays of unity and comradeship, tensions and frayed nerves often came to the surface in the heightened atmosphere of the factory workshops, revealing disharmony and divisions among the workers. It was widely recognized that relations between managers and ordinary workers were very strained in many of the British war factories.[46] In 1945 a report prepared by the Industrial Health Research Board drew attention to the 'lack of social unity between different levels of the factory society, and to the remote or non-existent contact between workers and other groups, such as supervisors and, in particular, managers'.[47] In fact, divisions existed not only between workers on the shop-floor, the office staff, the supervisors and the managers, but also between the 'tidy', respectable women and the 'common' or 'rough types', who were associated with illicit or even immoral behaviour.[48] Jean Wynne, who worked at a munitions factory in Sheffield, found it extremely difficult to cope with the whole experience:

> When you've been brought up in a sheltered way, and you're a quiet sort of person anyway, it is a shock to go into a munitions works. However

---

[42] Evidence of Respondent 1; *Aberdare Leader*, 9 October 1943.

[43] *Western Mail*, 6 October 1943.

[44] Having placed a slip of paper bearing her name and address in a box of shells, a munitions worker from Pontnewydd received a letter from 'Bill, George and the boys of "Mary"', who manned an anti-artillery site in the south of England. They explained that the 'excellent ammo' had 'done very well against the "doodle-bugs" for which we give you much credit', and to show their appreciation of her efforts they had named their gun after her. *Free Press of Monmouthshire*, 29 September 1944.

[45] Evidence of Respondent 7; *Western Mail*, 13 May 1941; *Free Press of Monmouthshire*, 15 August 1941.

[46] Lee, *This Great Journey*, p. 200.

[47] S. Wyatt et al., *A Study of Women on War Work in Four Factories*, MRC Industrial Health Research Board Report no. 88 (London, 1945), p. 1.

[48] A. P. Jephcott, *Girls Growing Up* (London, 1942), p. 77. See also ch. 4.

much I tried to hold my own, it was much rougher than I'd ever expected it to be.[49]

A former employee of Bridgend ROF remarked that, intially, she too found the language and subject matter of the everyday conversations of some of her fellow workers extremely shocking.[50] Recalling her first visit to the factory canteen, another former ROF worker explained how a group of older workers with whom she was acquainted took her under their wing until she 'found a nice girl of my standards' with whom she could sit.[51]

Clearly not all workers felt at home in the factory environment where women of all ages and 'character' laboured side by side. The fact that very few of the women employed in the war factories of south Wales had any previous experience of factory employment did not make matters any easier. A survey undertaken at one ROF in south Wales in June 1941 revealed that only 5 per cent of its female workforce had any previous experience of factory work: 85 per cent had been employed either in the 'luxury' trades, or as domestic servants, dressmakers, waitresses or clerical workers, while the remaining 10 per cent had never previously been employed.[52] The compilers of the *Beveridge Manpower Survey* of south Wales noted in 1940 that 'several cases were reported of women of the "better class domestic servant" type being unable to stand the strain, and especially the noise of work', in the Curran Works, Cardiff.[53] To many inexperienced workers, both the social and practical aspects of factory life must have appeared quite daunting. At the workbenches, new skills, work practices and even a whole new vocabulary needed to be acquired: the specially produced manual, *Munitions Girl: A Handbook for the Women of the Industrial Army* (1942), contained a detailed glossary of 'essential' technical terms for the new recruit.[54] As a reporter for the *Aberdare Leader* indicated in a 1943

---

[49] Evidence of Jean Wynne, in Nicholson, *What Did You Do in the War, Mummy?*, p. 204.
[50] Evidence of Respondent 4.
[51] Evidence of Respondent 5.
[52] *Western Mail*, 6 June 1941.
[53] *Beveridge Manpower Survey*, 1940.
[54] Caroline Haslett (adviser to the Ministry of Labour and National Service on women's training and past president of the Women's Engineering Society), *Munitions Girl: A Handbook for the Women of the Industrial Army* (London, 1942).

feature-article, the ROFs – and all that they entailed – were places which demanded description and definition:

> To most people, perhaps, 'R.O.F.' is hazy in its form and significance, a place quite often mentioned in the police courts when workers are fined for absenteeism, or prosecuted for pilfering, a place associated with unfamiliar sounding industrial terms, like labour manager, shopsteward, overlooker, tool-setter and worktaker, a place where fantastically high wages are paid; but above all, an indefinable place of obscure functions (except that it makes munitions), in an uncertain place ('Somewhere in Wales'), to which thousands of women and girls, and rather fewer men, from villages and towns within a wide radius, depart at fixed times, on different shifts by special R.O.F. trains.[55]

From the outset, therefore, there were signs that some of the Welsh factory recruits did not adapt easily to their new roles, and it appeared that there might be some foundation to the claim that Welsh girls were not 'factory-minded'. In November 1941 the Ministry of Supply revealed that it was experiencing great difficulty in trying to persuade the employees of Bridgend ROF to 'live in' at the newly built workers' hostels near the factory. Although accommodation for 2,000 workers was provided in the purpose-built units, only 300 young women had agreed to live in the hostels by that date.[56] A similar situation prevailed in Monmouthshire, where the hostels which had been built to house workers employed at Glascoed ROF were said to be only '2 per cent occupied' in December 1941.[57] The following year it was reported that construction work at hostels for 1,000 females employed at a south Wales munitions factory had been temporarily suspended because of the 'disinclination of the girls for whom it was intended, to leave their homes and take up residence'.[58] In the 1943 film, *Millions Like Us* – a production commissioned by the government to 'address the low recruitment and morale of women in factory work'[59] – Gwen Price

[55] *Aberdare Leader*, 9 October 1943.
[56] PRO, Lab 10/367.
[57] *Free Press of Monmouthshire*, 26 December 1941.
[58] *Western Mail*, 13 July 1942; SWCA, Ammanford, Llandybïe and District Trades and Labour Council (TLC) minutes, 8 June 1942. See, also, Office of the Minister of Reconstruction, *Welsh Reconstruction Advisory Council – First Interim Report* (London, 1944), p. 20.
[59] Sue Harper, 'The years of total war: propaganda and entertainment', in Gledhill and Swanson (eds.), *Nationalising Femininity*, p. 202.

(played by the Welsh actress Meg Jenkins) was to be seen remarking on the high standard of accommodation provided for
workers in factory hostels, where living conditions were far
superior to those she had previously experienced in her ordinary
Welsh mining home.[60] Despite such glowing commendation,
hostel life seemed to hold little attraction for the vast majority of
the factory girls of south Wales. The cost of staying at these
institutions may well have affected their popularity. As P. Inman,
the author of the official history of labour in the munitions
industries, noted, the hostel charge of '25s a week seemed more
to, say, a Welsh girl than to those in more prosperous districts;
many of the Welsh workers also made a practice of sending
money home.'[61] There were also other considerations which
might have caused some deliberation in the minds of this new
workforce. It was reported that the majority of the female
munitions workers of south Wales preferred to travel daily to the
factories from their homes some twenty or thirty miles away,
rather than endure the grim prospect of 'washing in front of
other girls' and sharing in the many other unappealing aspects of
'communal living'.[62] Two munitions workers from the Swansea
area, who were summonsed in December 1943 for leaving their
employment at a Monmouthshire factory without permission,
blamed the poor living conditions at the hostel for their departure. Not only had the food been of extremely poor quality, but
the lack of secure locks on their doors and the sound of 'men's
voices in the women's sleeping quarters' had been too much to
bear.[63]

The regime associated with factory life was not always readily
accepted and many factory employees resented the strict
discipline and enforcement of security regulations. In the filling
factories, where workers handled explosive materials, both safety
and security were of paramount importance. Workers were
searched as they entered and left the workplace and were also
subject to frequent random searches on the factory premises. At

[60] Peter Stead, 'The people as stars: feature films as national expression', in Philip M.
Taylor (ed.), *Britain and the Cinema in the Second World War* (London, 1988), p. 77.
[61] Inman, *Labour in the Munitions Industries*, p. 251.
[62] *Western Mail*, 13 July 1942; Mass-Observation, *People in Production: An Enquiry into
British War Production* (London, 1942), p. 293; Amabel Williams-Ellis, *Women in War
Factories* (London, 1943), p. 81.
[63] *South Wales Evening Post*, 15 December 1943.

the beginning of every shift, the munitions workers passed through a security barrier before entering the 'shifting house', where 'dirty' civilian clothes and personal belongings were left behind. All traces of life outside the factory were to be forgotten as the munitions workers, dressed in regulation overalls, turban and protective shoes, stepped into the 'clean' and orderly world of arms manufacture. One ex-munitions worker described her daily passage into Bridgend ROF as follows:

> We used to have to go down the 'dirty ways'. Now, when we'd start, we went into these where we changed our clothes, well, you had to take all your outdoor clothes off on this side of the barrier and then step over the barrier then and put these dungarees on and turbans in your hair, even change your shoes. So you'd strip your clothes off this end and go over, then put their clothes on. Well, then we'd go from there then, it was called the 'clean way'. You had the 'dirty way' and the 'clean way', but you had to make sure that there was no clips, combs, jewellery, you had to take your earrings off – if you could, take your wedding ring off, or they'd cover it for you.[64]

The enforcement of such tight security measures was essential in factories where workers were in direct contact with explosive materials. Every ROF employee was issued with a booklet which listed all the safety regulations and precautions to be taken inside the factory premises, and workers were made aware of the dangerous consequences of any irresponsible or careless behaviour.[65] At the factory benches the workers were closely supervised by passers, overlookers and inspectors, who ensured that all employees carried out their tasks according to the safety regulations.[66] Although the workers were fully aware of the need for such rigorous inspection, many felt that some individuals acted far too officiously towards those under their charge. Several of the former employees of Bridgend ROF described the female welfare officer at the factory as a formidable woman who behaved like a 'sergeant-major' and a 'prison officer', and who terrified many of the factory girls with her strict, disciplinarian

---

[64] Evidence of Respondent 7.
[65] See copy of the *Rules and Regulations of the Royal Ordnance Factories* (London, 1937), issued to Mary A. Evans on 5 February 1941. Aberdare Library, W. W. Price Collection, LH5/19.
[66] Evidence of Respondents 1 and 2.

approach.[67] Some workers may have had other grounds for resenting the interference of their superiors. In the early years of the war, many of the officials who were employed in the factories of south Wales were men and women who had been sent from established English factories to train the inexperienced Welsh workforce.[68] It is possible that the presence of these 'outsiders' created conflict which could have been avoided if the officials had been more familiar with the circumstances and background of those under their supervision. In truth, however, the feelings of the ordinary workers towards their supervisors – be they Welsh or English – were not likely to be very favourable. After all, regardless of their social background and origin, those in authority who gave orders, disciplined and frequently searched the workers and their belongings were unlikely to be popular with members of their staff. Moreover, the women who were employed as inspectors and security guards with the Ordnance Inspections Department and the War Department Constabulary, or were engaged as clerical workers in the administration offices, made up only a very small proportion of the workforce, and would, therefore, always be distanced from the majority of the workers on the shop-floor.

Once inside the factories, workers engaged in the production of munitions made their way to the small workshops where work was performed on the assembly-lines, either by hand or with small tools.[69] At Bridgend ROF, girls aged sixteen and seventeen were placed in the 'textile' section where they undertook various 'non-contact' tasks, such as sewing factory uniforms and powder bags, or pasting cardboard boxes. Once they reached the age of eighteen, these workers were moved to the factory 'sections' where the work of filling shells and detonators was carried out. In each of these small workshops, the workers either manufactured a specific component, or completed one of the many tasks involved in the production of munitions. A description of the female employees of one south Wales factory, busy at their tasks, was provided in the *Aberdare Leader* in October 1943:

---

[67] Evidence of Respondents 2, 3, 4 and 16.
[68] Some 400 workers were sent to Bridgend ROF from Woolwich Arsenal in October 1940. GRO, Maesteg UDC minutes, 15 October 1940.
[69] Postan, *British War Production*, p. 179.

this is one R.O.F. where bullets are made in astronomical quantities by
neat, speedy, trim machines set out in long rows, on acres of concrete floor,
on which the nimble fingers of women and girls work to good effect,
making the glittering little cases, which have to pass very strict tests, and
among which there are remarkably few rejects, showing the very high
quality of British products even when machines are operated by workers of
brief industrial experience. Some of these women tending the machines are
grey-haired; mothers, possibly grandmothers; the majority are younger.
They are all busy.[70]

For some munitions workers, their experiences of factory employment proved to be thoroughly enjoyable. Several of the
former employees of Bridgend ROF interviewed for this study
recalled with pride, and in great detail, the various tasks which
they had performed within the factory. Most of the workers had
been placed in more than one 'section' and many expressed a
preference for one particular job. Those workers who had been
appointed to positions of authority within the factory had a
particularly high regard for their experiences of war work. For
one woman who had been employed as an overlooker at
Bridgend ROF, the whole experience contrasted sharply with
her life before the war, and her memories of wartime service
were extremely positive:

> I lost my mother when I was eleven, so then I was having to look after my
> dad, who was a miner, and my brother, who was a miner, and washing all
> their clothes in the bath, under the tap with the old dolly. Oh! it was hard.
> But this was a doddle, and I did love explosives. I did like the job I was
> doing. Very interesting I found it – very.[71]

Other workers did not find the experience quite so engaging.[72]
Not only was the daily routine of life as a munitions worker
extremely wearisome, but most of the tasks upon which ordinary
workers were engaged were repetitive and downright boring. An

---

70 *Aberdare Leader*, 9 October 1943.
71 Evidence of Respondent 16.
72 See Diana Murray Hill's account of life in a munitions factory where she describes
in great detail the routine and repetitive nature of the work and its soul-destroying effects
upon the workforce. Yvonne M. Klein (ed.), *Beyond the Home Front: Women's Autobiographical
Writing of the Two World Wars* (Basingstoke, 1997), pp. 146–50. See also Hartley, *Millions
Like Us*, pp. 71–87.

investigation conducted by Mass-Observation at a Gloucester-shire factory in 1942 concluded that for many of its female employees, life had become

> a formless vista of days and weeks, from which most physical discomforts have been smoothed out, most cares lifted, and most pleasures and interests gone. Few gleams of aim or purpose lighten this vista, for their interest in the war has been blacked out by this sort of life as surely as their other interests. Instead of feeling 'in it' (as the newspapers would lead one to suppose working in a war factory makes one feel) they feel out of it, in every way, more than they ever have in their lives.[73]

In many factories, the low morale of the workforce could be attributed directly to the nature of the work which was being carried out. Workers who made small mechanical parts or items which appeared totally unconnected with munitions manu-facture were said to be particularly downhearted.[74] Realizing that output could be adversely affected, in February 1942 the Home Intelligence Unit of the Ministry of Information advo-cated more positive propaganda to emphasize the vital role of the individual war worker as a means of inducing a greater sense of purpose and involvement in the war effort:

> Many of the workers stand by their machines, day in, day out, week in, week out, making nothing but nuts and bolts or sprocket-holes, but often they ask in a tired sort of way, 'What good is this towards the war effort?' – They have not grasped the idea that their job, however small, is but one part of a great whole.[75]

One former employee of Bridgend ROF recalled feeling completely despondent after spending hours performing tasks which appeared to serve little purpose:

> Lots and lots of things that we did, we didn't even know what they were for . . . on the sewing machines, we made powder bags and all sorts of powder bags. I mean, all we knew was that they were for powder, some of them

---

[73] Mass-Observation, *War Factory*, 1st edn 1943 (London, 1987), p. 113.
[74] PP 1940–1 (III), *Twenty-first Report from the Select Committee on National Expenditure*, 'Output of labour', p. 17.
[75] PRO, Inf 1/292.

could be huge and others could be little tiny, little, little things. Sometimes, you'd be sitting there for hours and hours and hours, just putting tapes on them. But, I mean, what were they for?[76]

Given that much of the work undertaken on the assembly-lines was not only tedious but also extremely dangerous, the propagandists faced a formidable challenge in trying to make munitions work appealing. Workers who were employed in the production of shells and detonators in the filling factories faced serious risks to their health and safety as they handled poisonous materials such as tetryl, cordite and trinitrotoluene (TNT) and worked under the constant threat of an explosion. The health of workers who were in direct contact with TNT or 'yellow powder' was particularly affected, and the distinctive yellow discoloration of the skin marked them out from the other workers.[77] Although the government took many steps to minimize the unpleasant side-effects of working with TNT, by introducing improved washing facilities and health-care on factory premises and appointing factory welfare officers, the incidence of skin rashes and discoloration remained high.[78] In August 1941, the Home Intelligence Unit of the Ministry of Information reported that in some factories workers were said to be suffering from 'an illness in which the skin turns green'.[79] Former employees of the Welsh ROFs recalled that women who worked in the 'powder' or 'pellet' sections of the factories were easily distinguished by their yellow skin and tinged hair.[80] Despite being issued with protective clothing, turbans and shoes, it appears that it was almost impossible to escape the effects of this fine yellow powder, as one former employee of Bridgend ROF related:

[76] Evidence of Respondent 5.

[77] Skin discoloration caused by contact with TNT was extremely common among the female munitions workers who were employed during the First World War, earning them the name 'canary girls'. See Antonia Ineson and Deborah Thom, 'T.N.T. poisoning and the employment of women workers in the First World War', in Paul Weindling (ed.), *The Social History of Occupational Health* (Beckenham, 1985), pp. 89–107. For the same reason, the female munitions workers employed in south Wales during the Second World War were often referred to as 'budgies'.

[78] PP 1942–3 (III), *Third Report from the Select Committee on National Expenditure*, 'Health and welfare of women in war factories'.

[79] PRO, Inf 1/292.

[80] Evidence of Respondents 3, 4, 5, 6, 7, 16, 18 and 20. In an unusual case reported in March 1943, a munitions worker from Bryn-mawr who, it must be assumed, was engaged on 'non-contact' work in a local factory, was fined £4 after stealing a shilling's worth of TNT in order to tint her hair. *Free Press of Monmouthshire*, 16 March 1945.

Our overalls were supposed to be white, like drill. You had to cover your hair, otherwise you would be blonde. Even your hair went yellow. The powder used to get into everywhere. It was horrible. A lot of people couldn't stand it. They were ill and they were removed then. You had to do your turn in the powder shop, and we used to try and get out of it.[81]

Once the workers had been placed in the powder sections, most aimed to ensure that their stay there would be as short as possible. One twenty-year-old munitions worker from Penrhiwceibr decided to stay away from her place of work on the grounds that the powder was affecting her health. This course of action eventually led to an appearance before Abercynon magistrates' court in September 1942 where the young woman was fined £7 and ordered to return to the factory immediately.[82] Some workers developed an immediate skin reaction to the powder, whereupon they were moved to work in 'non-contact' sections. Those who remained desperately tried to 'create' their own skin conditions. One ex-worker recalled using a crêpe handkerchief to rub pepper into the skin around her eyes in a successful attempt to fake a 'pellet-rash'.[83] Those who remained in 'pellets' for longer periods took their own drastic measures to remove all traces of the yellow powder and used bleach and all manner of detergents on their skin.[84]

Although the munitions workers seemed to be mainly concerned with finding short-term solutions to the 'yellow powder' problem, the uncertainty surrounding the long-term effects of working with such unpleasant and noxious materials caused great anxiety. The Labour Research Department maintained in 1942 that in spite of all the talk about the potential health risks, few people seemed to know 'the up-to-date facts about the exact nature and extent of the dangers and the methods of combating them'.[85] A former nurse who worked in a hospital at Cardiff during the war recalled that members of the medical profession knew very little about these conditions and how best to treat them:

[81] Evidence of Mrs Jones in Pam Schweitzer et al. (eds.), *What Did You Do in the War, Mum?* (London, 1985), p. 71.
[82] *Aberdare Leader*, 5 September 1942.
[83] Evidence of Respondent 3.
[84] Evidence of Respondents 2, 3 and 7.
[85] Labour Research Department, *Women in War Jobs* (London, 1942), p. 16.

There was a patient in a side ward in whom there was a special interest because she had worked in the explosives factory at Bridgend where in one part they used phosphorus. She was extremely yellow in colour, and her internal organs were deteriorating. She developed a very bad abscess in her side. There was considerable concern to find the way of halting the deterioration as there was not much knowledge of the effects of those substances then.[86]

It is not known what happened to this patient, or any others who may have endured the same physical suffering. The South Western District branch of the National Union of General and Municipal Workers (NUGMW) reported in 1941 that many of its members who were employed at ROFs in south Wales had become incapacitated through inhaling TNT fumes.[87] At Blaina in 1942, Mollie Tarrant was informed by one local woman that many munitions workers were affected by the 'TNT rash', and that 'some girls have died of it here'.[88] The actual number of lives claimed in south Wales by TNT poisoning is unknown, for the stories of those workers, along with the men and women who suffered long-term health problems as a result of their experiences of war work, went largely unrecorded.[89]

However, for the majority of the munitions workers, the most frightening aspect of their life in the factory was that they worked under the constant threat of an explosion. Those who worked with live detonators or were employed in the powder sections knew full well that the slightest vibration, friction or spark could cause an explosion, the consequences of which could be extremely serious. In the detonator sections 'blow-ups' were common, as the evidence of munitions workers who were employed at filling factories across Britain reveals.[90] All the former

---

[86] NLW, MSS N23071E and N23072–3D.
[87] NLW, Minor Deposit A1994/81.
[88] M-O A, Topic Collection (TC) 64, Coal mining, Box 1, File C.
[89] The only reported fatality which has come to the attention of the author is that of a 61-year-old male, a former Bridgend ROF employee, who died in 1949. The medical evidence recorded that his death was due to carcinoma of the lung accelerated by TNT poisoning contracted whilst employed at the factory. *Glamorgan Gazette*, 2 December 1949.
[90] See the evidence of the following: Mrs Isabella Gilmour, 'Factory life', in Liverpool City Council, *Liverpool Women at War: An Anthology of Personal Memories* (Liverpool, 1991), p. 115; Mair Davies, 'The Royal Ordnance Factory, Bridgend', in Verrill-Rhys and Beddoe (eds.), *Parachutes and Petticoats*, pp. 81–2; Jean Wynne, '. . . and pass the ammunition', in Nicholson, *What Did you Do in the War, Mummy?*, pp. 201–6; Mildred Evans (b.1920), in Grenfell-Hill (ed.), *Growing Up in Wales*, p. 175.

employees of Bridgend ROF who were interviewed for this study had witnessed or heard explosions – incidents which they were officially forbidden to talk about once outside the factory. Some of the 'blow-ups' resulted in deaths, while many more caused horrific physical injuries. The report produced in 1941 by the People's Convention (an organization with strong links with the Communist Party) gave a rare insight into the dangers faced by munitions workers in the British war factories.[91] Its grim picture of 'What a war factory is really like' exposed tales of 'frequent' explosions which had resulted in 'some deaths' and many workers losing 'eyes, hands, fingers or thumbs'.[92] Given that most workers in the filling factories handled explosive materials every day, it is remarkable that only 134 munitions workers lost their lives in British ROFs during the Second World War.[93]

The total number of fatalities which occurred in the factories of south Wales is unclear, but reports of the deaths of twenty-two war workers who lost their lives as a result of explosions in the factories of the region have been found in local newspapers.[94] One explosion which took place at an unnamed factory in the area in August 1940 killed five men and seriously injured another three, while three women lost their lives and several others suffered serious injuries in May 1941 following a blast which may well have been at the same works. Fifteen of the twenty-two individuals whose deaths were reported in the local newspapers were males, who were generally responsible for the loading and carrying of large quantities of explosive materials. Although fewer females were reported to have lost their lives in factory accidents, women who worked on the assembly-lines ran a high risk of suffering physical injuries as a result of smaller explosions in the factory workshops. On only her third day at Bridgend ROF in December 1940, a 22-year-old woman from Trecynon was blinded, lost her right hand and badly maimed her left hand

---

[91] The People's Convention, 'What a war factory is really like', *Women Want 'Square Deal'* (1941), p. 3.
[92] Ibid.
[93] Angus Calder, *The People's War: Britain, 1939–1945* (London, 1992 edn), p. 326.
[94] *Free Press of Monmouthshire*, 26 September 1941; *South Wales Echo*, 22 August 1940, 5 July 1941, 1 November 1941, 12 July 1943, 16 November 1943, 20 December 1943, 30 April 1945, 1 June 1945, 22 March 1946, 23 October 1946; *South Wales Evening Post*, 11 August 1943.

in an explosion which killed five and injured fourteen.[95] In May 1943, Winifred Thomas, a 39-year-old from Porth in the Rhondda who worked as an overlooker at the factory, lost one eye and both her lower arms when the box of detonators which she was handling suddenly exploded.[96] Small wonder, therefore, that Bridgend ROF – a filling factory which specialized in the production of detonators and fuses for mortar bombs – was known to many as 'the suicide club'.[97] One woman who volunteered to work with detonators so that she could leave the unpleasant surroundings of the 'pellets' section was soon to regret her decision:

> I remember working down in pellets, in the yellow powder and we used to have our hair going yellow in the front. Then, I volunteered to go into the detonators where they were making the dets. to go for the bombs and that. It was a dangerous section. Well, I had a blow-up there. I was doing the dets. and you had to count them now into twenties . . . Well, I think I'd done about five boxes and I come to the last one with twenty, and, of course, you had to pick these twenty up . . . and the last one blew up in the air. It blew the box up. So, I remember I had that [top of thumb] hanging off, stitched all round there, and all these steel splinters through the eyebrows. But, otherwise, I was lucky, I was, because the poor people that was down there had limbs blown off and blindness. It was terrible down there, mind.[98]

For all the tight security and safety measures, it appears that many of the accidents which occurred in British munitions factories during the Second World War could have been prevented. The evidence of former employees of Bridgend ROF suggests that many workers took unnecessary risks when handling explosives and ignored safety regulations in a bid to reach production targets. Indeed, by awarding financial incentives, prizes and distinctions to workers who exceeded output targets, the factory authorities may be said to have encouraged

[95] BBC Radio Wales broadcast, 'The girls who made the thing-ummy-bobs'; *Aberdare Leader*, 27 November 1943; *Western Mail*, 8 March 1997.

[96] In January 1946 Winifred Thomas was awarded the British Empire Medal in recognition of her bravery and wartime service. *Porth Gazette and Rhondda Leader*, 26 January 1946.

[97] Richard Rees, 'Suicide club: the stirring story of Wales's unsung heroines of the war', *Empire News and Sunday Chronicle*, 8 September–13 October 1957.

[98] Evidence of Respondent 7.

negligence. One munitions worker, who was awarded the distinction of being 'the fastest war worker in Britain' in 1940, was often asked to take over from slower workers, even though the only way she could work quickly was by breaking safety regulations:

> They kept on taking me off the production line to go on the detonators and I refused to do it, because they were asking me all the time and I used to say, 'Well, let one of the other girls do it.' But, they'd say, 'you get on there, because you can do it quicker.' But of course, I used to do it, not the safety way. I used to have the detonators in my lap and just go like this in fact. Well, they had the head-boss, they fetched him to me because the foreman had said I had to do it . . . anyway, the head-boss, and he was from Woolwich, he came and he said, 'you've got to do it, you can't say no.' So I said, 'fair enough, I'll do it, but I'll do it the safety way.' And of course, I did it the way it was supposed to be done, taking one out, putting one in, taking one out and of course they realized what I was doing before.[99]

Considering the grave risks posed to their health and safety, it was not surprising that many munitions workers felt very uneasy about working in the dangerous environment of the factory workshops. The fears of these workers were heightened by the fact that munitions factories were prime targets for enemy air-bombings. An overlooker at Bridgend ROF recalled how the Nazi propagandist, 'Lord Haw Haw' (William Joyce), frequently mentioned the factory in his radio broadcasts: 'He'd be saying, "Hello, you pretty girls up in Bridgend! We know where you are. We are coming to get you!" '[100] In the opinion of some workers, it seemed that the dangers they faced every day in the munitions factories were not always appreciated by other members of the community. One worker, who had been incensed by the comments made in a local newspaper about the high wages undeservedly earned by women in munitions factories, wrote

[99] Evidence of Respondent 4.
[100] Evidence of Respondent 16. In her autobiography, Rachael Ann Webb (b.1903) also recalled hearing such threats being made in wartime radio broadcasts: 'Several times . . . Lord Haw Haw had called out over the airways, "You people of Maesteg think you are safe, but we're coming to blow up your collieries soon, and your arsenal in Bridgend." ' Rachael Ann Webb, *Sirens Over the Valley* (Port Talbot, 1988), pp. 122–3. Further evidence that Bridgend ROF was targeted by the Germans is provided by the existence of a reconnaissance photograph of the arsenal taken by the Luftwaffe on 20 August 1940. The photograph is reproduced in D. Glyn Williams (Foreword and Commentaries), *Old Bridgend in Photographs* (Barry, 1978), [plate 173].

back to inform the readers of the less than favourable conditions which she and her colleagues endured for their money: 'We work a nine-hour night shift from Sunday night to Saturday morning filling and pressing explosives and are liable to get a rash, turn yellow or get blown up, for a little over four pounds a week.'[101]

Not surprisingly, very few of the negative aspects of munitions work were disclosed in either the visual or the literary propaganda which was produced to attract new recruits to the factories. Few of the munitions workers who laboured alongside Diana Murray Hill at one British factory resembled the 'glowing figures of the posters and the documentaries', and the grinding routine of factory life had turned the majority into 'very poor shadows of the War Effort girls'.[102] Films which were produced by the Ministry of Information and shown before a full house at Fernhill Workmen's Hall, Tynewydd, in July 1941, portrayed the lighter side of life in the war factories and explained how entertainment in the form of concerts and radio broadcasts was provided for factory workers.[103] Even the film *Danger Area* (1944), a production filmed for the Ministry of Information at a Welsh factory, concentrated on praising female war workers for their part in supporting the fighting soldiers, rather than dwelling upon the actual dangers involved in the production of shells and detonators.[104] In this sense, the short film *Night Shift*, produced for the Ministry of Information by Paul Rotha's production company and filmed at Newport ROF, proved to be something of an exception. The film historian David Berry notes that *Night Shift* was an unusual production because it focused 'on the arduous nature of the women's work rather than on technical detail in the gunmaking factory'.[105] In the opinion of Susan L. Carruthers, however, *Night Shift* was no different from any of the other carefully produced films which concentrated upon the more positive aspects of factory life. Despite the dirt, grime and noise of the machinery, the film reassured its female audiences that friendship, and even romance, could be found in the British war factory. Moreover, as Susan L. Carruthers points out, potential

[101] *South Wales Echo*, 25 July 1942.
[102] Klein (ed.), *Beyond the Home Front*, p. 148.
[103] *The Rhondda Leader*, 26 July 1941.
[104] *Glamorgan Gazette*, 21 April 1944.
[105] David Berry, *Wales and Cinema: The First Hundred Years* (Cardiff, 1994), p. 195.

recruits could also take comfort from the scenes which showed female factory workers 'busily rearranging their hairstyles before work – a note that factory work was not synonymous with loss of femininity'.[106] The Ministry of Information seemed convinced that such representations of female factory workers, whose 'feminine' identities remained unaffected by their new masculine, industrial environment, would make factory work appear more attractive to the female audience. Indeed, in the summer of 1941 the ministry's Home Intelligence Unit suggested that the 'stigma' of factory work 'might be removed by more flattering references in the press to "young ladies on war work"'.[107] Some factory managers even adapted the machinery in their workshops in their attempts to make factory work more appealing to women. The managing director of one factory in south Wales claimed that by 'remodelling' his welding machines, 'what was once a distasteful, dirty and dangerous-looking job' had become one 'for which women readily volunteer'.[108]

Since the majority of female munitions workers were actually undertaking dirty work in very 'masculine' industrial environments, the attention which was paid to their traditionally 'female' characteristics was particularly interesting. In effect, the reports and descriptions of female war workers penned by contemporary commentators, seemed almost to overemphasize their femininity. Two newspaper reporters from south Wales who had visited several factories in the region remarked that female employees brought 'a smile into the factory', and created a lighter, cheerier atmosphere:

> Most people who see anything of our big war factories will agree that they are brighter places since women entered them in large numbers. Neat and trim in business-like overalls, they contrive amid the bustle of the workshop to retain about them colourful individual touches.[109]

Although the majority of women war workers wore functional, 'unfeminine' clothes in the factories, the descriptions of the

---

[106] Susan L. Carruthers, '"Manning the factories": propaganda and policy on the employment of women, 1939–1947', *History*, 75, no. 244 (1990), 240.
[107] PRO, Inf 1/292.
[108] *Glamorgan Advertiser*, 11 December 1942.
[109] Ibid.; *Western Mail*, 24 February 1941.

women at their workplaces often concentrated on their attempts
to reject these mannish looks. Following her visit to a fuse factory
in the Midlands, Peggy Scott remarked in detail upon the effort
made by one young woman to 'keep up appearances' under-
neath her factory uniform:

> the pretty girl at the machine wore high-heeled shoes with the trousers,
> and a white silk-shirt and a pale blue tie under her navy overall. Her hair
> was waved and curled, as was that of every other girl in the factory.[110]

As Pat Kirkham has argued, the emphasis placed on personal
appearances remained at the fore of women's culture throughout
the war. Even the government encouraged women to take time
with their appearance as a means to maintain morale.[111] Marilyn
Wells, the *Western Mail*'s 'beauty correspondent', declared in
1940 that Welsh women had a 'duty' to 'Keep the colours flying!'
throughout the wartime emergency.[112] For the female munitions
workers who had suffered skin problems after working with
explosive powders, the decision of the authorities to permit the
use of high-grade make-up in some factories was much appreciated, as was the advice provided in the 1942 pamphlet issued by
the Ministry of Supply, *R.O.F. Beauty Hints: Look to Your Looks*.[113]
Beauty competitions held in some of the munitions factories were
a further boost to the morale of these workers, many of whom
felt that their 'looks' had been adversely affected by their working
conditions.[114] In large factories, where women wore government-
issued overalls, turbans and shoes, and were identified by a shift
colour and number, the desire to retain some sense of indi-
viduality was strong. Although factory authorities rarely allowed

---

[110] Peggy Scott, *British Women in War* (London, 1940), p. 153. It was also widely
reported that some female workers refused to wear protective head-clothing which was
deemed to be unflattering, even though many accidents were caused when loose hair
became entangled in machinery: ibid., p. 176; Douie, *Daughters of Britain*, p. 105.

[111] Pat Kirkham, 'Beauty and duty: keeping up the (home) front', in eadem and David
Thoms (eds.), *War Culture: Social Change and Changing Experience in World War Two Britain*
(London, 1995), pp. 13–28; Pat Kirkham, 'Fashioning the feminine: dress, appearance
and femininity in wartime Britain', in Gledhill and Swanson (eds.), *Nationalising Femininity*,
pp. 152–74.

[112] *Western Mail*, 1 and 11 May 1940.

[113] Kirkham, 'Beauty and duty', p. 15; evidence of Respondent 1.

[114] In August 1944, Nora Roberts of Ynys-hir was crowned the 1944 Beauty Queen of
Bridgend ROF by the factory superintendent on the steps of the Embassy cinema,
Bridgend. *The Rhondda Leader*, 12 August 1944.

workers to wear non-regulation clothing or jewellery, the former employees of Bridgend ROF recalled that most women made some effort to ensure a 'personal touch' by wearing coloured ribbons or scarves in their hair.[115] Some individuals were even prepared to take great personal risks by carrying contraband materials, such as hair-grips, eyebrow pluckers or jewellery, into the factory, even though these items could cause friction on contact with explosive powders.[116] Richard Rees, an ex-miner from the Rhondda who worked at Bridgend ROF, recalled how many women found ways around the restrictions and passed these items on to their male colleagues whenever the factory searchers appeared on their rounds:

> The urgent whisper, 'Women Searchers on the line!' would send the lasses everywhere scurrying to find the nearest man.
> 'Searchers Dick! Mind these for me in your money-bag . . . hurry please!' It was no good arguing. Into my little canvas money-bag hung round my neck went rings, lipstick, face powder, hair clips, curlers – all the feminine bric-a-brac imaginable. And all of it contraband.[117]

In many ways, these overtly 'feminine' representations of female war workers served not only to maintain traditional gender identities, but reinforced the notion that the work performed on factory-benches was well suited to the female character. Women were not only regarded as being physically better adapted for the intricate work required on factory assembly-lines, but were also deemed to be blessed with the ideal temperament for undertaking monotonous and repetitive work.[118] In the opinion of one official from a south Wales munitions factory, the young female employees were not only 'much more conscientious and thorough in their work than boys', but were 'more adaptable and capable when it comes to unskilled labour . . . and better able to stand up to the monotony

---

[115] Evidence of Respondents 3, 4 and 5. See also Douie, *Daughters of Britain*, p. 105.

[116] NLW MSS N23071E and N23072–3D; M-O A, FR 1498, 'Blaina', p. 97; evidence of Respondent 2; BBC Radio Wales broadcast, 'The girls who made the thing-ummy-bobs'.

[117] Rees, 'Suicide club', *Empire News and Sunday Chronicle*, 15 September 1957.

[118] Gertrude Williams, *Women and Work* (London, 1945), p. 24; International Labour Office, *The War and Women's Employment: The Experience of the United Kingdom and the United States* (Montreal, 1946), p. 9; Douie, *Daughters of Britain*, pp. 102–3; Postan, *British War Production*, p. 218; Hay, *R.O.F.*, p. 42.

of the job than men'.[119] The efficiency of the Welsh female war
workers was often remarked upon during the war, and particular
attention was paid to the fact that this inexperienced workforce
had adapted so quickly to factory employment. A newspaper
reporter who visited an ordnance factory 'Somewhere in Wales'
in 1941 was clearly impressed by the competence shown by the
young female workers he had seen:

> It is amazing to watch the efficiency of these girls. They go through a short
> training course before being put on the benches, and there is even a school
> at the factory where the girls receive instructions and learn about decimal
> fractions . . . The factory superintendent told me that their adaptability
> surprised him. They were neat and precise in their work and were keen
> and enthusiastic to do as much as possible.[120]

The women who were employed at one ordnance factory in
south Wales – many of whom had worked as shop assistants
before the war – were given special praise in June 1944 by
members of the Select Committee on National Expenditure, who
remarked that the Welsh factory was the most efficient of the
three factories they had visited during the course of their wartime
investigations.[121]

In effect, such comments reaffirmed prejudices which had
been established in the manufacturing industries during the
inter-war years, when low-skilled and low-paid employment on
factory assembly-lines came to be regarded as 'women's work'.
As Miriam Glucksmann has argued, this 'sex-typing' of the work-
process meant that the skills which women brought to their
workplace were often dismissed as being 'innate sexual characteristics' and were never really valued.[122] During the war,
when thousands of women turned their hands to unfamiliar tasks
in munitions factories, the skills which they applied to the work
were often compared with the skills they had used in their
traditionally 'female' pre-war occupations. During her visit to
one British war factory, Peggy Scott observed former typists,

---

[119] *South Wales Argus*, 26 May 1942.
[120] Ibid., 13 May 1941. The 'happy' female war workers of Dowlais whose photograph
appeared in the local newspaper in 1941 were also praised by the factory manager for
their 'adaptability'. *Merthyr Express*, 18 January 1941.
[121] *Parliamentary Debates* (Hansard) (5th series), vol. 400, 1450 (7 June 1944).
[122] Glucksmann, *Women Assemble*, p. 209.

dressmakers and 'women who had only made up women's faces in beauty parlours', using 'their nimble fingers' to the same effect on engine parts.[123] A reporter from the *South Wales Argus*, who visited a south Wales factory was informed by 'labour experts' at the plant that 'in engineering work requiring delicately precise adjustment, deft-fingered young seamstresses, stenographers, and musicians often prove more reliable than the most experienced of horny-handed mechanics'.[124]

As Ruth Roach Pierson has argued in her examination of the propaganda of the Canadian War Departments, this 'domestication' of women's industrial work reinforced the notion that female war workers did not acquire any new skills in the workplace, but simply applied old techniques to new tools.[125] The fact that a 'frivolous female' plucked from a hairdressing parlour had proved herself to be 'as efficient with a drilling machine as with curling pins' was seen as evidence that the skills required to use the two instruments were fundamentally the same.[126] It was also implied that reverting to using the latter when the stint at the drilling machine was over would not prove to be a difficult transition for this Welsh female war worker.

The role of female war workers as temporary industrial substitutes was made explicit, therefore, not only in the type of work allocated to them, but in the commentaries which stressed that their services were required 'for the duration' only. The attitudes of both the female employees and their employers towards their wartime work must have been influenced by such thinking. An inquiry into wartime production conducted in 1942 found that in many factories there was 'no spirit of female effort as such', because many women were of the opinion that they were merely 'helping the men and *temporarily* taking over for the men to do something more important'.[127] Employers were also not likely to invest in workers whose period of service could be very short, and few female war workers received the opportunities of training or promotion. Indeed, only 29 per cent of the 2,609 women war workers interviewed by the Wartime Social Survey in 1943

[123] Scott, *British Women in War*, p. 10.
[124] *South Wales Argus*, 3 July 1943.
[125] Pierson, 'Embattled femininity', p. 203.
[126] *Glamorgan Gazette*, 13 July 1945.
[127] Mass-Observation, *People in Production*, p. 106.

had received any formal training for their job.[128] Very few of the
ex-munitions workers interviewed for this study were given any
formal instruction or training in their workplace. More often
than not, those who were occupied on unskilled work were
simply shown what to do and left to carry on. As the Ministry of
Labour's recruitment propaganda made clear, the work carried
out by women in shell-filling factories was 'a straightforward job,
easily picked up. No long training is required.'[129]

Yet, in spite of the many practical and ideological obstacles
which hindered the progress of female war workers, the mere
fact that thousands of females were employed in the war factories
of south Wales at all was a source of tension in the local community. Even though female munitions workers might only be
employed temporarily, they were at least being given a chance to
learn about factory work and to acquire new skills and knowledge of industrial work processes – an opportunity which the
vast majority of the men of south Wales were denied. In the
mining districts, younger and healthier members of the male
population were either conscripted for the armed forces or were
drawn back into the coal mining industry. Elderly miners, and
those incapacitated by illness who had been deemed unfit both
for active service and work underground, faced a more uncertain
future. As an age-limit of fifty-five years was applied to ROF
employees, many of the older unemployed men in the area were
immediately excluded from taking up factory employment.[130]
But even younger men faced difficulties in being placed in munitions factories which preferred a female workforce. In response
to his question why unemployed men from his constituency had
not been considered for the vacant positions at Bridgend ROF
in November 1941, the Ministry of Labour informed Ness
Edwards, the Caerphilly MP, that the 'light work' which was
available at the factory demanded 'nimbleness and dexterity',
and was thus 'particularly suitable for women'.[131] The following
year, the unemployed men of Aberdare, who were similarly

[128] Geoffrey Thomas, 'Women at work: the attitudes of working women towards post-
war employment and some related problems. An inquiry made for the Office of the
Minister of Reconstruction' (Central Office of Information, Wartime Social Survey, June
1944), p. 5.
[129] South Wales Echo, 10 March 1941.
[130] Parliamentary Debates (Hansard) (5th series), vol. 357, 430 (8 February 1940).
[131] Ibid., vol. 376, 430 (20 November 1941).

aggrieved by the preference given to female labour in local factories, were also informed that women were more suited to the work because 'they had more nimble fingers'.[132] As an ex-forewoman from Bridgend ROF explained, ex-miners were not the ideal workforce to carry out delicate manual operations:

> I remember having some retired miners, they had retired through dust or something because they weren't that old . . . The fuses then, on the naval side, well . . . they had tiny little screws that you screwed in and had to seal them up, and I always remember this gentleman saying to me . . . 'It's a shovel I want in my hand, not this little screw-driver. I can't feel it!' And his hands were hard with the coal and that, and it was true, he just couldn't feel that screw-driver in his hand. It was so tiny to his shovel that he'd been used to having.[133]

It was not surprising that men who were denied the rights to factory employment felt threatened by the creation of the large and conspicuous body of female industrial workers. In 1940 the compilers of the *Beveridge Manpower Survey* in south Wales observed that there were 'already some signs of resentment at the spectacle of bus-loads of women going off to munition works . . . while men remain unemployed at home'.[134] The unfamiliar sight of thousands of female workers pouring in and out of the new factories was clearly galling to many unemployed men. As growing numbers of women entered the munitions factories, calls to check the employment imbalance became more urgent. The fear that the end of the war could leave the male workforce unskilled, untrained, unemployed and undermined led many to seek remedial action. At a meeting of the Aberdare Trades and Labour Council (TLC) in September 1940, members of the Aberdare Unemployment Advisory Board complained that hundreds of local men remained unemployed while women were taken on at the town's cable works.[135]

Similar complaints were voiced in the Rhondda, where the level of male unemployment among elderly and disabled miners was causing grave concern. In December 1940 a public

[132] *Aberdare Leader*, 12 September 1942.
[133] Evidence of Respondent 16.
[134] *Beveridge Manpower Survey*, 1940.
[135] *Aberdare Leader*, 14 September 1940; *Western Mail*, 7 September 1940.

demonstration was held in the Rhondda Fach under the aegis of the Ferndale, Maerdy and Tylorstown lodges of the South Wales Miners' Federation (SWMF).[136] The fact that Bridgend ROF employed 10,137 workers by that time – nearly 70 per cent of whom were female – merely added to their frustrations.[137] The Rhondda men took their complaints directly to R. J. Humphreys, district controller of the Ministry of Labour in Wales, and discussions were held on the regulations which governed the employment of labour at munitions works. Although the controller maintained that 'every possible effort was being made to utilise all unemployed workers and, in doing so, the committee were not overlooking the Rhondda and other mining valleys', his response failed to appease the unemployed men of the district.[138] In the opinion of one local unemployed man, who voiced his concern in March 1941, it was 'a disgrace to see hundreds of women leaving the Rhondda Valley every day in buses, while thousands of men, like myself, are allowed to remain idle'.[139] The protests from the Rhondda continued and, two months later, a petition signed by several hundred disabled men from the area was sent to the minister of labour, urging him to provide them with work.[140] Their demands seem not to have been met, however, since a year later, in May 1942, yet another appeal was made to the minister in a letter from the secretary of the Rhondda East Divisional Labour Party, in which the grievances of 'the forgotten men' were aired. It was claimed that some 2,000 unemployed men from the Rhondda were immediately available for work in local factories but that 'no serious efforts' had been made to place them in employment in the area.[141] Speaking at a public meeting held at Porth a month later, W. H. Mainwaring, the Rhondda East MP, put forward his own solution to the unemployment problem facing his male constituents:

> It is my view that no woman ought to be taken in to industry until every man is supplied with a job. I would go further; if it were in my power to

[136] *Glamorgan County Times*, 7 December 1940.
[137] PRO, Lab 12/82.
[138] *Glamorgan County Times*, 21 December 1940.
[139] *South Wales Echo*, 26 March 1941.
[140] *The Rhondda Leader*, 24 May 1941.
[141] Ibid., 30 May 1942.

stop it, no girl would leave the Rhondda to take a job until every man had left.[142]

Similar opinions were voiced at meetings held in other parts of the coalfield as factory managers continued to overlook the substantial numbers of unemployed men who were available for light labouring work or 'for work normally done by women'.[143] At a meeting of the Aberdare TLC in September 1943, councillors renewed their earlier appeal for the minister of labour to employ local unemployed men in war industries before 'compelling married women with domestic responsibilities and other women who were already in reasonably-paid, less essential jobs to take up war work'.[144] In the opinion of Councillor T. J. Morgan, 'it was a social anomaly that men were idle while women were working', and he demanded an immediate solution to the problem.[145] Although some efforts were eventually made to employ greater numbers of elderly and incapacitated miners at Bridgend ROF in 1943–4, following the 1943 decision to suspend all miners certified with pneumoconiosis from further employment within the mining industry, the lack of jobs deemed suitable for the unemployed men of south Wales remained a stubborn problem throughout the war.[146]

It was not only unemployed, incapacitated or elderly men who found it difficult to obtain work at the war factories of south Wales. Following the passing of the Essential Work (Coalmining Industry) Order of May 1941, working miners were also to be denied access to other forms of employment and were tied to their 'reserved occupations' in the coal mines.[147] Many miners were resentful of the order for it prevented them not only from enlisting for active service but also from entering munitions factories where both working conditions and wages were more favourable.[148] Most pits lacked the facilities on offer in modern state-run factories where girls complained of being 'welfared to

[142] Ibid., 13 June 1942.
[143] PRO, Lab 12/82.
[144] *Aberdare Leader*, 11 September 1943.
[145] Ibid.
[146] Inman, *Labour in the Munitions Industries*, p. 186; Francis and Smith, *The Fed*, p. 439.
[147] *Ministry of Labour Gazette*, May 1941, pp. 95–6.
[148] Stuart R. Broomfield, 'South Wales in the Second World War: the coal industry and its community' (unpublished Ph.D. thesis, University of Wales, 1979), p. 27.

death'.[149] Talk of luxuries such as tea-breaks, rest-rooms, *Music While you Work* and factory concerts did much to highlight the inferior working conditions of the colliers. As B. L. Coombes, the south Wales miner and author, made clear in his wartime publication, *Those Clouded Hills* (1944), the south Wales miner considered himself very poorly treated in comparison with the female munitions workers of the region:

> Out of over a hundred and fifty pit canteens in South Wales – either working or in course of construction – only eight can provide a warm and full meal. Within a couple of miles in either direction of this place are factories, some run by the R.O.F. and others by private firms and all of them give meals to their workers . . . so the men go home hungry and tired, there sometimes to listen to their wives or sisters praising the meals at their canteen and to note that those same wives or sisters have brought home more pay after working in a new job than their menfolk get for work that has taken them years to learn. No wonder that it sounds, through the canteen and in all places where the men gather, like a Greek chorus: 'Something wants altering about this b— lot anyway.'[150]

In the wartime study conducted by Mass-Observation at the coal-mining town of Blaina, Monmouthshire, Mollie Tarrant reported that comparisons of this nature had given rise to considerable tension between local miners and munitions workers.[151] One local trade union leader gave the following description of their contrasting working conditions:

> the munition workers have all the amenities that the miners are denied. The miners have rotten working conditions, artificial ventilation, the stench of the water, smoke and its effect on chest and lungs, most miners get some kind of bronchial trouble at an early age. The munition workers have good working conditions, canteens and entertainment.[152]

The miners of Blaina were particularly angered by the fact that the weekly earnings of munitions workers were often higher than those paid in the mining industry. As one miner remarked, 'We're getting nothing like we should have. Look now, what the

[149] Williams-Ellis, *Women in the War Factories*, p. 39.
[150] B. L. Coombes, *Those Clouded Hills* (London, 1944), p. 41.
[151] M-O A, FR 1498, 'Blaina', pp. 41–60.
[152] Ibid., p. 51.

munition workers gets. Much more than we do.'[153] The evidence presented by the Mineworkers' Federation of Great Britain (MFGB) before the 1942 investigation into the wages of the coal industry, revealed that females employed in filling factories were paid the weekly wage of £3 10s. for unskilled work, while semi-skilled workers took home £4 10s., and sometimes £5 or more.[154] The miners' representatives concluded that

> the earnings of workers in ROFs in the coalmining districts, while affording only a moderate standard of life, are much higher than those of most miners, and this brings home afresh to the miner how low his wages are. Especially is this the case when women are bringing home more money from a ROF than the miner from the pit.[155]

Within the munitions factories themselves, however, female workers usually took home less money than their male colleagues. Harold Smith calculated that the vast majority of female industrial workers received only around 50 to 70 per cent of the rates paid to men in British war factories.[156] The inequality between the wages of male and female war workers was firmly enshrined in the agreements signed by the trade unions and industry representatives in the early years of the war. Even though wartime dilution policies drew greater numbers of lower-skilled female workers into the semi-skilled and skilled workforce, the agreements struck between the unions and employers ensured that the strict segregation between both the work and wages of men and women was maintained. In effect, therefore, the agreements drawn up between the various trade unions and workers' representatives, protected the wages and jobs of their male members.[157] In May 1940 the wage rates of females employed in the engineering trades during the war were agreed in

---

[153] Ibid., p. 41.
[154] SWCA, Mineworkers' Federation of Great Britain (MFGB) minutes 1942, written evidence presented to the Board of Investigation into Wages and Machinery of the Coalmining Industry, June 1942, p. 12.
[155] Ibid., Appendix 7, p. 106.
[156] Harold Smith, 'The problem of "equal pay for equal work" in Great Britain during World War II', *Journal of Modern History*, 53, no. 4 (1981), 652–72.
[157] See Norbert C. Soldon, *Women in British Trade Unions, 1874–1976* (Dublin, 1978), pp. 148–215; Sarah Boston, *Women Workers and the Trade Union Movement* (London, 1980), pp. 185–218; Clare Wightman, *More than Munitions: Women, Work and the Engineering Industries, 1900–1950* (London, 1999), ch. 7.

negotiations with members of the Engineering and Allied Trades Employers' Federation and the NUGMW, the Amalgamated Engineering Union (AEU) and the Transport and General Workers' Union (TGWU). The wage agreement stipulated that all women brought into the industry under its terms should be regarded as temporarily employed. Females employed on work normally performed by men were required to serve a probationary period of thirty-two weeks during which they were paid a fixed proportion of the men's rate. Only after the probationary period was over, and provided they were able to perform the work equally well and without additional assistance, would female workers be entitled to the basic rate and national bonus paid to men.[158]

Thus, despite the fact that many women were performing skilled work which had previously been undertaken by men, most female war workers continued to be regarded as temporary, lower-skilled members of the workforce and rarely received male wage rates. In the ROFs, wages were controlled by a 'group system' which ensured that rates of pay in each factory were related to the wages schedule of the sex which formed the majority of the workforce.[159] However, given that the majority of women employed at ROFs were engaged in unskilled work, their average wage rates remained comparatively low. Furthermore, as Penny Summerfield has argued, female workers were least likely to benefit from weekend work, overtime and bonus payments because of the greater demands placed on their free time by their heavier domestic responsibilities.[160]

In many ways, therefore, the wartime agreements struck by employers and trade unions served to confirm the temporary and inferior position of the female war worker. After all, the main priority of the large trade unions was to defend the interests of their male members, and female war workers were unlikely to be fairly represented by such organizations. As Miss V. Holmes of

---

[158] The provisions of this agreement were later adopted in agreements between the Engineering and Allied Trades Employers' Federation and the following unions: the National Union of Foundry Workers, the Electrical Trades Union, the National Union of Brass and Metal Mechanics, the National Union of Scale Makers, the National Society of Boilermakers and Iron and Steel Shipbuilders. International Labour Office, *The War and Women's Employment*, p. 67.

[159] Inman, *Labour in the Munitions Industries*, p. 359.

[160] Summerfield, *Women Workers in the Second World War*, p. 135.

the Engineering Branch of the Ministry of Labour argued in 1941,

> through not being independently organised or powerfully represented, they [females] have no real say in negotiation and their wages are therefore settled by two powerful bodies each considering male interests. The poor wages, the anomalies and much unfairness are the results.[161]

Although female membership of the Trades Union Congress (TUC) grew from 552,585 in 1939 to 1,340,729 in 1945, female war workers were often represented as temporary and marginal members of the trade union movement.[162] The large craft union, the AEU, excluded female members completely until 1943, while the females drawn into the large general unions continued to be on the periphery of union organization and policy-making. The Communist Dora Cox remarked that the majority of the female war workers of south Wales either remained outside the movement altogether, or took no real part in the organization once they had become members.[163] However, the reasons for their apparent disinterest in the trade union movement were too easily dismissed and the many practical and ideological obstacles which prevented many female war workers from playing an active role in their trade unions were never really removed.

Despite the strong tradition of male trade unionism in south Wales, the few attempts which had been made to organize the female workers of the region in the years before the war had proved largely unsuccessful.[164] However, as wartime conditions suddenly transformed the employment experiences of the local female population, trade unionists were soon awakened to the possibilities of organizing this large body of workers. Members of this new workforce also quickly realized the need for trade union protection and representation. Elizabeth Andrews reported in

---

[161] PRO, Lab 8/378.

[162] Boston, *Women Workers and the Trade Union Movement*, pp. 209–10.

[163] NLW, Idris Cox Papers, 36, lectures by Dora Cox on the history of women, 'Women under capitalism' [*c.*1940].

[164] For example, representatives of the TGWU who met at Pontypool in February 1939 to discuss the position of employees of the Weston's Biscuit Factory, Llantarnam, claimed that it was 'ten times harder' to organize female workers than males. According to J. E. Edmunds, secretary of the TGWU Newport District Branch, 'girls regard work merely as an interval between school and marriage and have no real concern about the conditions of employment'. *Free Press of Monmouthshire*, 10 February 1939.

1939 that females who were employed at the Polikoffs clothing factory in the Rhondda had been warned that they would be given notice if they joined a trade union, and she appealed to local representatives to take up their case.[165] A metal plastics factory on the Treforest trading estate was also reported to be exploiting its young female workforce, and members of the Pontypridd Trades Council heard in March 1940 that the female employees were paid the meagre daily wage of 2s.[166] Faced with a growing incidence of similar cases, the local trade union movement clearly needed to act, not only to defend the rights of these young females, but in order to protect the wages and jobs of their male members which were threatened by the increased use of cheaper female labour.

In the absence of a clear regional policy, the first moves to organize the female war workers of south Wales were initiated by individual trades councils who demanded immediate action in the matter. For example, in October 1940, the New Tredegar TLC called upon the Monmouthshire Federation of Trades Councils to arrange a conference to discuss the organization of female war workers.[167] By the spring of 1941, the South Wales Regional Council of Labour had entered into discussions with representatives of the two large general unions, the NUGMW and the TGWU, regarding the employment conditions of female war workers and their organization within the labour movement.[168] In June 1941 a meeting between representatives of the Glamorgan and Monmouthshire Federation of Trades Councils and officers of the NUGMW and the TGWU was held at Transport House, Cardiff, where the means by which female organization could best be achieved were discussed in detail. Each of the union officials present at the meeting reported that grave practical difficulties had been experienced in organizing women workers in the area – problems which were to obstruct the progress of the unions throughout the war.

---

[165] NLW, Labour Party of Wales Archive, South Wales Regional Council of Labour Executive Committee minutes, 22 September 1939.
[166] Pontypridd Public Library, Pontypridd Trades Council and Labour Party minutes, 11 March 1940.
[167] SWCA, New Tredegar TLC minutes, 2 October 1940.
[168] NLW, Labour Party of Wales Archive, South Wales Regional Council of Labour Executive Committee minutes, 18 February 1941, 11 March 1941, 8 and 22 April 1941, 13 and 27 May 1941.

A major obstacle facing the unions in their attempts to recruit female workers was that they were not always permitted to organize on factory property. Under the regulations of the Emergency Powers (Defence) Act of May 1940, factory meetings were prohibited without the consent of the management, and the circulation and distribution of literature and notices were illegal.[169] The South Western District Council of the NUGMW reported in March 1941 that 'extreme difficulty' had been experienced in trying to organize the female workers of Bridgend ROF 'due to the fact that the holding of meetings upon factory enclosures is strictly prohibited'.[170] In a bid to overcome this problem, members of the Women's Section of the Aberdare TLC distributed union literature to female workers as they travelled into the factories on buses and trains.[171] Even after the managers of Bridgend ROF had granted permission for local trade unions to hold meetings on the factory premises difficulties remained.

Since the majority of the employees lived considerable distances away from the workplace and from each other, the organization of successful meetings outside working hours was said to be 'impossible'.[172] Speaking at a conference held by the Glamorgan Federation of Trades Councils at Cardiff in October 1941, the secretary of the Aberdare TLC maintained that the difficulties in contacting women who lived in scattered and distant areas was 'a big problem' to their organization within the unions.[173] Moreover, given the long working hours and the time spent in travelling to and from the workplace, many munitions workers had little time or inclination to attend political meetings after arriving home, as the lack of interest recorded at several of the meetings organized especially for female war workers in their home districts confirmed. A gathering for female workers at the Lesser Hall, Mountain Ash, in July 1942 succeeded in attracting an audience of only nine. Even though it must have been difficult for many female war workers to attend the meeting, the poor turnout was evidently a great disappointment to union leaders,

---

[169] Wal Hannington, *Industrial History in Wartime* (London, 1940), pp. 99–100.
[170] NLW, Minor Deposit A1994/81, 26 March 1941.
[171] *Aberdare Leader*, 11 October 1941.
[172] NLW, Labour Party of Wales Archive, South Wales Regional Council of Labour Executive Committee minutes, 23 June 1941.
[173] *Aberdare Leader*, 11 October 1941.

particularly since George Hall, the local MP, had been invited specifically to address women on the importance of union membership and the issue of female transference to factories in England. As a local correspondent noted, 'It may be that working hours made it difficult for a large number of women to attend, but even then it seems that it should have been possible for more than nine to attend.'[174]

It was widely believed that the lack of interest shown by female war workers in union activities and working conditions stemmed from the fact that they regarded their period of wartime employment as purely temporary. As a departmental secretary at the Ministry of Labour remarked in March 1941:

> For men, their work is a life matter. For the average woman it is regarded as a temporary necessity. It is for this reason that, except in women's industries, women are apathetic to organisation and it is misleading to suggest that this is not the case.[175]

Female war workers were perceived, therefore, as having few grievances, concerns or even ambitions regarding their positions of employment and working conditions. Female factory workers observed by Mass-Observation researchers in 1942 were reported to be 'less opinionated' than their male colleagues and were 'more satisfied all through' with their wage rates, conditions of employment and factory managers.[176] None of the female munitions workers interviewed by Mollie Tarrant at Blaina had any complaints to make regarding their earnings, and it is likely, as Tarrant suggested, that those employed at Glascoed ROF found the basic wage rates of £2 4s. 9d. for the day shift, £3 for the afternoon shift and £3 12s. for night shifts to be quite acceptable.[177] To many women, the working conditions and wages of the war factories were far superior to those of their pre-war 'blind alley' occupations, while females who had not previously been occupied were well satisfied with the security of a steady wage. In fact, the female war workers of Blaina were far more concerned with issues relating to child-care arrangements,

---

[174] Ibid., 25 July 1942, 1 August 1942.
[175] PRO, Lab 8/378.
[176] Mass-Observation, *People in Production*, p. 31.
[177] M-O A, FR 1498, 'Blaina', p. 91.

travelling difficulties and health problems than with matters relating to factory management and wage-rates which male trade unionists were more eager to champion. In many ways, therefore, the priorities of male and female war workers often differed greatly, a fact which those who chose to compare the attitudes of both parties towards their experiences of work and trade union involvement failed to recognize.

However, considering that only a small proportion of the female war workers of south Wales had been members of trade unions before the war, the growth in wartime female membership was far from disappointing. In August 1941 the NUGMW reported that 'substantial progress' had been made at Newport ROF, where all women and unskilled workers at the factory had joined the union, while at Bridgend ROF, where the union had made concerted efforts to organize the large female workforce, membership was said to have increased by 400 per cent since March 1941.[178] Some successes were also reported at the smaller, privately owned factories, such as the cartridge-case factory at Aberdare, owned by the Cardiff-based Curran Works, where union members totalled 1,200 by October 1942.[179] As female membership of local trade union branches grew, many women began to take a more active role in union organization. The call-up of local male activists may also have been a determining factor in allowing several women the opportunity to take up positions of some authority within local branches.[180] Since many of the female war workers of south Wales had been brought up in homes and communities where a strong tradition of male trade unionism prevailed, it is not surprising that membership of the labour movement formed an important part of their wartime experience of work. During the First World War the female war workers from the mining valleys who were employed at the Nobel explosives factory at Pembrey were alleged to have been

---

[178] NLW, Minor Deposit A1994/81, 26 March, 6 August 1941. However, in May 1942 it was revealed that no more than 10,000 of the workers employed at Bridgend ROF had joined trade unions – a small proportion of the total workforce, which exceeded 30,000 by that date. Pontypridd Public Library, Pontypridd Trades Council and Labour Party minutes, 11 May 1942.

[179] NLW, Minor Deposit A1994/81, 17 October 1942.

[180] For example, Hettie Jones was elected president of the Caerphilly TLC in 1940, while a Mrs Sandercock was elected chair of the Aberdare TLC in January 1941. SWCA, Caerphilly TLC Executive Committee minutes, 1940; Aberdare TLC minutes, 1941.

'full of socialist theories and very great on getting up strikes'.[181] Although instances of industrial disputes in Welsh war factories during the Second World War were rare and short-lived,[182] it would appear that many members of the younger generation of females from these areas shared the political ideals of their mothers and aunts. Indeed, for some individuals, their wartime involvement in the work of the trade unions inspired a lifelong commitment to the labour movement.[183]

As growing numbers of unskilled workers joined the ranks of the NUGMW and the TGWU, the AEU finally decided to open its doors to female workers. Only months after the AEU had taken this decision in January 1943, the two general unions were locked in a fierce debate with the craft union on matters relating to the organization and recruitment of female workers in south Wales. In March 1943, the AEU was accused of being 'actively engaged in attempting to poach' female members of the NUGMW at the Curran Works at Aberdare, and by May 1943 it was reported that 'serious inroads' had been made into the NUGMW membership at these works and at Lucas Ltd, Cwmbrân.[184] The NUGMW was at pains to stress that it had organized and safeguarded the rights and conditions of women workers from the outbreak of the war, and it appealed to its female members to remain loyal. As the district secretary maintained in October 1943, the NUGMW had been 'the pioneer organisation for the semi-skilled engineering workers, both male and female' and, unlike the AEU, it was dedicated to permanent membership.[185]

Yet, despite having played a 'pioneering' role in the organization of female war workers, the general unions had, in fact, remained preoccupied with issues which primarily concerned their male members. As Sarah Boston has argued, both the NUGMW and the TGWU remained 'curiously silent' on the problems of women workers throughout the war.[186] Although the

[181] Angela Woollacott, *On Her Their Lives Depend: Munitions Workers in the Great War* (London, 1994), p. 39.
[182] For example, in November 1942 it was reported that thirty women employed at Lucas Ltd, Cwmbrân, had gone on strike for a day after the management had refused to meet their union representative to discuss a wages increase. PRO, Lab 10/368.
[183] See Hilda H. Price, 'Experiences in World War II', 110–13.
[184] NLW, Minor Deposit A1994/81, 13 March 1943, 8 May 1943.
[185] Ibid., 30 October 1943.
[186] Boston, *Women Workers and the Trade Union Movement*, p. 210.

NUGMW made great efforts to recruit the female war workers
of south Wales and negotiated some wage agreements and
compensation claims on their behalf, there is little evidence that
the union campaigned forcefully on issues such as child-care and
shopping leave, which were of particular concern to the female
workforce. Indeed, at a meeting of the Aberdare TLC in May
1942, it was alleged that local unions took little action on behalf
of their female members once they had recruited them. In the
opinions of Councillors Islwyn Williams and T. J. Morgan (chairman), the 'overloaded' unions were failing their female members
by 'doing little to cater for them after enrolling them and
collecting their sixpences'.[187] Over a year later, members of the
Aberdare TLC renewed their demands for the unions to take a
greater interest in the problems of their female members, following the prosecution of young female munitions workers from the
area. One young woman from Robertstown, who, after being
transferred to war work in the Midlands, had left her place of
work after completing only one shift, was fined £5 with costs by
Aberdare magistrates even though her own doctor and the
works' doctor had agreed that she was too ill to work. Members
of the Aberdare TLC resolved to send a 'strong letter' to the
south Wales headquarters of the NUGMW urging more effective
representation for female members who were involved in
industrial prosecutions.[188]

In many ways, the failure of the trade unions to represent
adequately the interests of their female members reflected a
general lack of commitment to the wartime female workforce. In
the wage agreements and working codes negotiated by the
unions and employers, the two parties made it clear that they
regarded female war workers as temporary employees who were
unlikely to remain members of either the trade unions or the
industrial workforce at the end of the conflict. The visual and
literary images of female workers presented in the powerful
wartime propaganda produced by the state did much to support
this view. A Ministry of Labour advertisement which appeared in
the south Wales press during the summer of 1941 noted that the
services of women war workers were required only 'for the

---

[187] *Aberdare Leader*, 16 May 1942.
[188] Ibid., 16 October 1943; SWCA, Aberdare TLC minutes, 7 October 1943.

duration',[189] and as soon as the war was over, the munitions worker was expected either to return to her pre-war occupation or to retire completely from the occupied workforce. Many of the literary and visual representations of female war workers at their positions in the factories had reinforced such expectations. By focusing on the efforts of female workers to retain traditionally 'feminine' expressions of appearance and behaviour, wartime audiences were reassured that women remained unaffected by their employment experiences and could easily make the transition from war worker back to home-maker when the conflict ended. Such representations of female war workers also served to confirm the prejudices of many employers regarding the future role of women as industrial workers. Although many female war workers had shown themselves to be highly efficient and capable in their work, there was never any real suggestion that the skills and knowledge which they had acquired in the war factories were to be applied in future careers.

In truth, however, the workers involved in the manufacture of munitions and armaments knew from the outset that when peace was restored and the demand for their products would cease, so too would the need for their services. In this sense, most munitions workers regarded their time at the factory workbenches as a temporary stint. The work they undertook in the munitions factories played a vital role in securing peace, and the female war workers of south Wales were glad to have been given the opportunity of making such a direct and important contribution to the war effort. Although the Welsh munitions workers would sorely miss the social and economic advantages of wartime employment, many would be relieved to be free of the rigorous routine, the long hours and the unpleasant and often dangerous work involved in the manufacture of munitions. For those war workers who had the additional strain of managing a double life as housewives and mothers, the whole experience had proved all the more demanding and difficult. Although their entry into the war factories had been heralded as a grand departure from their pre-war lives and labours, the reality was that most female war workers continued to shoulder heavy domestic burdens

---

[189] Ministry of Labour and National Service recruitment poster, 'Where IS Mrs Jones going?', *Glamorgan Advertiser*, 25 July 1941.

throughout their years of wartime service. In this sense, the revolution which wartime employment was said to have initiated in the lives of the Welsh female workforce failed to upset traditional expectations regarding their role in the domestic sphere. Women war workers were also mothers, wives and daughters, who returned home from the factories to face a daily round of domestic and household chores. Although there is no denying that the wartime employment experience brought about many new challenges and opportunities in the lives of the women of south Wales, the notion that their primary responsibilities rested with their homes and families remained unaltered.

III

'FILLING THE SHELL AND THE SHOPPING BASKET': WORKERS ON THE HOME AND FACTORY FRONTS

In an article entitled 'Metamorphosis of women', which appeared in the *South Wales Argus* in July 1943, the columnist Alexander M. Thompson (Dangle) reflected on the transformation which had taken place in the working lives of Welsh women since the outbreak of the war.[1] By 1943 thousands of local women had taken up unfamiliar work in factories, offices and farms across Britain and, whilst appreciating their valuable contribution to the war effort, Dangle feared for the 'consequences of this revolution in national habit and economy'. In his opinion, wartime conditions had not only initiated many changes in traditional employment practices but had also transformed 'the functions and social status of women'. Such shifts in traditional gender roles and responsibilities were sure to have serious implications for the future; after all, women who had 'tasted the sweetness of independence', as a result of wartime employment, were unlikely to welcome a return to their pre-war posts as 'unpaid drudges to conjugal bosses, at the washtub, the sink, the kitchen fire, and the cradle', when peace was restored.

In reality, however, very few of the female war workers of south Wales who entered the unfamiliar world of the munitions factory, abandoned their roles and responsibilities on the 'home front' in the crude manner implied in such a commentary. Women who worked shifts of eight hours or more at the munitions factories, and who endured long and tiring journeys to and from the workplace, were still charged with all the chores involved in the running of a busy household and in the care of children and other family members. Despite the dramatic changes which had taken place in the working lives of such women, traditional expectations regarding their primary responsibility towards their homes and families remained unchallenged. This chapter will examine in detail the means by which the female munitions workers of south

---

[1] *South Wales Argus*, 3 July 1943.

Wales coped with the conflicting demands made upon them on the home and factory fronts. Although women with domestic responsibilities and mothers of children under fourteen years of age were exempt from compulsory wartime service, many thousands volunteered for work in the war factories of Britain in response to the Ministry of Labour's urgent demand for labour. It has been estimated that around 81 per cent of all married women (aged between eighteen and forty) without children under the age of fourteen, and *c.*750,000 married women with children under the age of fourteen, worked in British industries during the war.[2] These women workers faced many practical difficulties in combining their roles as factory workers and as housewives and mothers. Additional domestic burdens had already been placed on the shoulders of many women following the call-up of male members of their households, when wives and mothers suddenly found themselves entrusted with all the responsibilities involved in the practical and financial management of their homes and in all aspects of parental supervision and discipline. In truth, therefore, as the more informed wartime commentators were to point out, women who took up industrial employment during the Second World War found themselves 'being called upon to do two jobs: to work in the factories, and to run their homes as well'.[3]

The important work which British women performed in their homes did not go unnoticed during the war. Indeed, the British housewife received much attention in wartime propaganda which urged her to 'keep the home fires burning' in the name of the war effort. In many ways, therefore, as Antonia Lant has argued, wartime conditions brought an 'acknowledgement' of the domestic responsibilities shouldered by ordinary women: 'Instead of the labour of home being invisible vis-à-vis waged and public work, shifting women into a patriotic category gave equal

[2] Sheila Ferguson and Hilde Fitzgerald, *Studies in the Social Services* (London, 1954), p. 23; Douie, *Daughters of Britain*, p. 16. A survey of 2,576 female workers conducted in the autumn of 1943, found that 43 per cent of those questioned were married. Thomas, 'Women at work', p. 3.

[3] The words of Megan Lloyd George, MP for Anglesey, *Parliamentary Debates* (Hansard) (5th series), vol. 382, 74 (22 July 1942). See also Scott, *British Women in War*, p. 8; Labour Research Department, *Women in War Jobs*, p. 15; Goldsmith, *Women at War*, p. 194; Williams-Ellis, *Women in War Factories*, p. 85; J. B. Priestley, *British Women Go to War* (London, 1943), pp. 37–8; Gertrude Williams, *The Price of Social Security* (London, 1944), p. 126.

representational weight to domestic labour, nursing, or riveting.'[4] However, this wartime reappraisal of the value of female domestic labour did little to reduce the burden of the work and, in many ways, it actually contributed to it by placing women war workers under even greater pressure to perform well both in their homes and at the workplace. Those who succeeded in combining their two roles quietly and efficiently were awarded high praise for their labours.[5] For example, in an advertisement for the Hoover vacuum cleaner which appeared in the south Wales press in 1944, women war workers were 'saluted' for the fine work which they performed outside the factory workshops – 'with no glamour of uniform' – where they tackled 'shopping queues, cooking, cleaning, mending and the hundred and one other household jobs'.[6]

However, the means by which the female war workers of Britain coped with the heavy demands of this 'double life' were not something which the wartime propagandists and advertisers chose to dwell upon. Although officials in the Ministry of Labour were aware that efforts would have to be made to assist women with some of their domestic responsibilities in order to release them for war work, questions relating to the type of assistance which should be offered, and to whom, generated lengthy discussions. Did wartime production needs warrant an intrusion into the 'private' affairs of the home and, if so, to what extent should the traditional role of wives and mothers be affected by such plans? In the event, as the detailed research undertaken by Penny Summerfield has shown, British policy-makers 'searched for a compromise between the two spheres of activity, domestic and industrial, such that neither would be profoundly changed'.[7]

---

[4] Antonia Lant, 'Prologue: mobile femininity', in Gledhill and Swanson (eds.), *Nationalising Femininity*, p. 21.

[5] See the wartime advertisement, 'No medals for mother', issued by the National Savings Committee, *Cambrian News*, 16 July 1943.

[6] See the wartime advertisement, 'The hand that held the Hoover turns out shells!', *Western Mail*, 10 March 1944.

[7] Summerfield, *Women Workers in the Second World War*, p. 29. See also eadem, 'Women workers in the Second World War: a study of the interplay in official policy between the need to mobilise women for war and conventional expectations about their roles at work and at home in the period 1939–45' (unpublished D.Phil. thesis, University of Sussex, 1982); eadem, 'Women, work and welfare: a study of child care and shopping in Britain in the Second World War', *Journal of Social History*, 17, no. 2 (1983), 249–69; Denise Riley, 'War in the nursery', *Feminist Review*, 2 (1979), 82–108; eadem, '"The free mothers": pronatalism and working women in industry at the end of the last war in Britain', *History Workshop Journal*, 11 (1981), 58–118.

Although provisions were made to care for the young children of working mothers, very little action was taken to relieve war workers of the burden of responsibilities and the actual labour involved in the running of their homes. Moreover, since the steps which were taken in this field were regarded strictly as temporary wartime measures, the state upheld the ideal that 'in normal times' women should be held responsible for the care of their children and their domestic affairs.

The reluctance of the state to interfere in British family and domestic life had been made clear in the mobilization policies announced during 1941. All pregnant women and mothers of children under fourteen years of age were granted exemption from compulsion, and the domestic and family ties of the remaining females were considered carefully before they were conscripted. The task of deciding exactly what sort of domestic responsibilities entailed exemption from wartime service fell to members of the Women's Consultative Committee who advised the Ministry of Labour on all aspects of the wartime registration and conscription of females. Following lengthy discussions, the committee members finally agreed the criteria which would justify exemption, and only women whose domestic or household responsibilities met those requirements could be placed in what became known as the 'Household R' category.[8] As Penny Summerfield and Margaret Allen have argued, the committee's definition of a 'household' was very much rooted in traditional male terms and, consequently, the only females who were 'protected' from compulsion were those whose roles within the household 'conformed to male-defined norms', as wives and mothers.[9]

Since the husbands of many married women were away on active service, the Women's Consultative Committee conceded that it was difficult to justify their total exemption from war work.

[8] For a detailed discussion of the precise definition of the 'Household R' category and of the debates which led to this classification, see Margaret Allen, 'Woman's place and World War Two' (unpublished MA thesis, University of Essex, 1979), pp. 21–62; eadem, 'The domestic ideal and the mobilization of womanpower in World War II', *Women's Studies International Forum*, 6, no. 4 (1983), 401–12; Summerfield, *Women Workers in the Second World War*, pp. 48–9; eadem, 'The girl that makes the thing that drills the hole that holds the spring . . .', pp. 38–40.

[9] Summerfield, 'The girl that makes the thing that drills the hole that holds the spring . . .', p. 39; Allen, 'The domestic ideal and the mobilization of womanpower in World War II', 401–12.

However, in view of the fact that they were 'responsible' for the care of a household, it was decided that such women would be regarded as immobile females who could be directed to war work in their home districts only. The feelings of the absent husbands played a significant part in the formulation of this policy, for it was reported in March 1941 that married servicemen were 'expressing anxiety and even indignation at the prospect of their wives being called up'.[10] In the event, therefore, the childless wife of an absent serviceman was granted the right to remain in her home district to perform her wartime service. The single female, on the other hand, was not protected by her marital status and, even though her domestic responsibilities may have been greater than those of her married female neighbour, she was liable to be sent away to work somewhere else in the country.

As the shortage of labour in the war factories of Britain became more acute, the Ministry of Labour realized that fewer exemptions would have to be granted to members of the female population, and many wives, mothers and women with household responsibilities eventually found themselves under great pressure to volunteer for war work. By the spring of 1942, it had been decided that the only females who could remain in the 'Household R' category were those who cared for other individuals in their homes and, eventually, as the official war historian M. M. Postan pointed out, 'the immunity was narrowed down still further to women who looked after children living at home.'[11] From March 1942, mothers of children under fourteen years of age were asked to consider taking up part-time work in their home areas and, similarly, women who were responsible for a household, but were not caring for any young children, were called forward for interviews at local employment exchanges and asked whether they would be willing to take up war work.[12] By April 1943 women who had not yet volunteered for war work were liable to be 'directed' to take up part-time employment locally under the Control of Engagement (Directed Persons) Order. The Ministry of Labour was also under pressure to place some immobile married women in the mobile category of labour.

[10] PRO, Inf 1/292.
[11] Postan, *British War Production*, p. 222.
[12] Allen, 'The domestic ideal and the mobilization of womanpower in World War II', 408–9.

In March 1942 members of the Select Committee on National Expenditure argued that 'the number of women in this category is considerable and that, on the grounds of national emergency, it may be necessary to reconsider the policy.'[13] In the event, however, married women and those with certain 'domestic responsibilities' continued to be regarded as immobile females who were available for work in their home districts, while only single females could be transferred to work anywhere in the country.

The issue of mobility was of particular concern to the women of south Wales.[14] In 1942 the Ministry of Labour established its 'coloured area' transfer scheme and classified each of its twelve 'regions' into one of three groups, according to the local supply and demand for labour. Wales was classed as a 'green' or 'supply area' from which mobile workers were to be transferred to 'amber' or 'scarlet' regions where a shortage of labour had been reported. In effect, therefore, all Welsh mobile females were to be exported to fill vacancies in the demand areas, while vacancies in the war factories of Wales were to be filled by local, immobile females. In order to release a greater number of mobile workers for employment away from their home districts, the Ministry of Labour needed to recruit many more immobile females to work in local factories, and in south Wales attention focused on the unoccupied married women who formed a large untapped source of labour in the region.

The Ministry of Labour had already made a concerted effort to target this large reservoir of unoccupied women during 1941, when a severe shortage of labour at Bridgend ROF led to a big recruiting drive in the area.[15] The full-time employment of married women was not a familiar concept in the region, however, and it appears that the wartime propagandists were fully aware that they needed to prepare their appeal for volunteers carefully. In view of the economic crises which had gripped the inhabitants of the industrial communities of south Wales for a decade or more, it was hardly surprising that the posters used in

[13] PP 1941–2 (III), *Seventh Report from the Select Committee on National Expenditure*, 'Supply of labour', p. 7.
[14] For local and national reaction to the wartime transference of the Welsh 'mobile' female population, see ch. 4.
[15] See the following for examples of recruiting posters, *Glamorgan Advertiser*, 11 and 25 July 1941.

the recruitment campaign focused on the economic benefits of wartime employment. An attempt was also made to reassure married women that it would be possible for them to combine their duties in their homes with their work in the factories, since 'time for shopping' could be 'arranged'.[16] The Ministry of Labour was evidently aware of the fact that some domestic assistance would have to be given to married women if they were to be persuaded to volunteer for war work. The unoccupied married women of south Wales who were questioned in 1940 by the authors of the *Beveridge Manpower Survey* had made it clear that their first priorities lay with their homes and families:

> Home ties, the need to prepare meals for husbands coming home from work and for young children, and also the difficulty of working night shifts when there are children home, appear to make many women feel it is impossible for them to take up employment.[17]

The survey investigators also noted that since the arrival of hundreds of child evacuees to the area, these domestic ties had become considerably greater. At Merthyr Tydfil, where some 1,600 evacuees from Kent had arrived in June 1940, unofficial sources claimed that 'ordinary home ties in a mining district, together with the additional claims on women's time due to the presence of evacuee children, would preclude many married women from taking up full-time employment.'[18] The women of the Rhondda no doubt shared their feelings, for hundreds of women in the valley had also 'thrown open' their homes to care for the *c*.2,500 official evacuees who had been sent there by the summer of 1940.[19]

In the event, the campaign to comb out the immobile female population of south Wales proved to be particularly successful, and a large proportion of the female workers who laboured in the war factories of the region were married women. At Blaina, for example, Mollie Tarrant reported that at least half the 500

[16] The words of a Ministry of Labour and National Service poster, *Aberdare Leader*, 1 November 1941.
[17] *Beveridge Manpower Survey*, 1940.
[18] Ibid.
[19] Cyril E. Gwyther, *The Valley Shall Be Exalted: Light Shines in the Rhondda* (London, 1949), p. 36; *The Rhondda Gazette*, 22 June 1940.

female munitions workers of the town were married women.[20] Former employees of Bridgend ROF confirmed that married women comprised a considerable proportion of the female work-force and, in several instances, their mothers and grandmothers worked alongside them on the factory workbenches.[21] To many such women, the assurance contained in the government's recruitment propaganda that they would be 'happier – and very likely more prosperous – in the great Munitions Army', greatly influenced their decision to volunteer for work in the munitions factories.[22] After all, the wages which could be earned 'on munitions' were far superior to the inadequate allowances and earnings which were received by the wives of servicemen and miners, and could provide opportunities for many women to make up for the economic hardships they had endured over recent years. Evidence of the financial benefits which munitions work could bring to the ordinary working-class families of south Wales soon became apparent to contemporary observers. At Blaina it was reported that 'for the first time in years people have been able to pay off arrears of rent, get new curtains, and feed their children properly', while a former munitions worker from Seven Sisters in the Dulais valley, who was interviewed during the 1970s, recalled that 'with women going to work, there was [sic] no more patches on the back of their children's trousers.'[23] There is no doubt, as W. H. Mainwaring, the Rhondda East MP, was to point out in 1946, that 'one reason why the women of Wales became available for work in their thousands is because they had lived on such a narrow economic base that they were glad to welcome an added shilling.'[24]

In some households, the only major source of income had been provided by the earnings of young female members who worked in low-paid occupations as domestic servants or shop

---

[20] M-O A, FR 1498, 'Blaina', p. 48.

[21] Evidence of Respondents 4, 7, 9 and 15.

[22] The words of a Ministry of Labour and National Service poster which appeared in the south Wales press during 1941, Glamorgan Advertiser, 25 July 1941. Several of the former employees of Bridgend ROF interviewed for this study maintained that local married women entered the munitions factories 'for the money'. Evidence of Respondents 4, 7 and 15.

[23] M-O A, FR 1196, 'Blaina investigation', 2 April 1942, p. 1; SWML, tape no. 148, interview with Nancy Davies, Seven Sisters. See also the evidence of Jill John in Davies (ed.), The Valleys Autobiography, p. 74.

[24] Parliamentary Debates (Hansard) (5th series), vol. 428, 390 (28 October 1946).

assistants. The higher wages paid in the munitions factories proved to be a great temptation to the mothers of these young girls and many mothers were persuaded to enter the industrial workforce. A fifteen-year-old girl from Maesteg gave up her job as a shop assistant in 1941 to look after her two younger brothers, thus enabling her mother to take up work at Bridgend ROF.[25] The incidence of this practice was said to be so common at Merthyr Tydfil during the war that members of the town's Juvenile Employment Committee feared that the young girls of the district were losing out on the opportunity to learn about factory work. In January 1944 the committee urged local mothers, who were 'keeping young girls at home so that they can themselves take up lucrative work at the factories', to think of the future employment prospects of their daughters and to give up their own positions.[26]

The wives and mothers of south Wales who volunteered for munitions work had clearly come to the conclusion that its economic advantages far outweighed the inconvenience and disruption caused by the long hours spent away from their homes and families. Under the regulations of the 1937 Factories Act, women were not permitted to work more than forty-eight hours a week, and as well as being banned from working night shifts, they could only work a limited period of overtime. By 1939, however, wartime production demands had enforced an extension of these working hours, and females over sixteen years of age were permitted to work up to fifty-seven hours per week.[27] In the early years of the war, the majority of the munitions factories of south Wales worked two ten-hour shifts. Clearly, female workers who were employed at such works had very little free time to spend on essential household chores at the end of their working day. Although a three-shift system of fifty-six hours a week was introduced at some factories from March 1940 onwards, the vast majority of the munitions factories of Britain continued to work a two-shift system which, with the addition of overtime, involved

---

[25] Evidence of Respondent 6.
[26] *Merthyr Express*, 29 January 1944.
[27] PP 1939–40 (IV, Cmd. 6182), *Report on Hours of Employment of Women and Young Persons in Factories during the First Five Months of the War.*

long hours for their employees.[28] A report produced by members of the Select Committee on National Expenditure in July 1942 revealed that women in two-thirds of the sixteen ROFs which they had visited worked over fifty-five hours a week and, in two factories, they were employed for sixty-six hours per week.[29]

The working of such long hours was deemed unacceptable by members of the wartime industrial workforce and their representatives, and the factory authorities came under increased pressure to reduce their working hours. In February 1941, the South Wales Regional Council of Labour called on the trade unions who represented female workers to press for eight-hour shifts in all factories in the area, in a bid to ensure that women were not kept away from their homes for more than fourteen hours a day.[30] The factory authorities appear to have taken little action in the matter, however, for in October 1942 demands for factories in the area to change over to the three-shift system continued to be voiced. According to Ness Edwards, the Caerphilly MP, the requests of his female constituents for local factories to adopt a three-shift system had fallen on deaf ears, for the largest ordnance factory in the district continued to work two ten-hour shifts. However, the representative from the Ministry of Supply who investigated this complaint, appeared to be unaware of any such requests and maintained that the majority of females were quite happy with the existing situation:

I have looked further into the proposal and find that there is only a very small minority of women workers at R.O.F. who wish to work on a three shift basis. The great majority desire no alteration in the present hours of work on a two shift basis. There would, in fact, be considerable difficulties in the way of running three shifts. Skilled labour is scarce and to make it go round it would have to keep to a two shift basis. Transport arrangements too, have to be fitted in with requirements of other industrial undertakings in the locality.[31]

[28] PP 1940–1 (III), *Seventeenth Report from the Select Committee on National Expenditure*, 'Labour problems in filling factories', p. 1; *Parliamentary Debates* (Hansard) (5th series), vol. 371, 851 (7 May 1941); PP 1940–1 (VIII, Cmd. 6310), *Memorandum by the Ministry of Labour and National Service on Welfare Work Outside the Factory, June 1940 to August 1941*, p. 8.
[29] PP 1941–2 (III), *Eleventh Report from the Select Committee on National Expenditure*, 'Royal Ordnance Factories', pp. 15, 21.
[30] NLW, Labour Party of Wales Archive, South Wales Regional Council of Labour executive committee minutes, 18 February 1941.
[31] *Caerphilly Journal*, 24 October 1942.

The needs of the female workers themselves did not appear to be the primary concern of this government official, who seemed to attach more importance to organizing factory shifts according to the requirements of local transport operators.[32] Admittedly, the factory authorities faced many difficulties in organizing transport in a region where the geography as well as the lack of investment in road and rail building created many problems. Although new railway halts were built to serve Bridgend, Glascoed and Hirwaun ROFs, the war factories of south Wales continued to rely heavily on road transport. In March 1940 the bus services of south Wales were in the hands of 288 independent small operators who owned approximately 2,500 vehicles between them. As the majority of these operators owned only one or two vehicles each, and had no spare vehicles or reserves of drivers, the task of organizing road transport in the region proved to be extremely difficult, and caused grave problems both for the recruitment and subsequent transport of war workers to and from the factories.[33]

The investigators who carried out the *Beveridge Manpower Survey* of south Wales in 1940 found that many 'dependent' females from the Rhondda had been deterred from volunteering for war work at Bridgend ROF because of severe transport difficulties between the two destinations.[34] Indeed, poor transport arrangements from Merthyr Tydfil, the Rhondda, the Cynon and neighbouring valleys were to have a detrimental effect on efforts to recruit female labour to Bridgend ROF throughout the early years of the war.[35] In March 1941 Ivor Thomas, the divisional welfare officer of the Ministry of Labour in Wales, informed ministry officials that many women who might have volunteered for war work at Bridgend and Glascoed ROFs had been discouraged from doing so after learning how their working day would be extended because of the time spent travelling to and from the factories.[36] It was even reported that women from the Rhondda who had volunteered and had been accepted for work

[32] Conversely, officials from the Ministry of Labour advocated the adoption of a three-shift system and the staggering of working hours at individual factories as a means of reducing transport problems. See PP 1940–1 (VIII, Cmd. 6310), p. 8.

[33] PRO, Lab 26/90; Parker, *Manpower*, p. 404

[34] *Beveridge Manpower Survey*, 1940.

[35] PRO, Lab 12/82, 26/90 and 26/91; *Aberdare Leader*, 14 December 1940.

[36] PRO, Lab 26/91.

at Bridgend ROF had subsequently been unable to take up their positions in the factory because of the inadequate transport arrangements.[37]

Although some of these early transport problems were eventually solved, little could be done to shorten the length of the journeys which so many of the female war workers of south Wales made each day to and from the war factories. Given that much of the labour employed at Bridgend and Glascoed ROFs was drawn from a wide geographical area within the region, the journeys of some female war workers could exceed over sixty miles each day.[38] In a report sent to the Ministry of Labour in April 1941, Eirwen Owen, the Welsh regional organizer of the Women's Voluntary Service, drew attention to the particular problems facing many of the munitions workers who were employed at Bridgend ROF:

> Bridgend, for instance is served from Ammanford, Merthyr and Rhondda. The time of travelling thus varies from three-quarters of an hour to one and a half hours. In some cases, the journey itself involves two changes as for instance from Ammanford to Bridgend. However, it is not the difficulty of the journeys which are the main problems but the actual physical distances people have to travel . . . billeting near the factories is difficult because houses are scarce and people will not leave their homes to go into lodgings.[39]

For women who had families and a host of domestic chores to attend to on arrival back home, lodging or hostel accommodation[40] was not a viable option, and they had little choice, therefore, but to put up with long bus or train journeys which kept them away from their homes for a substantial portion of the day. George Daggar, the Abertillery MP, complained in December 1940 that many female war workers from his constituency were 'at work and on the road for about 15 hours a day'.[41] The long hours of travel, often in blackout conditions,

[37] *Parliamentary Debates* (Hansard) (5th series), vol. 370, 1667–8 (10 April 1941).
[38] PRO, Lab 26/90 and 26/91; *Beveridge Manpower Survey*, 1940.
[39] PRO, Lab 26/90.
[40] Writing in 1942, the Minister of Labour expressed his opinion that the provision of billets and lodging accommodation could help relieve working women of some of their domestic responsibilities. Ernest Bevin, *The Job to be Done* (Kingswood, 1942), pp. 21–2.
[41] *Parliamentary Debates* (Hansard) (5th series), vol. 367, 1207 (18 December 1940).

made some women feel that life had become a daily journey 'from bed to work', and this inevitably took its toll on the health of the workers.[42] In November 1941 officials at Bridgend ROF reported that many employees were suffering from 'travel-tiredness', which had not only reduced their efficiency and productivity at the factory, but had also given rise to absenteeism, which was said to have reached 26 per cent in some cases.[43]

Local concern for the effects which long working hours were having on the health and general well-being of female war workers grew when it became clear that little action was being taken either to reduce their working or travelling hours. In the opinion of the editor of the *South Wales Evening Post*, the factory managers had only themselves to blame for the high levels of absenteeism recorded among female war workers in the area. Very little regard had been shown for the welfare of local women who, after their journeys home on buses and trains, often faced 'long walks in the rigours of winter mornings and evenings from stations or bus terminals to their homes'.[44] The father of one factory girl from the Rhondda was so incensed with the lack of concern shown for his daughter and her fellow workers that he voiced his opinions publicly in April 1942:

> They leave home four days in the week at 6.40am. and do not arrive home in the evening until 9.10. On Wednesday, they may get home at 7pm. and on Saturday at 5pm. The time spent in travelling and working amounts to 86½ hours each week. If their bus is three minutes late arriving at the factory, 15 minutes is deducted from their time. Their bus fare amount [sic] to 8s. a week and they generally have to stand most of the way home. For all these hours of work and discomfort, they do not receive £3 per week even when they are lucky enough to have no deductions. Does the Government take any interest in the girls that they send to these factories?[45]

[42] Evidence of Respondents 1, 8 and 11. Claims that 'travel-weariness and exposure to weather' were having a deletrious effect on the health of some 350 married women who travelled daily about sixty miles each way to a south Wales factory were made at a meeting of the Welsh National Memorial Association at Aberystwyth in January 1942. *South Wales Evening Post*, 30 January 1942.

[43] *Western Mail*, 27 November 1941; PRO, Lab 10/367.

[44] *South Wales Evening Post*, 2 January 1942. In October 1941, Ada Williams, a 'dauntless' 32-year-old war worker whose story had appeared in the south Wales press, was presented with a bicycle by Lord Bennett, the former premier of Canada, in order to spare her the ten-mile 'daily tramp' from the bus stop to her home. *Western Mail*, 21 and 22 October 1941.

[45] *South Wales Echo*, 7 April 1942.

Many war workers were of the opinion that their transport problems could be solved if existing transport schemes were co-ordinated more effectively. A female war worker from Ferndale in the Rhondda wrote directly to Ernest Bevin, the minister of labour, to explain how a more flexible transport system could be of benefit to elderly workers like herself who would prefer to travel to work by bus rather than by train:

> The Rhondda Valley people are willing to know is it possable [*sic*] that women in their 50 and over cannot get on the bussies [*sic*] if they live a long way from the train and the trains start so early in the morning at 5 o'clock. Several people are loosing [*sic*] work through that Bussies are running with just a few people in them, we think it is a shame to see people 50 and over running like mad and passing the bus and shall not get on them, we think that when busses run by the door should [*sic*] have a bus ticket. Some people pass the bus to go by train and some pass the train to go by bus . . . Young girls can run to the train but people with household duties over 50 should have a bus ticket.[46]

Other female workers did not wait to receive official permission before changing their transport arrangements and took matters into their own hands. In November 1941 two married women from the Rhondda were fined £1 each by Ystrad magistrates after they admitted giving false information to the National Registration Officer 'for the purpose of changing their mode of transport'. In their defence, the women explained that they had deceived the local official in order that they could travel to and from their place of work by bus, which provided a quicker service than the train and got them home earlier.[47] Another Rhondda war worker, who was fined £1 at Porth police court in February 1944 for failing to attend the local ROF, explained that she had had enough of travelling by train to and from Tylorstown when a bus could get her home half an hour earlier, thus leaving her more time to do her shopping.[48] In mining districts, it appeared that greater co-ordination of the transport services provided for factory workers and colliers could also have improved matters for both parties.[49] In December 1942 four

[46] PRO, Lab 26/90.
[47] *The Rhondda Leader*, 15 November 1941.
[48] *Free Press and Rhondda Leader*, 12 February 1944.
[49] PRO, Lab 26/90.

female war workers from Heolgerrig, Merthyr Tydfil, who were employed at Hirwaun ROF, wrote to the Ministry of Labour to ask why they could not be picked up by the half-empty colliers' bus which passed them every day, rather than wait in all weathers for their own transport to arrive.[50]

Given these circumstances, it is hardly surprising that the long journeys to and from the munitions factories became too much for some war workers to bear. In February 1941 it was reported that over a thousand women had left Bridgend ROF 'mainly on account of transport difficulties which extend the working day to unreasonable lengths'.[51] Female war workers who were later conscripted to work in local factories were unable to take such action and had to put up with the grinding routine which left them feeling constantly tired and worn out. In 1942, commenting on the effect which wartime employment was having on the health of the local female workforce, a councillor from Blaina drew attention to the problems faced by women war workers who also shouldered considerable domestic responsibilities:

> The girls are getting run down. Some of the young women are looking quite old. And what can you expect when they're up at 4.45 in the morning and not back here again until 4.30. And then they've got their bits of shopping and housework to do . . . I begged the women to stand for factories nearer home, but of course, they wouldn't do anything. I am sure there are hundreds of women who could do part-time work.[52]

The introduction of part-time employment would clearly have been a great help to many women, yet this was not an option which was made widely available to the female war workers of south Wales. Part-time work was offered only to those females whose parental or domestic responsibilities had already granted them exemption from full-time employment. As such, part-time employment schemes were introduced as a means of making greater use of all available female labour, rather than as an initiative to assist female war workers with their domestic responsibilities. There was plenty of evidence to suggest that a considerable number of the women who were exempt from

[50] Ibid.
[51] PRO, Lab 12/82.
[52] M-O A, FR 1498, 'Blaina', p. 94.

compulsion would volunteer for war work, but they would only do so if working hours were arranged so that they also had time to attend to their homes and families. In its guide to the call-up of females, the Labour Research Department pointed out that, although 'the great majority of housewives feel now that they want to be doing a real war job outside their home', they also felt that their families needed 'good, well-cooked meals and a comfortable home to come back to'.[53] It appeared that the housewives of south Wales would also have considered taking up work in local war industries if working hours and journey times to and from the factories could be shortened. At Nant-y-glo and Blaina, in July 1943, it was revealed that an estimated 900 non-mobile women would willingly accept either full-time or part-time employment 'if it were near enough to their homes to enable them to deal with their domestic responsibilities in addition'.[54]

However, the enthusiasm shown by members of the female population for part-time work was not always shared by the factory managers and employers who would have to make the necessary adjustments to existing shift-times and working practices. Six hundred female war workers who had registered for part-time work in the borough of Merthyr Tydfil in November 1942 found that few employers in the area were willing to avail themselves of their services.[55] Managers of the state-run factories proved to be rather more accommodating and a 'Housewives' Brigade' of part-time workers was formed at some ROFs in south Wales. The scheme was launched at Bridgend ROF in November 1941, when housewives from the district were invited to attend a public meeting at the Embassy cinema in the town where they could learn more about the special working hours and conditions which could be arranged for their convenience.[56] The scheme proved extremely successful and some 400 women were recruited to the factory almost immediately.[57] As this was a scheme which had been 'evolved' to enable the ordinary housewife to take up war work 'in her spare time', potential recruits were assured that the remainder of the day could be dedicated to

[53] Labour Research Department, *A Complete Guide to the Call Up of Women*, p. 7.
[54] M-O A, TC 64, Coal mining, Box 1, File C, report of the Nantyglo and Blaina UDC post-war reconstruction conference of former Special Areas, 20 July 1943.
[55] *Merthyr Express*, 21 November 1942.
[56] *Glamorgan Advertiser*, 7 November 1941.
[57] PRO, Lab 12/82.

their usual domestic tasks. Women worked shifts of four and a half hours' duration, five days a week, either from 9 a.m. to 1.30 p.m. or from 1.30 p.m. to 6 p.m., and were permitted to 'select whichever period of duty is most suitable to them', safe in the knowledge that their families and homes received their attention during the remainder of the working day.[58] One 58-year-old woman from Bridgend, who had joined the brigade in 1941, took part in a Welsh-language radio broadcast to publicize the benefits of the scheme for married women. She reassured her audience that this was work which any housewife could manage, since she was left with plenty of time to 'do the housework and look after the family' ('Pedair awr a hanner yw ein shifft ni wragedd y Brigade ac y mae hyn yn rhoi cyfle i wneud gwaith y tŷ a disgwyl ar ôl y teulu').[59]

The female war workers who remained tied to their full-time posts in the war factories of south Wales were given little relief from the demanding routine of wartime employment and were left to carry on as best they could. It was not long, however, before the physical and emotional strain of this gruelling lifestyle took its toll on the health of the female workers. Shift-work left many women feeling permanently tired as their bodies struggled to adjust to changing sleep-patterns, while others found that their eating habits were severely affected by the disruption to their normal hours.[60] A member of the medical profession who voiced his concerns on such matters in 1943 believed that most British factory workers went to work on an empty stomach, took only a few sandwiches for their lunch, then ate nothing else until they returned home, when they found that they were 'usually too tired to eat'.[61] During the course of her wartime investigation at Blaina and Nant-y-glo, Mollie Tarrant, the Mass-Observation investigator, heard plenty of evidence to suggest that similar problems plagued the female munitions workers of the district, and led many to stay away from the workplace:

> Digestive troubles and over-tiredness were frequent causes of absenteeism . . . Another suggestive sidelight on the question of fatigue came from a

[58]   *Glamorgan Advertiser*, 7 November 1941.
[59]   NLW, BBC (Wales) Archive, script of radio talk by Mrs Llewelyn, Bridgend, broadcast on 10 December 1941.
[60]   Evidence of Respondent 5.
[61]   *British Medical Journal*, 3 April 1943.

morning visit to munition workers' homes. A road was picked at random and the first six houses in which munition workers lived, visited. All except one of the workers had been away for as long as a fortnight in the past three months. All complained of the long hours of travelling, the strain of the work, the food.[62]

Eventually, however, growing concern for the high level of female absenteeism recorded in the war factories of Britain, led the government to commission several investigations into the causes of the problem. The findings of the two studies conducted by the Industrial Health Research Board confirmed that sickness absence was a particular problem among female war workers, many of whom were said to be suffering ill-health as a result of 'the stresses and strains associated with war-time conditions of work'.[63] A detailed inquiry into the sickness absence of female workers at five munitions factories in 1944, which involved an examination of the records of over 20,000 employees, found that absences due to sickness and accidents accounted for more than half the total time lost, with respiratory diseases (including colds and influenza) accounting for 28.6 per cent of the total number of absences among both married and single females in a period of six months. Many women war workers also suffered from 'psychological disorders' which were attributed to general war-time anxieties.[64]

In south Wales, where the general physical condition of the population had suffered as a result of the poverty of the inter-war years, standards of health appear to have improved considerably following the outbreak of the war. Some regarded the wartime diet to be far superior to that to which they had been accustomed, since regular wages and the introduction of the rationing system ensured that all individuals received the basic needs of a balanced and healthy diet.[65] The medical officers of health for the Rhondda and the Ogmore and Garw UDCs were agreed that the

[62] M-O A, FR 1498, 'Blaina', Appendix: 'The latest news', September 1943, pp. 20–1.
[63] S. Wyatt et al., *A Study of Certified Sickness Absence among Women in Industry*, MRC Industrial Health Research Board Report no. 86 (London, 1945), p. 31. See also idem, *A Study of Women on War Work in Four Factories*, pp. 40–1.
[64] Idem, *A Study of Certified Sickness Absence among Women in Industry*, pp. 33–4.
[65] See M-O A, FR 1498, 'Blaina', p. 117; evidence of Margaret Lloyd in Verrill-Rhys and Beddoe (eds.), *Parachutes and Petticoats*, p. 39.

additional income generated by the wartime employment of hundreds of local women had had a 'beneficial' effect on health standards.[66] Even so, there was no denying that the physical and emotional condition of some members of the population, including many female war workers, had shown little sign of improvement. Speaking to Mollie Tarrant, a 35-year-old married woman and mother explained how the strain of managing her dual role as housewife and war worker was becoming too much to bear:

> I dunno, I don't want to eat, and I can't sleep. I never eat up there. I wouldn't go to the canteen. I've never seen anything like the way they dish up the stuff. Makes you feel ill to see it. Most people take their food up with them. I do sometimes, but I never feel I want to eat there. And then, when I get home I'm too tired to eat. And then when I get up again I still don't feel like it. It's a lot to do when you've got your house to look after and child to go to school.[67]

From the outset of the war, it had become evident that female war workers were far more prone to sickness and 'unaccountable' absenteeism than their male colleagues. In July 1941 it was reported that the female absenteeism rates at British filling factories were between 60 and 90 per cent higher than the male rates.[68] The official war historian noted that in the first five months of 1943, absenteeism at filling factories (as a percentage of manpower hours worked) was 9.36 per cent among the male workforce and 19.96 per cent among female workers.[69] Another inquiry, carried out at British war factories by the Factory and Welfare Advisory Board of the Ministry of Labour during the period June–October 1943, confirmed that absence from work was almost twice as high among women as among men.[70] It was also clear that absenteeism was significantly higher among married than among single females.[71] A study conducted by the Industrial Health Research Board into the sickness absence of

[66] *Annual Report of the Rhondda Medical Officer of Health, 1944*, p. 19; *Annual Report of the Ogmore and Garw Medical Officer of Health, 1944*, p. 5.

[67] M-O A, TC 64, Coal mining, Box 1, File C.

[68] PP 1940–1 (III), 'Labour problems in filling factories', p. 1. See also M-O A, FR 1163, 'Women in industry', 19 March 1942, p. 4.

[69] Inman, *Labour in the Munitions Industries*, p. 279.

[70] PRO, Lab 26/132.

[71] Ibid.

women at four war factories found that a large proportion of the female workers who were absent from work due to sickness were women who were 'wholly responsible for housework and shopping'.[72] Married women probably accounted for the vast majority of such females. The Wartime Social Survey of 1944 found that while 52 per cent of the 2,609 female war workers they questioned were mainly responsible for the housework, the proportion was as high as 83 per cent among married women, compared with only 22 per cent among single women.[73] Another investigation, carried out by the Industrial Health Research Board in 1944, also revealed that the incidence of sickness absence was 65 per cent higher among married women than among single women. Moreover, married women were found to suffer most from diseases of the generative, locomotory and circulatory groups, and from functional nervous disorders including 'fatigue'. The survey investigators concluded that the high rates of sickness absence among married females had to be attributed to the 'additional strains of married life':

> Much has already been said about the difficulties of those married women who do factory work and run a home in their spare time. The physical and mental effort required by this dual task is undoubtedly severe, and it is not surprising that several were unable to bear the strain and were either discharged or had long periods of illness.[74]

The absenteeism rates of male and female workers employed at two of the largest ROFs in south Wales were typical of the general pattern recorded elsewhere in Britain.[75] As table 3.1 shows, the absenteeism rates recorded among female workers at Bridgend and Glascoed ROFs during January 1942 were generally much higher than those of the male workforce.[76]

---

[72] Wyatt et al., *A Study of Women on War Work in Four Factories*, p. 41.

[73] Thomas, 'Women at work', p. 6.

[74] Wyatt et al., *A Study of Certified Sickness Absence among Women in Industry*, pp. 31, 34. A report received by the Ministry of Information's Home Intelligence Unit from the Wales Regional Office at Cardiff in May 1940 also noted that married women were 'feeling strain most'. PRO, Inf 1/264.

[75] The aggregate planned hours lost by men and women employed at factories in the 'Wales Division' during June and October 1943 were very similar to those lost at factories in England during the same period. PRO, Lab 26/4.

[76] PRO, Lab 26/131.

Table 3.1: Percentage of aggregate planned hours lost by employees at Bridgend and Glascoed Royal Ordnance Factories, January 1942

Week ending	Bridgend ROF		Glascoed ROF	
	Males	Females	Males	Females
	%	%	%	%
10 January 1942				
Sickness	2.0	3.4	6.3	9.3
Injury	–	–	0.7	–
Leave	0.2	0.8	0.4	1.1
Absence	6.5	22.4	3.7	16.8
17 January 1942				
Sickness	1.7	3.4	7.0	11.1
Injury	–	–	0.8	0.1
Leave	0.5	1.2	0.3	1.1
Absence	6.6	23.0	4.3	15.3
24 January 1942				
Sickness	1.6	3.2	7.0	12.8
Injury	–	–	0.9	–
Leave	0.4	0.7	0.4	1.1
Absence	8.7	26.7	5.9	19.1
31 January 1942				
Sickness	2.3	3.6	7.6	13.6
Injury	–	–	0.8	0.1
Leave	0.5	0.5	0.4	1.1
Absence	6.2	24.0	3.8	15.4

Source: PRO, Lab 26/131.

It is immediately apparent that the female employees of both Glascoed and Bridgend ROFs were not only more likely to be absent from work owing to sickness but also lost far more hours than their male colleagues on the grounds of 'unaccountable absenteeism', that is, absenteeism which was not due to sickness, injury or leave. The situation was particularly bad at Bridgend ROF, where the female workforce had lost almost a quarter of planned hours due to such unexplained absences. Female absenteeism was clearly a stubborn problem at the factory.[77] In December 1942, when a number of female employees were brought before the local police court and fined £5 each for 'absenting themselves from work without reasonable excuse', it was alleged that the absenteeism rate of some of the workers had been as high as 80 per cent.[78]

It was evident from the vast differences recorded in the rates of absence of the male and female employees of Bridgend and Glascoed ROFs that the additional domestic responsibilities shouldered by the female war workers were making it extremely difficult for them to cope with the demanding routine of a full week's work. For many female munitions workers, the only way to take control of their domestic affairs was to lose an hour or two's work each week. The inquiry into wartime production conducted by Mass-Observation in 1942 found that 62 per cent of married women attributed their absence from work to reasons other than sickness, injury or leave.[79] Some women stayed away from work when their husbands came home on leave, but the majority were found to absent themselves regularly in order to undertake essential domestic chores. The Select Committee on National Expenditure reported in July 1941 that females were most likely to be absent during weekends, a time which they 'like to devote to domestic duties and to family life'.[80]

In view of the rigidity of working hours and the lack of domestic assistance to female war workers, it was hardly surprising that such high levels of female absenteeism were recorded at the factories of south Wales. Yet, persistent absentees received very little assistance or sympathy from government officials and factory managers, who seemed intent on disciplining the offenders, rather than on investigating the reasons behind their absences. A 38-year-old miner's wife from Blaina, who was

[77] In a bid to conquer absenteeism, factory officials awarded prizes and distinctions to employees who achieved full attendance. Bridgend ROF's monthly newsletter, *R.O.F. 53 News*, published pictures of workers who had achieved full attendance during the month. In February 1943, photographs of the Brackla 'A' women workers who had lost no time during December 1942 were proudly displayed, and a challenge was issued to workers of the high-explosive fuse section to emulate their achievements during the following month. *R.O.F. 53 News*, February 1943, 4. I am grateful to Deborah James of the University of Glamorgan for providing me with a copy of this publication.

[78] *South Wales Echo*, 15 December 1942.

[79] Mass-Observation, *People in Production*, p. 167.

[80] PP 1940–1 (III), 'Labour problems in filling factories', p. 3.

employed at a factory at Rogerstone, near Newport, highlighted the problems faced by working mothers whose employers showed little consideration for their domestic situations:

> I've been in there six weeks now, and I like it very much. The only thing I don't like is the way they treat you when you stay away. You have to go up before the absentee officer each time, and they don't seem to see you have any real excuse. I mean if you have children and one of them has a cold, well, you don't feel you like to leave them to the care of other people all the time . . . They say you can have a day off if you ask for it, but you never get it. Lots of them have tried. There's always some excuse. The foreman said to me when I'd stayed away, 'Mrs——— if you had twelve children the wheels of industry would have to keep on going.' 'That's all very well,' I said, 'but they won't stop going if I stay away for one day.' The charge-hand's nice. He says he appreciates the problems of married women. But the foreman – he just had a milk-round before the war. The war's made him and he don't really know how to deal with things.[81]

Married women and mothers were not the only female war workers whose household responsibilities affected their attendance at the war factories. Many single females were also involved in the upkeep and management of their homes and assisted their families with various domestic chores on their return from work.[82] In 1942 the county youth organizer of Glamorgan reported that many young women in the district 'performed heavy household duties after working in factory or office', and in this respect they were 'more unfortunate than their brothers'.[83] Daughters of miners were perhaps the most 'unfortunate' of all for, despite being engaged on full-time employment at local munitions factories, many continued to assist their mothers with the heavy domestic chores associated with life in a mining household. Since only one female from each household could be granted exemption from wartime service on the grounds of her domestic responsibilities, the daughters or other female members of a mining household could not be excused from compulsory war work if the miner's wife was already at hand to care for the

[81] M-O A, TC 64, Coal mining, Box 1, File C.
[82] Evidence of Respondents 1 and 5.
[83] GRO, Glamorgan County Council, annual report of the director of education for 1942, report of the county youth organizer, 4 December 1942.

men of the house. Although the cases of several miners'
daughters were brought before tribunals in south Wales, their
appeals for exemption from wartime service rarely succeeded. In
1942, members of the Rhondda East Divisional Labour Party
received many complaints from local families regarding the
treatment that young women had received at the tribunals, and it
was alleged that the authorities had failed to give adequate
consideration to their domestic situation when a claim had been
made that a girl was required at home.[84]

Given these circumstances, it was not surprising that many
young women absented themselves from their place of work on a
regular basis, even though their actions incurred the wrath of
their employers and Ministry of Labour officials. Several young
females were brought before magistrates in south Wales to face
charges of non-compliance with government orders as a result of
their poor attendance at local munitions factories.[85] In January
1943 a 23-year-old munitions worker from Nant-y-glo was fined
by Pontypool magistrates after she stayed home from the factory
to assist her 62-year-old mother with the care of her two
brothers, both of whom were employed in local collieries.[86] In
her defence, the woman argued that it was impossible for her to
carry out her daily chores around the home in the few spare
hours that were left at the end of the long working day. Moreover, since the shifts worked at the collieries and the war factories
often clashed, women like herself who needed to be on hand to
care for the returning miner(s) had little option but to stay home
occasionally to attend to their needs.[87]

Such difficulties were exacerbated by the fact that single
females were classed as 'mobile workers' who were deemed to be
free of all domestic and family ties and who could, therefore, be
directed to undertake essential war work anywhere in Britain.
The plight of many miners' daughters was highlighted by a case

[84] *Parliamentary Debates* (Hansard) (5th series), vol. 380, 340–1 (21 May 1942); *The Rhondda Leader*, 30 May 1942, 6 June 1942.

[85] See the following for reports of such court cases: *Aberdare Leader*, 16 January 1943, 3 April 1943; *Porth Gazette and Rhondda Leader*, 17 February 1945.

[86] *Free Press of Monmouthshire*, 15 January 1943.

[87] A miner who worked at a colliery in the Ogmore and Garw district during the war recalled that he rarely got the opportunity to meet his fiancée who worked at Bridgend ROF because their working hours clashed: 'It was all shift work see, and very often we'd be clashing – I'd be days, she'd be afternoons, perhaps the other way around.' Evidence of William Gibson in Davies (ed.), *The Valleys Autobiography*, p. 74.

which was brought before the police court at Aberdare in November 1943, when Blodwen Lloyd, a 28-year-old munitions worker from Hirwaun, was fined £3 for refusing to work in a factory away from the district. As a single woman who lived with her widowed mother, her sister and brother, Lloyd felt that several important factors regarding her domestic situation had not been taken into account by the local Ministry of Labour officials. In her opinion, she should have been regarded as an immobile female, for she was solely responsible for attending to the needs of her collier brother since her sister, who was in poor health, did not have the strength to look after him and their ailing mother:

> I work eight hours at a factory . . . I have a brother working underground and I must look after him because my sister is not strong enough to do it. I have everything to do when I get home from the factory. I have to do the shopping and see to the home. I stay up till one in the morning to see to my brother when he comes in from the afternoon shift at the Empire colliery and then, I must get up at five the same morning to go to my own work at the factory. Everything depends on me.[88]

In stark contrast to the experiences of Blodwen Lloyd, the popular wartime representation of the young, single, female war worker offered a very different picture of her lifestyle and character. Young female munitions workers were often portrayed as carefree and irresponsible workers who showed little interest or any sense of duty either towards their work or their families.[89] Conversely, older or married females were seen as reliable and conscientious workers who were believed to have a steadying influence on their younger colleagues.[90] In their study of the sickness absence of female war workers published in 1945, the Industrial Health Research Board concluded that:

> young single women and young married women without children and home duties, showed on the whole, less sense of responsibility than older women, and were less eager to come to work when feeling 'off colour' . . . The comparative indifference to work and to the war effort, shown by

[88] *Aberdare Leader*, 27 November 1943.
[89] *South Wales Evening Post*, 16 July 1942.
[90] See Douie, *Daughters of Britain*, p. 16; evidence of Respondent 7.

some of the younger women, would also tend to make them less eager to resume work after an illness.[91]

Factory managers 'up and down the country' were said to be full of praise for the married women who worked in their establishments, and who had shown themselves to be extremely loyal and diligent workers.[92] In the opinion of the chief labour officer employed at one Welsh factory, the 'middle-aged woman, who has carried out the arduous task of bringing up a family, can stick it better than a young person'.[93] Officials at another war factory in south Wales clearly shared this view for, in 1943, Lillian Meyrick, a 53-year-old from Cardiff, was judged the most meritorious female worker at one of the war factories in the district, and was honoured with the official title of 'Miss Munitions'. As a widow who had lost her husband during the First World War, 'Gran' Meyrick set a fine example to all her younger colleagues, for despite travelling twenty miles to work every day, she also found time to care for her 75-year-old mother and her two young grandchildren.[94]

Overall, however, the highest levels of absenteeism were recorded among older and married female workers, who found it increasingly difficult not to lose some hours each week in order to attend to their various domestic affairs. In the opinion of many women workers and their representatives, this was a situation which could have been avoided if adequate provision had been made for the special needs of female workers in the first place. During the first month of the war, members of the National Women's Advisory Council of the TUC urged the government to make special arrangements to meet the requirements of female workers, 'particularly in view of the dual responsibility of the home and employment'.[95] Several months later, however, little action had been taken by the government to address this central issue. As thousands of females entered the war factories during the spring and early summer of 1941, the Home Intelligence Unit of the Ministry of Information reported an urgent

[91]   Wyatt et al., *A Study of Certified Sickness Absence Among Women in Industry*, p. 33.
[92]   Mass-Observation, *People in Production*, p. 166.
[93]   *Western Mail*, 27 November 1941.
[94]   Ibid., 19 February 1943; *South Wales Evening Post*, 19 February 1943.
[95]   Trades Union Congress (TUC), National Women's Advisory Council minutes, 19 September 1939 (Harvester Microfilms).

demand for the establishment of day nurseries and the introduction of flexible working hours, which would give women
more time to undertake essential household tasks such as shopping.[96] It was clear that unless steps were taken in such matters,
potential female war workers would be deterred from volunteering their services, while those already employed in munitions
factories would continue to absent themselves from the workplace or perhaps even leave the workforce completely.

Ultimately, therefore, it was the growing concern for the effect
which female absenteeism was having on recruitment and
production targets at the war factories of Britain which eventually prompted officials at the Ministry of Labour to take a closer
look at the special needs and demands of the female workforce.
Reports from both official and unofficial sources across the
country suggested that one of the most pressing problems facing
female war workers was that of finding time to carry out their
shopping.[97] Wartime food shortages and the introduction of
rationing had made the task all the more tiresome and time-
consuming for working women. Indeed, in the opinion of Vera
Douie, 'shopping for a family became in wartime quite a major
operation, requiring considerable tactical ability and a good
information service.'[98] In the early months of the war in particular, before many essential foodstuffs were rationed, women
waited their turn for hours in long queues, only to find that
the goods which they required had already sold out. One commentator, who visited the Rhondda in December 1941, noticed
how housewives had to 'scout round' the shops of the area
'stepping on and off crowded buses' in their search for 'some tit-
bit for their men'.[99]

Women who were engaged in full-time work at the large war
factories in the region had little time or energy to shop around in
this manner, and many had little option but to take time off work
in order to get their shopping done. In the Rhondda, munitions
workers who worked night shifts at a local ordnance factory

[96] PRO, Inf 1/292.
[97] See *Parliamentary Debates* (Hansard) (5th series), vol. 368, 253 (22 January 1941);
ibid., vol. 370, 333–4 (20 March 1941); PRO, Lab 26/60 and Inf, 1/292; PP 1941–2
(III), 'Supply of labour', p.11; M-O A, FR 1163, 'Women in industry', p. 3.
[98] Douie, *Daughters of Britain*, p. 152.
[99] NLW, BBC (Wales) Archive, script of radio talk by John Griffith, 'The Rhondda
valleys', broadcast on 18 December 1941.

complained that they were often too tired to go into work because they had spent their days queuing for food in the shops.[100] In view of the long distances which the munitions workers of south Wales travelled to and from their place of work each day, it was also often the case that, by the time many women returned home from the war factories, the shops had either sold out of essential goods, or had already shut. For example, in May 1942, the female war workers of Merthyr Tydfil claimed that it was impossible for them to obtain goods in the shops after ending their shifts, since 'those who have nothing else to do' had already done their shopping 'and denuded the shops of all that is going'.[101] Women war workers from the Rhondda called on the Minister of Labour to provide a more efficient transport service to and from Bridgend ROF in order that they could arrive home before the shops had shut.[102] Female employees of Glascoed ROF who lived in the isolated settlement of Fochriw were also keen to change their transport arrangements for the same purpose, and in September 1942, they requested a 'shopping break' at the nearby town of Bargoed on their bus journey home from work on Friday evenings.[103]

One of the main difficulties facing the female munitions workers of south Wales was the lack of co-ordination between the hours worked at the factories and the opening hours of local shops. In November 1941, the production executive of the Wales Regional Board of the Ministry of Labour officially recognized that the high absenteeism rates of the Welsh female war workers were 'largely due' to the 'clashing of their working hours with those during which their food shops are open'.[104] Whilst appreciating the difficult conditions under which local retailers were operating, the board urged Welsh chambers of trade and other retailers' representatives to consult with the Ministry of Labour before recommending the adoption of revised opening hours in the future. Officials from the Ministry of Labour were no doubt keen to avoid any repetition of the situation which had arisen in south Wales in previous months, when local traders had shown

[100] *The Rhondda Leader*, 24 February 1945.
[101] *Merthyr Express*, 9 May 1942.
[102] PRO, Lab 26/90.
[103] GRO, Gelligaer UDC minutes, 15 September 1942.
[104] *Glamorgan Advertiser*, 28 November 1941.

little regard for the needs of female workers when deciding on shop opening hours. Female factory workers had reported shopping difficulties at Merthyr Tydfil in November 1940, following the decision of the local authority to act on the recommendations of local trading interests and to close all shops at 1 p.m. on Thursdays and 6 p.m. on every other evening.[105] A storm of protest had also followed the decision taken by the Swansea Chamber of Trade and Grocers' Association in September 1941 to close grocery shops at 1 p.m. on Saturday afternoons and 3 p.m. on weekdays. Only months previously, the managers at Bridgend ROF had agreed to abolish Saturday afternoon working in order that female employees could carry out their shopping. The factory workers who lived in the Swansea area would clearly not be able to benefit from this scheme and, in the opinion of Alice Huws Davies, welfare officer at the Ministry of Labour offices in Cardiff, there was no doubt that 'the case of the factory worker' had been 'entirely overlooked'.[106]

In the months which followed, however, the appeals of the Ministry of Labour officials themselves were also 'overlooked' by some shopkeepers and local authorities, as they continued to place their own interests before those of local factory workers. In October 1942 the decision of the Aberdare UDC to close all shops in the town at 1 p.m. on Thursdays and 6 p.m. on every other weekday met with stern criticism from opponents such as Councillor J. Rhys James, who championed the cause of local war workers. In his opinion, the new proposals would cause 'great hardship' to the men and women who worked long hours at munitions factories in the area and would lead to even higher levels of absenteeism:

> Some men and women are losing Saturday morning in order to do their shopping . . . It was all very well for people in comfortable jobs, working ordinary hours, to talk – they could go and do their shopping when they liked . . . What about these poor dabs working ten and twelve hours a day? . . . they get no consideration at all.[107]

[105] *Merthyr Express*, 30 November 1940.
[106] PRO, Lab 26/61.
[107] *South Wales Echo*, 13 October 1942; *Aberdare Leader*, 17 October 1942.

In November 1942 councillors at Tredegar voiced similar grievances in protest at the decision of the local Chamber of Trade to
close all shops in the town at 5.30 p.m., causing 'great inconvenience' to a large proportion of the local working population.[108]

Yet, not all working women were in favour of extending the
opening hours of shops in the evenings. A married woman from
Cardiff maintained that time was more scarce at the end of the
day, as evenings were spent on 'the usual household duties', and
she advocated opening shops earlier in the mornings.[109] An
official from the Ministry of Labour was also of the opinion that
the late opening of shops was not always the best solution to the
problem. In a letter to Eleanor Rathbone MP in October 1942,
J. J. Taylor argued in favour of changing working hours, rather
than shop opening hours, since 'so many of the women war
workers have other domestic duties to perform in addition to
shopping and are unwilling to break or delay their journey home
after having carried out a full day's work.'[110]

Although officials at some factories, including Bridgend and
Glascoed ROFs, responded to the needs of their female workers
by providing 'controlled absences' which gave women time to
carry out their shopping and other household chores,[111] other
employers remained unsympathetic to such schemes. The Home
Intelligence Unit of the Ministry of Information reported in July
1941 that a distinct 'lack of understanding' had been shown for
the shopping problems of female workers by factory managers
across Britain.[112] Married women who were employed at a
civilian air-base in south Wales were only too aware of the difficulties which could arise if officials proved to be uncooperative
and failed to acknowledge their needs. The arrival of a new
civilian accountant officer at St Athan aerodrome marked the

---

[108] GWRO, Tredegar UDC minutes, 24 November 1942.
[109] *South Wales Echo*, 20 February 1942.
[110] PRO, Lab 26/61.
[111] Ibid.; *Caerphilly Journal*, 24 October 1942. A clerical officer employed at Glascoed
ROF assured Mass-Observation investigators in 1942 that any female employee who
regularly absented herself from the factory was asked if she had special reasons for doing
so: 'If she has, and it may be something to do with the shopping or the family we say to
her that it would be more satisfactory if we knew that she would always take that day off
and then we could make our arrangements accordingly. I think that will solve things
better.' M-O A, FR 1498, 'Blaina', p. 95.
[112] PRO, Inf 1/292.

end of the 'shopping time' which his predecessor had arranged for married female employees, and the protest of one married woman against the sudden change in policy eventually resulted in her dismissal from the workplace on the grounds of 'industrial misconduct'.[113]

In its bid to find a solution to the 'shopping problems' of the female war workers, the Ministry of Labour proposed several other schemes, which included the establishment of shops at the factories themselves and giving war workers preferential service in local shops.[114] Neither scheme was particularly successful in south Wales. At Merthyr Tydfil in 1942 the proposal to establish shops at local war factories caused much ill-feeling among local retailers and never got off the ground.[115] In other districts, local authorities experimented with a 'priority' system which permitted war workers who wore special badges or armlets to move to the front of shopping queues at designated times.[116] However, the scheme was declared a failure at Pontypridd in September 1942, following widespread abuse of the system.[117] Oral evidence suggests that the scheme also failed in other towns in south Wales, as both shopkeepers and other shoppers were not always willing to co-operate with the programme.[118]

Ultimately, therefore, in view of the failure of the Ministry of Labour to introduce a clear policy on shopping which might have forced retailers or factory managers to change their working practices, the problems of the female war workers remained largely unsolved. Those who were fortunate enough managed to rely on family members, friends or neighbours to assist them with

[113] Price, 'Experiences in World War II', 111–12.

[114] One of the schemes which was supported by the TUC proposed granting war workers permission to reserve items with their local shopkeepers which they could collect at their convenience. TUC Workmen's Compensation and Factories Committee minutes, Factory and Welfare Advisory Board, 18 March 1941 (Harvester Microfilms); *Free Press of Monmouthshire*, 15 August 1941.

[115] *Merthyr Express*, 9 May 1942.

[116] *Glamorgan Advertiser*, 15 August 1941.

[117] Pontypridd Public Library, Pontypridd Trades Council and Labour Party minutes, 14 September 1942.

[118] Evidence of Respondent 1. An insight into the ill-feeling which preferential treatment for war workers could arouse among 'ordinary' housewives is provided in the following extract from an anthology of wartime recollections: 'A Cardiff housewife remembers a long wait in a queue [at a bus-stop] which ended in her being 'the last permitted passenger. Just as I was about to get on, a woman from behind me pushed to the fore. "I've been working on cranes all day at the Dowlais. I want to get home. Housewives can wait!"' Norman Longmate, *How We Lived Then: A History of Everyday Life during the Second World War* (London, 1971), p. 318.

the task, and, as one commentator was to remark in 1943, this was the only way which most British war workers managed to 'keep the Larder more or less supplied' throughout the war.[119] In the close-knit communities of the south Wales valleys, where the ties of kith and kin were strong, female war workers were particularly dependent on the assistance of their relatives and neighbours. A shops inspector from Blaina told Mollie Tarrant that 'nearly all' the female war workers could 'quite easily get someone else to do their shopping for them, a mother or a daughter. So many of them are related, you see, to someone else living nearby.'[120] One 38-year-old munitions worker from the town explained that her two sons were left in charge of the shopping and, as well as filling in the ration books, they also waited in the queues.[121] Reports that children were being kept home from school to 'look after the home' and 'run errands' for their working parents, became increasingly common.[122] In the Afan valley in 1941, several parents who were engaged on war work were fined by justices at Port Talbot for keeping their children away from school to act as 'housekeepers' in their absence.[123] Meanwhile, one thirteen-year-old boy from Pontnewydd, who appeared before Pontypool juvenile court in February 1942 after stealing two bicycles, was said to be in a 'state of rebellion' against having to do the housework while his parents both worked at a local factory![124] Not all women workers were in a position to rely on the assistance of family members in this respect, however, and as an increasing number of 'unoccupied' females were drawn into wartime service, many war workers found that they were left with little option but to carry out their own shopping whenever they could find the time.

Perhaps one of the most striking aspects of the whole issue of wartime shopping was the failure of the state to propose any measures which would have relieved female war workers of the actual burden of shopping. Changing the opening hours of shops or arranging more flexible working hours, were merely proposals which made the task more convenient and less onerous for

[119] Egert P. Booth, *Women at War: Engineering* (London, 1943), p. 26.
[120] M-O A, FR 1498, 'Blaina', p. 100.
[121] M-O A, TC 64, Coal mining, Box 1, File C.
[122] *Free Press of Monmouthshire*, 25 April 1942, 22 May 1942.
[123] *South Wales Evening Post*, 25 March 1941.
[124] *Free Press of Monmouthshire*, 6 March 1942.

working women, and did nothing to challenge the notion that they should be held solely responsible for carrying out the shopping and a host of other household chores. No schemes were proposed to provide domestic assistance to women within their own homes, and the suggestion that any male members of the household might help their womenfolk with domestic chores was never really addressed.[125] Unless friends or relatives could help out, women war workers had little choice but to carry out their own domestic chores in the few spare hours they had left at the end of their long shifts. Zelma Katin, a married woman and mother who worked as a tram conductor in Yorkshire during the war, envied her colleagues 'who had mothers or other relatives at home to do at least some of the eternal household drudgery'.[126] Although the Ministry of Labour and the Ministry of Food co-operated to introduce innovations which relieved women of some of the burdens of cooking, in the form of communal feeding schemes such as British Restaurants[127] and factory canteens, their impact on eating and cooking arrangements in the homes of the majority of the female war workers should not be over-emphasized.[128] Moreover, the fact that such institutions were established purely on a temporary basis provided a clear message that it was only the emergency conditions of war which had brought about such concessions, and that, 'in normal times', the responsibility of caring for the family should rest firmly with the female members of the household.

In stark contrast to the solutions put forward to the shopping problems of the female war workers, the provisions which were made to care for the young children of working mothers did involve relieving women of some of their traditional parental and domestic responsibilities. Although mothers of children under fourteen years of age were technically exempt from compulsory direction to war work, Ministry of Labour officials were aware that production targets at the war factories of Britain could not be met

---

[125] See Allen, 'The domestic ideal and the mobilization of womanpower in World War II', 407–8.

[126] Zelma Katin, *'Clippie': The Autobiography of a War Time Conductress* (London, 1944), p. 48.

[127] By September 1945, sixty-one British Restaurants had been established in Wales, supplying an average of 10,300 main meals per day. PP 1945–6 (XX, Cmd. 6938), *Wales and Monmouthshire, A Summary of Government Action, 1 August 1945–31 July 1946*, p. 45.

[128] See Summerfield, *Women Workers in the Second World War*, pp. 100–3.

unless such women undertook some form of wartime employment. The provision of child-care facilities would have to be ensured, therefore, in order that the mothers of young children could volunteer their services at the war factories and, from 1940 onwards, the Ministry of Labour pressed for the establishment of wartime nurseries to care for children aged between two and five.

By September 1944, 1,450 full-time and 109 part-time nurseries had been established in England and Wales, providing accommodation for a total of 71,806 children.[129] Given that the number of nurseries in England and Wales totalled only fourteen in October 1940, it is clear that the war experience initiated dramatic changes in the provision of collective child-care in Britain.[130] Yet, as the research undertaken by both Penny Summerfield and Denise Riley has revealed, the civil servants who were responsible for the child-care policy implemented during the war were often far more concerned with resisting pressures to change pre-war child-care policy than with taking positive steps to meet the new wartime needs.[131] Although Ernest Bevin was a keen advocate of wartime nurseries, Ministry of Labour officials such as Mary Smieton, assistant secretary in the Factory and Welfare Department, favoured using 'minders' rather than nurseries, and even expressed her opposition to the notion that the mothers of young children should be encouraged to work at all.[132] However, it was the Ministry of Health which was ultimately responsible for the establishment of day nurseries under the provisions of the 1918 Maternity and Child Welfare Act, and the views of its ministers and officials were, therefore, of crucial importance in the search for a wartime policy on collective child-care. Officials from the Ministry of Labour could only inform the Ministry of Health of the demand for a nursery in a particular area, and it was the Ministry of Health which decided whether or not to act upon that information and make the necessary arrangements with the local authority on matters relating to the premises, their running costs

---

[129] A further 34,877 children were cared for at nursery classes and schools. Ferguson and Fitzgerald, *Studies in the Social Services*, p. 190.

[130] Summerfield, 'Women, work and welfare', 250.

[131] See ibid., 250–8; eadem, *Women Workers in the Second World War*, pp. 67–98; Riley, 'War in the nursery', 83–7.

[132] Summerfield, *Women Workers in the Second World War*, p. 68. See also Shena D. Simon, 'Married women and munition making', *Industrial Welfare and Personnel Management*, XXII (1940), 356–7.

and staffing. Medical officers of health and councillors who served on the maternity and child welfare committees of their local authorities were also key players in this procedure, for unless they supported the Ministry of Labour's recommendation to establish a nursery in their area and presented the case before the Ministry of Health, no action would be take in the matter.

As in other parts of Britain, the opinions of the councillors and medical officers of health of south Wales could differ greatly from one district to another and, consequently, nursery provision, particularly during the early years of the war, was unevenly distributed throughout the region. Some local authorities welcomed the wartime expansion of child-care provision which they saw as building on the foundations laid during the inter-war years, and gave their wholehearted support to nursery schemes. Such enthusiasm contrasted sharply with the stern opposition voiced by other local officials who opposed full-time nurseries on the grounds that they denied mothers their 'natural' responsibilities and deprived children of 'proper' maternal care. It is also clear that the conflict of opinion which existed between government officials at the Ministry of Labour and Ministry of Health in London existed in their regional offices. For example, when assessing the demand for nursery provision in the area, the views of civil servants employed at the Ministry of Labour offices in Cardiff and those of their counterparts at the Welsh Board of Health (who answered to the Ministry of Health) often contradicted each other.

In the early summer of 1940, when the Ministry of Labour issued its first official demand for wartime nurseries to be established as a means to encourage the recruitment of married females, the Ministry of Health reported that there was 'no immediate need' for nurseries in any of the Welsh districts it had surveyed. This was a cause of some relief to Zoë L. Puxley, assistant secretary in charge of maternity and child welfare at the ministry, as she confided to Mary Smieton, her opposite number at the Factory and Welfare Department of the Ministry of Labour, in July 1940: 'I notice that the Welsh districts are all in brackets [i.e. no immediate need] which comforts me for I had not succeeded in persuading the Welsh Board to take any immediate action. I shall make another effort later.'[133] In another

---

[133] PRO, MH 55/695.

letter written to Mary Smieton only a few weeks later, Zoë Puxley repeated her claim that no action needed to be taken in the industrial districts of Wales. After all, this was an area where there was 'always a large reservoir of female labour', and as this had not yet been used up, Puxley felt that 'a drive for the young married woman is unnecessary and perhaps undesirable'.[134] Only months earlier, however, officials at the Ministry of Labour in London had received very different reports of the demand for nurseries from their representatives in the Welsh districts. Indeed, in June 1940, Ministry of Labour officials identified Wales as one of the wartime 'regions' where nursery provision was 'most urgently required'.[135]

The attitude of the two ministries towards the provision of collective child-care differed greatly in many respects and, whilst the Ministry of Labour was eager to establish wartime nurseries as a means to reduce female absenteeism and increase recruitment, the Ministry of Health upheld its pre-war views that nurseries should be provided to meet the needs of children rather than working mothers. In view of the differences in the priorities and interests of the two ministries, it was not surprising that the provision of child-care did not progress as swiftly as many women workers might have hoped.[136] In south Wales, the difficulties which resulted from the conflicting opinions of the representatives of the Ministry of Labour and the Welsh Board of Health regarding the demand for nurseries in the area were compounded by allegations that the Welsh local authorities were 'dilatory' in setting up nurseries. In April 1941 Ivor Thomas, welfare officer for the Ministry of Labour in Wales, vehemently denied the accusation which had been made by Mary Smieton, and pointed out that the Welsh Board of Health had only just received a formal request from the Ministry of Health in London to look into the question of establishing nurseries in Welsh districts. Moreover, since the Welsh Board of Health was insisting upon 'specific data' regarding attendance figures at proposed nurseries, and had inquired how the Ministry of Labour was

---

[134] Ibid.
[135] PRO, Lab 26/57.
[136] For evidence of the growing demand for day nurseries among female war workers and potential female recruits during 1941–2, see PRO, Inf 1/292; *Parliamentary Debates* (Hansard) (5th series), vol. 376, 1083 (2 December 1941).

'going to prove any need for nurseries', Ivor Thomas felt that the Board should take some responsibility for the delays in the establishment of wartime nurseries in Wales:

> We have pointed out that it is almost impossible to gauge the potential need. Even if one canvasses women who might take work if their children were catered for . . . the whole idea of day nurseries is new to South Wales and we are certain that women will not really make up their minds until and unless some nurseries are actually opened.[137]

The whole question of 'proving' demand for a nursery also worried Elizabeth Andrews, the Labour Party's women's organizer in Wales. In a letter to Ernest Bevin in November 1940, she argued that since day nurseries were unfamiliar institutions to the majority of the mothers of south Wales, greater emphasis should be placed on creating a demand for nurseries among local women, rather than waiting for mothers to request their establishment:

> We have asked all our women councillors to interest themselves and press the authorities to get them [nurseries] set up. The reply to them has been – *that the need has not yet arisen*. Some of us feel that we got to [*sic*] create the need by extensive propaganda among the women who are already in factories and the women who may be called upon during the coming months.[138]

In the event, a number of surveys were carried out both by Ministry of Labour officials and by representatives of the Welsh local authorities, in a bid to assess the actual demand for wartime nurseries among the women of south Wales. Initially, the Ministry of Labour concentrated its efforts on finding out whether females who were already at work at some of the largest factories in the region could be assisted by the provision of childcare facilities.[139] In April 1941 Ivor Thomas reported that whilst managers at Bridgend ROF had proved extremely helpful and had provided the names and addresses of female workers who had young children, the efforts to obtain returns at Glascoed and

---

[137] PRO, Lab 26/58.
[138] Ibid.
[139] PRO, Lab 12/82 and 26/91.

Newport ROFs had not been so successful, while factories in Cardiff had 'not shown any interest in the provision of nurseries'.[140]

Local authorities and voluntary organizations conducted their own surveys to assess the current and potential demand for child-care provision among the female population of south Wales.[141] It is not always clear, however, if the women themselves were questioned during such inquiries, or whether the surveys relied solely on the evidence of factory managers, local medical officers of health or members of the maternity and child welfare com-mittees, who gave their own personal and sometimes biased judgements on the situation prevailing in their own districts. At Caerphilly, for example, it appears that the negative response to the inquiry regarding the need for nurseries in the area may well have reflected the opinion of Dr W. R. Nash, the medical officer of health, and not the views of local women. Having assured members of the local maternity and child welfare committee that there was no need for a nursery in the area, he claimed that its establishment would not be a 'practicable proposition', for not only were there serious problems in matters relating to the premises, staffing and the opening hours of nurseries, but 'enquiries show that many parents would not regard the propos-ition with favour'.[142]

However, the opinion of the medical officer of health of Caerphilly was evidently not representative of that held by all mothers in the district, for only two months after Dr Nash had presented his report before the local councillors, members of the Caerphilly Labour Women's Federation resolved to take action to impress upon the local authority the urgent need for wartime

---

[140] PRO, Lab 26/58.

[141] For example, at Maesteg the medical officer of health assessed demand purely on the basis of the number of mothers who were already employed at factories in the district. GRO, Maesteg UDC minutes, 8 July 1941. Other local authorities, such as the Pontypridd UDC, canvassed mothers who had already taken up war work as well as those who would be prepared to do so if their children could be cared for in a nursery, and found that 10 working mothers and 145 non-working mothers would send their 225 children to wartime nurseries if they were established in the area. GRO, Pontypridd UDC minutes, report of medical officer of health, 2 February 1942. At Abergwynfi and Blaengwynfi in the Glyncorrwg UDC, a representative of the Women's Voluntary Society prepared a report on the demand for nurseries in the district on behalf of the local authority. West Glamorgan Record Office, Glyncorrwg UDC minutes, 27 January 1942, 19 May 1942, 9 and 16 June 1942.

[142] GRO, Caerphilly UDC minutes, 30 July 1940, 23 September 1941.

nurseries in the Gelli-gaer and Caerphilly area.[143] Members of the women's sections of the Labour Party championed the cause of working mothers elsewhere in south Wales, and several local authorities in Glamorgan and Monmouthshire were urged to establish nurseries without delay. In April 1941, the Monmouth-shire Labour Women's Advisory Council brought pressure to bear on the Tredegar and Abertillery UDCs, while the Bridgend and Nantyffyllon women's sections of the Labour Party de-manded the immediate establishment of nurseries in the urban districts of Bridgend and Maesteg respectively.[144] The Women's Group of the Labour Party at Bridgend presented local coun-cillors with the results of its own independent survey of a third of the residents of the town, which revealed that nursery accom-modation was urgently required for the 169 children of 80 mothers who were engaged in full-time war work.[145]

In spite of the additional pressure which was exerted on local authorities by the supporters of wartime nurseries, not one full-time nursery had been opened in Wales by the end of October 1941.[146] Officials at the Ministry of Labour, who had grown increasingly frustrated with the lack of progress in the Welsh districts, concluded that the only possible explanation for the delay was the 'reluctance' and 'opposition' of some local councillors and medical officers of health to the wartime nursery scheme, 'on the grounds that they do not approve of the employment of married women with children and do not, even in these times, recognise the need for it'.[147] Dr Edith Summerskill, the Labour MP who was a strong supporter of wartime nurseries, was also of the opinion that the personal prejudices of a small minority of local officials had impeded progress in the provision of child-care assistance. Speaking in Parliament in March 1942, she stated her views clearly: 'My diagnosis is simple, but I think it is a correct one. The delay is due to the reluctance of reactionary councillors to intro-duce a reform which they think is calculated to spoil women.'[148]

[143] GRO, Gelligaer UDC minutes, 25 November 1941; SWCA, Caerphilly Labour Party Women's Section minutes, 29 November 1941.
[144] GWRO, Tredegar UDC minutes, 25 April 1941; Abertillery UDC minutes, 28 April 1941. GRO, Bridgend UDC minutes, 6 May 1941, 17 June 1941; Maesteg UDC minutes, 18 March 1941, 1 July 1941.
[145] GRO, Bridgend UDC minutes, 17 June 1941.
[146] PRO, Lab 26/58.
[147] Ibid.
[148] *Parliamentary Debates* (Hansard) (5th series), vol. 378, 851 (5 March 1942).

In view of the fact that the full-time employment of married women was in itself a new phenomenon in the industrial districts of south Wales, it would appear that Welsh councillors and local authority officials reacted less favourably to the wartime proposals to establish nurseries than their counterparts who served in districts where there was a greater tradition of employing married women and mothers. There is certainly plenty of evidence to suggest that this was indeed the case.[149] In April 1941 a member of the Abertillery UDC declared that he was not in favour of the wartime nursery scheme since it encouraged the mothers of young children to take up work which would keep them away from their homes all day.[150] Members of the Aberdare UDC Education Committee, which met in June 1941 to discuss the establishment of wartime nurseries in the district, shared this view. During the meeting, several councillors urged committee members to give careful consideration to the effect which the employment of mothers would have on the welfare of young children in the area. Councillor William Lawrence opposed the establishment of day nurseries on the grounds that the provision of child-care at such institutions militated against the traditional social conventions of the area: 'I don't want to see South Wales becoming a replica of cotton Lancashire. We do want to keep the Welsh tradition as far as home life is concerned.'[151] Another member of the committee, Councillor D. J. Morse JP, even argued that 'every obstacle should be placed in the way of such mothers', in a bid to prevent them from taking up factory employment.[152] Even after nurseries were eventually established in the Aberdare area, it was made clear that they were facilities which would be provided purely 'for the duration'. At the opening ceremony of the Robertstown nursery in July 1942, Councillor D. J. Morse, who now served as chairman of the authority, stressed that 'in normal times' the mother should remain at home to look after her children; after all, 'the home was the mother's place and a child needed a mother's care.'[153]

---

[149] Councillor J. Jones Edwards of Port Talbot described the provision of nursery facilities in the town as 'throwing money down the drain. Nursery schools may be necessary in large English industrial centres but results show they are not wanted in Port Talbot'. *South Wales Evening Post*, 23 July 1942.
[150] GWRO, Abertillery UDC minutes, 28 April 1941.
[151] *Aberdare Leader*, 28 June 1941.
[152] Ibid.
[153] Ibid., 11 July 1942.

The medical officer of health for the Ogmore and Garw UDC also questioned the 'desirability' of employing women with household responsibilities, and intimated that once peace was restored this practice should not be encouraged.[154]

However, not all Welsh councillors greeted the wartime expansion of nursery provision in such a hostile manner, and it must be emphasized that many local authorities were extremely supportive of attempts to establish nurseries in their districts. In December 1941, in response to pressure from the Ministry of Labour for action to be taken to increase the number of nurseries, the Ministry of Health decided to pay a 100 per cent grant to local authorities to assist them with the cost of equipping, building or adapting suitable premises. This offer of financial assistance was quickly taken up by several Welsh local authorities and, by June 1942, sixty-one full-time nurseries were in operation in the counties of Glamorgan and Monmouth alone.[155] At the official opening of the wartime nursery at Cae-du Park, Ogmore Vale, in October 1942, Councillor Mrs H. W. Thomas, who chaired the local maternity and child welfare committee, expressed her joy at the establishment of such a fine institution to care for the children of local mothers who were engaged on war work.[156] Although some of the opponents of wartime nurseries had voiced their anxieties as to the standard of care which would be provided at the new centres, the fact that the Ministry of Health favoured the appointment of qualified nurses and insisted on high staffing ratios meant that most nurseries were very well run and the children well looked after. One mother from Cardiff, who worked at a local shell-making factory, was clearly delighted at the standard of care and attention which her two-year-old daughter received at one of the city's nurseries:

> I should not have time, even if I was not working, to look after her as she is looked after at the nursery. With the rest of my children to attend to and the house to keep in order, I could not wash her three times a day, keep her hair and teeth brushed, and teach her to say, 'Pardon Daddy?', as they do at the nursery.[157]

[154] *Annual Report of the Ogmore and Garw Medical Officer of Health, 1944*, p. 5.
[155] *Merthyr Express*, 27 June 1942.
[156] *Glamorgan Advertiser*, 2 October 1942.
[157] *South Wales Echo*, 24 February 1942.

Working mothers elsewhere in the county of Glamorgan also came to appreciate the advantages of nursery care. In her annual report to members of the Glamorgan County Council in 1942, Margaret M. James, the county welfare officer, noted that, although some mothers had initially been apprehensive about sending their children to day nurseries, they had soon overcome their prejudices when they saw that 'the tiny tots throve and loved being there', and had subsequently made 'good use' of the new service.[158]

The use which Welsh mothers made of the wartime nurseries was not, in itself, a reliable indicator of the level of demand or support for child-care provision in the area. Attendance figures at nurseries were dependent upon a whole host of factors, and circumstances could vary considerably from one district to the next. Some nurseries fared badly right from the outset. For example, concern was expressed at Port Talbot in July 1942 when it was revealed that only one child was in attendance at the newly opened nursery school.[159] The proposed opening of the wartime nursery at Gelli-gaer in the Rhymney valley was delayed in April 1942 when it was revealed that only a handful of mothers were likely to make use of the service.[160] Similar problems were reported in the area several months later, when it emerged that only three mothers had made applications to send their children to the nursery which was due to open at Bargoed. Although the Bargoed nursery eventually attracted the support of enough local mothers to justify its opening in December 1942, its success was short-lived, and by March 1943 the nursery was forced to close due to low attendance figures.[161] The reasons why the working mothers of Bargoed showed such little interest in their wartime nursery are not known, but it may well have been the case that many women were not even aware of its existence. Investigations undertaken at Cardiff in 1942 revealed that the local authority and factory managers had taken very little action to publicize wartime nurseries among working mothers, and

---

[158] GRO, Glamorgan County Council, annual report of the director of education for 1942; report of the county welfare officer, 15 October 1942.

[159] *South Wales Evening Post*, 23 July 1942.

[160] *Merthyr Express*, 4 April 1942.

[161] SWCA, Caerphilly Labour Party, Gelligaer Area Committee minutes, 7 January 1943; GRO, Gelligaer UDC minutes, 5 January 1943, 26 January 1943, 2 March 1943; PRO, Lab 26/133.

many of the city's nurseries were consequently underused.[162] This inaction contrasted sharply with the efforts which were made by employers and local councils in other parts of south Wales. Penybont RDC co-operated with officials at Bridgend ROF to publicize its nurseries during 1942–3, by distributing handbills among female employees of the factory and displaying posters on factory notice-boards.[163] In the Ogmore and Garw district, the local council promoted its wartime nurseries in a series of films, lectures and public meetings held under the auspices of the Ministry of Information, while all eligible mothers in the Rhondda were leafleted and provided with a barrage of information in the form of press advertisements, posters, public meetings, open days and the use of a loudspeaker van.[164]

Although such campaigns must have had some influence on the initial popularity of nurseries, the use which mothers made of them in the long term depended on the standard and type of service which they could provide. In a letter to Ernest Bevin in November 1940, Elizabeth Andrews predicted that many of the female war workers of south Wales would find it difficult to make use of nurseries unless opening hours could be arranged to suit their needs. She explained that, since most Welsh workers travelled long distances to their place of employment, they left their homes very early in the morning and would have 'no chance', therefore, of taking their children to the nurseries before leaving for work.[165] Ivor Thomas, welfare officer for the Ministry of Labour at Cardiff, shared this view and, in a letter to Mary Smieton in January 1941, he pointed out that the nurseries due to be established by Welsh local authorities were 'not proposing to provide a mid-day meal or to open for sufficiently long hours to be of any use to industrial workers'.[166]

---

[162] M-O A, TC 19, Day nurseries, Box 1, File D, Cardiff day nursery position, 9 February 1942; ibid., FR 1151, 'The demand for day nurseries', 11 March 1942; *South Wales Echo*, 24 February 1942.

[163] GRO, Penybont RDC minutes, 5 March 1942, 4 March 1943, 1 April 1943, 14 October 1943.

[164] GRO, Ogmore and Garw UDC minutes, 7 January 1943; *The Rhondda Leader*, 1 August 1942; *Annual Report of the Rhondda Medical Officer of Health, 1942*, pp. 33–4. Among the speakers who addressed public meetings in the Rhondda were Lillian Hayward of the Ministry of Information and Elizabeth Andrews, who represented the Labour Party on the Welsh Regional Advisory Council of the ministry.

[165] PRO, Lab 26/58.

[166] Ibid.

Demands for opening hours to be extended appear to have fallen on deaf ears, for the majority of the nurseries which were eventually established in south Wales were open only from 9 a.m. to 5 p.m., five days a week. For working mothers who were engaged on shifts of eight or ten hours per day at factories several miles away from their homes, the wartime nurseries served little purpose. At Cardiff, where the opening hours of nurseries clashed with the shifts worked at local factories, it was claimed that many of the nurseries were 'half empty'.[167] The reporter from the city's evening newspaper who made this allegation in February 1942 drew attention to the fact that few of the mothers employed at Cardiff's Curran Works could use the facilities:

> Women working on the morning shift leave home too early to take their babies to the nursery on the way to work: afternoon shift workers do not leave work in time to collect their babies on the way home. Workers on the night shift, although the day-time nursery hours give them a rest while they are off duty, have no nursery facilities for their children while they are at work.[168]

Similar difficulties were reported elsewhere in the region. The opening hours of the nurseries at Caerphilly were also incompatible with the hours worked at local factories, making it impossible for mothers to take their children to a nursery in the morning, or to pick them up at the completion of their shift.[169] In February 1943, an absentee inspector who was employed at one of the munitions factories in the region maintained that the nurseries which had been opened in the Pontypridd and Rhondda district served 'very little purpose', since the majority opened only from 9 a.m. to 5 p.m.[170] Although the hours of two nurseries in the Pontypridd area had been extended to open from 7 a.m. to 9 p.m. every weekday, the fact that many local factories continued to work two ten-hour shifts made it extremely difficult for female war workers to avail themselves of the service.[171]

---

[167] *South Wales Echo*, 24 February 1942; M-O A, TC 19, Day nurseries, Box 1, File D, Cardiff day nursery position, 9 February 1942.
[168] *South Wales Echo*, 24 February 1942.
[169] GRO, Caerphilly UDC minutes, 23 September 1941, 4 March 1942.
[170] *Western Mail*, 10 February 1943.
[171] Ibid., 16 February 1943; *The Rhondda Leader*, 10 April 1943; PRO, Lab 26/133.

The cost involved in accommodating children at wartime nurseries also appears to have deterred some mothers from sending their children there.[172] Although most nurseries charged only 1s. a day per child, the cost could vary from one nursery to another, according to their hours of opening and the services which they provided.[173] Extensive provision was also made for the admission of children aged between three and five at the public elementary schools of south Wales during the war, and many mothers appear to have sent their children to such nursery classes where no payment was required.[174] A survey conducted by the Ministry of Education in January 1945 revealed that 13,966 children under the age of five were attending ordinary public elementary schools in Wales: 700 at nursery schools, 525 at nursery classes and 822 at play centres.[175] The provision of nursery care which extended beyond ordinary school hours could not, however, be met at these nursery classes and schools, for opening hours were even shorter than those of the day nurseries, and were equally inconvenient for the working mother.

Under the circumstances, it is not surprising that the vast majority of mothers relied on their relatives or friends to care for their children, either throughout the whole of the day, or during the period between the ending of school hours and their return from the factory.[176] In April 1943 officials from the Ministry of

[172] This was the reason given for low attendance at the nurseries of Cardiff by one 55-year-old woman interviewed by Mollie Tarrant in March 1942, M-O A, TC 19, Day nurseries, 10 March 1942. In April 1944 the Penybont RDC informed the Welsh Board of Health that the fall in attendance at its wartime nurseries was chiefly due to the increased charges which had recently been introduced, GRO, Penybont RDC minutes, 27 April 1944.

[173] David W. Greenaway, 'The impact of the Second World War on nursery, elementary and secondary education in Glamorgan' (unpublished M.Ed. thesis, University of Wales, 1985), p. 63. For example, at the Hirwaun wartime nursery each child was provided with a midday meal, milk, cod-liver oil and orange juice for the charge of 1s. per day. The same services – at the same charge – were provided at nurseries which opened for a 'full day' in the Penybont RDC, while those which opened only for 'school hours' charged 9d. GRO, Logbook of the Cwmaman and the Hirwaun wartime nurseries, 17 March 1944; Penybont RDC minutes, 4 March 1943.

[174] Greenaway, 'The impact of the Second World War on nursery, elementary and secondary education in Glamorgan', pp. 58–70; PRO, Lab 26/133; *Annual Report of the Rhondda Medical Officer of Health, 1945*, p. 34.

[175] PRO, MH 55/1708.

[176] GRO, Ogmore and Garw UDC minutes, 23 and 28 May 1941; Caerphilly UDC minutes, 4 March 1942; *Annual Report of the Rhondda Medical Officer of Health, 1942*, p. 34; evidence of Respondent 18. This was also the case elsewhere in Britain: only 5 per cent of the children of working mothers interviewed by the Wartime Social Survey in the autumn of 1943 attended nurseries, 59 per cent of the children were at school and either looked after themselves or were cared for by relatives in the period between the ending of

Health admitted that 'the principal reason' why the Welsh nurseries were not filling up was 'undoubtedly that most of the mothers seem to be able to make private arrangements'.[177] In fact, this was exactly what the Ministry of Health had hoped would happen; after all, if mothers made their own child-care arrangements either with relatives, neighbours or private child-minders, there would be no need for an expansion in the provision of collective child-care.[178] The truth of the matter, however, was not that the mothers of south Wales 'preferred' to make their own arrangements for the care of their children, but that they had little choice in the matter since the wartime nurseries could not provide a comprehensive child-care service which met their needs. In view of the high standards which the Ministry of Health insisted upon in the premises and staffing of wartime nurseries, it was ironic that the care which children received in the homes of their relatives and neighbours was not subject to any official scrutiny and, although such provision sounded ideal, it often proved to be far from satisfactory. Children could be cared for in overcrowded homes by women who already had their own domestic charges to attend to. Moreover, as Mrs J. L. Adamson, MP for Dartford, pointed out in February 1942, private arrangements made between mothers and carers could 'break down on the slightest pretext', giving rise to even greater levels of female absenteeism.[179] The authors of the *Beveridge Manpower Survey* of south Wales had noted that during the summer months of 1940, several cases were reported where the strain of looking after the children of their relatives or neighbours had proved too much for some carers, with the result that the working mothers had been forced to retire from the workforce.[180]

Although the majority of the working mothers of south Wales managed to make adequate arrangements for the care of their children by securing the assistance of reliable and competent

school hours and their mothers' return, 16 per cent were cared for by grandmothers, 7 per cent were cared for by other relatives, 5 per cent were cared for by neighbours, while the remainder had either been evacuated or were cared for by a child-minder. Thomas, 'Women at work', p. 7.

[177] PRO, Lab 26/133.

[178] See PRO, MH 55/884.

[179] *Parliamentary Debates* (Hansard) (5th series), vol. 377, 1558 (12 February 1942). See also ibid., vol. 378, 839–40 (5 March 1942).

[180] *Beveridge Manpower Survey*, 1940.

child-carers,[181] others were not so fortunate. Since such a large proportion of the adult female population was engaged on some form of wartime service, it was often the case that the children of working mothers were placed in the care of elderly women or teenagers. At a meeting with representatives of the Welsh Board of Health in December 1940, members of the Ogmore and Garw UDC pointed out that in the absence of a war-time nursery, a number of the mothers who were employed at Bridgend ROF had been forced to leave their young children 'in the charge of older children or aged persons with unsatisfactory results in some instances'.[182] Although she clearly had some reservations about the standard of care which her young child-minder could provide, a thirty-year-old munitions worker from Blaina placed her children in the charge of a teenage girl: 'I have somebody in to look after the children, but she's only sixteen and she can't do the work at all.'[183] In June 1941 the school managers of the Eastern Valley of Monmouthshire heard evidence that many working mothers in the area placed their youngest children in the care of their older siblings.[184] School attendance had been severely affected by this practice and it was reported that the eldest daughter of a family of ten children had hardly attended school since her mother had started working at a local factory.[185]

Elsewhere, the failure of working mothers to ensure that their children were properly supervised during working hours was alleged to be the cause of the wartime increase in truancy and juvenile crime.[186] In October 1942 the Home Intelligence Unit of the Ministry of Information reported that, in many parts of Britain, 'the neglect of children and the increase in juvenile delinquency' were being attributed to the recruitment of women into industry, since 'no attempt is made by the authorities to find out whether the children will be properly looked after in the

---

[181] GRO, Pontypridd UDC Education Committee minutes, 9 December 1942.
[182] GRO, Ogmore and Garw UDC minutes, 9 December 1940.
[183] M-O A, FR 1498, 'Blaina', p. 94.
[184] *Free Press of Monmouthshire*, 27 June 1941.
[185] Ibid.
[186] *Western Mail*, 27 March 1943. See David J. V. Jones, *Crime and Policing in the Twentieth Century: The South Wales Experience* (Cardiff, 1996), pp. 68–9, 79.

mother's absence'.[187] In south Wales, councillors at Pontypool, Aberdare and Abertillery shared the view that truancy and juvenile crime had increased in their areas since local mothers had taken up war work.[188] At a meeting of the Aberdare TLC in September 1942, Councillor Sam Wilcox launched an attack on local mothers who had, in his opinion, placed financial gain before the interests of their children. He knew of one 'disgusting' case in which both the father and mother worked at a local factory, leaving their nine children unsupervised and free to roam the streets.[189] Local councillors did not need to look further than their local courts to find plenty of evidence to support their views, as reference was often made to the fact that the mothers of young offenders were engaged on full-time work in the munitions factories.[190] In 1942, when the parents of several persistent truants were brought before the juvenile courts of Aberdare and Abercynon, it was observed that the majority of the young offenders had merely been taking advantage of the fact that their mothers were away all day at the war factories.[191] The mothers of two young boys who appeared before the juvenile court at Aberdare, charged with stealing a bicycle and some coal in May 1942, were also revealed to be engaged on full-time work in local munitions factories. The police sergeant who gave evidence against the eleven-year-old bicycle thief remarked that since the mothers of the area had taken up war work, local children had been 'getting out of hand'.[192]

For many contemporary observers, such evidence merely served to reinforce their belief that the rightful place of wives and

---

[187] PRO, Inf 1/292. Speaking in Parliament on 20 March 1941, Mrs J. L. Adamson MP warned of the inevitable outcome of 'the effects of factory life on the mothers of this country and on the children of those mothers'. In her opinion, the wartime increase in juvenile crime was 'down to the fact that the father of the family may be in one of the Services or working long hours and often at week ends, and that the mother too may be in a factory, so that there is no guiding hand over the children. The result is that they get into mischief and come before the court, and unconsciously those young people are being turned into criminals.' *Parliamentary Debates* (Hansard) (5th series), vol. 370, 391 (20 March 1941).

[188] GRO, Aberdare UDC Education Committee minutes, 9 April 1941, 9 July 1941; GWRO, Abertillery UDC minutes, 28 April 1941. Similar comments were made by members of the Pontardawe branch of Undeb Dirwestol Merched y De (the South Wales Women's Temperance Union) in October 1941, NLW MS 16594D, 14 October 1941.

[189] *Aberdare Leader*, 12 September 1942.

[190] Ibid., 5 July 1941; *Free Press of Monmouthshire*, 6 November 1942.

[191] Ibid., 25 April 1942, 24 October 1942.

[192] Ibid., 2 May 1942.

mothers was in the home with their husbands and children.[193] The wartime employment of thousands of Welsh wives and mothers was interpreted as a temporary aberration, and pre-war notions regarding the 'proper' role of women in the domestic sphere remained intact. The female munitions workers of south Wales continued to shoulder considerable domestic responsibilities throughout their years of service in the war factories, and their function and social status as mothers and housewives were clearly not transformed as a result of their entry into full-time employment. The cumulative strain of juggling with the conflicting demands made on them as wives, mothers and war workers proved extremely difficult to bear and gave rise to anxiety in the home and absenteeism from the workplace. In the event, it was the urgent need to reduce female absenteeism rates and release greater numbers of women for wartime employment which eventually prompted government policy-makers and employers to make some allowances for their female employees. The services which were provided were far from satisfactory, however. For example, the provisions which were made to assist female war workers with the care of their children proved to be wholly inadequate, while no action whatsoever was taken to relieve women of their responsibilities and workload in the home. Moreover, as the state placed much of the responsibility for establishing child-care and shopping schemes upon local authorities, the response to the needs of the female population was often tempered by local conditions, convention and prejudice. Ultimately, therefore, despite acknowledging the need to meet wartime production demands, the representatives of several local authorities, trade unions, retailers and employers in south Wales proved to be extremely resistant to the introduction of any measures which challenged traditional social and cultural norms regarding the role of married women and mothers in the industrial and domestic workforce.

---

[193] Anxieties regarding the impact of the war on family life, and more particularly on the welfare of children, would place renewed emphasis on the role of the mother and the importance of maternal care in the post-war period. Theories espoused by psychologists such as John Bowlby, who saw a direct link between 'maternal deprivation' (that is, the wartime separation of mothers and children) and juvenile delinquency, proved a potent ideological force to discourage the mothers of young children from going out to work. See John Bowlby, *Forty-Four Juvenile Thieves: Their Characters and Home Life* (London, 1946), pp. 37–44; idem, *Maternal Care and Maternal Health* (Geneva, 1951), p. 11.

Tremains Railway Halt: workers arriving for the 2.05 pm shift (up platforms), at Bridgend ROF, 3 June 1942.
© Great Western Railway Collection, National Railway Museum.

4,000 Welsh girls, conscripted and sent to England by Bevin's Ministry of Labour, will never return (according to the New Wales Union)

'Bevin's Breakfast', *The Welsh Nationalist*, July 1945.

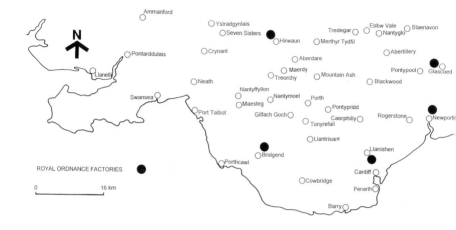

Location of the Royal Ordnance Factories of south Wales.

Women making ammunition shells *c*.1939, probably at the Curran Works, Cardiff.
© National Museums and Galleries of Wales.

"Where IS Mrs. Jones going?"

Like so many others who know their duty, *she's off to make munitions.* Now she has a job "for the duration," and she is bringing nearer the day when her soldier-husband comes back home.

It's as easy for you to get a job of *real* importance! Thousands of women are wanted for factories in or near your district. No previous experience is needed. Good hostel accommodation is provided for those whose homes are beyond daily travelling distance.

You'll be happier—and very likely more prosperous—in the great Munitions Army. Go, telephone or write for advice to your local office of the Ministry of Labour and National Service, and enrol to-day.

YOUR DUTY NOW IS

ISSUED BY THE MINISTRY OF LABOUR & NATIONAL SERVICE

Glamorgan Advertiser, 25 July 1941.

£3 A WEEK

average pay

OFFERED TO 6,000 WOMEN

in South Wales

SIGNING ON NOW

Light work on munitions

HERE in South Wales we are making munitions. Guns and shells. Some for the Red Army. Some for our men going overseas. Some for this island which has to be a fortress.

We must help Russia. We must equip our own forces.

We have all this to do and it has to be done fast.

Come and help us. Take one of these jobs. They're good jobs with decent pay and decent conditions. Light work that any woman of 18 to 60 can do. You can take this work whether you have registered or not.

The first week the hours are 7½ a day; second week 8, a day; third week 9½ a day, then back to 7½ and so on. Pay is by the hour and averages £3 a week.

The factories are in a district served by buses and trains (exact locations cannot be stated, for obvious reasons). Excess of fares over 3s a week is paid. Excellent hostels are available. Time for shopping can be arranged.

Taking this job may mean a change in your way of living — but it's to prevent a greater change — it's to save us all and our children from passing into Nazi slavery. We can defend ourselves only by making the arms to do it.

Don't wait till it's too late —

APPLY NOW

AT ANY EMPLOYMENT EXCHANGE

ISSUED BY THE MINISTRY OF LABOUR AND NATIONAL SERVICE

Aberdare Leader, 1 November 1941.

"Let's show 'em what South Wales can do"

The Ministry of Labour wants thousands of women for vital work in local war industries.

The men in the Services need munitions of all kinds. Those women who have not yet been called to National Service now have a grand opportunity to play their part.

No previous experience is necessary. If you live beyond daily travelling distance from the factory, excellent hostel accommodation is provided. Ask your local office of the Ministry of Labour and National Service for full particulars and rates of pay. There is a job for you.

YOUR DUTY NOW IS

ISSUED BY THE MINISTRY OF LABOUR & NATIONAL SERVICE

Glamorgan Advertiser, 11 July 1941.

No medals for Mother

Her cares are many,
her tasks beyond number.
Every hour, every minute
She is on duty—
She sees the children
off to school
She makes the meals
She makes the beds—
and the planes !
Sees to the laundry
and the lathe.
Fills the shell—
and the shopping basket.
a tiring business
these days.
Cuts sandwiches
for her man
going on night duty.
and wakes at once
if her child
cries in the night.
Tired yet tireless,
She holds the fort
of the family ;
the citadel
of the hearth.
She has no medals,
only the pride
of working and striving
beside her menfolk
in a great enterprise—
to save the homes
and the children
of all the world.

*   *   *

The women of Britain are making enormous
contributions to the war effort—not least of
these is what they are doing for Savings.
We thank them . . .

Save for Victory

HOUSEWIFE 1944

The Hand that held the Hoover turns out Shells !

With no glamour of uniform, with all the burdens and responsibilities of running a home, thousands of housewives in 1944 are war-workers too. They are doing a double job. They get no medals for it. But if ever women deserved especial honour, these do. So to all war-workers who also tackle shopping queues, cooking, cleaning, mending and the hundred and one other household jobs

Salute ! FROM HOOVER

Hoover users know best what improvements they would like in the post-war Hoover. Suggestions are welcome.

BY APPOINTMENT TO H.M. KING GEORGE VI AND H.M. QUEEN MARY
HOOVER LIMITED, PERIVALE, GREENFORD, MIDDLESEX

Western Mail, 10 March 1944.

Try YOUR hand at Reconstruction !

You've every right to have your say about the sort of post-war home you want.   After all, *you've* got to live in it, and *you've* got to run it.

So why not try *your* hand at reconstruction ? You've always wanted a cleaner, easier-to-run kitchen. You've often thought how nice it would be to have less housework to do. You've thought of a hundred and one improvements in the way of constant hot water and constant cosy warmth. Electricity can help you. Electricity can save you time, labour, trouble and expense. Visit your Electricity Showroom and discuss your ideas.

ELECTRICITY
IMPROVES

IV

'CHANGING THE LIFE OF WALES':
WOMEN, WAR AND SOCIAL CHANGE

Traditional expectations regarding the domestic responsibilities of the women workers of south Wales may not have altered dramatically as a result of wartime conditions, but there can be little doubt that many other aspects of their daily lives were profoundly affected by the experience of war and wartime employment. To the overwhelming majority of the female war workers, their entry into the unfamiliar surroundings of the vast munitions factories constituted a dramatic departure from their pre-war working lives. After all, munitions work not only presented new practical challenges and the chance to acquire new skills and work interests, but it also provided the women with the opportunities for far greater measures of social freedom and financial independence than they had previously enjoyed.

The new leisure and social opportunities which were created as a direct result of factory employment and wartime conditions initiated many changes in the social experience and outlook of the Welsh female population. Yet, such developments were not always regarded favourably by contemporary observers. Indeed, in the opinion of several commentators, the war experience presented a direct challenge to many aspects of the social, economic and cultural life of Wales and seemed set to lead to a weakening of traditional social and cultural ties. In an article which appeared in the *Aberdare Leader* in October 1943, a reporter went so far as to maintain that the war factories were 'changing the life of Wales', adding that the three letters 'ROF . . . signifying one of His Majesty's Government's wartime Royal Ordnance Factories' had 'come to hold rather oddly-contrasted meanings for the people of coalmining, conservative, non-conformist South Wales'.[1] Members of the Welsh nationalist community would no doubt have agreed with such sentiments. As the historian K. O. Morgan has noted:

---

[1] *Aberdare Leader*, 9 October 1943.

the pressures of wartime merely added to the doubts and fears of patriots for the future of their country and its culture. Whatever 'the Welsh way of life' comprised, it was clearly being swamped by the collectivist, centralizing forces entailed in another total war.[2]

In a bid to counteract what was considered to be the destructive impact of such forces on the social and cultural life of Wales, a group of prominent Welsh nationalists convened a meeting of Pwyllgor Diogelu Diwylliant Cymru (the Committee for the Defence of the Culture of Wales) in December 1939. By August 1941, members of the Defence Committee had joined ranks with Undeb Cenedlaethol y Cymdeithasau Cymraeg (the National Union of Welsh Societies) to form Undeb Cymru Fydd (the New Wales Union), a society which was to wage a high-profile campaign to safeguard various aspects of the Welsh-language culture throughout the war years.[3]

Although the concerns of Undeb Cymru Fydd mainly focused on the impact of the war on the lives of those who lived in the predominantly rural and Welsh-speaking heartlands of north and west Wales, the effects of the war on the people and the social and cultural patterns of the industrial and largely Anglicized communities of south Wales were no less profound. The call-up of thousands of men and women to wartime service in distant lands and cities, coupled with the increased mobility of the civilian population, seemed set to lead to the adoption of new social mores and the further weakening of Welsh cultural and linguistic allegiances. In a radio script penned during the early years of the war following a return visit to his home town of Rhymney in Monmouthshire, the poet Idris Davies (1905–53) reflected on the changes which had already become evident in the life of his native community:

> It has been said many times that a mining valley, and especially a Welsh one, lives a unique life of its own, that it is a self-contained community, with its own outlook on life and even its own language. And I think that

---

[2] Kenneth O. Morgan, *Rebirth of a Nation: Wales, 1880–1980* (Oxford, 1982 edn), p. 271.
[3] For a detailed examination of the objectives, activities and membership of Undeb Cymru Fydd, see R. Gerallt Jones, *A Bid for Unity: The Story of Undeb Cymru Fydd, 1941–1966* (Aberystwyth, 1971), pp. 18–29; John Davies, *A History of Wales* (London, 1993), p. 603.

that is largely true; though the great crisis of 1926, and the years following 1926, with widespread unemployment and the great exodus of workers to the factories of England, did bring about some modifications. And the present war has already brought some more important changes. The mountain walls, as it were, have been pierced here and there. Through them have gone out thousands of young men, and many young women too, to join the Forces. Through them have come in thousands of evacuated children from other parts of the country. Such changes will perhaps have lasting effects on the everyday life of the mining valleys.[4]

The traditional social, cultural and religious activities of the region had already been severely disrupted as a result of wartime conditions.[5] Attendance at the chapels and churches of south Wales declined sharply during the early months of the war and, in their annual report for 1940, the officials of one Welsh Non-conformist cause in the Rhondda noted that wartime conditions had 'breached and weakened' almost every aspect of the work of the chapel.[6] In addition to the call-up of hundreds of local men, large numbers of females had been drawn into the munitions factories of the region, where the working of shifts of eight or ten hours' duration, seven days a week, had made it impossible for many to continue to worship regularly. Such was the impact on attendance at one Nonconformist chapel in Dowlais that the church elders, in association with other members of the local Free Church Council, approached the factory authorities to discuss the possibility of holding religious services at their industrial establishments.[7]

Although officials of the churches and chapels of south Wales did not voice publicly their objections to the introduction of Sunday working, many were no doubt extremely concerned about the wider social, cultural and spiritual implications of this wartime development. Workers who were engaged in the manufacture of weapons and armaments found it increasingly difficult

[4] NLW, MS 22413E.
[5] See the scripts of 'Home fires burning' (1939) and 'Wales marches on' (1941), the 'radio pictures' written by Jack Jones in collaboration with T. Rowland Hughes, which provide both a 'snapshot' of life in the mining communities of wartime south Wales, and give an insight into local 'reaction to the new conditions imposed by war'. NLW, Jack Jones MSS 88 and 144.
[6] *Adroddiad Blynyddol Jerusalem M.C, Ton* (Pentre, 1941), p. 6.
[7] J. Ronald Williams and Gwyneth Williams, *History of Caersalem, Dowlais, Welsh Baptist Church* (Llandysul, 1967), p. 64.

to reconcile their actions at the workplace on Sundays with the
'respectful' behaviour which was expected of them outside the
factory walls. A former employee of Bridgend ROF who worked
in the 'textile section' of the factory, recalled how the issue
became the source of considerable tension in her home, and
eventually led her to challenge her family's strict observance of
the Sabbath:

> I mean, on a Sunday, you weren't allowed to put a bit of cotton through
> the eye of a needle on a Sunday. So, if you wanted to wear something and
> you had a button off it . . . you went upstairs, in the bedroom with the door
> shut all quiet, you know, to sew this button on and nobody knew about it.
> But, Sunday afternoons of course, from three o'clock until ten o'clock, I
> was sewing at the factory! So of course, I came down one day now, 'Oh!
> Button off my blouse, I'll sew that on now.' I got the sewing box out, then,
> 'What do you think you're doing?', said my mother. 'I'm going to sew my
> button on, Mam.' 'It's Sunday!' I said, 'I know that. What is it, out of sight
> out of mind with you? You don't mind me going into the arsenal and
> sewing for hours, but you're not willing for me to sew a button on?'[8]

The introduction of Sunday working led others to challenge
the Sabbatarian values upheld in society at large, and many of
the local authorities of south Wales came under increased
pressure to lift their restrictions on Sunday entertainments, particularly with regard to the Sunday closure of cinemas. Although
a few local authorities bowed to the wartime demands of their
residents, others firmly resisted all calls for a relaxation of pre-
war conventions. In February 1944 the Home Intelligence Unit
of the Ministry of Information reported that support for the
ideals of the Lord Day's Observance Society was particularly
strong among the people of Wales, many of whom had expressed
'misgivings at the "growing clamour" for Sunday entertainments
and favouring closing all places of entertainment on Sundays'.[9]
However, the firm stand taken in this matter by several local
authorities in the urban and populated districts of south Wales
met with stern criticism by some members of the public.

---

[8] Evidence of Respondent 5.
[9] PRO, Inf 1/292. Stephen Ridgwell notes that as late as 1952, only 8 per cent of
cinemas in Wales ran regular Sunday programmes, compared with 97 per cent in
London and the south-east of England. Ridgwell, 'South Wales and the cinema in the
1930s', 611.

Members of the Pontypridd UDC, who had voted over-whelmingly against a proposal to open cinemas on Sundays in November 1940, were accused by one local resident of 'hypo-critical' behaviour and of failing to face up to the social needs of wartime life. According to R. E. Arnott, a supporter of the Sunday opening scheme, the scenes which he had witnessed along the length of Taff Street, Pontypridd, on Sunday nights revealed an urgent need for some form of organized enter-tainment for the young people of the town: 'Doorways are full with young men and girls, and I would rather see them indoors under control and supervision.'[10]

Such changes in the social and cultural aspirations of the people of south Wales were closely linked to the new social and economic opportunities which had been created by wartime employment. Inquiries into the effects of the war on the social life of the region conducted by Undeb Cymru Fydd, Mass-Observa-tion and local authority officials found that the wartime increase in less 'desirable' leisure activities, such as drinking, smoking and dancing, and a corresponding decrease in more traditional and 'respectable' pursuits, such as 'serious reading', sports events and musical activities of a 'high standard', could be attributed directly to the employment of large numbers of the local popula-tion in munitions work.[11] The anxieties of middle-class com-mentators regarding the long-term social and cultural effects of the war were exacerbated by the fact that the overwhelming majority of the workers employed at the munitions factories of south Wales were females. The elevated economic and social profile of the younger female population caused particular con-cern to those in authority, and fears that the stability of Welsh home and family life was in danger of being subverted led to attempts to regulate the social behaviour of the female work-force. To members of the Welsh nationalist community, the wartime shift in the social and economic experiences of the Welsh female population had grave linguistic and cultural

---

[10] *Glamorgan County Times*, 9 November 1940.
[11] NLW, Undeb Cymru Fydd Papers (November 1960 Collection), 165, responses to the Undeb Cymru Fydd inquiry into the condition of the social life of Wales, 1943; M-O A, FR 1498, 'Blaina', p. 162; GRO, Glamorgan County Council, annual report of the director of education for 1942, report of the county youth organizer, 4 December 1942.

implications. Welsh women were being removed from their 'traditional' roles as guardians of the Welsh language and culture in the home, and in the opinion of many prominent nationalists, the British government had not only 'violated Welsh family life', but had struck a 'death-blow to the life of the nation' ('Dywedwn yn ddi-betrus, dyma'r ergyd fwyaf marwol ar fywyd ein cenedl ni').[12]

To the people of the industrial communities of south Wales, it was the high wages earned by women in the war factories which presented the most immediate threat to the established social order. Very few females had previously had the opportunity to earn such wages and their new-found economic gains were not looked on favourably by all members of the community. The issue caused grave concern to those who worked in the coal mining industry, where rates of pay were particularly low. The Essential Work (Coalmining Industry) Order of May 1941, which tied miners to their place of work for the duration of the war, prevented them from sharing the economic benefits of munitions work, and many colliers viewed the wartime situation as a serious affront both to their industry and their manhood. Jack Jones (1884–1970), the Merthyr-born writer who toured the south Wales valleys during the war in his capacity as an itinerant Ministry of Information speaker, found that many miners had been angered by this wartime development:

> . . . we've had about enough of it, said one. There's no workers' playtime down there where we work, Jack, but there is where my daughter works and earns more money than I do.
>
> That was how miners in all parts of the South Wales coalfield were talking, I found as going from one mining valley to the other. A new layer of resentment was forming over the old and deep layers formed by indignities suffered by long years of unemployment between the wars, and this new layer, the creation of a new kind of indignity, that of paying them less than was being paid to many female munition workers, had roused the

---

[12] Cathrin Daniel, 'Ffarwel cartrefi Cymru', *Y Ddraig Goch*, XV, no. 4 (1941), 3. Similar sentiments were expressed in the following: *Yr Efrydydd*, VII, no. 2 (1941), 2–3; P.L.S., 'The war on women', *The Welsh Nationalist*, September 1941; *Baner ac Amserau Cymru*, 30 July 1941, 10 December 1941; *Y Ddraig Goch*, XVI, no. 1 (1942), 2; Gwenan Jones, 'Benywaeth – gwir a gau', *Yr Efrydydd*, II, no. 3 (1942), 14–18; Plaid Genedlaethol Cymru, *Gorfodaeth Filwrol ar Ferched Cymru* (Caernarfon, 1945), p. 5.

smouldering fires of ancient grudges and an eruption which might seriously affect the national war effort was imminent.[13]

The arguments and evidence put forward by the miners of south Wales during their wartime campaign for a wage increase, placed a great deal of emphasis on the disparity between their earnings and those of the female war workers. In a letter written to the executive council of the SWMF in April 1941, members of the Caerau (Llynfi valley) lodge of the federation drew attention to the fact that workers employed at ROFs in the area received far higher wages than men who laboured in local collieries.[14] The lower financial rewards earned by the miners for their part in the war effort contributed greatly to the demoralized state of the mining workforce.[15] Speaking in Parliament in July 1941, Ness Edwards, the Caerphilly MP, drew attention to the psychological effects of this inequality:

> In my street there is a collier who is being asked to work himself to death in order to produce more coal. He receives £4 a week, yet his daughter who works in a munition factory and comes home and says that she has been gossiping all day, gets more money than he does. What effect will that have on the enthusiasm which ought to be brought to our national effort?[16]

This popular, if inaccurate, interpretation of the contrasting work experiences and wartime contribution of the miners and the female munitions workers became central to the miners' wartime campaign for a wages increase. Speaking at a rally organized by the Communist Party at Aberdare in March 1942, Will Paynter, the miners' agent for the Rhymney valley, referred to the 'fed-upness' of the miners who:

---

[13] Jack Jones, *Me and Mine* (London, 1946), pp. 202–3. Similar grievances relating to the contrasting wage rates and working conditions of the south Wales miners and munitions workers were highlighted in Coombes, *Those Clouded Hills*, p. 41; idem, *Miners Day* (London, 1945), p. 15.

[14] SWCA, South Wales Miners' Federation (SWMF), executive committee minutes, 22 April 1941.

[15] For a detailed account of the wider issues which led to problems within the coal industry and discontent among the miners during the Second World War, see Broomfield, 'South Wales in the Second World War'; W. H. B. Court, *Coal* (London, 1951); R. Page Arnot, *The Miners in Crisis and War* (London, 1961); Calder, *The People's War*, pp. 431–43.

[16] *Parliamentary Debates* (Hansard) (5th series), vol. 373, 250 (9 July 1941).

on the one hand were told that coal was the most vital industry in the matter of increasing production, and then on the other hand, miners came home after six days hard grind at the coal-face with less money in their pay-packets than a girl of eighteen working in a munitions factory.[17]

His sentiments were echoed two years later by another miners' agent from Monmouthshire. Speaking at the opening ceremony of the Mynydd Maen colliery canteen in February 1944, Obadiah Evans JP referred to the fact that 'wives and daughters were taking home more money than some miners' and expressed the view that 'the miners had been looked upon as the scum of the industry as to conditions and wages'.[18] Although this was an issue which concerned miners across Britain, Evan Williams, general secretary of the SWMF, was of the opinion that discontent was greatest in the South Wales Coalfield where there was no tradition of female industrial employment.[19] The chief conciliation and industrial relations officer of the Ministry of Labour in Wales shared this view:

> This feeling is probably stronger in South Wales than elsewhere, because, in the mining valleys the economic dependence of the women upon the men has hitherto been absolute, but with the establishment of the munitions factories, employing women, the miner finds that his womenfolk are not only independent economically, but in many cases, their earnings capacity is greater.[20]

As tensions mounted in the coalfield, the SWMF stepped up its efforts to secure a new wage agreement. In May 1942 telegrams were sent to the president and general secretary of the MFGB demanding a national delegate conference to press for an urgent general flat-rate increase.[21] The younger members of the Welsh mining workforce took matters into their own hands and gave vent to their frustrations by holding a series of unofficial strikes and demonstrations during the summer months.[22]

[17] *Aberdare Leader*, 4 April 1942.
[18] *Free Press of Monmouthshire*, 25 February 1944.
[19] *Western Mail*, 13 May 1942.
[20] PRO, Lab 10/368.
[21] *Western Mail*, 13 May 1942.
[22] See Stuart Broomfield, 'The apprentice boys' strikes of the Second World War', *Llafur*, 3, no. 2 (1981), 53–67.

Although such actions had a direct impact on wartime production, public support and sympathy for the cause of the
striking miners was much in evidence.[23] The view expressed by a
columnist who wrote in the weekly newspaper of Aberdare in
June 1942 was no doubt shared by many local inhabitants:

> The collier is as great a lover of his own country and its democratic
> institutions as any man in the land: if he seems to threaten the war effort by
> his demands, it is because he has bitter memories, wants a square deal, and
> sees other workers, who do not labour half as strenuously at the factory
> machine (even if they do work longer hours) as he does at the conveyor-
> face, get a much larger pay packet.[24]

In June 1942, following the rejection by the coal owners of the
MFGB's claim for a minimum wage of £4 5s., the wages dispute
was placed in the hands of the new Board of Investigation
established under Lord Greene.[25] Although the Greene Award of
18 June 1942 provided some hope for the miners of south Wales,
with the granting of a weekly minimum wage to which they had
never before been entitled, their subsequent demands for the
minimum rates of £4 3s. per week for all underground workers
(aged over twenty-one), £3 18s. for surface workers and a flat-
rate increase of 2s. 6d. were refused and their grievances arising
from the disparity between their wages and those of the female
munitions workers remained unresolved.[26] During a return visit
to Blaina in August 1942, Mollie Tarrant found that complaints
regarding the high earnings of female munitions workers were 'as
much in evidence' as they had been earlier in the year.[27] Stories
relating to the handsome wages earned by women at the war
factories continued to be circulated, and there was little evidence
to suggest that local tensions between the miners and the munitions workers had been defused.

Although it must be acknowledged that many mining households warmly welcomed the additional economic contributions
of their womenfolk, there is evidence to suggest that the issue was

[23] *South Wales Echo*, 19 May 1942; *Baner ac Amserau Cymru*, 10 June 1942; PRO, Inf
1/292.
[24] *Aberdare Leader*, 13 June 1942.
[25] Arnot, *The Miners in Crisis and War*, pp. 342–3.
[26] Francis and Smith, *The Fed*, p. 399.
[27] M-O A, FR 1498, 'Blaina', Appendix II, August 1942.

a source of tension within some families. The ordinary miner felt that his traditional position as breadwinner and head of the household had been undermined by the wartime employment of females who had previously been his dependants, and the psychological effect of this blow to his status had placed a great strain on family relations.[28] A miners' representative from Blaina told Mollie Tarrant that he knew of two cases where 'the woman brings home more than the man. In one case, they've parted.'[29] In another household, a miner's wife explained how she had been forced to adopt certain tactics when dealing with her wages in order to avoid confrontation:

> Now, I might sometimes get a little more than my husband but what I do is to come in and I just put my wages up on the mantelpiece. I don't say how much I've got. If I did, my husband would just say, 'All right, you don't go out to work then.' The way I look at it is, we're both working for the home and to bring up the boys. What we do is to live on my husband's money, and we're saving mine for after the war. You never know what it may come in useful for then. We want to buy a house of our own. But in some houses, there may be women who'd say, I've earned all this, I've got a right to so and so. And then it'd be all up.[30]

However, elderly or disabled miners who had been unable to find work at either local collieries or factories had little choice but to suffer the indignity of 'living on the earnings' of their wives and, in the opinion of Ness Edwards, the growing incidence of this intolerable situation was set to lead to a 'grave social problem'.[31] One ex-miner from Aberdare gave vent to his feelings on the matter in an interview with a local newspaper reporter in 1943: '"I'm one of the unemployables; but I reckon they're wrong. I could do some of the jobs the women are doing." He spat reflectively. "You know, since my old woman has been working, my life has been just hell." '[32]

---

28 See PRO, Inf 1/292; M-O A, FR 1498, 'Blaina', pp. 47–50; Harold Wilson, *New Deal for Coal* (London, 1945), p. 50; Court, *Coal*, pp. 222, 329; England, 'The Merthyr of the twentieth century', p. 99; Broomfield, 'South Wales in the Second World War', pp. 26–7.
29 M-O A, FR 1498, 'Blaina', p. 50.
30 M-O A, TC 64, Coal mining, Box 1, File C.
31 *Parliamentary Debates* (Hansard) (5th series), vol. 392, 357 (23 September 1943).
32 *Western Mail*, 18 March 1943.

Men who found themselves being supported by the wages of their daughters suffered the greatest humiliation of all.[33] Speaking in November 1940, Alderman Degwel Thomas warned that south Wales was on the verge of witnessing 'a cultural revolution' as young daughters, who had once been regarded as 'liabilities to the families of miners until they married', now became the main breadwinners.[34] Some fathers found it extremely difficult to come to terms with this state of affairs and their deep sense of personal shame proved impossible to conceal. One miner's daughter recalled the reaction of her father when she returned home from Bridgend ROF with her first pay-packet of £2 19s.: 'it was more than my father was earning in the colliery – two pounds fourteen he was bringing home. I'll never forget his face when I brought my pay home . . . terrible it was.'[35] Such scenes were not confined to mining households. Another employee of Bridgend ROF who took home more money than her father, who was employed as a railway guard, recalled that the matter was regarded as 'a big thing' within the household.[36] Tensions also ran high between siblings and 'sweethearts' as young colliers grew resentful of the fact that their sisters and girlfriends could earn higher wages than themselves.[37]

In some instances, the conflict which arose from this issue caused deep divisions. Relations between friends and neighbours who had shared many hardships during the years of the depression could be severely tested as their contrasting experiences of wartime employment brought equally contrasting financial rewards. At Blaina, Mollie Tarrant found that 'feelings of resentment' had arisen wherever miners and munitions workers lived next door to one another. Such feelings were said to be particularly strong when more than one member of a family worked 'on munitions' and took home 'double money'.[38] Similar circumstances were reported to be the source of considerable ill-feeling at Aberdare. Speaking at a meeting of the Aberdare TLC in September 1942, Councillor Sam Wilcox drew attention to one

[33] M-O A, FR 1498, 'Blaina', p. 49.
[34] *Western Mail*, 21 November 1940.
[35] Evidence of Kitty Bishop in Davies (ed.), *The Valleys Autobiography*, p. 73.
[36] Evidence of Respondent 4.
[37] PRO, Lab 10/368 and Inf, 1/292; *South Wales Evening Post*, 25 May 1942; Broomfield, 'The apprentice boys' strikes of the Second World War', 56.
[38] M-O A, FR 1498, 'Blaina', p. 49.

particularly 'galling' case, where an unemployed family from the Gadlys district of the town lived alongside a household comprising several munitions workers whose total earnings were alleged to amount to £30 a week.[39] As if to add insult to injury, the female war workers of the town were also said to be 'revelling in the good money' they were earning and 'saying – "they don't mind if the war goes on for a few years"'.[40]

Concerns that the benefits of wartime employment were not being evenly distributed among the residents of south Wales were heightened by the fact that it was some of the female population who were making the greatest financial and social gains from the wartime experience. Mollie Tarrant noted that many of the people of Blaina regarded the changes which had been initiated in the lives of the female population as breaking with the 'traditional background' of the area.[41] The clearest indication of that 'break' with tradition had come as a result of the increased earnings capacity and spending power of the female population. As the former employees of Bridgend ROF confirmed, the wages which young women could earn at the war factories were far greater than any they had received before the war, and the feeling that they had suddenly 'become rich' had a profound effect on their general outlook and behaviour.[42] Moreover, female war workers were not only being given the opportunity of earning wages which exceeded those paid to many adult males, but were also exercising an unprecedented measure of financial and social independence by choosing how and where to spend their money. The contrast with their pre-war experiences was striking and it was perhaps not surprising, therefore, that the changing lifestyle of a section of the Welsh female population attracted so much attention. Speaking at a public meeting at Aberdare in April 1942, the Communist Isobel Brown observed that it was precisely because most Welsh women had been 'brought up in an atmosphere that women's place was in the home' that they were now 'rather ostentatiously enjoying their new won freedom'.[43] In the opinion of Mollie Tarrant, the female munitions workers of

---

[39] *Aberdare Leader*, 12 September 1942.

[40] Ibid., 8 August 1942. The female munitions workers of Blaina were also alleged to have made similar remarks in 1942; see M-O A, FR 1498, 'Blaina', p. 130.

[41] M-O A, FR 1498, 'Blaina', p. 106.

[42] Evidence of Respondents 1, 4, 5, 12, 13, 14, 15, 16 and 22.

[43] *Aberdare Leader*, 2 May 1942.

Blaina were also behaving as though they had 'suddenly awakened to quite new possibilities'.[44]

This sudden and dramatic shift in the economic and social
profile of the female population of south Wales was not welcomed
by all members of society. Indeed, many onlookers despaired
of the type of social conduct which the new independence of
the female munitions workers seemed to be encouraging. The
behaviour of young, single women, who had fewer family responsibilities, and thus showed a greater tendency to spend their wages
on personal 'luxuries', caused particular concern. Members of the
Cardiff Education Committee were of the opinion that the high
wages earned by young women were 'encouraging a feeling of
independence' and giving them 'a false sense of being "grown
up"'.[45] Employers and factory officials complained of a consequent increase in unpunctuality, absenteeism and indiscipline
among their female employees. In May 1941 it was reported that
some young war workers were staying away from work on the
grounds that they could 'well afford to lose a few days pay when
they feel like it'.[46] The situation at Bridgend ROF was said to be
'particularly bad, it being a matter for boasting among the girls
that they can absent themselves whenever they like, and a number
of employees have been fined for false clocking-in'.[47] The view that
young war workers were not mature or responsible enough to be
earning, let alone spending, such high wages was shared by a local
newspaper columnist, who feared that:

> the receipt of high wages may tend to place the juvenile in a false position
> in the home. An assumed superiority over other (and senior) members of
> the family is liable to produce lack of discipline and stability of character.
> This, together with an ignorance of values, frequently results in a frittering
> away of prevailing income . . . It would be desirable to appropriate part of
> the earnings as savings for use of the young people after the war.[48]

Given the social and economic hardships which had been
endured by the people of the Welsh industrial communities in

---

[44] M-O A, FR 1498, 'Blaina', p. 203.
[45] Cardiff Central Library, City of Cardiff Education Committee annual reports for
1943 and 1944, Juvenile Employment Committee reports.
[46] PRO, Inf 1/292.
[47] Ibid.
[48] *Merthyr Express*, 18 April 1942.

the years before the war, such criticism of the spending habits of the female war workers was understandable. The fact that the women of Blaina had had 'no money at all for anything other than absolutely necessary spending' during the inter-war years explained the significance which local residents attached to the idea of wartime saving and the 'semi-hostility' that was directed towards female war workers who appeared to be 'spending recklessly'.[49]

As evidence of the new prosperity of the female war workers became more apparent, the 'extravagant' lifestyle of a minority became the focus of intense public attention and scrutiny. The apparent lack of respect shown by the female munitions workers of Blaina for the wartime mood of 'austerity' riled many local residents. The woman who ran 'the only up-to-date dress shop' in the town admitted that a considerable amount of money had been spent in her shop before the introduction of clothing rations in June 1941: 'It's ridiculous . . . Of course, you can't do anything about it, but sometimes I feel I'd like to refuse to serve them.'[50] Local housewives were equally disapproving of the spending habits of the young munitions workers. One married woman told Mollie Tarrant: 'You can easily see people have been spending more on clothes since the war. Women you'd know had only one pair of shoes for Sundays and weekdays at one time, now they might have half a dozen.'[51] An increase in the amount of money which the young women of south Wales spent on luxuries such as 'silk stockings, powder and lipstick' was also remarked upon and attracted widespread criticism.[52] One of the strongest condemnations came from members of the Pontardawe branch of Undeb Dirwestol Merched y De (the South Wales Women's Temperance Union), whose total incomprehension of the desire among young Welsh women to paint their faces like 'Red Indians' was itself a powerful indicator of the way in which the social and cultural aspirations of the female population were being rapidly modernized by the wartime experience.[53]

[49] M-O A, FR 1498, 'Blaina', p. 97.
[50] Ibid., p. 104.
[51] Ibid.
[52] Ibid., p. 203; South Wales Echo, 6 December 1943, 18 March 1944.
[53] NLW, MS 16594D, 8 September 1942.

In their actions, behaviour and attitudes, the young female war workers of south Wales represented a 'new way of life' and, as such, were seen to present a direct challenge to the old social and moral order. Contemporary observers spoke of the 'emancipatory' effect which the wartime employment experience had on the behaviour and outlook of local women; indeed, in many ways, the Welsh female munitions worker could be regarded as the 'modern girl' or 'flapper' of her generation.[54] Freed from many of the social and economic constraints which had previously restricted her opportunities to take part in various leisure activities, the war years proved particularly 'liberating' for the young, single Welsh war worker. After all, wartime employment not only granted a measure of financial autonomy, but also brought increased mobility and enabled young women to interact and socialize with their contemporaries to a far greater extent than had been possible before the war.

The workplace was itself an important meeting-place, and employees of the larger war factories formed their own recreational clubs and societies in order to pursue their leisure activities both during and outside working hours. In addition to the myriad singing and dancing troupes which had been formed to entertain fellow workers in the factory, Bridgend ROF boasted a swimming club and a successful operatic society which gave several public performances at Porthcawl Pavilion.[55] The 'cream' of the singers and musicians from the war factories of south Wales even competed against each other at the 'Welsh inter-factories eisteddfod', which was held annually at City Hall and Cory Hall, Cardiff, between 1943 and 1945.[56]

The war years also provided plenty of opportunities for the young munitions workers to enjoy some of the more commercial forms of public entertainment outside their working hours. Several of the former employees of Bridgend ROF interviewed during this study recalled how they frequently met their colleagues at a local cinema or dance before commencing, or even

[54] M-O A, FR 1196, 'Blaina investigation', p. 1; ibid., FR 1498, 'Blaina', pp. 89, 108.
[55] GRO, Bridgend UDC minutes, 28 May 1940; Porthcawl UDC minutes, 13 September 1943, 13 March 1944.
[56] *Western Mail*, 14 September 1943, 3 June 1944; *South Wales Echo*, 2 June 1944, 30 June 1945. The Welsh inter-factories eisteddfod continued to be held after the cessation of the war, drawing competitors from many of the new works established on the sites of the former munitions factories.

after ending, their long shifts.[57] Indeed, given the difficult and hazardous conditions under which the munitions workers worked every day, it was hardly surprising that many were eager to take full advantage of their free time and 'make whoopee' once outside the factory gates.[58]

The factory authorities, however, took a dim view of the carefree attitude adopted by many of their young female employees. Indeed, the 'hectic' social lives led by some of the more 'irresponsible' workers was widely reported to be the root cause of their absenteeism from the workplace. In a newspaper article published in November 1940, Beverley Baxter, MP for Wood Green, claimed that 'in certain districts' young factory girls

> gave trouble by remaining away from work at odd times and coming late at others. They missed their contact with ordinary life and gave the management frequent headaches by staying away to get their hair done or to see their favourite film star.[59]

The female war workers of south Wales were often accused of 'slacking' in this manner. Indeed, it was alleged that the high absenteeism rates recorded among the young munitions workers of the Rhondda, Merthyr Tydfil and Blaina resulted from the late-night dances which they frequently attended.[60] One thirty-year-old war worker from Blaina was severely critical of the conduct of the young women with whom she worked:

> The young girls are the worst to work. They've no inclination to think – 'This is my effort for the War.' The girls from the big families are a bit better, they've had to take more responsibility at home. With the others, it's all dancing, pictures and drink. Two girls I'm working with every day, last night they went to a cinema *and* a dance. They were dead when they came to work.[61]

---

[57] Evidence of Respondents 1, 3, 4, 5, 6, 7 and 15.
[58] Evidence of Respondent 5.
[59] *South Wales Echo*, 21 November 1940.
[60] *The Rhondda Leader*, 6 December 1941; *Merthyr Express*, 30 January 1943; M-O A, FR 1498, 'Blaina', p. 96.
[61] M-O A, FR 1498, 'Blaina', p. 96.

Cinema-going had established its position as one of the main recreational pursuits of the female population of industrial south Wales during the inter-war years, but its popularity during the war exceeded all previous records. Indeed, a visit to the cinema became a central feature in the social life of the British wartime public, and it is estimated that some twenty-five to thirty million cinema tickets were sold in Britain each week throughout the war.[62] Nearly 380,000 people were said to have attended the cinema at Tredegar Workmen's Hall during 1942 alone, and the income generated by the cinema during the war years enabled the hall to clear the debts it had incurred as a result of extensive building alterations.[63] Films such as *How Green was my Valley* and *Gone with the Wind*, both of which went on general release in south Wales in 1942, proved extremely popular with the local female war workers and, as Angus Calder noted, it is likely that many of the 'war-weary minds' who sat through all three hours and forty minutes of the epic, *Gone with the Wind*, were only too 'content to be swept away by its colour, costume and glamour'.[64] The former munitions workers interviewed for this study regularly visited their local cinemas during the war – some even attended almost on a daily basis – and it was not surprising, therefore, that many of the picture-houses of south Wales rearranged their schedules in order to fit in with factory shifts and presented special 'showings' and programmes for the factory workers.[65]

Having been considered out of bounds to all women of 'respectable' character in the years before the war, the dance-hall suddenly became one of the main social centres attended by the young women of wartime south Wales. Dances held at venues such as the Pavilion at Porthcawl, the Palais de Danse at Bridgend and at Pontypool, as well as the smaller town and village halls, attracted large numbers of young women during the war.[66] One former munitions worker remarked that she and her friends were all 'dance-mad' and to the accompaniment of the wireless at home and in the factory canteens the young war workers took advantage of every spare minute to practise their

[62] Calder, *The People's War*, p. 367.
[63] D. J. Davies, *The Tredegar Workmen's Hall, 1861–1951: Ninety Years of Endeavour* (Cardiff, 1951), p. 87.
[64] Calder, *The People's War*, p. 370.
[65] Evidence of Respondent 6.
[66] Ibid., and Respondents 3, 4, 5, 7, 15 and 20.

steps and routines.[67] Much time and effort was also spent upon experimenting with clothes, hairstyles and make-up in a bid to achieve a glamorous 'look', far removed from the drab and uniform appearance expected of the women in the factory workshops. Such emphasis upon personal presentation and 'grooming' was deemed vital if a young woman was to catch the eye of a male partner. Hundreds of servicemen who were stationed at nearby airbases and military camps attended dances in the Bridgend and Porthcawl district and, indeed, the relationships forged between some dancing partners were to lead to the more permanent partnerships of marriage.[68]

Although some Welsh parents appear to have modified their pre-war opinions on the 'evils' of the dance-halls – having concluded perhaps that it was far better to allow their daughters to attend organized events where their behaviour and associations with members of the opposite sex would be subject to some public scrutiny rather than to permit them to roam the streets unsupervised – such enlightened views were not shared by all members of the community. At their annual meeting held at Tonpentre, Rhondda, in 1941, representatives of Undeb Dirwestol Merched y De – a movement whose stated objective was to ensure 'The Moral Safety and Elevation of the Women of our Country' – delivered a stern warning to the women of Wales of the social and moral perils which lurked in the dance-hall.[69] The residents of Maesteg were made aware of such dangers in April 1943, when it was alleged that dances which had been organized by the military services at the town hall had been conducted in a 'disgraceful manner'. Local mothers, who had allowed their daughters to attend the dances on the strict condition that they would not frequent licensed premises, had been shocked to find out that 'beer was overflowing' in the hall and that young girls had been 'plied with drink' by the soldiers.[70] Problems also arose at licensed dances held at the Brangwyn Hall, Swansea, during the same year. Allegations that such events had encouraged female drinking and 'consequent moral laxity', eventually led

---

[67] Evidence of Respondents 5 and 19.

[68] Respondents 3 and 4 met their husbands, who were airmen based at Porthcawl, at dances held at Porthcawl Pavilion.

[69] NLW, MS 16594D, report of the annual meeting of Undeb Dirwestol Merched y De, held at Jerusalem, Tonpentre, May–June 1941.

[70] GRO, Maesteg UDC minutes, 6 April 1943; *Glamorgan Advertiser*, 9 April 1943.

councillors to vote in favour of discontinuing the licence in December 1943.[71]

Reports of such incidents, coupled with evidence of a large increase in female drinking and smoking, served to confirm the worst fears of the middle-class moralists who had warned against the social and moral dangers of allowing too much economic and social freedom to young, impressionable women.[72] In south Wales, where women had previously been considered 'as good as damned' if they smoked in public and all 'respectable' females had steered clear of the public houses for fear of being branded 'scarlet women', the sudden change in the social habits of a section of the female population attracted a great deal of public attention and widespread criticism.[73] Sensationalist accounts of the wartime 'epidemic' of female drunkenness were widely reported in the south Wales press.[74] The public houses of the Rhondda were said to be 'full of women drinking, swearing and smoking', while at Newport it was reported that gangs of females, dressed in dungarees 'as if they had just left work', regularly frequented the local hostelries.[75] Indeed, the impression given, was that the women of wartime south Wales 'poured into' the male preserves of the public houses on the same scale as they had entered the war factories.[76] Religious and temperance societies, as well as the officials and representatives of local authorities, were quick to condemn the growing incidence of such unacceptable behaviour.[77] In their

---

[71] *South Wales Evening Post*, 8 December 1943.

[72] For evidence of the wartime increase in female drinking, see PRO, Inf 1/292; Jephcott, *Girls Growing Up*, p. 136; 'M-O Bulletin: Women in public houses, February 1943', in Dorothy Sheridan (ed.), *Wartime Women: A Mass-Observation Anthology* (London, 1990), pp. 195–205; M-O A, FR 1611, 'Social change – women in public houses', 23 March 1943; ibid., FR 1635, 'Women in public houses', 30 March 1943.

[73] M-O A, FR 1498, 'Blaina', p. 107; ibid., Directive Reply (DR) 2678, 'Report on drinking habits among young people in your area', May 1943; ibid., TC 85, Drinking habits, Box 8, File A, 'Blaina survey, 1947–8'; GRO, Glamorgan County Council, annual report of the director of education for 1944, report of the county youth organizer, 21 July 1944; SWML, tape no. 88, interview with Reg Fine, Maerdy; evidence of Respondents 4, 16, 17 and 22.

[74] *Caerphilly Journal*, 27 February 1943.

[75] Ibid., 30 January, 11 September 1943; *South Wales Argus*, 5 February 1942.

[76] Gwyn A. Williams, *When Was Wales? A History of the Welsh* (Harmondsworth, 1985), p. 254. It should be noted that it was as a result of the wartime increase in female drinking that separate washing and lavatory facilities for women were first provided in many of the public houses of south Wales.

[77] See *Annual Reports of the South Wales Temperance and Band of Hope Union (Undeb Cymdeithasau Dirwestol a Gobeithluoedd Deheudir Cymru)* (Cardiff, 1939–45), and *Annual Reports of the South Wales Women's Temperance Union (Undeb Dirwestol Merched Deheudir Cymru)* (Rhymni and Treforys, 1939–45).

annual reports to the licensing sessions of south Wales, magistrates and senior police officers frequently referred to the wartime increase which had been recorded in female drinking in their areas, and voiced their concerns at the long-term social and moral implications of this unwelcome development.[78] James A. Wilson, the chief constable of Cardiff, despaired of the 'provocative spirit of independence' exhibited by the young female munitions workers of the city who considered it 'the thing' to 'indulge in beers and gins etc.'[79]

The strong public reaction against the wartime increase in female drinking and attendance at public houses was not un-expected given that such conduct challenged one of the central precepts of Welsh female respectability. Although similar social restrictions prevented women from entering public houses in many English working-class districts,[80] the strong Nonconformist values of the Welsh industrial communities appear to have enforced additional religious and moral limitations on the behaviour of the female population. As a reporter from the *Caerphilly Journal* pointed out in February 1943, the sight of women drinking openly in public houses was

> a most unusual feature here in Wales. There has always been drinking in pubs in Wales but such women were considered as low persons . . . It is not in any way held against a woman that she calls in an hotel in Birmingham or Bristol or Bath as it would be in Porth, or Tonypandy or Aberdare.[81]

The notion that the women of Wales upheld 'higher' social and moral values than their English sisters left some Welsh observers in no doubt as to who was to blame for bringing about the sudden wartime increase in female drinking. Since the outbreak of the war, several thousand English women had been

[78] See, for example, the annual reports of licensing sessions in Cardiff, Bedwellty, Carmarthen, Llanelli, Blackwood, Newport, Pontypool, Usk, Lower Miskin, Bridgend and Aberdare: GRO, City of Cardiff licensing sessions, minutes and reports 1939–45; *South Wales Echo*, 6 February 1941; *South Wales Evening Post*, 10 February 1941, 4 February 1943; *South Wales Argus*, 2 and 4 February 1942; *Free Press of Monmouthshire*, 13 February 1942, 5 February 1943, 12 February 1944; *Glamorgan Advertiser*, 13 February 1942; *Aberdare Leader*, 14 February 1942.
[79] GRO, City of Cardiff licensing sessions minutes, 6 February 1942, 5 February 1943.
[80] See Andrew Davies, *Leisure, Gender and Poverty: Working-class Culture in Salford and Manchester, 1900–1939* (Buckingham, 1992), pp. 61–73; Roberts, *A Woman's Place*, p. 115.
[81] *Caerphilly Journal*, 20 February 1943.

evacuated with their children to the rural and urban districts of Wales, and it was they who were deemed to have introduced the 'drink habit' to the local female population. Differences in the customs and attitudes of the English evacuees towards drink had become apparent during the early months of the war. In their 'evacuation survey' prepared for the Fabian Society in 1940, Richard Padley and Margaret Cole noted that, whilst adult evacuees who had been sent to Wales had been greatly irritated to find that all public houses in the country closed on Sundays, the local residents had in turn 'felt that their moral standards were being attacked by strangers'.[82] The members of the Committee for the Defence of the Culture of Wales were keen exponents of that view, and in a memorandum published in 1940, they warned of the 'moral havoc' being caused in the Welsh rural communities by English evacuees whose background and traditions were 'completely alien' to those of the Welsh people.[83]

The conduct of the female evacuees who were sent to the more urban environment of industrial south Wales was judged to be equally unacceptable by many local residents. In a letter to his local weekly newspaper, the *Merthyr Express*, a resident of Merthyr Tydfil attributed the unwelcome and unfamiliar sight of 'women in slacks smoking in our streets' to the female evacuees of the town.[84] At Pontypool in Monmouthshire, where a marked increase in the number of women frequenting public houses had been reported during 1942–3, Police Superintendent Edward Casey pointed out that the females in question were evacuees who were 'carrying out the custom of other districts'.[85] Elsewhere, the behaviour of the female visitors gave even greater cause for concern. Speaking at the annual meeting of the Blackwood brewster sessions in February 1942, Police Superintendent L. Spendlove accused female evacuees who lived in the

---

[82] Richard Padley and Margaret Cole (eds.), *Evacuation Survey: A Report to the Fabian Society* (London, 1940), p. 237.

[83] Executive Committee of the Conference for the Protection of Welsh Culture, *Evacuation Schemes and Service of Youth* (Denbigh, 1940), p. 7. Similar friction arose in the rural towns and villages of England where the behaviour of female evacuees from the large, urban areas was also deemed to be at odds with that of the local female population. See 'War comes to a Norfolk village: the diary of Muriel Green, 1939', in Sheridan (ed.), *Wartime Women*, p. 58.

[84] *Merthyr Express*, 22 November 1941.

[85] *Free Press of Monmouthshire*, 12 February 1943. Similar remarks were made in the annual reports of the Aberdare and the Blackwood brewster sessions. *Aberdare Leader*, 14 February 1942; *Free Press of Monmouthshire*, 11 February 1944.

Blackwood and Aber-carn area of 'pub-crawling'.[86] A few months later at Aberdare, the stipendiary magistrate condemned the evacuee mothers who took their young children with them when they went drinking at the public houses of the town and pointed out that this practice was totally unacceptable to the local residents: 'The standard of propriety of evacuees here may not be as high as that of us in Wales. We have a strong sense of propriety. Wales is a deeply religious country.'[87]

The worst fears of such prominent local officials were soon confirmed, however, when it became evident that members of the local female population were adopting many of the alleged social customs of the English evacuees. Indeed, one senior police officer from Carmarthen went so far as to accuse the English female evacuees of 'teaching local women to drink'![88] Speaking to Mollie Tarrant in 1942, an official from the Blaina labour exchange maintained that:

> There's more smoking and drinking among the women now, especially smoking. I think it's a lot to do with the evacuees. They'd been used to going into pubs, whereas down here, they'd never seen a woman in a pub, and the only drinking was furtive.[89]

Oral evidence supports this viewpoint. A former munitions worker from Aberkenfig was in no doubt that the female evacuees, 'who were used to going into pubs and leading a different life', had played an important part in changing local customs.[90] This opinion was shared by a miner from Maerdy in the Rhondda Fach, who remarked in an interview recorded during the 1970s that attitudes towards female drinking were 'altered during the war when the evacuees came down here'.[91]

If the social habits and outlook of the Welsh female population could be so adversely affected merely through their casual associations with English women, the decision to transfer Welsh women to work alongside their English sisters in the factories of England seemed set, to some, to lead to social and cultural ruin.

86 *South Wales Argus*, 2 February 1942.
87 *Aberdare Leader*, 13 June 1942.
88 *South Wales Evening Post*, 10 February 1941.
89 M-O A, FR 1498, 'Blaina', p. 156.
90 Evidence of Respondent 4.
91 SWML, tape no. 88.

From January 1942, the Ministry of Labour assumed powers to direct Welsh 'mobile' females – the overwhelming majority of whom were single women aged between nineteen and thirty – to factory employment in districts where there was a shortage of labour, such as the south and Midlands of England. To the people of south Wales this development evoked bitter memories of the inter-war transference schemes.[92] Anxious parents repeated their pre-war concerns for the social and moral welfare of their daughters who were to be sent away to hostels and lodging-houses in the large English industrial centres, while politicians and community leaders decried the implementation of a policy which seemed set to lead to yet another exodus of the young Welsh female population.

By June 1942, only six months after the transfers began, it was reported that the residents of Mountain Ash and Aberdare had become 'intensely irritated' by the fact that so many local girls had been transferred to work in 'distant spots in England and Scotland', while the English girls who had been sent to the area at the beginning of the war to train the 'green' Welsh workforce continued to be employed locally.[93] The matter was immediately taken up by members of the Mountain Ash TLC who sent telegrams of protest to Ernest Bevin, the Minister of Labour, and arranged an urgent meeting with George Hall, the local MP. Ultimately, however, both courses of action proved futile. Speaking at the emergency meeting convened by the TLC on 13 June, George Hall denied all claims that Welsh girls were being forced to go to England while English girls remained in Welsh factories, and he declared such allegations to be nothing but 'twaddle'.[94] The dismissive attitude of the Aberdare MP greatly angered the relatives of local girls who had been sent to work in English factories 'contrary to their wishes'.[95] One father, whose daughter had been 'directed' to war work in England, sent the following response to the local evening newspaper:

> Mr George Hall MP was recently reported to have stated that girls who have been transferred to employment in various parts of England have

---

[92] Office of the Minister of Reconstruction, *Welsh Reconstruction Advisory Council – First Interim Report*, p. 21.
[93] *Aberdare Leader*, 13 June 1942.
[94] Ibid., 20 June 1942.
[95] *South Wales Echo*, 15 June 1942; *Merthyr Express*, 27 June 1942.

done so voluntarily. He appealed to his listeners not to listen to 'twaddle' about girls being compelled to take up employment in England. I am the father of a girl who since the war started has been doing essential work in South Wales. She was told a few weeks ago that she had to take up employment in England or go to the Forces. If this is not compulsion then what is?[96]

During the months that followed, the compulsory direction of the 'mobile' female population of south Wales to war work outside the region continued at a swift pace, and although only 1,455 Welsh females had been transferred to employment in England by June 1943, the figure was to exceed 5,000 by May 1945.[97] The transference policy was implemented with particular vigour during 1943–4. The Ministry of Labour transferred hundreds of female war workers from Bridgend ROF to the Midlands and elsewhere and filled their positions by drawing on both the local immobile female population and an increasing number of retired and disabled miners.[98] Not all the young female war workers accepted their fate quietly.[99] One young war worker from Swansea who, along with 'a large batch of girls', had received her direction order to leave for the Midlands in April 1943, called on the Welsh people to unite in their opposition to this policy:

I feel rather bitter over the whole affair as I volunteered to go to my present factory . . . my one reason being that I was near my home. Why is it that Welsh girls are pushed around in this manner? All I hope is, that Wales will stand firm and act at once and demand that the youth of Welsh factories be left where they belong and allow no more transfers. I have, like all Welsh women, been a conscientious worker and have been proud to do my share towards the war effort but I cannot say I feel the same way now I

---

[96] *South Wales Echo*, 23 June 1942.
[97] *Parliamentary Debates* (Hansard) (5th series), vol. 390, 331 (3 June 1943); *Western Mail*, 9 May 1945.
[98] Inman, *Labour in the Munitions Industries*, p. 186.
[99] Letters of protest from Welsh female war workers appeared in the following: *Aberdare Leader*, 27 June 1942, 11 July 1942; *South Wales Evening Post*, 28 June 1943, 21 December 1943. A group of young war workers from the Llanelli district who had been transferred to Birmingham wrote to their local trades council in the autumn of 1943, to ask for assistance to be given to get them returned to Llanelli to work. NLW, Minor Deposit 1992, Deian R. Hopkin Papers, Llanelly Trades Council and Divisional Labour Party minutes, 14 October 1943.

am being sent to the Midlands, so I, like a lot more, will hope and pray that some Welshman will do something to prevent us going.[100]

As the number of transfers increased, Welsh trade unionists, public officials, politicians and nationalists stepped up their efforts to bring to an end the compulsory direction of the mobile female population. In April 1943 a deputation of Welsh MPs led by James Griffiths, the member for Llanelli, met Ernest Bevin and Oliver Lyttelton, the minister of production, to protest against the 'denudation' of the young Welsh population.[101] Strong opposition to the transference scheme was voiced at meetings convened during the year by the Monmouthshire Federation of TLCs, the Rhondda West Divisional Labour Party, the Merthyr Tydfil branch of the NUGMW, and the Aberdare TLC.[102] Representatives of the chambers of trade of the Merthyr Tydfil CB who met to discuss the matter in June 1943, voted unanimously to submit the following resolution to the relevant government ministries:

> this conference of traders in the Borough of Merthyr views with alarm the proposed transfer of our mobile labour to factories in England, particularly in view of the fact that many thousands that were transferred from the Borough in the years of the depression have been totally lost to us, and if this exodus is to be again repeated, it will mean the utter and complete disintegration of the life of the Borough.[103]

However, the strongest opposition to the movement of hundreds of Welsh females to factories in England came from members of the Welsh nationalist community. Addressing a meeting organized by Undeb Cymru Fydd at Shrewsbury in July 1943, Gwynfor Evans (who was elected vice-president of Plaid Genedlaethol Cymru the following month) successfully proposed a motion protesting against the removal of Welsh workers to

---

[100] *South Wales Evening Post*, 29 April 1943.
[101] Ibid., 12 April 1943.
[102] *South Wales Argus*, 5 July 1943; NLW, Minor Deposit 1995/62, Rhondda West Divisional Labour Party, Executive Committee minutes, 6 July 1943, 7 September 1943; *Merthyr Express*, 11 September 1943; SWCA, Aberdare TLC minutes, 2 September 1943, 7 October 1943.
[103] *Merthyr Express*, 26 June 1943. See also Merthyr Tydfil Town Public Library, Merthyr Tydfil CB minutes, 24 May 1943, 25 June 1943, 13 September 1943.

England – a policy which was, in his opinion, 'having a grievous effect on the life of Wales'.[104] Those members of Plaid Genedlaethol Cymru who were opposed in principle to the inclusion of Wales in 'this English war', launched a bitter attack on the 'deportation' scheme which they believed would deprive Wales of its future mothers and, thus, lead to 'the tragic destruction of our nation and the integral communities within it'.[105] As the Home Intelligence Unit of the Ministry of Information reported in April 1943, many Welsh people viewed the transfers 'as an almost systematic denudation of the nation of some of the essentials of its continued existence'.[106] Similar sentiments were expressed by sections of the Scottish community, for, like Wales, Scotland was also designated as a wartime 'supply region' and thousands of Scottish 'mobile' females were directed to war factories in the English Midlands.[107] Yet, despite the strong appeals launched by both Welsh and Scottish MPs in defence of the rights of their female war workers to remain in their own countries, the Ministry of Labour refused to reconsider its policy.[108] Speaking in Parliament in March 1942, Ernest Bevin made his position on the matter clear: 'I cannot treat this problem as Scottish, Welsh or English. I have to treat it as British. It is a British war and I have to look at the population of the country as a whole.'[109]

The attitude of the minister of labour appalled members of the Welsh nationalist community. Many gave vent to their frustrations in the Welsh-language and nationalist press where they accused the government of treating Welsh girls as 'salvage' by sending them away against their will on the 'slave trains' which took them on their journeys to the English industrial centres.[110] Since those

---

[104] *South Wales Evening Post*, 12 July 1943.

[105] *The Welsh Nationalist*, September 1943. Similar views were expressed in the following works written by members of the Welsh Nationalist Party: D. J. Davies and Noëlle Davies, *Wales . . . The Land of our Children? A Survey of Welsh Population Problems* (Caernarfon, 1942), p. 16; Wynne Samuel, *Transference Must Stop* (Caernarfon, 1943), p. 9.

[106] PRO, Inf 1/292.

[107] W. K. Hancock and M. M. Gowing, *British War Economy* (London, 1949), p. 284; Calder, *The People's War*, p. 333.

[108] See *Parliamentary Debates* (Hansard) (5th series), vol. 370, 354 (20 March 1941); vol. 377, 398 (22 January 1942); vol. 378, 884 (5 March 1942); vol. 388, 351 (1 April 1943).

[109] Ibid., vol. 378, 895 (5 March 1942).

[110] *Baner ac Amserau Cymru*, 18 February 1942; *The Welsh Nationalist*, December 1943; *Y Ddraig Goch*, XVIII, no. 1 (1944), 1. Some individuals expressed their anger in verse: see Gwilym R. Jones, 'Y Gaethglud' ('Captivity'), in Alan Llwyd and Elwyn Edwards (eds.), *Gwaedd y Lleiddiad* (Llandybïe, 1995), p. 108.

who failed to comply with their direction orders were liable to be prosecuted, Plaid Genedlaethol Cymru claimed that a 'halo of fear' surrounded the Welsh mobile female population.[111] Government sources were quick to refute such claims. A divisional officer employed by the Ministry of Labour in Wales pointed out in December 1943 that English and Scottish mobile females received the same treatment as the Welsh girls and were also liable to be directed to work in factories away from their homes.[112] Although many Welsh women appealed against their direction orders – mainly on the grounds that they should have been classed as 'immobile' rather than 'mobile' females[113] – it appears that only a very small proportion of those who were issued with their transfer papers actually refused to go. Of the handful of such women who appeared before the courts of south Wales on charges relating to their non-compliance with government orders, the majority received fines of less than £5.[114] The case of Katherine Foley of Plasmarl, Swansea, which was brought before Swansea police court in November 1943 and was championed by Plaid Genedlaethol Cymru, was clearly an exception. The stand taken by the 24-year-old, who had refused to obey a direction order to take up war work in Birmingham because she objected to working outside Wales, was condemned by Sir Marlay Samson, the stipendiary magistrate for Swansea, who imposed a fine of £25 or a month's imprisonment on the young woman.[115]

Having failed in their attempts to stem the flow of Welsh girls to the factories of England, members of the Welsh nationalist

---

[111] *The Welsh Nationalist*, May 1943.

[112] *Western Mail*, 18 December 1943.

[113] See ch. 3.

[114] For example, Alice Griffiths of Pontardawe was fined 40s. with costs for failing to comply with a direction to go to a factory in England, *The Welsh Nationalist*, August 1943; Queenie Webber of Pontnewydd was fined £3 for failing to obey an order to take up work at a Coventry factory, *Free Press of Monmouthshire*, 10 September 1943; Blodwen Lloyd of Hirwaun was fined £3 for refusing to work in a factory away from her home, *Aberdare Leader*, 27 November 1943; and Elizabeth Singh of Porth, Rhondda, was fined £5 for failing to comply with an order to work in a factory at Birmingham, *Porth Gazette and Rhondda Leader*, 4 March 1944.

[115] *South Wales Echo*, 17 November 1943; *South Wales Evening Post*, 17 November 1943; *Western Mail*, 18 November 1943; *The Welsh Nationalist*, December 1943. A collection started by Katherine's work colleagues at Tre-boeth, Swansea, raised enough money to pay her fine, while Plaid Genedlaethol Cymru paid her legal fees. NLW, Plaid Cymru Archives, M69.

community concentrated their efforts on safeguarding the social and moral welfare of the young women who found themselves placed in the 'alien' surroundings of English industrial centres. If, as many Welsh people claimed, the transfers involved 'a change not only of locality' but of a 'way of life', urgent measures needed to be taken in order to care for the Welsh girls who had been up-rooted from their home districts.[116] The moral and sexual dangers which the wartime removal of young women from their usual 'protective environments' might involve greatly concerned anxious parents and prompted calls for action to be taken to oversee the leisure activities of the exiled war workers.[117] After all, if Welsh girls were to be placed in hostels or lodgings with war workers and families whose social customs and moral values were regarded as being very different from their own, the assumption was that the consequences could prove disastrous. Although the residents of hostels were subject to tight regulations and close supervision by wardens and matrons, the communal atmosphere of these large, impersonal institutions did not lend itself to self-discipline and restraint. The evidence of a sixty-year-old male from Pen-coed, near Bridgend, who was a member of Mass-Observation's volunteer panel of observers, suggests that the female residents of the ROF and Land Army hostel situated near his home enjoyed a far greater measure of social freedom than the war workers who were billeted with local families. In his reply to a Mass-Observation directive on the drinking habits of young people in his area in May 1943, he reported that the young women who filled the pubs were 'not local girls, very few of whom have adopted the pub habit, but the girls imported to work at the factory' who resided at the hostel. He added that the war workers who lodged with local families were rarely seen in the public houses, for 'a good deal of the family discipline im-posed on them in their own homes by their own parents' was applied by their hosts.[118]

---

[116] PRO, Inf 1/292.

[117] Clearly, such fears were shared by the parents of transferred war workers and servicewomen from all parts of Britain. For a fuller exposition of this theme, see George Ryley Scott, *Sex Problems and Dangers in War-Time: A Book of Practical Advice for Men and Women on the Fighting and Home Fronts* (London, 1940), pp. ix, 39.

[118] M-O A, DR 3450, 'Report on drinking habits among young people in your area', May 1943.

The parents of exiled Welsh girls who had been billeted with English families hundreds of miles away from their homes were unlikely to draw much comfort from such observations, for the fact remained that their daughters had been directed to live and work among people whose social and moral standards they considered to be 'alien' to their own. The experience of one Welsh war worker who arrived at her digs in Birmingham in January 1944 only to find that her landlady had gone to Blackpool for the week, leaving the key to the house with her next-door neighbours and a note telling her to 'make herself at home', had no doubt served to confirm such prejudices.[119] The social problems which could arise from such situations had become immediately apparent to one Welsh resident of Birmingham. In a letter written to Undeb Cymru Fydd officials in October 1943, the Revd Idris Hopcyn of Handsworth drew attention to the fact that Welsh girls who were placed in lodgings with local families quickly adopted the customs and habits of their hosts, even though such behaviour would have been deemed unacceptable back home in Wales:

Er iddynt fod yn ddigon cysurus yn eu llety, yn fynych iawn, disgwylir iddynt fyned allan gyda'r nos. Nid oes angen pwysleisio'r perigl a gyfyd drwy hynny. Onid adwaenant deulu Cymreig yn y cylch, nid oes iddynt ond rhodio'r stryd neu fyned i'r sinema neu geisio diddanwch mewn lleoedd mwy amheus. Clywsom hefyd, fwy nag unwaith yn ddiweddar, am rai o'r teuluoedd a letya'r merched yn eu cymell i ddifod [*sic*] gyda hwy i dreulio'r hwyrnos yn y dafarn – heb lwyddo bob tro. Gwneir hyn, weithiau er mwyn eu gwneuthur yn gartrefol yn eu llety. (Mae barn y Canoldir am ferched yn diota yn wahanol i eiddo Cymru.)[120]

(Although they are comfortable enough in their lodgings, very often, they are expected to go out in the evenings. We need not stress the dangers which may consequently arise. Unless they know a Welsh family in the area, there is no option open to them but to stroll along the streets, visit the cinema or look for entertainment in more dubious places. We have also heard, on more than one occasion recently, that some of the families with whom the girls lodge, persuade them to go along with them to spend the evening in the public house – although they do not always succeed. This is sometimes done in an attempt to make the girls feel at home in their

[119] NLW, Undeb Cymru Fydd Papers (November 1960 Collection), 150.
[120] Ibid., 152.

lodgings. (The people of the Midlands hold very different opinions on female drinking from the Welsh.))

It was in the light of such evidence that Undeb Cymru Fydd resolved to take steps to ensure that adequate social and welfare services were made available to the young women conscripted from Wales. In May 1942 Undeb officials made several representations to the Ministry of Labour calling for special welfare officers to be appointed to take care of the Welsh girls who were called up for war service away from their homes, but the response from the ministry proved extremely disappointing. In contrast to the situation in Scotland, where the demands of Scottish nationalists for similar provision to be made in connection with their exiled female workers were met with the appointment of welfare workers, the Ministry of Labour paid little heed to the calls for such assistance to be provided for the Welsh girls.[121] Undeb Cymru Fydd decided to take matters into its own hands and, during the summer of 1942, three committees were set up in the north, the south-west and the south-east of Wales, to investigate the social problems which had arisen as a result of the compulsory direction of the female population. The findings of the three committees confirmed the worst fears of Undeb members, for it was reported that 'the sudden shift from country to town, and the sudden stretching – if not breaking – of old roots and old conventions, had caused a most unsatisfactory state of affairs, particularly in regard to social morality and religious belief.'[122]

The situation spurred Undeb Cymru Fydd into action, and in May 1943 a special Joint Committee comprising Undeb officials and representatives of the Welsh churches, the Young Women's Christian Association (YWCA), and the Welsh Temperance Union met to discuss how best to organize welfare services for the Welsh war workers who had been sent to England.[123] The work of the Joint Committee was supported purely by voluntary financial donations and generous contributions were received

[121] International Labour Office, *Transference of Labour in Great Britain* (Montreal, 1942), pp. 123–4; Calder, *The People's War*, p. 333.
[122] Jones, *A Bid for Unity*, p. 25.
[123] Undeb Cymru Fydd, *Undeb Cymru Fydd, 1939–1960* (Aberystwyth, 1960), pp. 8–10; NLW, Undeb Cymru Fydd Papers (1951 Collection), 259.

from members of the Welsh Nonconformist chapels, including those at Aberdare, Merthyr, Ferndale, Treherbert, Tredegar, Pontlotyn and Nant-y-moel in the industrial south.[124] Funds raised by the Joint Committee eventually supported the appointment of two full-time 'liaison' or 'welcoming officers' to work among the Welsh women who had been sent to the Midlands and to the south-east of England. Mair Rees Jones, a qualified social worker who took up her post as welcoming officer at Birmingham in January 1944, was able to build on the work already accomplished in the Midlands since July 1943 by Mai Roberts, the secretary of the YWCA in north Wales. In co-operation with members of local Welsh societies and the YWCA, Mai Roberts had helped to establish several 'welcoming committees' in the Birmingham, Coventry and Wolverhampton area.[125] The welcoming committees continued to work closely with Mair Rees Jones during 1944–5 to ensure that all Welsh war workers were presented with bilingual 'welcoming pamphlets' containing the names and addresses of local Welsh individuals, churches and societies on their arrival at the large train stations of the area.[126] A 'Welsh centre' was also opened in Birmingham in November 1944 under the auspices of the YWCA, in order to provide the Welsh war workers of the district with a central meeting-place.[127]

With the eventual co-operation of the Ministry of Labour and factory authorities, the welcoming officers also visited factories in their respective areas and addressed all new arrivals from Wales. Only a few months after commencing her work in the Midlands, Mair Rees Jones had visited forty-three factories in the region, while Emma Williams, the welcoming officer who took up her post in the south of England during 1944, was reported to have held meetings with the Welsh war workers who were being sent in increasing numbers to factories at Aylesbury, Banbury, High Wycombe, Luton, Oxford, Reading, Slough and Thame.[128] The

[124] NLW, Undeb Cymru Fydd Papers (April 1963 Collection), 226.
[125] Jones, *A Bid for Unity*, p. 26.
[126] *Western Mail*, 15 December 1943.
[127] Ibid., 6 November 1944. See also Idris Hopcyn, *Hanes Eglwys yr Annibynwyr Cymraeg, Wheeler Street, Birmingham, 1860–1960* (Maesteg, n.d.).
[128] Undeb Cymru Fydd, *Undeb Cymru Fydd*, pp. 12–13. A list of 'submissions of women transferred from Wales during November–December 1944' to factories in the south-east of England is to be found among the papers of Emma M. Williams, NLW, Undeb Cymru Fydd Papers (November 1960 Collection), 152.

welcoming officers also encouraged the leaders of factory societies and clubs to organize special events for the Welsh workers
who were, according to the testimony of several English factory
officials, '*without exception*, far more prone to homesickness than
the Scottish and Irish girls' ('Tystiai awdurdodau y ffatrïoedd *yn
ddieithriad* fod y Cymry yn fwy hiraethus o lawer na'r merched
o'r Alban neu'r Iwerddon').[129] The south Wales newspapers
reported several cases of Welsh girls who had returned home
from the English districts without official permission only days
after commencing their work at the factories. A nineteen-year-
old factory worker from Garndiffaith returned home from the
Midlands only a day after her arrival, complaining bitterly about
the unsatisfactory living arrangements. A girl from Robertstown,
Aberdare, was fined £4 for returning home from Coventry
after completing only one shift at a factory, while Mary Don-
ovan, a 22-year-old from Rhydfelen, near Pontypridd, was fined
10*s*. after leaving her employment at Wolverhampton without
permission.[130] Gwyneth Cull, a 21-year-old from Porth, was
sentenced to a month's imprisonment in November 1943 when
she defied a second direction order to take up war work at
Wolverhampton. Only a month earlier, Cull had been granted a
fortnight's remission by the home secretary on a prison sentence
she had received in September for leaving her work at an English
factory after only four days.[131]

   The opportunities which Undeb Cymru Fydd provided for
Welsh war workers to socialize together aimed to ease such
settlement problems while at the same time ensuring that Welsh
girls who were sent to England were 'kept to the Welsh way of
life'.[132] The notion that the women of Wales needed to be
protected from the subversive influences of their English host
families and fellow workers underlay much of the welfare work
carried out by the Joint Committee in the English industrial districts, and it was a theme voiced constantly throughout the war

---

[129] NLW, Undeb Cymru Fydd Papers (1951 Collection), 259; ibid. (November 1960 Collection), 152.
   [130] *Free Press of Monmouthshire*, 13 August 1943; *Aberdare Leader*, 2 October 1943; *Free Press and Rhondda Leader*, 21 August 1943.
   [131] *Free Press and Rhondda Leader*, 25 September 1943; *Rhondda Gazette*, 27 November 1943.
   [132] NLW, Undeb Cymru Fydd Papers (1951 Collection), 259; *Baner ac Amserau Cymru*, 26 April 1944.

by those who opposed the transfers. Indeed, the English factory workers alongside whom the exiled Welsh girls lived and worked, were often portrayed in the Welsh nationalist press as women of low moral standards who posed a serious threat to the superior character of the Welsh. Writing in *Y Ddraig Goch* in April 1941, Cathrin Daniel painted a grim picture of the type of working environment which awaited the Welsh girls who were sent to the factories of England:

> Yno, fe gyfarfyddant â merched trefi diwydiannol Lloegr. Nid oes yn y rhai hyn na diwylliant na moesoldeb. Fe fyddai wythnos o gymdeithas ffatri arfau Lloegr yn ddigon i sgubo Cymraesau cefn gwlad Cymru oddi ar eu traed. Yn ddiweddar iawn, gwelais ddisgrifiad mewn papur Saesneg o awyrgylch ffatri yn Lloegr lle gweithia merched yn unig. Testun beunyddiol y sgwrs yno oedd pleserau rhywiol a sut orau i'w mwynhau heb ganlyniadau.[133]

> (There, they will meet girls from the industrial towns of England. These women have no conception of culture or morality. A week spent in an English munitions factory will be enough to sweep the girls from rural Wales off their feet. Recently, in an English newspaper, I read a description of the atmosphere in a factory in England where only females are employed. The daily topic of conversation was sexual pleasure, and how best to enjoy it without consequences.)

D. J. Williams (1885–1970), a prominent Welsh-language writer and one of the founding members of Plaid Genedlaethol Cymru, took this 'nightmare vision' one step further in his short story 'Ceinwen', written and published in 1949, in which he traced the social and moral decline of a young Welsh girl who had been sent to work at a munitions factory at Dudley.[134] Set in 1943, the story is related by Jo, a young mother from Aber Rheidol in west Wales; she visits Ceinwen, her childhood friend, who has returned home from the English Midlands in poor health. From her sickbed, Ceinwen shares with Jo her unhappy experiences of life as an exiled war worker. She points out that 'things started to go wrong right at the beginning', when she was placed in a hostel among women whose language and behaviour she found shocking:

[133] Daniel, 'Ffarwel cartrefi Cymru', 3.
[134] D. J. Williams, *Storïau'r Tir Du* (Aberystwyth, 1949), pp. 79–114.

' 'Rwyt ti'n gweld, fe aeth pethe'n rong o'r start, rywfodd, wedi i fi orfod gadael Aber Rheidol,' meddai hi, gan ddechre ar ei stori:

'Mewn rhyw fath o hostel merched 'roedden ni yn aros yn Dudley, fel y gwedais i wrthot ti yn 'yn llythyron, – ugeiniau ohonon ni gyda'n gilydd, – merched o'r Sowth, lawer iawn ohonyn nhw, ond heb fawr o Gymraeg, – yn gymysg â'r merched o Saeson, wrth gwrs, wedi'u hanfon yno o bob man, fel ninne. 'Roedden nhw'n ferched digon neis yn'u ffordd am 'wn i, ond bod 'u hiaith nhw'n ofnadw i'nghlustie i, ar y cynta, nad oedd yn gyfarwydd â chlywed pethe o'r fath. 'Roedden ni'n gweithio orie maith, mewn gwaith afiach; a'r blitsis ac ambell ddamwain erchyll yn y sheds yn whalu nerfs dyn yn waeth wedyn.

'Y prif atyniad, wrth gwrs, oedd y tŷ tafarn – y tŷ tafarn a'i ole glas gwan, – a'r cwrw a'r dynion yno. 'Doedd yno fawr o siarad am ddim arall, – ond y pethe diweddar yn y sinema, weithie. 'Rown i'n teimlo fel brân o unig ynghanol y crowd; a fe fues bron â danto'n llwyr ar y cynta.'[135]

('You see, things started go wrong right at the beginning somehow, after I had to leave Aber Rheidol,' she said, starting on her story:

'We were staying in a sort of women's hostel in Dudley, as I told you in my letters, tens of us together, girls from the South, many of them, but few were Welsh-speaking, mixed with English girls, of course, who had been sent there from everywhere, like us. They were nice enough girls in their own way I suppose, but their language was terrible to my ears at first, not being used to hearing such things. We worked long hours, doing horrible work; and the blitz and the odd frightening accident in the sheds played havoc with your nerves.

'The main attraction, of course, was the public house – the public house with its weak blue light, – and the drink and the men inside. There wasn't much talk of anything else, except for the latest showings at the cinema sometimes. I felt as lonely as anything among the crowd; and I almost gave up completely at first.')

It is not long, however, before Ceinwen has adopted the social customs and moral standards of those around her, and her adulterous relationship with Stanley Fordson, a foreman at the factory, eventually leads to her downfall. The climax of the story is reached when Ceinwen reveals the nature of her illness to Jo: she is dying from a venereal disease which has already claimed the life of her illegitimate baby and, after spending the past few weeks at a special hospital and sanatorium in Dudley, she has come home to Aber Rheidol to die.

[135] Ibid., p. 92.

Essentially, this fictional account of the wretched experiences of an exiled Welsh war worker was a reworking of a familiar theme in Welsh-language writing: that of the Welsh girl's inevitable fall from grace in an urban, industrial and Anglicized society.[136] Torn from her friends and family and placed in an 'alien' environment, Ceinwen had quickly succumbed to the temptations and influences which surrounded her. As the following report of an address delivered by Mair Rees Jones at a factory near Rugby in March 1944 reveals, the welfare work carried out by Undeb Cymru Fydd in the English districts during the war clearly aimed to protect Welsh girls from a similar fate:

> [Mair Rees Jones] appealed to the young girls present to remember their responsibilities and duty to Wales. The moral and educational standards are recognised as being higher than those of many countries but we must remember that and make every endeavour to uphold that reputation by living a pure, clean life. By living a loose life we not only lose our most precious possession in life, our character, but we also lower the standard of our country. I well know the temptations that beset young girls in a town like this and I know the courage and strength of mind needed to lead a good life but if we attend a centre such as the one we hope will start as a result of this meeting, we will gain strength from fellowship with each other and fellowship with God.[137]

By November 1944, in response to the demands of Mair Rees Jones for greater assistance to be given with the provision of moral and spiritual guidance to Welsh workers in the Midlands, Undeb Cymru Fydd had appointed the Revd D. Jones Davies of Wrexham to serve as chaplain at Coventry, where a thousand transferred workers were said to reside in seventeen hostels by that time. Appeals for more chaplains to be sent to neighbouring industrial districts fell on deaf ears, however, and Davies soon found himself ministering to the needs of war workers further afield at Birmingham, Leamington Spa, Leicester, Redditch, Rugby, Warwick and Wolverhampton.[138] While it remains difficult to assess accurately how many Welsh women took

---

[136] For example, see the following short stories and essays: 'Y Fagdalen o Gymru', *Aberdare Leader*, 3 and 10 March 1917; H. Griffith, 'Ymgom rhwng dwy ferch', *Y Gymraes*, XXX, no. 352 (1926), 12–13; A. E. Hughes, 'Ymgom: cartrefi cysegredig', *Y Gymraes*, XXI, no. 362 (1926), 170–1.

[137] NLW, Undeb Cymru Fydd Papers (November 1960 Collection), 151.

[138] Undeb Cymru Fydd, *Undeb Cymru Fydd*, pp. 13–14.

advantage of the welfare and recreational services provided by Undeb Cymru Fydd and the Welsh chapels and societies in the English districts, it would appear that those who chose to participate in such activities took great comfort from the meetings.[139] The parents of the exiled Welsh girls were also extremely appreciative of the work carried out by the welcoming officers and their committees. One mother from Broughton in Flintshire wrote to Undeb officials to express her thanks for the provisions which had been made to care for her daughter:

> I don't know how to thank you and your Welsh club for taking the trouble of looking after the Welsh girls who are working so far away from there [*sic*] homes as it is a big worry to us parents when they have been sent to large towns and have not been away from there [*sic*] home . . . With Iris, she is a senceable [*sic*] girl and is old enough to look after herself. But we never know in such a big place or town and that why [*sic*] I feel my self contended [*sic*] and her father as there is such a club as you'rs [*sic*] to look after our girls, I say thanks again.[140]

Occasionally, however, the welcoming officers were called upon to deal with situations which they would no doubt have hoped their work could have prevented. During 1944 Mair Rees Jones assisted five young Welsh girls at Wolverhampton and Coventry who had fallen pregnant, one of whom had allegedly had a relationship with a married RAF officer who denied all responsibility for the child.[141] Had Mair Rees Jones been appointed to her post some months earlier, it is possible that she would also have been able to help the 23-year-old war worker from Miskin, near Llantrisant, who was charged with concealing the birth of her illegitimate child at Birmingham in January 1944. The young woman had hidden the stillborn baby under her bed for two days before burying the body on wasteland.[142]

While it could be argued that the welfare work carried out by Undeb Cymru Fydd played some part in ensuring that such incidents were extremely rare, the fact remains that the

---

overwhelming majority of the thousands of Welsh girls who were directed to war work in the English industrial towns did not drift into the life of moral turpitude which some prominent nationalists envisaged. Gladys Perrie Hopkin Morris, chair of the South Wales Advisory Committee of the Ministry of Labour, who was given special permission by the Welfare Department of the ministry to report on the settlement of Welsh girls in the Midlands during the spring of 1944, failed to find any evidence to justify the sensationalist reports of immorality and vice which had been circulated in the Welsh nationalist press.[143] In an article penned in April 1944 following several visits to factories where Welsh girls were employed, she reassured Welsh parents that conditions in the English factories and towns were no worse than those which could be found in the industrial and urban districts of Wales:

> To mothers with daughters of 20, press statements about moral and social conditions in factory areas cause deep anxiety. Undesirable happenings and ways of life can be seen any night of the week in Cardiff – but that is not a reflection of the real life of Cardiff.
>
> Ways of life and social conditions and conventions may be different in English factory areas but the vast majority of the English girls who work and live there are as jealous of the high standard of their own life as are the girls sent there from Wales. There are poor types of individuals among the four nationalities, but they are in the minority.[144]

These words were unlikely to bring much comfort to Welsh parents who had heard horrifying tales of the kind of lifestyle led by the 'poor types' who seemed to have found their way into war factories on both sides of Offa's Dyke. Indeed, the munitions factories of Britain were depicted in some quarters as dens of iniquity, where the female workers indulged in all manner of debauchery and revelry. In July 1941 the Home Intelligence Unit of the Ministry of Information reported that mothers were preventing their daughters from entering the munitions factories 'on the grounds that immorality goes on there', while Mass-

---

[143] See *Western Mail*, 11–13 April 1944, for three articles compiled by Gladys Perrie Hopkin Morris OBE (wife of Rhys Hopkin Morris, regional director of the BBC in Wales, 1936–45), following her visit to the Midlands.
[144] Ibid., 13 April 1944.

Observation and the Wartime Social Survey investigators found that potential recruits had been similarly dissuaded from taking up factory employment.[145] Such expressions of opposition to munitions work were particularly strong in those areas where there was no tradition of female industrial employment.[146] Celia Fremlin, the Mass-Observation investigator who spent a short period during 1942 working at a radar equipment factory in Gloucestershire, noted that many local residents were of the opinion that 'factory workers are a very low class of people; that the girls are "not nice"; that it is a low sort of occupation altogether'.[147] Some of the women who worked at the plant admitted that both they and their families had had grave misgivings about entering factory employment. The husband of one factory worker had told his wife that 'it would degrade him' if she were to take up industrial work, while another woman had faced similar opposition from her son, who was unhappy that his mother would be working alongside the 'terrible types' whom he associated with factory work.[148]

Similar opinions were held in south Wales. The investigators who conducted the *Beveridge Manpower Survey* in the region during 1940, reported that in the commercial coastal towns of Cardiff, Penarth and Newport, 'where there is a more complex social stratification . . . factory work was felt to be beneath the dignity of some women, such as unemployed and unskilled clerks and shop assistants and women at present unoccupied.'[149] Women from the mining valleys had expressed a similar disinclination

[145] PRO, Inf 1/292; Penny Summerfield and Nicole Crockett, ' "You weren't taught that with the welding": lessons in sexuality in the Second World War', *Women's History Review*, 1, no. 3 (1992), 439.

[146] M-O A, FR 533, 'Women and the war effort', December 1940; Summerfield, 'Women workers in the Second World War', p. 86.

[147] Mass-Observation, *War Factory*, p. 16.

[148] Ibid., p. 152.

[149] *Beveridge Manpower Survey*, 1940. A Mass-Observation diarist who worked as a clerk at the parcel office of the Great Western Railway at Newport, made the following entry in her diary in July 1942: 'The social status of clerks is always insisted upon and we are the clerks, they are the uniformed staff. Recently a new male forced two female clerks in my office, four of us, to queue up for our pay-checks [*sic*] outside the office in what was almost the public road. We were all rather annoyed by this as it did not seem at all necessary and no other of the two office women had to do so. This at last came to the ears of the senior clerk who was outraged. "Making our girls queue up like a lot of factory girls!" We don't queue any more. Apparently he'll stop us queuing if he has to go to Paddington about it. What amused me was the slur on factory girls. Not quite true that if I were to volunteer for factory work I would be considered very much beyond the pale.' M-O A, Diary 5460, 26 July 1942.

towards factory employment. Writing in 1944, Councillor Iorwerth Thomas noted that the entry of Rhondda women into the war factories had been 'the occasion for critical observations and cynical comment. The superior females looked down their noses upon these munition girls with an air of contempt and an attitude of disdain.'[150] The oral evidence of women who were employed as munitions workers at the war factories of south Wales supports such views. In an interview conducted during the early 1980s, a native of the Afan valley (b. 1924) remarked that her parents had been unwilling to allow her to enter Bridgend ROF 'because they said you mixed with ruffians there', while a female war worker from the Ogmore and Garw district, whose oral recollections were published in 1992, maintained that women were regarded as 'common if they went to the factory to work'.[151]

Although many thousands of Welsh women – including those who may have regarded themselves as 'superior' or 'dignified' – were eventually drawn into the war factories of south Wales, such prejudiced views of female factory workers as women of 'rough' character and low moral standards remained. Rumours that the government was proposing to allow some factories to sell alcohol in their canteens and had installed contraceptive vending-machines in others, merely served to reinforce people's low opinion of the factory and its workforce.[152] At their annual meeting held at Siloah chapel, Tredegar, in May 1942, members of the Monmouthshire Baptist Association urged the government to reconsider its decision to sell alcohol on factory premises and, thus, save local munitions girls from 'going to the devil'.[153] Reports of the misdemeanours committed by gangs of female munitions workers within and outside the factory walls (which included fist-fighting, petty thieving, displaying 'indecent photographs' and using 'vile' language) also played their part in perpetuating the image of the factory workers as coarse, vulgar and

[150] *Porth Gazette and Rhondda Leader*, 16 September 1944.
[151] Beth Thomas, 'Accounting for language shift in a south Wales mining community', *Cardiff Working Papers in Welsh Linguistics*, no. 5 (1987), 63; evidence of Kitty Bishop in Davies (ed.), *The Valleys Autobiography*, p. 73.
[152] NLW, MS 16594D, 11 November 1941; *Baner ac Amserau Cymru*, 3 December 1941, 11 February 1942; PRO, Inf 1/292; T. Trefor Jones, *Iechyd yng Nghymru* (Liverpool, 1946), p. 52; *Free Press of Monmouthshire*, 30 January 1942.
[153] *Western Mail*, 27 May 1942; *Free Press of Monmouthshire*, 29 May 1942, 20 November 1942.

'loose' women.[154] At Aberdare 'wild stories' were said to be circulating in the area regarding the behaviour of some of the munitions girls, while at Blaina, where the female war workers were accused 'in order of gravity' of 'too much spending, too much drinking' and 'too great sexual promiscuity', Mollie Tarrant heard many tales concerning the improper behaviour of the females who travelled on the 'Budgie trains' to and from the factories: 'All kinds of stories are attached to these trains, all kinds of things are supposed to happen in them. Some people are amused by the stories, others are shocked and the whole subject arouses lively curiosity.'[155] The comments of a married man who worked at a munitions factory in the area and travelled daily on the 'Budgie train' gave some indication of the nature of such stories: 'There are young women in this street going for the same train as I do. Do you know, that if I was to walk down the street two days running with one of them somebody would be coming and saying to my wife, "D'you know your husband's got a budgie?"'[156]

Given that very few of the men and women of south Wales had the opportunity of working alongside members of the opposite sex, it was perhaps not surprising that their moral and sexual behaviour became the focus of such intense public scrutiny. Two south Wales men who were members of Mass-Observation's panel of 'volunteers' put forward their own observations on the impact which factory employment had had on relations between local men and women in their replies to a directive in April 1944. One of the observers, a 38-year-old accountant from Tredegar, noted that male and female factory workers who had been 'thrown together at work' also tended to make 'casual contacts' outside working hours.[157] The second

---

[154] *South Wales Echo*, 12 July 1941; *Glamorgan Gazette*, 18 July 1941; *Caerphilly Journal*, 4 July 1942; *Aberdare Leader*, 7 August 1943; *Free Press of Monmouthshire*, 21 May 1943, 6 July 1945, 21 December 1945.

[155] *Aberdare Leader*, 14 February 1942; M-O A, FR 1498, 'Blaina', pp. 102–3, 106–7. See also Brian Roberts, 'The "budgie train": women and wartime munitions work in a mining valley', *Llafur*, 7, nos. 3 and 4 (1998–9), 143–52.

[156] M-O A, FR 1498, 'Blaina', p. 107.

[157] M-O A, DR 3528, 'Opinions on sexual morality in recent years, changing standards etc.', April 1944. During a case heard at Pontypool Sessions in 1945, when a married woman summoned her philandering husband on the grounds of desertion, the fact that he came in daily contact with women in the factory where he worked was remarked on. According to the husband, it was 'only natural' for him to strike up associations with his female colleagues when he met them outside the workplace. *Free Press of Monmouthshire*, 27 April 1945.

observer, a county councillor and businessman from Pen-coed who was reported to be in his sixties, was rather more forthright in his opinions when he remarked on the frequency with which 'married men working in the factories with women, openly form associations and, apart from an occasional "flare-up", no one takes the trouble to even talk about it'.[158] Similar remarks were made by several of the former employees of Bridgend ROF who were interviewed during the course of this study.[159] As one respondent recalled,

> It [the ROF] was a funny place . . . there was some single men there, you know, but a hell of a lot of the married ones carried on down there. All the women there see, and the men there, they must have thought they were something special in these white jackets, white trousers and a white little cap! I mean, they were thrown together for hours and hours see, there was quite a lot of hanky-panky, if you know what I mean, going on there![160]

Newspaper reports of local court cases in which female factory workers summonsed married male colleagues in respect of their illegitimate children – some of whom were said to have been conceived on the factory premises – provide further evidence of the nature of the relations formed between some men and women at the workplace.[161]

More often than not, however, it was the female war workers who stood accused of instigating such illicit relationships. One 'Disgusted Wife', whose husband may well have conducted his own extramarital affair during working hours, wrote to the *South Wales Echo* in September 1943 to express her outrage at the conduct of the 'certain class of women' who could be found in the factories 'throwing themselves at other women's husbands'.[162] In reality, however, it appears that young female workers were far more likely to be troubled by the unwanted attention and sexual advances of male colleagues who were

---

[158] M-O A, DR 3450.
[159] Evidence of Respondents 1, 4, 5, 6, 18 and 20.
[160] Evidence of Respondent 6.
[161] *The Rhondda Leader*, 14 March 1942; *South Wales Echo*, 11 March 1946, 29 May 1946.
[162] *South Wales Echo*, 9 September 1943.

usually their superiors both in terms of age and occupational status and, more often than not, were married men.[163]

Although female members of the armed forces were subject to a similar body of criticism regarding their moral and sexual behaviour, it is clear that female factory workers, the majority of whom came from more lowly social and economic backgrounds, were also regarded as women of lower moral standards.[164] In his report before the annual licensing sessions at Cardiff in February 1942, James A. Wilson, the chief constable, noted that the behaviour of the young female munitions workers who frequented the hostelries of the city contrasted sharply with the 'exemplary' conduct of the servicewomen who exercised 'commendable self-control' during their leisure hours.[165] The intemperance of the female war workers was clearly not the only aspect of their behaviour which concerned the chief constable and other local social and moral leaders. In March 1943 representatives of the Cardiff Police Court and Rescue Mission expressed their anxieties regarding the moral welfare of young women who became 'unduly excited and befuddled' as a result of drinking alcohol and, consequently, 'lost control' of themselves and 'indulged in immodest and immoral behaviour'.[166] Similarly, at Bridgend in February 1944 local magistrates heard evidence that the young munitions girls of the town were drinking 'to such an extent as to be quite irrational or irresponsible'.[167] In his report before the Bridgend licensing sessions the following year, Police Superintendent William C. May drew attention to the problems which had arisen in the public houses of the town as a result of such disorderly conduct:

[163] Evidence of Respondents 1, 5 and 18. See also the short story based on the experiences of night-shift workers at an ordnance factory in south Wales where Jeff, a married man, is depicted as the 'Casanova' of the works and preys on the 'more susceptible girls'. Idris Williams, 'The sleepers awake', in Davies Aberpennar (ed.), '*Look You': A Miscellany Concerning Wales* (Caernarfon, 1948), pp. 14–17.

[164] Evidence of Respondents 4 and 5. The character and moral conduct of female members of the armed forces were sternly defended in parliament by Ernest Bevin, the minister of labour, see *Parliamentary Debates* (Hansard) (5th series), vol. 376, 1574–5 (10 December 1941); and in a government report of 1942 by Violet Markham: PP 1941–2 (IV, Cmd. 6384), *Report of the Committee on Amenities and Welfare Conditions in the Three Women's Services*, pp. 49–51. There is no evidence, however, that any prominent government officials made similar public representations in defence of the female factory workers.

[165] GRO, City of Cardiff licensing sessions minutes, 6 February 1942.

[166] *Western Mail*, 27 March 1943.

[167] *Glamorgan Gazette*, 11 February 1944.

it is not uncommon to see women sitting in the public bars with the men, consuming pints and half pints of beer. The mixing of the sexes in drinking rooms draws a certain class of custom, and there is a danger of reducing public houses from being reputable places of recreation to haunts and hunting grounds of sharks and loose women, whose business consists of exploiting the follies and weaknesses of the unsuspecting.[168]

Such critical observations on the behaviour of the 'good-time girls' and 'loose women' of south Wales – who were usually identified as munitions workers – became central to the public debate which raged throughout the war concerning changing standards in sexual morality and the consequent increase in illegitimacy and adultery.[169] The six Mass-Observation 'volunteers' from south Wales who expressed their opinions on such matters in April 1944 were agreed that there had been a definite loosening of moral standards since the outbreak of the war, and several of them cited examples of the 'lax' moral behaviour exhibited by members of the local female population as evidence of the 'steady decline in moral outlook' among the people of the region.[170] One male observer from the Pen-coed area claimed that married women with husbands in the forces 'openly and blatantly co-habit with men who are left', while 'girls in their teens associate with men stationed in the district and no one apparently cares a hoot about it'.[171] A civil servant in his early twenties who hailed from nearby Bridgend, was equally outspoken in his criticism of the conduct of the young women of the district:

no longer is the woman who prostitutes herself shunned as a social outcast – maybe lewd remarks are made – but this is becoming the accepted thing. I have known 'firewatching' used as an excuse for absence from home for a

---

[168] Ibid., 9 February 1945.
[169] See the following for comment on the 'slackening' of sexual mores in the region: Gwenan Jones, 'Purdeb – gwir a gau', *Yr Efrydydd*, IX, no. 5 (1944), 13–18; Cardiff Central Library, *Annual Report of the Cardiff Medical Officer of Health, 1944* (Cardiff, 1945), p. 40; *Glamorgan County Times*, 9 November 1940; *Aberdare Leader*, 8 February 1941; *Glamorgan Advertiser*, 1 August 1941; *Caerphilly Journal*, 4 July 1942, 30 January 1943; *Merthyr Express*, 14 March 1942, 12 December 1942, 6 February 1943, 8 and 15 July 1944; *Western Mail*, 27 March 1943; *South Wales Echo*, 6 and 8 September 1943; *Rhondda Gazette*, 11 September 1943.
[170] M-O A, DR 2678, 3137, 3419, 3450, 3527, 3528, 'Opinions on sexual morality in recent years, changing standards etc.', April 1944.
[171] Ibid., DR 3450.

night and the absence of one or both parents has resulted in a lessening in home control. I would think that it is a case of young women are growing up [*sic*] to accept a lower standard of sexual morality than say even after the first year of war.[172]

Significantly, however, the men who consented to such sexual relationships were rarely criticized. Writing in December 1943, the columnist 'Aberdarian', who contributed a weekly article to the *Aberdare Leader*, could find little fault with the men who succumbed to the charms of the young 'temptresses' of the town and merely appealed to local parents to exercise greater control over their wayward daughters: 'It is no use blaming Servicemen when there is trouble. Girls – especially young ones who make themselves look older than they are – are too often the mischief makers and there is need for strict supervision by parents.'[173] Reports that the young girls of Llanelli 'could be seen absolutely throwing themselves at members of the Forces and other men' every night of the week generated a similar response from local residents.[174] The defiant conduct of these young, headstrong females, who were portrayed as relentlessly pursuing and harassing soldiers, was seen to present a direct challenge to the accepted norms of female sexual behaviour and, in the opinion of many social commentators and moralists, immediate action was required to control such 'deviant' behaviour.[175]

The arrival of American troops on Welsh soil in 1942 expedited such demands.[176] By December 1943 nearly 21,500 American soldiers were stationed at camps in Glamorgan and

---

[172] Ibid., DR 3527.

[173] *Aberdare Leader*, 11 December 1943.

[174] *Western Mail*, 27 March 1943; *Llanelly and County Guardian*, 1 and 8 April 1943. The question of the 'morality of young girls with the soldiers' was raised at a meeting of the Llanelly and District Trades Council and Divisional Labour Party in May 1944. The minutes of the meeting record that a 'long and interesting discussion ensued on the whole position and it was agreed that the matters shall be discreetly raised in committees'. NLW, Deian Hopkin Papers, Llanelly Trades Council and Divisional Labour Party minutes, 11 May 1944.

[175] Parallels may be drawn with the situation which arose during the First World War, when fears that the young women of Britain had been gripped by a wave of sexual excitement – 'khaki fever' – led to demands for measures to be taken to control their sexual behaviour. See Angela Woollacott, ' "Khaki fever" and its control: gender, class, age and sexual morality on the British homefront in the First World War', *Journal of Contemporary History*, 29, no. 2 (1994), 325–47.

[176] See Sonya O. Rose, 'Girls and GIs: race, sex, and diplomacy in Second World War Britain', *The International History Review*, XIX, no. 1 (1997), 146–60.

Monmouthshire and, by the following April, their numbers had increased to 48,524.[177] With their 'Hollywood' accents and fine serge uniforms, and bearing gifts of chocolate, tinned fruit, cigarettes and nylon stockings, the well-paid 'Yanks' immediately won the hearts of the women of south Wales.[178] Indeed, in reply to the social survey questionnaire distributed throughout Wales by Undeb Cymru Fydd in December 1943, one respondent from the Hengoed and Ystradmynach area in the Rhymney valley claimed that 'the Yanks' had become one of the most popular wartime attractions in the district![179] The innocent fascination which the 'Yanks' held for the majority of Welsh females was overshadowed, however, by reports that gangs of 'good-time girls' – defined by the official war historians as 'semi-prostitutes' who 'thrived on the presence of well-paid servicemen from Overseas'[180] – travelled the country hounding American troops. At the Maindy Barracks, Cardiff, where hundreds of black soldiers were stationed, the problem was reported to have escalated beyond all control by 1945 as crowds of 'girl tramps' and 'harpies' swarmed around the camp.[181]

A possible solution to the problem lay in the appointment of female police officers with powers to interrogate women and the authority to clear from the streets those who behaved in a socially unacceptable manner. The Welsh MPs were keen proponents of such a scheme. In May 1943, when a deputation representing the Welsh Parliamentary Party met the home secretary to discuss the problem of drinking among young

---

[177] David Reynolds, *Rich Relations: The American Occupation of Britain, 1942–1945* (London, 1995), pp. 110–11.

[178] Evidence of Respondents 6, 15 and 16. See also the evidence of a Welsh female ATS volunteer quoted in Juliet Gardiner, *'Over Here': The G.I.'s in Wartime Britain* (London, 1992), p. 53.

[179] NLW, Undeb Cymru Fydd Papers (November 1960 Collection), 165.

[180] Ferguson and Fitzgerald, *Studies in the Social Services*, p. 95; PRO, Inf/292.

[181] *South Wales Echo*, 12, 15, 17, 20 and 22 September 1945; *Western Mail*, 12 September 1945. Local residents were greatly aggrieved by this situation and it is clear that many looked forward to the removal of black American servicemen from the district. The following message was delivered to the soldiers in a cartoon by J. C. Walker entitled 'Letter to a coloured ally', which appeared in the local press in September 1945: 'Dear Coloured Ally, Many Cardiff residents a few years ago would have welcomed your presence had the "Beasts of Belsen" shown up on the horizon but as such a possibility has passed a few grateful citizens would like to show their hospitality by removing you to a camp in the wilderness . . . Soon, very soon, I trust a ship will take you home to a climate more in keeping with your complexion . . . [where] maidens of your own race will be wanting to steal your hearts instead of your money.' *South Wales Echo*, 20 September 1945.

people, they impressed on him the urgent need to appoint female police officers in areas where large numbers of young women were employed in war factories, as a means to counter female intemperance and the associated problems of prostitution and venereal disease.[182]

In south Wales, as in many other parts of Britain, a sharp increase in reported cases of venereal diseases (notably syphilis and gonorrhoea) had been recorded since the outbreak of the war.[183] Often referred to as 'the camp-follower of war', the incidence of venereal disease was reported to be particularly high in areas where large numbers of troops were stationed, such as Cardiff, Porthcawl and Bridgend.[184] From late 1942 onwards, in accordance with Ministry of Health guidelines, local authorities were charged with a responsibility to take immediate action in the matter, and a subject which had previously been regarded as strictly taboo was given much public exposure in 'VD Propaganda' campaigns.[185] In addition to organizing lectures and films which aimed to increase public awareness of the problem, the Welsh local authorities held public meetings and conferences where residents, councillors and medical officers of health came together to consider what steps should be taken to halt the spread of infectious diseases. Significantly, however, while discussions at such meetings usually centred upon the importance of 'safeguarding' the troops from the dangers of infection by restricting

[182] *Western Mail*, 26 May 1943. The deputation consisted of Megan Lloyd George, MP for Anglesey, D. O. Evans, MP for Cardiganshire, and James Griffiths, MP for Llanelli. This view was shared by the Cardiff VD almoner and social worker, see Cardiff Central Library, *Annual Report of the Cardiff Medical Officer of Health, 1944*, p. 32. Similar motives lay behind the movement to appoint females to serve as police officers in certain parts of Britain during the First World War; see Woollacott, ' "Khaki fever" and its control', 333–40; Philippa Levine, ' "Walking the streets in a way no decent woman should": women police in World War I', *Journal of Modern History*, 66, no. 1 (1994), 34–78.

[183] PP 1941–2 (IV, Cmd. 6340), *Ministry of Health, Summary Report for the period 1 April 1939–31 March 1941*, p. 7; E. Wyn Jones, *Yr Afiechydon Gwenerol a Dirwest: Rhai Agweddau Meddygol* (Liverpool, 1943), p. 3.

[184] Sydney M. Laird, *Venereal Disease in Britain* (Harmondsworth, 1943), p. 33. For evidence of the increased incidence of venereal disease in these districts, see Cardiff Central Library, *Annual Report of the Cardiff Medical Officer of Health, 1941*, p. v; *Annual Report of the Cardiff Medical Officer of Health, 1945*, pp. 36–7; GRO, Bridgend UDC minutes, 17 June 1941; Porthcawl UDC minutes, 25 January 1943.

[185] For the reaction of the residents of Newport to the VD propaganda campaign launched in their area, see M-O A, TC 1, 'Sexual behaviour', Box 1, File G.

the movements of the local female population,[186] there was rarely any suggestion that male members of the armed forces should be subjected to similar limitations on their social and sexual freedoms in order to protect local women.[187]

Stern measures were eventually taken to deal with the female offenders. Women who were found 'loitering' near or trespassing on US army premises were immediately arrested and, having been brought before local magistrates, they were usually imprisoned for their crimes.[188] Four 'girl pests', all of whom had previously served terms of imprisonment for trespassing on US army property, were brought before magistrates at Penarth on similar charges in April 1945, when they received the maximum sentence of six months' imprisonment.[189] The evidence which was put forward during several of the court cases held in south Wales attested to the sexual intentions of the perpetrators. An eighteen-year-old girl from Llanelli, who was sentenced to two months' imprisonment in September 1944 for loitering near premises occupied by American soldiers, had been found along with three other girls 'in various stages of undress' inside a disused aeroplane crate. Similarly, two nineteen-year-old girls from Gilfach-goch, who received the same prison sentence for trespassing in October 1944, were reported to have been wearing no underclothing when they were discovered in the company of two American soldiers at a US Army camp.[190] Older and even married women were among those who were brought

[186] *Western Mail*, 24 February 1941, 15 September 1943; GRO, Bridgend UDC minutes, 17 June 1941. See also the poster used as part of the Ministry of Health's VD propaganda campaign, *c*.1943–4, reproduced in Raynes Minns, *Bombers and Mash: The Domestic Front, 1939–45* (London, 1980), p. 177, which warned the male population of the dangers posed to the health of the nation by the 'easy' girlfriend who 'spreads Syphilis and Gonorrhoea, which unless properly treated may result in blindness, insanity, paralysis, premature death'.

[187] One notable exception was the suggestion by a Miss M. A. Williams of Llanelli that local girls should be 'protected' from the unwanted advances of troops. However, her remark drew a swift response from a local newspaper columnist who argued that it was the soldiers who desperately needed protecting from members of the female population. *Llanelly and County Guardian*, 8 April 1943.

[188] See the following for reports of cases which were brought before the south Wales courts: *Free Press of Monmouthshire*, 7 April 1944, 13 October 1944, 8 December 1944, 2 February 1945, 30 March 1945; *Glamorgan Advertiser*, 9 June 1944, 2 March 1945, 9 and 23 March 1945; *Porth Gazette and Rhondda Leader*, 1 April 1944; *South Wales Echo*, 28 August 1944, 7 and 14 October 1944, 12 and 24 February 1945, 11 June 1945, 13 September 1945.

[189] *South Wales Echo*, 25 April 1945.

[190] *Glamorgan Advertiser*, 22 September 1944, 26 October 1944.

before the south Wales courts charged with trespass or other offences related to their relationships with American soldiers.[191] A married woman from Merthyr Tydfil was sentenced to six months' imprisonment by local magistrates in July 1944 for 'neglecting and abandoning' her two young children while she went out drinking with American soldiers.[192] The following June a married woman and mother of five children was sentenced to two months' imprisonment at Barry police court for trespassing at a camp for black American soldiers.[193]

Although the majority of the police authorities of south Wales supported the principle of imposing curfews and controls on the local female population, not all were agreed that women police officers should be appointed to enforce such measures. Even at Newport and Swansea, where the borough constabularies first appointed females in 1940–1, the women officers rarely patrolled the streets, and were employed mainly as auxiliaries to assist in administrative and communication work in order to relieve men for outside duties.[194] At Merthyr Tydfil and Cardiff, however, the chief constables vehemently opposed suggestions that females should join their police forces in any capacity.[195] James A. Wilson, the chief constable of Cardiff, was keen to protect females from the dark and seedy underworld of crime and immorality, and he maintained that the 'forceful character' of the duties which female officers would be expected to perform were 'beyond the physical capacity of women police and they were unsuitable for it'.[196] Even after Herbert Morrison, the home secretary, had ruled in April 1944 that police forces should ensure an adequate number of female officers in order to 'check

---

[191] An American soldier who was stationed in Wales during the war recalled that 'it was no uncommon thing for a guy to get propositioned three times in an evening. We never got over how easy it was to make it with the girls, and not just the single ones either.' Gardiner, *'Over Here'*, p. 119.

[192] *Merthyr Express*, 15 July 1944.

[193] *South Wales Echo*, 11 June 1945.

[194] Phyllis Gamble (who had two years' experience in the metropolitan force), and Joan Bartlett, the two females appointed at Newport in 1940–1, were the first women to be appointed to full-time police work in Wales. *Western Mail*, 24 February 1941; *South Wales Echo*, 30 August 1941. See also Walter William Hunt, *To Guard My People: An Account of the Origin and History of the Swansea Police* (Swansea, 1957), p. 89; evidence of V. Harvey in Verrill-Rhys and Beddoe (eds.), *Parachutes and Petticoats*, pp. 84–5; PP 1945–6 (XIV), *Report of His Majesty's Inspectors of Constabulary for the year ended 29th September 1945*, pp. 18–21.

[195] *Merthyr Express*, 14 September 1940, 15 April 1944; *Western Mail*, 7 December 1943, 13 and 18 January 1944.

[196] *Western Mail*, 13 January 1944.

misbehaviour which is likely to give rise to public scandals and to maintain standards of order and decorum among certain young British girls and women', Wilson reiterated his contention that the employment of female police officers in the city of Cardiff was not justified.[197]

The chief constable of Cardiff was also extremely unwilling to make any changes to the gendered nature of police work on the basis of what he regarded as purely 'temporary' wartime needs. In his report before the Cardiff licensing sessions in February 1944, he expressed his belief that the increase in female patrons in the public houses of the city was 'only a war-time phase', and that with the resumption of peacetime conditions, the women of Cardiff would stop their 'excessive and promiscuous drinking' and revert to leading more orderly and respectable lives.[198] Similar sentiments had been voiced a year earlier by Llewellyn Jones, the chairman of the Bridgend magistrates. Speaking at the Bridgend annual licensing sessions in February 1943, Jones remarked that 'it was not a good augury for the future mother-hood and happiness in the homes' to see the young women of the town 'drinking as freely as any man of mature age', but he expressed his hope that 'when things become normal and high wages have been reduced, they will amend their ways'.[199]

The notion that many of the social and sexual problems facing the communities of wartime south Wales would disappear when life returned to 'normal' and women went back to their homes became a familiar theme in the misogynist rhetoric of the Second World War and served as a useful weapon in the hands of those who despaired of the social and economic changes which war had initiated in the lives of the Welsh female population. As Joan W. Scott has argued, this representation of the war as 'the

---

[197] Ibid., 11 May 1944.

[198] GRO, City of Cardiff licensing sessions minutes, 4 February 1944.

[199] *Glamorgan Gazette*, 12 February 1943. On the perceived association between high wages and immorality, it is interesting to compare the findings of G. H. Armbruster, an American sociologist who carried out research in the Blaenavon and Pontypool area during the late 1930s. Commenting on the fatalistic attitude he encountered among local miners with regard to their ability to handle large sums of money, Armbruster noted: 'Chapel teachings are often referred to, to the effect that the miner when he has too much becomes immoral, indulges in gambling and drink, or even if he is "respectable" and saves he will only lose it in a strike.' G. H. Armbruster, 'The social determination of ideologies: being a study of a Welsh mining community' (unpublished Ph.D. thesis, University of London, 1940), pp. 162–3. I am grateful to Steven D. Thompson for this reference.

ultimate disorder' implied that the restoration of peace and
'normality' would see an immediate 'return to "traditional"
gender relationships, the familiar and natural order of families,
men in public roles, women at home, and so on'.[200] A correspondent from Cardiff who wrote to the *South Wales Echo* in
April 1943 to decry the fact that while women's experiences
of factory employment had given them a 'deep knowledge of
cosmetics, films, stockings, boyfriends, dancing, beer and the
various brands of cigarettes, the skill needed to manipulate the
scrubbing brush or cook a decent meal is entirely absent', clearly
hoped for an immediate post-war resolution of this 'unacceptable' state of affairs when women were returned to their 'rightful'
positions in the home.[201]

Yet, this popular view of the Second World War as a force
which disrupted conventional gender roles and relations, and
one which brought about the social and sexual 'liberation' of the
female population, tells us little about the real effects of the war
on the daily lives of the women of south Wales. Admittedly,
significant shifts in the general social outlook and behaviour of
the female population did take place during the Second World
War, but it is evident that the attention devoted to such changes
was grossly exaggerated and was scarcely representative of the
wartime experiences of the majority. Furthermore, the distorted
representation of the war as a period of sexual and social
disorder, when all inhibitions and social constraints were suddenly cast aside, presented an equally false image of life in pre-
war south Wales as respectable, chaste and religious. The busy
ports of Cardiff and Swansea had their share of prostitutes and
'good-time girls' long before the outbreak of the war, and even a
cursory glance at the records of the police and magistrates' courts
of the region reveals that they were frequently visited by female
drunks, gamblers and abortionists, and young women seeking
affiliation orders in respect of their illegitimate children.[202] The
strict social and moral values upheld by the strong Welsh
Nonconformist tradition evidently had little bearing on the
conduct of a section of the Welsh female population before or

[200] Joan W. Scott, 'Rewriting history', in Higonnet et al. (eds.), *Behind the Lines*, p. 27.
[201] *South Wales Echo*, 28 April 1943.
[202] See GRO, City of Cardiff licensing sessions minutes, and also the minute books of
the Glamorgan Quarter Sessions.

during the war. As Michael Lieven noted in his study of the social history of the mining village of Senghennydd between 1890 and 1930, 'so far as sex was concerned, the code of the chapels was widely ignored among young people, despite varying degrees of disapproval by the older generations.'[203]

The behaviour of the 'respectable', law-abiding majority could hardly be regarded as newsworthy, however, and it is not altogether surprising that wartime media and public attention focused on the conduct and activities of those individuals who challenged accepted social, cultural and sexual norms. Remarking on the attention which the wartime increase in female drinking at Blaina had attracted among local residents, Mollie Tarrant concluded that

> what is now taking place in Blaina, is not necessarily a decided increase [in drinking] among women in general and among women war workers in particular, but rather the imminent break-down of a social taboo is leading to over-concentration on whatever appears to threaten a long established attitude. The smallest trickle of water through the dyke will inevitably arouse a much greater anxiety than the size of the hole would appear to warrant.[204]

Clearly, not all the female munitions workers of south Wales were hell-bent on spending their wartime wages on cigarettes and alcohol, and the majority either invested their money in wartime savings schemes or continued their pre-war custom of contributing part or all of their wages to their families, receiving only a small personal allowance to spend or save as they wished.[205] Mrs L. Gomer Evans, leader of the Women's Voluntary Service in the Rhondda, was keen to point this fact out and in May 1942, in response to press allegations of intemperance and immorality among the Welsh female war workers, she sprang to the defence of the young women of her area:

---

[203] Michael Lieven, *Senghennydd: The Universal Pit Village, 1890–1930* (Llandysul, 1994), p. 124. See also, idem, 'Senghenydd and the historiography of the South Wales Coalfield', *Morgannwg*, XLIII (1999), 29.

[204] M-O A, FR 1498, 'Blaina', p. 105.

[205] Inman, *Labour in the Munitions Industries*, p. 251; Rosemary Crook, 'Women in the Rhondda valley between the wars' (unpublished MA thesis, University of Leeds, 1980), p. 46; evidence of Beatrice Manderella, *Wales on Sunday*, 25 June 1995; evidence of Respondents 3 and 4.

I think that Welsh girls are doing a fine job of work in our Government factories and to pick out a few exaggerated cases and libel as a whole a perfectly respectable section of the community is unjust and unfair. I have yet to see a Rhondda girl the worse for drink. I know of several workers who are putting their money in savings groups rather than spending it in the ways suggested. It is an unnecessary slur on a fine body of workers who are definitely doing their bit.[206]

The oral testimony of several former war workers provides further evidence that the lives of many of the young women of wartime south Wales remained bound by traditional notions of female respectability.[207] As one respondent from Treherbert in the Rhondda explained,

The problem was, we were earning more money, but we didn't have anything to spend it on! We couldn't buy clothes, we couldn't buy sweets, and if you went into the pub – which you wouldn't do – you'd be judged, you just couldn't.[208]

While such accounts, which stress the continuities between pre-war and wartime society, provide an alternative interpretation of the role of the Second World War as an instigator of social change and guard against simplistic assumptions that the war 'revolutionized' the lives of the women of south Wales, there can be no denying that the war experience had a profound effect on the expectations and ideals of the thousands of Welsh women who undertook essential war work in the munitions factories of England and Wales. After all, munitions work not only allowed them greater mobility and a measure of financial and social independence, but it also broadened their social networks and interests and awakened them to new possibilities in their social and working lives. The official war historians, and more recent commentators such as John Costello and Cate Haste, have argued that the war 'set patterns of behaviour that could not be expected to cease with the gunfire' and promoted an inevitable

---

[206] *Western Mail*, 28 May 1942.
[207] Evidence of Respondents 5, 14 and 18.
[208] Evidence of Respondent 22.

'reappraisal' of previously held social, cultural and moral values.[209] The south Wales which emerged in the aftermath of war was certainly very different from that which had entered the conflict in 1939. In the opinion of Dai Smith, 'the late 1940s stand out as the last authentic years of that distinctive culture which had been fashioned in South Wales.'[210] Many of the old, traditional values had been swept aside as the war accelerated changes already afoot in the social, linguistic and religious life of the region.[211] The heightened economic and social profile of the female population of south Wales stood out as one of the most striking features of this process of social and cultural change. Given the nature of the work and leisure experiences of Welsh women in the years before the war, it is small wonder that many contemporary observers viewed the changes in the lives of the female population as the ultimate expression of the war's destructive impact on familiar concepts of Welsh cultural life.

---

[209] Ferguson and Fitzgerald, *Studies in the Social Services*, p. 26; John Costello, *Love, Sex and War: Changing Values, 1939–45* (London, 1985), p. 14; Cate Haste, *Rules of Desire: Sex in Britain, World War I to the Present* (London, 1992), pp. 137–8.

[210] Dai Smith, *Wales! Wales?* (London, 1984), p. 124.

[211] See W. Morgan Davies, 'Pride of race', in Davies Aberpennar (ed.), *'Look You'*, pp. 5–8; Katie Olwen Pritchard, *Y Glas a'r Coch (Darlith Flynyddol Llyfrgell Penygroes, 1980/81)* (Cyngor Sir Gwynedd, 1981), p. 30.

V

A 'NEW SOUTH WALES'?

The cessation of hostilities in Europe in May 1945 signalled the end of an era for the female munitions workers of south Wales. After some five years of service at the factory benches and workshops which had ensured a steady supply of armaments for the Allied forces, the services of the munitions workers became surplus to requirements, and the process of releasing the labour force from temporary wartime posts began.[1] By mid-summer 1945, several thousand Welsh women – the majority of whom were married or had domestic responsibilities or were aged over fifty – had already left their positions in the factories as production in the war industries was gradually run down.[2] Although some factories, including both Glascoed and Llanishen ROFs, were to retain the services of a proportion of their workforce as reserve capacity,[3] the future of the vast majority of the plants and their employees hung in the balance as the end of the war grew imminent. The surrender of the Japanese on 14 August 1945 sealed the fate of the munitions industries of south Wales and the effective disbandment of the wartime army of Welsh female industrial workers got under way.

In many ways, the ending of the war marked a new beginning in the lives of many Welsh female war workers, for the changing nature of the social, economic and political fabric of post-war south Wales was to have a profound effect on their experiences of work and home life. Although the scale of female employment opportunities could never match that recorded at the height of

---

[1] *Western Mail*, 16 and 17 May 1945.

[2] Thomas, 'War and the economy', p. 258. Such was the impact of the drastic curtailment of work orders that employees in some factories had no work to occupy them. For example, in June 1945 it was alleged that workers employed at Bridgend ROF were 'playing the piano' and 'dancing to fill in their time'. *Western Mail*, 21 June 1945; *South Wales Echo*, 26 June 1945; *Glamorgan Advertiser*, 6 July 1945.

[3] In the immediate post-war period, Glascoed ROF manufactured concrete railway sleepers and items which were directly related to the government's reconstruction programme, such as concrete units for prefabricated homes and electrical home fittings. Llanishen ROF, an engineering plant, produced items such as oil engines and rolling stock for railways. Both factories resumed armament production during the 1950s.

the conflict, women's involvement in the industrial labour
market increased significantly in the years following the war as a
direct result of the interventionist policies of the government's
post-war reconstruction programme. Writing in a supplement of
the *Western Mail* in 1953, Doreen Stiven, personnel manager at
the Dunlop Rubber Company, Hirwaun, concluded that:

> The last fifteen years or so have seen a complete economic and social
> revolution in our Welsh national life. Not only has the balance of the
> old economic structure been radically altered, but the domestic scene has
> been re-orientated and re-formed . . . The 'new look', although having a
> significant impact on our menfolk had its most profound influence on the
> life of women in Wales . . . The writer ventures some criticism, but would
> express an honest opinion that it was the coming of the large armament
> factories and the Essential Work Order which had the greatest effect in re-
> shaping the domestic scene.[4]

One of the most striking trends of the post-war era was
the growing number of married women who took up paid
employment. By 1954 it was estimated that married women
comprised 43 per cent of the occupied female population of
England and Wales, compared with a mere 16 per cent in 1931.[5]
This development appeared to signal a gradual breaking down of
pre-war conventions and attitudes towards female employment.
At the same time, however, concerns about the dislocating effects
of the war on home and family life placed renewed emphasis on
women's traditional role and social status as wives and mothers.
Advances in the fields of social security, health and housing, and
the advent of a new age of consumer goods and appliances for
the home, served to reaffirm such ideals and further complicated
the interrelationship between home and work and the problems
of balancing their often conflicting demands and interests.[6] In

---

[4] *Western Mail (Commercial and Industrial Review)*, 19 January 1953.

[5] E. M. Harris, *Married Women in Industry*, Institute of Personnel Management
Occasional Papers no. 4 (London, 1954), p. 13; *Census of England and Wales, 1931,
Occupation Tables*, p. 1.

[6] For an overview of these themes and other aspects of the history of British women in
the post-war period, see Jane Lewis, *Women in Britain since 1945: Women, Family, Work and the
State in the Post-war Years* (Oxford, 1992); Pat Thane, 'Towards equal opportunities? Women
in Britain since 1945', in Terry Gourvish and Alan O'Day (eds.), *Britain since 1945* (London,
1991), pp. 183–208; eadem, 'Women since 1945', in Paul Johnson (ed.), *Twentieth-Century
Britain: Economic, Social and Cultural Change* (New York, 1994), pp. 392–410; Penny Summerfield, 'Women in Britain since 1945: companionate marriage and the double burden', in
James Obelkevich and Peter Catterall (eds.), *Understanding Post-war British society* (London,
1994), pp. 58–72.

short, as Teresa Rees has argued, the post-war years were
'characterized by both major changes and continuities in the
lives of women in Wales'.[7] This chapter will examine the contradictory impact of issues such as industrial restructuring, the
expansion in female work opportunities, and the prevalence of
pre-war attitudes towards women's role as workers and home-
makers on the domestic and work experiences of the women of
industrial south Wales in the years immediately following the
war.

One of the most important long-term legacies of the Second
World War for the people of south Wales was the fact that it
virtually eliminated unemployment. Wartime conditions had
involved dramatic changes in the nature of the industrial
economy of south Wales, and the impact on the future social,
economic and industrial prospects of the region was to prove
immense.[8] The economic benefits of the war had brought
immediate relief to industrial communities which had been
devastated by the effects of mass unemployment and poverty
and, as the authors of the Welsh Reconstruction Advisory
Council Report of 1944 noted, hopes were high that 'such a
wholesale frustration of human desires and ideals' would never
again have to be endured.[9] The redrawing of the political map of
Britain elicited promises that such optimism was not unfounded.
The Labour Party achieved a landslide victory in the general
election of July 1945 and the new government was returned to
Parliament with an unprecedented majority. In Wales, Labour
captured twenty-five of the thirty-six seats and its share of the
vote rose to 58.5 per cent (compared with 48 per cent for the
United Kingdom as a whole).[10] Some of the largest Labour

---

[7] Teresa Rees, 'Women in post-war Wales', in Trevor Herbert and Gareth Elwyn
Jones (eds.), *Post-War Wales* (Cardiff, 1995), p. 78.
[8] See Colin Baber and Dennis Thomas, 'The Glamorgan economy, 1914–45', and
Colin Baber and Jeffrey Dessant, 'Modern Glamorgan: economic development after
1945', in A. H. John and Glanmor Williams (eds.), *Glamorgan County History, Volume V.
Industrial Glamorgan, 1700–1970* (Cardiff, 1980), pp. 519–79, 581–658.
[9] Office of the Minister of Reconstruction, *Welsh Reconstruction Advisory Council – First
Interim Report*, p. 9. James Griffiths, MP for Llanelli, noted that similar sentiments were
expressed at the reconstruction conferences organized by the Labour Party in south
Wales during 1942. Griffiths recalled that a 'note of confidence' had pervaded each
meeting and that the main feeling of the delegates had been that 'out of this blood and
sweat and tears we must build a new and better Britain'. NLW, James Griffiths Papers,
B3/9, 'Impressions of the reconstruction conferences' (1942).
[10] Morgan, *Rebirth of a Nation*, p. 300.

majorities were recorded in the south Wales valleys, where the
Labour victory became a symbol of hope for the creation of a
'new south Wales'.[11] This mood of expectancy was captured in
January 1946 by the local newspaper columnist 'Aberdaria':

> As we enter 1946 with a Labour government in power pledged to intro-
> duce great and sweeping social reforms, the air is charged with the spirit of
> reconstruction. Coming soon are a great social insurance scheme to banish
> want, coupled with family allowances and higher compensation for injured
> workers, long-looked for nationalisation of the mining industry, a broader
> and better education system, a comprehensive national health service,
> more houses . . . The horizon looks bright; we walk into this New Year full
> of hope of better times to come.[12]

Without doubt, the substantial increase in the number of
females who entered full-time employment was one of the most
significant developments of the post-war period. As economists
such as Dennis A. Thomas have argued, the war proved instrumental in realizing 'the potentialities of female labour in south
Wales, releasing a major source of virtually untapped labour'.[13]
Wartime conditions also initiated changes in the character of
female employment in the region. At the war factories, women
had acquired new skills and work practices associated with the
precise and repetitive work of the assembly-line, and had grown
familiar with 'working to the hooter' and commuting to and
from the workplace.[14] The creation of this new 'factory mental-
ity'[15] proved a significant asset to the future prospects of the
south Wales economy and was attractive bait for persuading
wartime firms to remain in, and new industrialists to come into,
the area in the years immediately following the war.[16]

---

[11] Evidence of Respondent 17. See 'New South Wales?', *The Economist*, 11 May 1946;
Kenneth O. Morgan, 'Post-war reconstruction in Wales, 1918 and 1945', in Jay Winter
(ed.), *The Working Class in Modern British History: Essays in Honour of Henry Pelling* (Cambridge,
1983), pp. 82–98.

[12] *Aberdare Leader*, 5 January 1946.

[13] Thomas, 'War and the economy', p. 263.

[14] Office of the Minister of Reconstruction, *Welsh Reconstruction Advisory Council – First
Interim Report*, pp. 20, 71.

[15] The words of Councillor Sweet, vice-chairman of the South Wales TUC Advisory
Committee, at a meeting with the Board of Trade, 30 September 1946. PRO, Lab 43/1.

[16] PP 1947–8 (XVI, Cmd. 7267), *Wales and Monmouthshire, Report of Government Action for
the year ended 30 June 1947*, p. 17; *Western Mail*, 27 May 1949; Dunning, 'Employment for
women in the Development Areas 1939/51', 276.

In addition to creating a large and efficient female industrial workforce, the wartime experience left another important legacy in south Wales, namely, a large number of empty industrial buildings. The nature and scale of wartime investment in the region had been significant and the sites and premises of the large war factories provided a ready-made base for industrialists who wished to capitalize on the plentiful supply of experienced factory workers in the post-war years.[17] The conversion of wartime factories to civilian production was given a considerable boost by the industrial restructuring programme initiated by the government. The passing of the Distribution of Industry Act of 1945, which designated the whole of industrial south Wales as a Development Area and empowered the Board of Trade to establish new factories and industrial estates in the region and to provide grants and loans to new industrialists, was instrumental in creating the opportunities for future investment. Although many problems were experienced in the difficult transition period which immediately followed the end of the war, progress was steady and the conversion of some of the large war factories from wartime to peacetime production soon got under way. Newport ROF was allocated to Standard Telephones and Cables Ltd, while Bridgend and Hirwaun ROFs were converted into trading estates, where units ranging from 100 to 208,000 square feet in size were allocated to prospective industrialists.[18]

Elsewhere across the region, new manufacturing industries producing goods and appliances, ranging from radio and television equipment to zip fasteners, tinsel and artificial flowers, were established at over sixty brand-new government-financed factories. In the mining valleys, where few wartime industries had been located, such developments had a dramatic impact on the industrial landscape. Contemporary observers drew particular attention to 'the changing face' of the Rhondda, where the erection of new factories at Blaenrhondda, Dinas, Ferndale, Llwynypia and Treorci brought new life and prosperity to communities which had previously been wholly dependent on

---

[17] Graham Humphrys, *Industrial Britain – South Wales* (Newton Abbot, 1972), p. 37.
[18] PP 1945–6 (XX, Cmd. 6938), pp. 66–71.

coal.[19] By July 1947 almost all the government-owned space which was readily available for industrial use had been allocated, and by June of the following year it was revealed that 24,151 people were employed at the sites of the old munitions factories which had been converted, allocated, sold or otherwise disposed of for civilian production.[20]

Although females accounted for less than half the total number of employees who had found work at the new industrial projects, their entry into the industrial workforce nonetheless signalled a dramatic departure from the pre-war work situation.[21] In Wales as a whole the number of occupied females had increased by 83 per cent between 1939 and 1946, compared with an increase of only 14 per cent in England and Wales.[22] Nowhere was this increase more apparent than in the industrial communities of south Wales. In a series of articles tracing the 'Changing face of Wales' which appeared in the *Western Mail* in 1949, J. Alun Jones drew particular attention to the transformation which had taken place in the work experiences of women in the industrial south.[23] In the Rhondda approximately half the 5,000 workers employed in the new factories of the Valleys were women, while some 60 per cent of the 2,000 workers employed at the Hirwaun trading estate and half the 3,127 employed at the Bridgend trading estate on the sites of the old ROFs were females.[24] The contrast with the situation prevailing before the war, when few employment opportunities existed for females in these industrial communities, was striking. Indeed, between 1932 and 1948, the number of females employed in the South Wales and Monmouthshire Development Area had swollen from 37,802 to 105,201, an increase of 178.3 per cent.[25]

[19] Dennis H. Morgan, 'The changing face of south Wales', *Wales*, VII, no. 27 (1947), 364–75; National Industrial Development Council of Wales and Monmouthshire, *Wales and Monmouthshire: An Illustrated Review of the Industries and Tourist Attractions of the Principality* (Cardiff, 1948/9), p. 26; Gwyther, *The Valley Shall Be Exalted*, pp. 86–7; Colin Wills, 'New life in the Rhondda valley', *The Listener*, 28 September 1950.

[20] Thomas, 'War and the economy', p. 260; PP 1948 (II, Cmd. 7540), *Board of Trade, Distribution of Industry*, p. 49.

[21] In total, 8,981 females and 15,170 males were employed at the 148 projects listed by the Board of Trade in June 1948. PP 1948 (II, Cmd. 7540), p. 49.

[22] Thomas (ed.), *The Welsh Economy*, p. 32; Dennis A. Thomas, 'Recovery in the Special Areas and the effects of the Second World War, with particular reference to south Wales' (unpublished M.Sc. (Econ.) thesis, University of Wales, 1973), p. 82.

[23] *Western Mail*, 20, 24, 27 and 31 May 1949, 3, 7, 10, 14, 17, 21, 24 and 28 June 1949, 1 and 5 July 1949.

[24] Ibid., 3, 10 and 17 June 1949.

[25] Thomas, 'War and the economy', p. 269.

Table 5.1: *Number of occupied males and females and percentage as total in age group[1],*
1931–1951

| Area | 1931 | | | | 1951 | | | |
| | Males | | Females | | Males | | Females | |
	Number	%	Number	%	Number	%	Number	%
Glamorgan	**415371**	**90.8**	**89529**	**19.8**	**386040**	**86.5**	**124121**	**25.9**
Cardiff CB	72622	90.0	27700	30.9	75562	87.6	31583	31.6
Merthyr Tydfil CB	24932	91.7	3913	15.3	19369	84.8	6162	25.2
Swansea CB	55195	90.8	15103	23.5	51848	86.6	17525	26.8
Aberdare UD	17597	92.0	2470	13.8	13287	84.0	3580	21.7
Bridgend UD	3209	88.2	1109	27.7	4320	86.7	1478	26.4
Maesteg UD	8723	91.3	1041	12.1	7509	87.3	1805	21.0
Mountain Ash UD	13390	91.9	1516	11.8	9815	84.9	2982	24.4
Neath MB	11528	91.6	2565	20.3	10829	87.9	3563	26.8
Ogmore & Garw UD	9766	93.3	944	10.8	7462	87.2	1647	19.4
Pontypridd UD	14004	89.5	2593	17.3	12289	85.6	4314	28.1
Rhondda UD	50461	92.4	5484	11.4	35237	85.3	10412	23.5
Monmouthshire	**149475**	**91.3**	**27731**	**17.9**	**138007**	**87.0**	**39887**	**24.3**
Newport CB	30013	91.4	9079	26.2	34501	89.1	12186	28.9
Abertillery UD	11450	93.7	1221	11.6	9183	87.4	2080	20.1
Blaenavon UD	4049	92.1	461	12.1	3400	88.8	725	19.4
Ebbw Vale UD	11164	92.4	1316	12.5	9954	89.7	2112	19.2
Nantyglo & Blaina UD	4466	89.8	481	10.7	3767	85.8	867	20.1
Pontypool UD	2337	94.1	472	19.8	14121	87.7	4144	24.9
Tredegar UD	8108	91.2	1000	12.9	6516	85.7	1632	21.1

[1] 1931: 14 years and over; 1951: 15 years and over.
Source: 1931 and 1951 Census Occupation Tables.

As table 5.1 shows, between 1931 and 1951 the proportion of
employed females rose from 19.8 per cent to 25.9 per cent in the
county of Glamorgan and from 17.9 per cent to 24.3 per cent in
Monmouthshire. The highest increases were recorded in mining
areas such as the Rhondda, the Ogmore and Garw, Mountain
Ash and Aberdare UDs. Overall, an additional 46,748 females
had been drawn into the workforce of Glamorgan and Monmouthshire since 1931.[26] Conversely, the number and proportion of employed males decreased during the same period, with
the greatest rates of decline recorded in the mining districts.

[26] *Census of England and Wales, 1931, Occupation Tables*, pp. 395, 410; *Census of England
and Wales, 1951, Occupation Tables* (London, 1956), pp. 336–7.

Table 5.2: Occupational distribution of females shown as percentage of total females occupied in age group[1], 1931–1951

Occupation group	Glamorgan and Monmouthshire		England and Wales	
	1931 %	1951 %	1931 %	1951 %
Personal service	44.0	22.4	34.4	23.3
Commerce and finance	19.4	16.7	10.8	12.1
Clerks, typists etc.	8.4	19.8	10.3	20.3
Professional occupations	12.2	11.1	6.9	8.3
Clothing manufacture	5.5	6.5	9.7	7.0
Metal, electrical and textile workers	1.0	4.0	12.7	8.9
Transport and communications	1.3	2.0	1.2	2.1
% occupied females in age group	19.3	25.2	34.2	34.9
Total number occupied females in age group	117,260	164,008	5,606,043	6,272,876

[1]1931: 14 years and over; 1951: 15 years and over.
Source: 1931 and 1951 Census Occupation Tables.

Not only had the number of females engaged in full-time employment increased substantially, but the nature of the work which they performed had also undergone a dramatic change.[27] As table 5.2 shows, the proportion of females who were employed in the personal service occupation group fell significantly in the counties of Glamorgan and Monmouth between 1931 and 1951, while the proportion employed in the rapidly expanding clerical and manufacturing sectors increased.

The shift in the occupational distribution of the female population was most apparent in the mining districts, where employment opportunities had not only been extremely scarce but had been limited almost entirely to the service industries.[28] For example, in the Rhondda UD, the proportion of females who

[27] For a detailed commentary on the changing nature of female work opportunities in south Wales, see *Western Mail (Industrial and Commercial Review)*, 31 January 1955.
[28] A detailed breakdown of the occupational distribution of the female workforce in some UDs and RDs of Glamorgan and Monmouthshire in 1951 is provided in the Appendix.

were occupied in the personal service sector – the vast majority
of whom were domestic servants – fell from 43 per cent to 16.3
per cent between 1931 and 1951. At the same time, the proportion employed as clerks and typists increased from 5.6 per
cent to 16.2 per cent, and those engaged in the manufacturing
industries, notably clothing manufacture, increased from 4.9 per
cent to 13.8 per cent. The post-war expansion of light industries
in the district clearly had a marked impact on the female work
experience. It is known that Polikoff's clothing factory at Treorci
employed over a thousand women by the late 1940s, and their
numbers were expected to double following the completion of an
extension to the works.[29] Writing in 1949, a local newspaper
reporter concluded: 'The outlook for Rhondda women is bright.
Thousands of them have already fitted neatly into the industrial
pattern and the indications are that when the factories' plan
materialises, more and more will be absorbed.'[30]

The industrial prospects of the female population had not
looked so bright in the months immediately following the end of
the war. Indeed, as production in the munitions factories ground
to a halt, the future looked extremely bleak for the thousands of
female war workers who were made redundant almost overnight.
In its first report in 1944, the Welsh Reconstruction Advisory
Council estimated that between 40 per cent and 50 per cent of
the employees of the new industries of the region worked in
factories which would 'almost inevitably either close down or
drastically curtail their activities at the end of the war'.[31] The
temporary nature of the wartime employment situation gave
little hope for the future, therefore, and in June 1945 the chief
conciliation and industrial relations officer of Wales noted that
'the uncertainty of the continuity of their employment' was
having 'a sobering effect on the minds of industrial workers'.[32]

As unemployment rose sharply, fears mounted that a return to
the dark days of the pre-war economic situation was inevitable.[33]

[29] *Western Mail*, 10 June 1949.
[30] Ibid.
[31] Office of the Minister of Reconstruction, *Welsh Reconstruction Advisory Council – First
Interim Report*, p. 30.
[32] PRO, Lab 10/555.
[33] *Glamorgan Gazette*, 5 July 1946. For an insight into the general 'fears for the future'
which dominated public opinion in south Wales during this period, see Office of the
Minister of Reconstruction, *Welsh Reconstruction Advisory Council – First Interim Report*,
pp. 8–9, 30–1; NLW, Thomas Jones Papers, class H, vol. 9, no. 168, Pontypridd and

The transition from wartime to peacetime production proved difficult and it was evident that the peacetime concerns which would eventually be established in south Wales would employ only a small proportion of the total number of women who had worked in the war factories of the region. A rough approximation of the post-war employment situation, based on the assumption that servicewomen and women employed in war production would require work after the war, was submitted to the Welsh Reconstruction Advisory Council in October 1944 by representatives of the local authorities of south Wales. It was estimated that over 50,000 women from thirteen districts in the region would require industrial employment after the war but, given that the estimated female employment capacity of basic industries in these districts was only 19,691, it was clear that the jobs which would become available would fall far short of the estimated demand for post-war industrial employment.[34]

Wartime inquiries had indicated a general desire among Welsh women to continue in factory employment after the war and few appeared to have changed their opinions following the end of the conflict.[35] Roma Sanders, a reporter with the *Western Mail* who interviewed several former south Wales war workers in January 1946 – many of whom were unemployed – found that the vast majority were eager to find work in the new factories which were being established in the region:

> Welsh women released from their wartime jobs in factories and free to choose their own work for the first time in several years are looking for new employment – in other factories. This despite the fact that they were

District Educational Settlement, 9th Annual Report, 1 April 1945–31 March 1946; class H, vol. 12, no. 159, Merthyr Settlement, Mortimer Jones, 'Report of men's clubs, 1943–44'; Labour Party of Wales Archive, South Wales Regional Council of Labour Executive Committee minutes, 24 November 1945; A. Beacham, 'The future of the South Wales Coalfield', *The Welsh Review*, V, no. 2 (1946), 138–44; W. Idris Jones, 'The future pattern of Welsh industry', ibid., V, no. 3 (1946), 208–16.

[34] GRO, Industrial Development Council of Wales and Monmouthshire Papers, memorandum on 'Some aspects of post-war employment policy in Special Areas submitted to the Welsh Reconstruction Advisory Council', October 1944. The thirteen local authorities and their estimated post-war industrial female populations were as follows: Abercarn UD – 1,500; Abertillery UD – 2,000; Bridgend UD – 1,500; Brynmawr UD – 500; Llantrisant RD – 2,200; Merthyr Tydfil CB – 6,491; Mountain Ash UD – 850; Nantyglo and Blaina UD – 1,250; Ogmore and Garw UD – 3,500; Pontypridd UD – 14,000; Rhondda UD – 15,000; Rhymney UD – 1,000; Tredegar UD – 2,008.

[35] M-O A, TC 2, Reconstruction, Box 3, File E, Cardiff survey, 19 September 1942; ibid., FR 1498, 'Blaina', p. 101; *Western Mail*, 10 March 1945.

directed often against their will to take up factory work during the war.
Moreover, they know they will not get the high wages of wartime. All this
came to light as I chatted with women outside employment exchanges, in
cafés and on buses during the past few days. And the reason they gave for
wanting to return to the factory bench was that they liked working with
other women. They laughed as they recalled their reluctance to switch
over from comfortable offices, shops and the home. Then they disliked the
idea of factory life and would not be able to get on with other women.
Now, having gone through some hectic years in the war effort they have
made good friends and are anxious to carry on a peacetime job with the
same team.[36]

Assessing the post-war ambitions of women war workers on the
basis of such subjective evidence is a problematic exercise, however, and raises many important questions regarding methods of
historical reconstruction. Women's own responses to questions
relating to their post-war intentions could vary considerably,
depending on personal and family circumstances or the nature of
their experiences of war work. The views of one group of Welsh
women might therefore be totally unrepresentative of the
opinions of women from a different age group or social class
whose voices were not expressed publicly and made available to
the historian. Problems of interpretation have also been identified
in the body of literature which was published during and after the
war about women and their post-war work ambitions.[37] The
conclusions drawn by several wartime surveys were that the vast
majority of women did not want to remain in post-war employment, with wives and mothers and women who were engaged on
low-skilled, repetitive work expressing a greater desire to return to
their homes than did single, childless women or those who held
professional or 'responsible' jobs.[38] It was also claimed that the
vast majority of women had regarded their experiences of factory
life as an exceptional 'wartime interlude' and, having served the
needs of their country, welcomed their release from the rigours of
factory routine and the return to 'normality'.[39] Yet, as Penny

[36] *Western Mail*, 16 January 1946.
[37] See Summerfield, 'Approaches to women and social change in the Second World
War', pp. 71–2 ; eadem, 'The girl that makes the thing that drills the hole that holds the
spring . . .', pp. 47–8.
[38] Thomas, 'Women at work', pp. 14–17; PRO, Inf 1/292.
[39] M-O A, FR 1163, 'Women in industry'; ibid., FR 2059, 'Will the factory girls want
to stay put or go home?', 8 March 1944.

Summerfield has shown, the data collated by the 1944 Wartime Social Survey provided little conclusive evidence to support these generalizations: 'Only 36 per cent of married women and 7 per cent of single women did *not* want to go on in paid work after the war. The rest either definitely wanted to, or were undecided, answering "if possible" or "may have to".'[40] It is also worth noting that only 90 (3 per cent) of the 2,609 women interviewed by the Wartime Social Survey of 1944 were from Wales.[41]

One crucial point to remember is that the post-war intentions and desires expressed by women war workers were not necessarily realized. Many of the women who retired from the workforce after the war and returned to their homes may have had little choice in the matter. Even if they so desired, those who had domestic or family responsibilities found it extremely difficult to remain in full-time employment, while opposition from trade unions, employers or unemployed males gave others little incentive to continue working. Conversely, working-class women who may have wished to remain at home may have been forced to continue in low-paid, low-status jobs because of economic pressures. Whether women continued working or left paid employment after the war was not, therefore, an accurate measure of their true preferences. Although the post-war years witnessed significant changes in both the scale and nature of female employment in south Wales, women continued to face considerable practical and ideological obstacles to fulfilling their ambitions. Consequently, they either remained in subordinate positions in the workplace, or were discouraged from taking up full-time work completely.

In post-war south Wales, the young unmarried woman accounted for the largest proportion of the occupied female population. Although the age profile of working women in England and Wales had grown steadily older in the years following the war, the pre-war pattern of a predominantly young, female workforce remained relatively unchanged in south Wales.[42] According to the 1951 census, more than two-thirds of

---

[40] Summerfield, 'The girl that makes the thing that drills the hole that holds the spring . . .', p. 47.
[41] Thomas, 'Women at work', Appendix 1: Regional distribution of interviews, p. 31.
[42] In 1931, 41 per cent of the occupied female population of England and Wales was aged under twenty-five, but by 1951 this proportion had fallen to approximately 34 per cent. Summerfield, *Women Workers in the Second World War*, p. 188.

the occupied female population of England and Wales was aged over twenty-five, but in the counties of Glamorgan and Monmouth, women under the age of twenty-five accounted for 43 per cent and 44.3 per cent of the female workforce respectively, while approximately a quarter of occupied females were 'juveniles' aged between fifteen and nineteen.[43]

In the immediate post-war period, work was not easy to come by in the industrial communities of south Wales. Such were the difficulties which young women encountered in finding employment in the district that the government was forced to introduce a voluntary transfer scheme in April 1946 in order to alleviate rising unemployment. Between July 1945 and July 1946 the number of unemployed women in Wales increased from 6,835 to 29,079 and it was clear that urgent measures were required to deal with the problem.[44] Although the rate of unemployment remained lower than it had been before the war (in July 1938 the female unemployment rate stood at 12.4 per cent in the South Wales and Monmouthshire Development Area compared with 4.5 per cent in July 1945 and 8.7 per cent in July 1948), a far greater number of females were now insured and registered as unemployed, and female unemployment thus represented a greater proportion of the total unemployed.[45] Under the provisions of the Voluntary Temporary Transference Scheme, unemployed workers from the Development Areas were given assistance to take up employment away from their home districts for a minimum period of three months. Between April and July 1946, 1,346 Welsh females were transferred to work elsewhere in Britain under this scheme.[46] The Ministry of Labour also assisted an additional 2,112 females to find work outside Wales between August 1945 and July 1946.[47]

Although the transferred workers were promised a return journey when work became available in their home districts, there were several elements of this new post-war transference scheme which greatly concerned the people of the industrial valleys of south Wales. In a letter to his local newspaper in

[43] *Census of England and Wales, 1951, County Report, Glamorganshire* (London, 1954), p. xliii; *Census of England and Wales, 1951, County Report, Monmouthshire* (London, 1954), p. xliii.
[44] PRO, Lab 43/1.
[45] See Thomas, 'War and the economy', pp. 265, 269.
[46] PP 1945–6 (XX, Cmd. 6938), p. 6.
[47] Ibid.

March 1946, Tom Davies, secretary of the Hirwaun branch of the NUGMW, drew attention to the fact that some ninety girls from the Merthyr and Dowlais district had received notice that, unless they took up work at the Lucas factory, in Birmingham, their unemployment payments would be stopped.[48] Reports from other districts suggested that these were not idle threats. At a meeting of the Ogmore and Garw UDC in March 1946, Councillor Mavis Llewellyn made a formal complaint about the 'flippant' treatment of local women by officials of the Courts of Referees, who interviewed young girls who had refused to leave the area to work and, consequently, had had their benefits stopped.[49] In May 1946, the Revd T. Alban Davies, minister of Bethesda Welsh Congregational chapel, Tonpentre, claimed that some 200 girls from the Rhondda had been denied unemployment benefit because they had refused to take up work in England.[50] Similar allegations were made at a meeting of the Aberdare TLC in February 1946, when local trade union representatives were urged to take urgent action to prevent the 'mass transfer' of female labour from the area to the English Midlands.[51] According to a council member, the present transference system was 'more ridiculous than any previous similar action' and had grave implications for the future social and economic prospects of the district:

> Daily we read in the newspapers that South Wales is looked upon as a special area, where they are going to build factories. The fact that they are transferring masses of females from this district to the Midlands will mean that when these factories are established here we won't have any labour here unless they transfer the women back again.[52]

Members of Undeb Cymru Fydd, the society which had campaigned tirelessly on behalf of the Welsh girls who were sent to the English industrial districts during the war, were equally incensed at the continuation of the industrial transference scheme. Concerns had already been voiced that a large number

[48] *Aberdare Leader*, 9 March 1946.
[49] *Glamorgan Gazette*, 29 March 1946, 5 April 1946.
[50] *Western Mail*, 29 May 1946; *Porth Gazette and Rhondda Leader*, 1 and 8 June 1946.
[51] *Western Mail*, 8 February 1946; *Aberdare Leader*, 16 February 1946.
[52] *Aberdare Leader*, 16 February 1946.

of the Welsh girls who were transferred to England during the war would not be allowed to return to their home districts,[53] and the news that further transfers were to be implemented during 1946 enraged many Welsh people.[54] Although Undeb Cymru Fydd had initially proposed to disband its Joint Committee at the cessation of the war and bring to an end the welfare services which had been provided to Welsh workers in the English districts, the flood of Welsh girls who continued to arrive in the English industrial areas during 1945–6 was such that the committee decided to continue with its pastoral work until 1947.[55] Among the papers of Mair Rees Jones and Emma Williams, the two welcoming officers who were employed by Undeb Cymru Fydd in the English Midlands and Home Counties, are over 150 leaflets which were filled out by Welsh girls sent to English factories in the months immediately following the end of the war.[56] The vast majority of those sent to Birmingham hailed from the Bridgend and Maesteg area and almost all were former employees of Bridgend ROF. Redundant workers from Bridgend, Glascoed and Hirwaun ROFs also featured prominently among the ranks of those who found employment with firms such as Huntley and Palmers, Vauxhall Motors and A. C. Cossons in Reading, Luton and High Wycombe in the English Home Counties. A serious shortage of female labour was reported in many of these English districts, and the local newspapers of south Wales often advertised job vacancies for women in local factories.[57] Some unemployed Welsh women were sent further afield to find work. During the summer of 1946, some

---

[53] *Baner ac Amserau Cymru*, 18 and 25 July 1945. A cartoon, entitled 'Bevin's breakfast', by Dewi Prys Thomas appeared in *The Welsh Nationalist* in July 1945, showing transferred Welsh girls being 'sacrificed' at the table of Ernest Bevin, the Minister of Labour 1940–5.

[54] *Y Cymro*, 31 August 1945, 21 December 1945; *The Welsh Nationalist*, October 1945; *South Wales Echo*, 13 and 23 October 1945.

[55] NLW, BBC Wales Archive, script of radio talk by Elinor Evans, 'Cyd-bwyllgor Undeb Cymru Fydd a'r eglwysi' (the joint committee of Undeb Cymru Fydd and the churches), broadcast on 23 May 1946; Undeb Cymru Fydd Papers (1951 Collection), 259.

[56] NLW, Undeb Cymru Fydd Papers (1960 Collection), 150–2.

[57] For example, the Midland Co-operative Laundries Association urgently required women and girls to train as laundresses in Northamptonshire; BSA, the cycle and motorcycle manufacturing company, advertised for women and girls to undertake light assembly and light machine work at their factories at Birmingham; while the Rheostatic Co. Ltd of Slough required women and girls to undertake light machining work at their modern factory. *Aberdare Leader*, 5 January 1946, 22 February 1946; *The Rhondda Leader and Gazette*, 23 May 1946.

500 females, the majority of whom were former munitions workers who had been unemployed for up to six months, were sent to Jersey to pack tomatoes.[58]

Yet, such measures provided only short-term solutions to the unemployment problems of south Wales, and the female war workers grew increasingly impatient with the slow progress of the post-war programme to establish new industries in the region. The young, unmarried war workers of south Wales, particularly those who had entered wartime industries straight from school, had no desire to be pushed into the 'blind-alley' occupations of the pre-war years. As members of the Welsh Committee of the Communist Party noted in a memorandum to the Industrial Council of South Wales and Monmouthshire in November 1945, the days of '10/- and keep with one free evening', which had been the lot of the servant girl, were now doomed.[59] In Cardiff, where Ministry of Labour officials reported an acute shortage of domestic servants in the immediate post-war period, members of the local juvenile employment committee noted that it was becoming increasingly difficult to persuade young girls to train for domestic service.[60] In stark contrast to factory employment, where young women could enjoy the benefits of female companionship and a measure of personal and social freedom, domestic service was regarded as a lonely, laborious and inferior occupation, often subject to contempt and ridicule. The authors of an official wartime investigation into domestic employment knew of several instances where domestic servants 'had found themselves ostracised by shop or factory workers who refused to associate with them'.[61] Moreover, it was claimed that female servants were also snubbed by members of the opposite sex, who 'not infrequently indicated their preference to walk out with young ladies enjoying the superior status of the shop or workroom'.[62]

---

[58] *Western Mail*, 27 August 1946; *Aberdare Leader*, 31 August 1946; *The Rhondda Leader*, 9 and 23 August 1946; evidence of Respondent 7. A similar scheme operated in 1947 and 1948; see *Free Press of Monmouthshire*, 29 October 1948; PP 1948 (II, Cmd. 7532), *Wales and Monmouthshire, Report of Government Action for the year ended 30 June 1948*, p. 30.

[59] GRO, Industrial Council of Wales and Monmouthshire Papers, memorandum on 'The conversion of industry and redundancy in Wales', submitted by the Welsh Committee of the Communist Party, 13 November 1945.

[60] *Western Mail*, 16 January 1946, 10 January 1948; Cardiff Central Library, City of Cardiff Education Committee annual report for 1947, Juvenile Employment Committee report.

[61] PP 1944–5 (V, Cmd. 6650), *Report on Post-war Organisation of Private Domestic Employment*, p. 6.

[62] Ibid.

Given such circumstances, it was hardly surprising that a growing number of young Welsh women turned their backs on domestic employment, expressing a preference for the relatively amenable jobs which were becoming available in the new factories, and in the commercial and distributive trades. In the opinion of members of the South Wales Communist Party, the war had occasioned a great 'change' in the outlook and work expectations of the young female population: 'they are industrial workers – that is the change.'[63] In the Garw valley a group of unemployed women, the majority of whom were redundant workers from Bridgend ROF, demanded a voice on their local trades council in order to press their case for the right to employment in the new factories of the district. Speaking on behalf of her female members in May 1946, Winifred Thomas spelled out their post-war intentions: 'We resent being used as stop-gaps and want to take our place in industry with our menfolk on an equal footing.'[64]

The industrial ambitions of the female war workers of south Wales were not always appreciated, however, by the menfolk of this industrial society. The opinion expressed at a meeting of the Bridgend TLC in March 1946, when a male delegate warned that there would be much ill-feeling in the town regarding the employment of women in the forthcoming reorganization of industry, provided only a foretaste of what was to follow.[65] Male unemployment rose steadily as thousands of demobilized soldiers and war workers returned to their home districts, and disillusionment soon replaced their high hopes for a 'new south Wales'. Not only were serious delays experienced in the establishment of new industries in the area, but when the new works eventually opened their doors, it became apparent that they preferred to employ females at the factory benches. In January 1946 it was announced that all five of the firms which had agreed to establish manufacturing concerns at the site of the Hirwaun ROF were proposing to employ about 70 per cent female labour.[66] Indeed, by June 1946, females comprised 43.9

, [63] Communist Party of Mid-Glamorgan, *When War Jobs Finish: Contributions by the Communist Party of Mid-Glamorgan* (Abertridwr, 1944), p. 7.
  [64] *Western Mail*, 28 May 1946.
  [65] *Glamorgan Gazette*, 8 March 1946.
  [66] *Western Mail*, 2 January 1946.

per cent (7,049) of all those employed in surplus government factories in the South Wales and Monmouthshire Development Area.[67] As D. A. Price-White, Conservative MP for Caernarfon Boroughs, argued in May 1946, such developments did not augur well for the future industrial prospects of the Welsh male population:

> many of us are concerned with the situation in the light industries which are all too slowly appearing in Wales and which, though they help in the employment of women, do not in our view offer any real solution for male unemployment. Many of these light assembly factories employ women in as high a proportion as 80 or 90 per cent and while the employment they afford is very thankfully received, they don't represent the ultimate answer to general unemployment.[68]

As the number of women who were taken on at the new industries of south Wales gradually increased, efforts to ensure that future industrial projects provided greater employment opportunities for the idle male workforce intensified. Speaking in Parliament in May 1946, D. J. Williams, MP for Neath, asked Sir Stafford Cripps, the president of the Board of Trade, whether he was aware of the 'widespread concern' felt in south Wales at the high proportion of female labour to be employed in the new factories announced for the region, and he urged the minister to take urgent action to ensure that all future industrial projects designated for the area employed a higher proportion of males.[69] The representatives of the unemployed men of south Wales launched their own appeals and petitions to the appropriate government departments and, during 1946, a number of un-employment marches, demonstrations and public meetings were held throughout the district in protest at the delay in the establishment of industrial concerns which would provide work for local men.[70] Such was the gravity of the situation that a

---

[67] PP 1948 (II, Cmd. 7540), p. 49.
[68] NLW, BBC (Wales) Archive, script of radio talk by D. A. Price-White MP, 'Wales at Westminster', broadcast on 28 May 1946.
[69] *Parliamentary Debates* (Hansard) (5th series), vol. 422, 49 (6 May 1946).
[70] *Aberdare Leader*, 10 and 31 August 1946; *Free Press of Monmouthshire*, 19 April 1946, 10 May 1946; *Glamorgan Advertiser*, 21 June 1946; *Glamorgan Gazette*, 6 December 1946; *The Rhondda Leader*, 26 May 1946, 20 and 27 July 1946, 3 August 1946; *Western Mail*, 18 and 23 July 1946, 21 August 1946, 28 October 1946.

deputation of Welsh MPs met the prime minister, the president of the Board of Trade and the minister of labour and national service in July 1946 to impress on them the urgent need to alleviate male unemployment.[71]

At the same time, government ministers were embarking on a campaign to encourage the women of Britain to enter, or remain in, industrial employment until post-war export targets were reached.[72] After several appeals for women to come forward, the Ministry of Labour decided to press ahead with a national propaganda drive, and the 'Women in industry' campaign which was aimed at women aged between thirty-five and fifty was launched on 1 June 1947 in sixty districts where the labour shortage was most acute.[73] Although the women of Wales were not targeted in the post-war campaign,[74] the nationwide appeals for British women to go back to work incensed many of those who lived in the industrial communities of south Wales. Responding to a radio talk delivered by the prime minister in March 1946, the editor of *The Rhondda Leader* noted that 'one passage in an otherwise admirable broadcast' had 'struck a jarring note in the ears of the inhabitants of these valleys'.[75] Clement Attlee's appeal for women and elderly people to remain in industrial employment clearly made little sense to the people of the Rhondda valleys, where over 4,000 men were registered as being out of work at that time. The unemployed residents of Aberdare were similarly aggrieved by such appeals, as a local newspaper columnist explained in March 1947:

> The Prime Minister has appealed to the women of the country who have left the factories since the war ended to go back to work to help increase

[71] PRO, Lab 43/1. The deputation included the following MPs from south Wales: W. H. Mainwaring (Rhondda East); G. Daggar (Abertillery); D. R. Grenfell (Gower); J. Callaghan (Cardiff South); W. G. Cove (Aberavon); P. Freeman (Newport); W. John (Rhondda West); P. Morris (Swansea West); D. Ll. Mort (Swansea East); L. Ungoed-Thomas (Llandaff and Barry); and E. J. Williams (Ogmore). A deputation from the South Wales Regional Council of Labour met Sir Stafford Cripps, president of the Board of Trade, for similar talks in August 1946.

[72] PP 1946–7 (XIX, Cmd. 7046), *Economic Survey for 1947*, pp. 27–8.

[73] See William Crofts, 'The Attlee government's pursuit of women', *History Today* (1986), 29–35.

[74] In fact, by 1947, government officials had come to the conclusion that the time had come 'to resist the introduction of more firms requiring predominantly female labour' in parts of south Wales, and that efforts should be concentrated on attracting industries which provided jobs for unemployed males. PP 1947–8 (XVI, Cmd. 7267), p. 17.

[75] *The Rhondda Leader*, 9 March 1946.

the nation's production, but there is no need for this in Aberdare. We still have here a large army of unemployed men, many of them ex-miners unable to hew coal in the pits any longer because of dust-condition and various injuries, who are waiting anxiously and a little bitterly for the chance to work in lighter industries. Development at the Trading Estate, where about 2,000 people are now working, mostly women, has by-passed them.[76]

The realization that the new factories and light industries were failing to make 'any great contribution to the problem of male unemployment' in south Wales weighed heavily on the minds of the unemployed men of the mining districts where the crisis in the coal industry remained critical.[77] The war years had failed to provide the necessary stimulus to halt the steady decline of the industry, and both production and manpower rates had suffered as a result. Coal output at the pits of south Wales fell from 37,773,000 tons to 20,950,000 tons between 1937 and 1946 and, during the same period, the number of men employed in the industry fell from 135,901 to 107,642.[78] Although the nationalization of the coal industry on 1 January 1947 brought new hope for the future, the industrial outlook remained bleak, particularly for the elderly and disabled miners for whom there was little or no immediate prospect of securing alternative employment.[79]

The fact that the post-war reconstruction programme was bringing thousands of jobs to the female population of south Wales was of little consolation to those who regarded the provision of jobs for men to be a priority. As a local newspaper columnist argued forcefully in July 1946: 'Aberdare's need . . . is *employment for men.*'[80] Eva Bendix, a journalist from Aberdare's sister-town, Slaglesse in Denmark, who visited the nearby Hirwaun trading estate in the summer of 1946, agreed:

---

[76] *Aberdare Leader*, 29 March 1947.
[77] Beacham, 'The future of the South Wales Coalfield', 143; GRO, Rhondda UDC minutes, 14 March 1945.
[78] Francis and Smith, *The Fed*, p. 438.
[79] See the following for representations made on behalf of the unemployed, elderly and disabled miners of south Wales: NLW, Labour Party of Wales Archive, South Wales Regional Council of Labour Executive Committee minutes, 19 February 1946; *Aberdare Leader*, 19 January 1946, 9 February 1946; *South Wales Echo*, 12 February 1946; *Western Mail*, 9 and 12 February 1948.
[80] *Aberdare Leader*, 13 July 1946.

what lingers in my mind is so many women working there. Is that good? I
have a very disturbing picture in my mind of your unemployed, standing in
the street, smoking their pipes, waiting . . . I did not like that. I hope they
will have jobs soon.[81]

While the wartime employment situation could be written off
as a temporary anomaly, this 'disturbing picture' of life in post-
war south Wales posed a far more serious and long-term
challenge to the traditional employment patterns and industrial
structure of the region. Indeed, many interpreted such changes
as a threat to the area's social and cultural conventions. The
Welsh woman's 'traditional' position was regarded as being
firmly in the home, and the restoration of such an ideal became a
powerful notion to be championed by many disgruntled patri-
archs in the immediate post-war period. Addressing members of
the local Cymrodorion Society at the Mona café, Aberdare, in
November 1945, Wynne Samuel, a prominent member of Plaid
Genedlaethol Cymru, called for action to be taken to safeguard
the status of the *penteulu*, or head of the family. In his opinion, it
was 'a deadly blow to a famous Welsh tradition' to see young
girls in their early teens working while elderly men, the
traditional breadwinners, were unemployed.[82] 'Aberdaria', a
columnist with the *Aberdare Leader*, commented that while Wynne
Samuel's nationalist views were usually 'damned in the eyes of
most people', his opinions on this matter at least were widely
supported in the town.[83] Councillor Tom Davey, a member of
the Ogmore and Garw UDC, lent his support to this notion at a
special meeting of the authority held in July 1946, when he
expressed his concern that young females were now the main
breadwinners in many homes in the area. In his opinion:

The present trend of employing juvenile labour is undermining a vital
characteristic of life in the Welsh mining valleys. It has always been the

[81] Ibid., 31 August 1946.
[82] *Aberdare Leader*, 24 November 1945. See also the report of the meeting of the
executive committee of Plaid Genedlaethol Cymru held at Aberystwyth in December
1945, when Wynne Samuel repeated his concern that unemployed Welshmen who
wished to remain in their native districts would soon have no option but to endure the
indignity of staying home to undertake domestic chores while their wives and daughters
went to the factories to work. *South Wales Echo*, 31 December 1945.
[83] *Aberdare Leader*, 24 November 1945.

prerogative of the head of the family to be the chief wage-earner, very often today, we find that a girl of fifteen is the only wage-earner.[84]

Similar views had been expressed by an unemployed man from Neath in a letter to his local newspaper in September 1945. Angered that a factory which had recently opened in his locality employed 957 females but only 57 men, 'Redundant' urged the authorities to ensure that future projects employed a fair proportion of male labour: 'I do not forget the fine efforts of the women during the war, but after all, the man is the bread-winner and the Welsh idea is based on the woman's place in the home.'[85]

Essentially, therefore, the creation of a new body of female industrial workers, with its associated problems, reflected wider changes to the Welsh economic and social pattern. An uncertain future for the heavy industries meant that a very different industrial south Wales – and a very different industrial workforce – was being created, with greater emphasis laid upon factories and light industries. Indeed, by July 1947, only 22 per cent of the workforce employed in the South Wales and Monmouthshire Development Area was engaged in coal mining, while 21 per cent was employed in the manufacture of capital goods.[86] To many local residents this shift in the occupational distribution of the industrial workforce, which favoured the employment of females and juveniles, could not be regarded as providing a solid foundation for the long-term future of the industrial communities.[87] As the authors of the *Industrial Survey of South Wales* had predicted in 1932, this society's long history of economic dependence on the heavy industries and its predominantly male labour force would make it difficult for some people to accept the possibility of an alternative industrial structure:

> There exists in South Wales, whose population has for so long been engaged in the extraction of coal and the manufacture of iron and steel, a habit of thinking that the only kind of production which is dignified or worthwhile is the production of primary commodities . . . Such persons

[84] *Glamorgan Advertiser*, 26 July 1946.
[85] *Neath Guardian*, 21 September 1945.
[86] PP 1948 (II, Cmd. 7540), p. 24.
[87] *The Rhondda Leader*, 7 September 1946.

sometimes argue that the 'new' industries . . . cannot 'give employment' as coal mining, or shipbuilding, or cotton-spinning can do.[88]

Another government report published before the war had warned that some of the inhabitants of those areas traditionally associated with heavy industry might adopt a 'contemptuous outlook' towards light industries.[89] In the industrial communities of south Wales there was much evidence to suggest that this was indeed the case. Often viewed disdainfully as paltry solutions to the unemployment problems of the region, factories manufacturing goods such as 'dolls'-eyes', 'baby-linen' and 'buttons, pots and pans' failed to convince a disillusioned and demoralized body of unemployed men of their suitability as realistic or desirable forms of employment.[90] In the mining communities of south Wales where the labour process had traditionally been based upon heavy, manual work, such contempt for factory employment was perhaps not unexpected. At a meeting of the Ogmore and Garw UDC in February 1948, a councillor stressed the importance of placing disabled ex-miners in employment connected with the coal industry, rather than in 'pickle works and paper factories', with which he was 'not so enamoured'.[91] Furthermore, since factory work had become associated with the employment of female labour, it was clear that general perceptions of the nature and importance of the work had become devalued and debased. One ex-miner who had been directed to work in a factory during the war made his feelings on the matter clear in a conversation with Mass-Observation investigators at Blaina in September 1943:

> It's no work for a *man* in the factory. Bloody red tape everywhere. You can't call your soul your own up there. In the pit, if I get bloody fed up I can curse the manager. Up there, we're all a set of little ladies in pinafores.[92]

---

[88] Board of Trade, *Industrial Survey of South Wales*, p. 156.
[89] PEP, *Report on the Location of Industry*, p. 68.
[90] *Free Press of Monmouthshire*, 6 September 1946; *Glamorgan Advertiser*, 13 September 1946; *Western Mail*, 3 September 1948.
[91] *Glamorgan Gazette*, 6 February 1948.
[92] M-O A, FR 1498, Appendix, 'The latest news', September 1943, p. 13.

This scornful attitude towards factory employment changed very little over the years, as the evidence of social researchers who conducted an investigation in the Swansea area in the early 1950s suggests. In the opinion of the researchers, the 'often-heard sneer against "dolls'-eyes" factories by men who were more accustomed to the work-processes of heavy industry, was an indication of their contempt for work which was regarded as "not really men's work at all" '.[93] This view of factory work as being somehow beneath the dignity of the male population raises important questions about notions of masculinity within this changing industrial society. The researchers who undertook the social investigation in the Swansea area noted how the gradual decline of the old, heavy industries was seen to have led to a consequent 'decline in status of the older skilled manual worker'.[94] Writing in the late 1950s about the effects of the 'silent economic revolution' which had taken place in the Rhondda since the end of the war, E. D. Lewis also concluded that the decline in the numbers employed in the coal industry, and the increased employment of females in factories, had 'brought about a lowering of men's status in the community'.[95]

Such representations of factory work as demeaning and emasculating also ensured that, despite women's economic and social gains, the relative status of 'women's work' remained both socially and culturally subordinate to that of men.[96] At the factories, women workers were invariably engaged on 'unskilled', low-paid work which reflected the low social and cultural status attributed to such jobs. It must be recognized, however, as Jane Lewis has argued, that the concept and measure of 'skill' is itself 'socially constructed'.[97] Many women, particularly those who had previous experience of factory employment, were accomplished and highly competent assembly-line workers who possessed genuine skills. Yet, rather than being regarded as a measure of their painstaking efficiency and manual dexterity,

---

[93] T. Brennan, E. W. Cooney and H. Pollins, *Social Change in South-West Wales* (London, 1954), p. 4.
[94] Ibid., pp. 4–5.
[95] Lewis, *The Rhondda Valleys*, p. 274.
[96] For a detailed examination of the characteristics of 'women's work', see Lewis, *Women in England, 1870–1950*, pp. 162–217.
[97] Ibid., p. 171.

women's apparent suitability for 'monotonous, repetitive' work, which required 'nimble and delicate fingers', was merely dismissed as an indication of the low level of 'skill' required for the job.[98] Thus, regardless of the ability and expertise which women brought to the workplace, they were generally excluded from what were regarded as 'skilled' work processes and, consequently, were denied the higher rates paid to 'skilled' workers who were invariably men.[99] Women workers also often lacked the full protection and backing of trade union organizations in order to pursue their claims for fairer wage rates. Speaking at a meeting of the Maesteg UDC in January 1948, Councillor R. Mordecai alleged 'a lack of vigilance by trade unions' on behalf of the young women of the area, who he claimed were being 'exploited' and used as cheap labour in the factories of the district.[100]

Despite the substantial post-war increase in the number of working women and the shift in the occupational distribution of this workforce, the female workers of south Wales remained in sexually segregated, low-paid and low-status jobs. 'Women's work' continued to be regarded as work of secondary importance to that performed by the male workforce, whose claim to higher status and higher-paid employment remained largely unchallenged. This concept was firmly enshrined in state policy, as exemplified in the views of the authors of the report of the Royal Commission on Equal Pay, published in October 1946:

> The average male earner is a husband and father. The average woman in employment is not a wife and mother, and even the wives and mothers who are in employment are not normally the sole support of their families. It is moreover as well to remember that the average woman is not in employment at all . . . It is manifest that the welfare of many more persons depends on the level of the man's rate of pay than on that of the woman's rate, and in any estimate of the consequences of equal pay this numerical fact must be given due weight.[101]

[98] *Glamorgan Gazette*, 24 October 1947; *Aberdare Leader*, 12 June 1948.
[99] *Merthyr Express*, 4 October 1947.
[100] *Glamorgan Gazette*, 2 January 1948.
[101] PP 1945–6 (XI, Cmd. 6937), *Report of the Royal Commission on Equal Pay, 1944–46*, p. 133.

Women workers were also commonly regarded as temporary employees whose careers would inevitably be interrupted or cut short by their primary commitment to marriage, children and home life. The assumption that women's role as wage-earners was 'secondary to their reproductive function'[102] served to re-affirm their low status in the labour market and ensured that women workers were rarely regarded as long-term investments by employers and trade unions. As John Newsom, chief education officer for Hertfordshire, noted in 1948:

> Employers are themselves reluctant to train girls for highly skilled or responsible jobs, because they know from experience that the majority will leave to get married just when they reach their peak efficiency; and to be constantly recruiting and training young women for these posts, only to lose them at the critical period, is more trouble that it is worth.[103]

In addition to generalizing about the work capabilities and expectations of women workers, contemporary observers also expressed their shared beliefs that certain forms of employment were more suitable and acceptable for the female population to perform. A series of articles entitled 'Careers for women', which appeared in the *Western Mail* in 1949, urged young women to consider occupations in the service industry, such as hotel and shop work, which had traditionally been performed by females.[104] Despite the thousands of new job opportunities which were being created in the light industries of south Wales at the time, no mention was made of factory employment; such work was clearly not deemed to be an occupation worthy of considera-tion by any ambitious young woman. In this respect, the war experience had failed to bring about any profound shift in people's perceptions of the type of work which the female population should perform. Indeed, the emphasis which was placed on the need to 'rebuild' the family unit after the disloca-tion of war served to focus public attention even more squarely on the desirability of placing young women in domestic service. After all, in addition to being a career for which females were deemed naturally suited, domestic service provided young

---

[102] Lewis, *Women in England, 1870–1950*, p. 173.
[103] John Newsom, *The Education of Girls* (London, 1948), p. 37.
[104] *Western Mail*, 8 and 15 January 1949, 5 and 12 February 1949.

women with the training required for their future roles as wives and mothers.

Concerns that the female war workers of south Wales would not be 'qualified to become managers of middle-class or working-class households, or mothers of children', because their experiences of factory employment had deprived them of the 'opportunities of learning homecraft', troubled many observers during the war.[105] A columnist who wrote in the Bridgend-based *Glamorgan Gazette* in 1943 believed that many local women would find it difficult to make the transition from 'munition worker to housewife' in the future:

> We hear and know that many thousands of women do not know how to cook, have no tradition of home-making, prefer tinned food, consume large quantities of patent medicines and bring up children with little knowledge of cleanliness or decent behaviour . . . Is it a matter for astonishment that girls uneducated in domestic affairs often do not make good wives or home-makers? One is very mindful of the great war handicap which many thousands of young women have sustained during the past few years through going straight from school into industry . . . In fairness to these young women, in fairness to the young men whom they will eventually marry and in fairness to the traditions of British home life and comforts, they should be given an opportunity of learning all that a good housewife should know, and so given the capacity to enjoy to the full, the new houses they hope to occupy.[106]

Such anxieties were heightened at the end of the war when it became clear that a growing number of young women were choosing to remain in factory employment and were ignoring appeals to return to more 'traditional' female professions such as domestic service or nursing.[107] In the opinion of the educationalist, John Newsom, this shift in the nature of the work experience of the female population was having a 'pernicious' effect on the character and domestic capabilities of the future wives and mothers of Britain:

[105] *South Wales Argus*, 3 July 1943; *Glamorgan Gazette*, 2 July 1943.
[106] *Glamorgan Gazette*, 2 July 1943.
[107] *South Wales Echo*, 29 January 1946, 5 September 1947.

These sterile occupations are the immediate preliminary to marriage and the rearing of children, a job which makes demands far greater than the repetitive machine-minding of the factory; and even the demands of a husband, modest though they may be, will strain a mind numbed by ten years on an electric sewing machine for eight hours a day.[108]

The damaging effect on the stability and happiness of home and family life had become all too evident to contemporary Welsh observers. Speaking in February 1948, Elizabeth Andrews JP, chair of the Ystrad (Rhondda) Matrimonial Court, expressed her opinion that 'bad housekeeping' caused by the post-war increase in factory employment was the root cause of marriage separation in the district: 'The girls were not taught the elements of good housekeeping and when they fell in love and married, their limitations proved disastrous.'[109]

In a bid to counter this disquieting trend, strenuous efforts were made to 'impart the ideal of "home-making as a career" ' to young women in the years immediately following the war.[110] In addition to promoting domestic service as a 'skilled craft' and an occupation which fulfilled 'an essential service to the community',[111] the housewives and mothers of the future were provided with new opportunities to receive training and education in the essential art of 'homecraft'. The Norwood Report of 1943, which outlined proposals for the secondary school curriculum to be adopted by the 1944 Education Act, strongly advocated the teaching of domestic science to female pupils, for knowledge of the subject was considered 'a necessary equipment for all girls as potential makers of homes'.[112] Violet Markham and Florence Hancock, the authors of the government report which was commissioned to investigate the post-war organization of domestic employment, were agreed that such training proved invaluable 'for the girl who subsequently marries and has a home of her

---

[108] Newsom, *The Education of Girls*, p. 41.

[109] *Western Mail*, 10 February 1948. Such views were frequently expressed by Welsh-language commentators: see, for example, Robert Owen, 'Problem y cartref a'r teulu', *Y Drysorfa*, CXIX (1949), 255–9; and Kate Roberts's 'women's column' in *Baner ac Amserau Cymru*, 4 and 11 June 1947, 7 April 1948.

[110] Summerfield, 'Women in Britain since 1945', p. 61.

[111] PP 1944–5 (V, Cmd. 6650), pp. 3–4. See also *Glamorgan Gazette*, 19 January 1945.

[112] Board of Education, *Curriculum and Examinations in Secondary Schools: Report of the Committee of the Secondary School Examinations Council appointed by the President of the Board of Education in 1941* (London, 1943), p. 127.

own. Such a girl starts married life better equipped for the task ahead than the majority of those who have spent their days at automatic machines.'[113] The report also argued in favour of expanding education and training opportunities in this field and recommended that the National Institute of Houseworkers be established to ensure improved conditions and training for domestic servants.[114] In south Wales a number of post-war initiatives were set in place to teach domestic subjects to the housewives of the future and, by the autumn of 1947, a new training centre for domestic servants had been opened at Dan-y-coed, Swansea.[115] Commenting on the establishment of the new centre in an interview with a local newspaper reporter in February 1948, Elizabeth Andrews expressed her hope that young girls from the Rhondda would take advantage of the courses offered at the centre where, in addition to being taught the skills necessary to take up domestic service, they would be trained to become 'good housewives and mothers'.[116]

Upon achieving marriage and motherhood, it was assumed that women would retire from full-time employment and devote themselves entirely to their homes and families. Fuelled by concerns about the wartime break-up of families and the falling birth rate, women's traditional roles as wives, mothers and home-makers took on a new significance in the post-war period and gave additional force to the argument that married women should stay at home. Despite the fact that many married women and mothers had entered the industrial workforce during the war, attitudes towards their full-time employment remained generally discouraging and, as the results of the Social Survey of 1948 revealed, the notion that women's primary responsibilities lay with their homes and families continued to be upheld by both married women and their husbands.[117] At the same time, the sudden closure of wartime nurseries and the disappearance of

---

[113] PP 1944–5 (V, Cmd. 6650), pp. 3–4.
[114] Ibid., pp. 21–2.
[115] *Western Mail*, 11 September 1946, 1 August 1947.
[116] Ibid., 10 February 1948.
[117] Thomas, 'Women and industry: an inquiry into the problem of recruiting women to industry carried out for the Ministry of Labour and National Service' (Central Office of Information, Social Survey, 1948), p. 1. The results of the 1948 survey echoed those of two inquiries conducted in 1944 which found that marriage played a determining role in shaping women's attitude towards employment. Thomas, 'Women at work', pp. 14–15; M-O A, FR 2059, 'Will the factory girls want to stay put or go home?', pp. 6–7.

part-time shifts and shopping schemes designed to enable women to combine war work with their domestic and parental responsibilities made it impossible for many wives and mothers to continue working and emphasized the temporary and exceptional nature of their wartime role as workers.

Given the terms under which thousands of married women had entered paid employment during the war, it is not surprising that a conventional view of their 'rightful' role in the home survived. The wartime government had made explicit its aim to protect the family unit by ensuring that the wives of servicemen, mothers of young children, and women with domestic responsibilities were either exempt from national service or were protected from certain direction orders. The future role to be played by such women when the war ended had been further emphasized in the demobilization plans drawn up by the Ministry of Labour in November 1944, which stated that priority for release from war work should be given to women with household responsibilities, the wives of servicemen and women over the age of sixty.[118] Married women and working mothers had also been subjected to a constant barrage of wartime propaganda which reminded them that their services at the war factories were temporary and would not be required once the wartime emergency was over. One of the recruitment posters which featured prominently in the south Wales press during 1941 pointed out that the married woman who took up a job 'for the duration' was working to bring 'nearer the day when her soldier-husband' returned home and her life returned to normal.[119]

The married women war workers of south Wales who wished to challenge such notions of 'normality' by remaining in the labour market also faced the deadweight of local opposition and prejudice against their full-time employment. In the immediate post-war period, when the urgent need to provide work for the unemployed men of the district dominated discussion, the work ambitions of the married female population prompted heated debate in local newspapers, with many irate correspondents

---

[118] *Western Mail*, 17 November 1944; Calder, *The People's War*, p. 570.
[119] The words of the Ministry of Labour and National Service recruitment poster, 'Where IS Mrs Jones Going?', *Glamorgan Advertiser*, 25 July 1941. Similar sentiments were expressed in the article 'This one's for the housewife', *Glamorgan Gazette*, 1 January 1943.

advocating the swift return óf all married female workers to 'the kitchen front'.[120] According to a columnist who wrote in the *South Wales Echo* in January 1946, such action would be welcomed by many Welshmen who feared for their own future role in the home and workplace:

> They have seen womenfolk collaring office, factory and outdoor jobs in all directions and have had visions of themselves being shunted into household chores with the care of children, shaking of beds etc. while their wives and daughters enjoyed themselves on office stools and at the benches, drinking tea at regular intervals at their working places.[121]

Although commentators such as Gertrude Williams had expressed great optimism in 1945 at the post-war employment prospects of married women, in the wake of the wartime experience and the removal of the marriage bar in the teaching and civil service professions, there remained a great deal of opposition to their continued employment.[122] The strength of opposition in south Wales had already been highlighted during the war, when many local authorities and employers expressed a marked reluctance to implement even a temporary suspension of the marriage bar in some professions, and only reconsidered their position under pressure from government officials, or when labour shortages became acute.[123] Some employers proved far

[120] *South Wales Echo*, 28 January 1946. See also ibid., 26 and 29 September 1945, 24 November 1945, 21 February 1946, 1 March 1946, 9 April 1946.

[121] Ibid., 18 January 1946.

[122] Williams, *Women and Work*, p. 100. For evidence of this opposition, see PP 1945–6 (X, Cmd. 6886), *Marriage Bar in the Civil Service, Report of the Civil Service National Whitley Council Committee*, p. 13; Harold L. Smith, 'The womanpower problem in Britain during the Second World War', *Historical Journal*, 27, no. 4 (1984), 941–4.

[123] For example, in October 1940, members of the Pontypridd UDC voted unanimously in favour of preventing married women from taking up even temporary positions in the employ of the authority. It was only when the authority was faced with a desperate shortage of labour during 1941 that officials agreed that married women could take up temporary clerical positions in the council offices. GRO, Pontypridd UDC minutes, 1 October 1940, 18 November 1941. The wartime policy adopted by the Swansea CB Education Committee, whereby all female teachers were to resign upon marriage (unless they were marrying men who were in the armed services or were undertaking work of national importance), and no married women were to be appointed to wartime posts if single women were available, incurred the wrath of the Board of Education. It was only after Sir Wynn P. Wheldon, secretary of the Welsh Department of the Board of Education, communicated with the committee members and impressed upon them the urgent need to reconsider their policy that married women became eligible for engagement under the conditions applicable to temporary appointments. West Glamorgan Record Office, Swansea CB minutes, 9 September 1941, 6 October 1941, 8 December 1941, 12 January 1942.

more resistant to change. It was only after receiving an official warning from the Board of Education that if it did not agree to the retention of married female teachers it would not be permitted to appoint college-leavers to local teaching posts, that the Mountain Ash Education Committee finally resolved to appoint married women to fill temporary positions in July 1944.[124] A similar situation arose at Cardiff, where the local education authority also failed to accede to recommendations that women teachers should be allowed to continue in employment after marriage. The matter eventually came to a head in April 1943, when the Board of Education ruled that no new teachers could be appointed to Cardiff's public elementary schools until the local education committee gave an assurance to suspend the regulations governing the termination of services of married women teachers.[125]

The war experience had clearly not changed local opinions on this matter, for almost as soon as the war was over many Welsh employers and local authorities which had temporarily employed married women immediately terminated their wartime contracts. In March 1946, members of the Caerphilly UDC resolved to terminate the services of all married women, while six months later, members of the Merthyr Tydfil Education Committee decided to adopt the principle of employing single women or widows only in appointments connected to its further education scheme and 'Make do and mend' classes.[126] Similarly, the Monmouthshire Education Committee placed a ban on the appointment of married women to vacancies in the school canteens of the authority.[127] Despite the fact that the Education Act of 1944 provided for the abolition of the marriage bar in the teaching profession, south Wales clearly remained a problematic area. In May 1946 the Glamorgan Education Committee was accused of contravening the terms of the new Act, following its decision to dismiss married women who became pregnant.[128]

[124] GRO, Mountain Ash UDC Education Committee minutes, 7 July 1942, 6 October 1942, 2 February 1943, 19 April 1943, 6 July 1944.

[125] Greenaway, 'The impact of the Second World War on nursery, elementary and secondary education in Glamorgan', p. 24.

[126] GRO, Caerphilly UDC minutes, 12 March 1946; *Western Mail*, 22 October 1946.

[127] *Free Press of Monmouthshire*, 30 May 1947.

[128] GRO, Glamorgan County Council, annual report of the director of education for 1946, 13 May 1946; *Western Mail*, 14, 22 and 25 May 1946; *Parliamentary Debates* (Hansard) (5th series), vol. 423, 513–4 (23 May 1946).

The situation seems not to have improved significantly in the months that followed. As the testimony of one married woman who found herself consigned to 'the scrap-heap' in 1947 reveals, married women teachers continued to experience great difficulties in finding work in the area:

> There is no tradition of female labour in South Wales and, especially now that there are ex-Servicemen without employment, the prejudice against retaining married women in occupations is very strong. Scarcely a week passes without some indignant ratepayer writing to the postbag about pin-money women, and appealing for the dismissal of married women workers so that ex-Servicemen may have their jobs 'and thus become satisfied citizens . . .' A friend, with a good degree and qualified as a teacher, is in similar plight because of the reluctance to employ married women teachers in Glamorgan. We are both of us on the scrap-heap – wasting national assets – but does anybody care?[129]

Although some individuals and employers were prepared to champion the rights of married women to employment,[130] the negative stand taken by many of the Welsh local authorities met with the general approval of many of the residents of the industrial communities of south Wales. The representatives of the unemployed men of the district were prominent voices in the chorus of protest which called for married women to be suspended from their 'temporary' wartime posts. Speaking at a meeting of the Aberdare TLC in May 1946, Councillor Sam Wilcox expressed his opinion that 'no married woman should be in a job' while so many local men remained idle.[131] The grievances of the unemployed men of Merthyr Tydfil were voiced three months later at a meeting of the local TLC, when councillors complained that many married women continued to be employed in local factories and schools, while 'large numbers of young men who have been serving with H. M. Forces throughout the war' were 'compelled to sign on at the Labour Exchange'.[132] Many ex-servicemen were of the opinion that the jobs temporarily filled by married women should automatically

---

[129] *New Statesman*, 3 May 1947.
[130] See, for example, *Free Press of Monmouthshire*, 5 December 1947, 24 September 1948.
[131] *Aberdare Leader*, 1 June 1946.
[132] NLW, Labour Party of Wales Archive, South Wales Regional Council of Labour Executive Committee minutes, 9 September 1946.

be transferred to local men. In December 1945 the Merthyr Vale branch of the British Legion called on the councillors of the borough to vote in favour of a proposal to dismiss all married women who had been employed by the authority during the war and to fill their positions with ex-servicemen.[133] Similar views were expressed in December 1946 by an ex-serviceman from the Rhondda who had been incensed by the fact that the local authority continued to employ married women in its offices:

> Many an ex-serviceman who is now unemployed after 5–6 years in the Forces would be more than pleased to accept a job with the average rate of £6 per week in preference to the dole. To dispense with the services of the female employees would not create any undue hardship to these people as it would not be difficult for them to find other work in these valleys at the local factories who are not able to employ male labour but would willingly engage most, if not all, of the other sex who are desirous of obtaining work . . . Furthermore, I am informed that some of these female employees are now married and into their homes go a joint income of approx. fourteen pounds a week . . . This makes me ask the question – 'Is this what we have fought for?'[134]

Significantly, many of the female residents of the Welsh industrial communities were agreed on this point and argued that married women should now give up their positions to unemployed men.[135] At a conference of Women's Social Clubs held in Hertfordshire in September 1947, delegates from south Wales proposed a motion deploring the efforts of the government to urge married women to go back to industry 'while men unfit for heavy work were unemployed and in view of the rise in juvenile delinquency which had occurred during the war'.[136] A motion passed at the annual Wales Area conference of the Women's Section of the British Legion at Aberystwyth six months previously, also called on 'married women who are employed and whose husbands are earning sufficient to maintain wife, family and home' to give up their employment 'when it can be proved that an unemployed ex-serviceman or

[133] Merthyr Tydfil Town Public Library, Merthyr Tydfil CB minutes, 7 December 1945.
[134] *The Rhondda Leader*, 28 December 1946.
[135] *South Wales Echo*, 13 April 1946, 13 December 1946.
[136] *Western Mail*, 25 September 1947.

Table 5.3: Married female workers and percentage of total occupied female workforce
(aged fifteen and over), 1951

Area	Number of married female workers	% of total occupied female workforce	% married female workers who work full-time
Glamorgan	**36258**	**29.2**	**86.4**
Cardiff CB	10044	31.8	78.0
Merthyr Tydfil CB	1754	28.5	91.4
Swansea CB	4939	28.2	89.3
Rhondda UD	2881	27.7	93.1
Monmouthshire	**12233**	**30.7**	**87.2**
Newport CB	3814	31.3	83.6
Wales	**71870**	**27.7**	**87.3**
England and Wales	**2496799**	**39.8**	**75.7**

Source: 1951 Census Occupation Tables.

ex-servicewoman, qualified and prepared to take on the position is on the register of the employment exchange'.[137]

Given the strength of local feeling against the employment of married women, it seems remarkable that a growing number of Welsh wives entered the labour force during the post-war years. By 1951 some 30 per cent of occupied females in the counties of Glamorgan and Monmouth were married women and, as table 5.3 shows, the overwhelming majority were employed in full-time work. It is evident, however, that the proportion of married female workers remained far lower in Wales than in England and Wales as a whole. Considerable variation was also recorded in the proportion of married women who were employed in various parts of south Wales: married women accounted for 31.8 per cent of the female workforce in the Cardiff CB, while only 27.7 per cent of working women in the mining communities of the Rhondda UD were married. The increase in the number of married women workers was, in part, a consequence of changes

[137] Ibid., 15 February 1947.

in the Welsh marriage rate. The immediate post-war period witnessed a veritable 'marriage boom' as the proportion of married women increased and the average age at marriage fell.[138] In 1931 only 28.7 per cent of Welsh females aged between twenty and twenty-four were married, but by 1951 the proportion had risen to 46.9 per cent.[139]

Although changes in the marital composition of the female workforce were evident, closer examination of the nature of the work performed by married women, and of their attitudes towards work, reveals that traditional perceptions of their marginal role in the labour market remained firmly entrenched in the work culture of south Wales. It is impossible to give an accurate assessment of the occupational distribution of the married female workforce, but evidence suggests that the vast majority of wives who entered paid employment in the immediate post-war period were engaged in low-skilled, low-paid jobs in the new industries of the region, where the demand for female labour was great and often exceeded the local supply.[140] While their employment in large numbers in the factories of south Wales was a cause of great anxiety among the unemployed male population, it is significant that, in comparison with other occupations, such as the teaching profession, opposition to their appointment to low-status factory work was relatively subdued. Married women, particularly those who performed 'menial', repetitive tasks at factory benches, were not taken seriously as a workforce. The women themselves were unlikely to view such employment in terms of a 'career' and, so long as they continued to shoulder the double burden of paid employment and unpaid domestic labour, they would be regarded as a temporary and unreliable industrial workforce, prone to absenteeism and high labour turnover rates.[141] Moreover, since all married women were assumed to be financially dependent on their husbands, their status as wage-earners was also deemed subordinate and subsidiary to that of the male

---

[138] See J. M. Winter, 'The demographic consequences of the war', in Smith (ed.), *War and Social Change*, p. 153.

[139] John Williams, *Digest of Welsh Historical Statistics* (2 vols., Cardiff, 1985), I, pp. 35–6.

[140] See the following for reports of serious shortages of female labour at the Hirwaun trading estate, *Aberdare Leader*, 29 March 1947, 16 October 1948, 5 February 1949, 27 August 1949.

[141] Harris, *Married Women in Industry*, p. 26.

breadwinner. This concept was firmly enshrined in the Beveridge Report of 1942, where it was noted that:

> to most married women earnings by a gainful occupation do not mean what such earnings mean to most solitary women. Unless there are children, the housewife's earnings in general are a means, not of subsistence but of a standard of living above subsistence, like the higher earnings of a skilled man as compared with a labourer.[142]

Often referred to derogatorily as 'pin-money' or 'pocket-money', the earnings of the working wife were generally regarded as a supplement to the main family income, to be spent on non-essential items which were 'above regular family expenditure'.[143] No doubt many of the Welsh wives who desired to continue in industrial employment viewed their wages in this light. Wartime earnings had brought relative prosperity to impoverished homes and, having grown accustomed to this source of additional income, few wives wished to return to their straitened pre-war circumstances.[144] Looking back on the post-war years and the changes which the war initiated in the lives of many of her contemporaries, Maggie Pryce Jones, a young woman from Trelewis who married soon after the war ended, recalled that the chance to earn extra money to supplement the low wages of their husbands was a great inducement to the married women of the area to take up work in local factories:

> Previously they had relied upon their men to provide every penny they needed; there was never cash left over for luxuries. Now they could earn enough to pay for the extras for themselves; they could afford to buy the luxury goods which until now had been denied them.[145]

---

[142] PP 1942–3 (VI, Cmd. 6404), *Social Insurance and Allied Services, Report by Sir William Beveridge*, pp. 49–50.

[143] James, 'Women at work in twentieth century Britain', 297; PRO, Lab 10/367; *South Wales Echo*, 7 and 13 December 1946; Harris, *Married Women in Industry*, p. 27.

[144] Evidence of Respondent 4. The evidence of the chief constable of Neath suggests that many women sorely missed their wartime earnings. He noted that the number of shop thefts perpetrated by females had increased significantly since 'the withdrawal of women in industry and the shortage of clothing and domestic goods'. *Neath Guardian*, 29 April 1946.

[145] Maggie Pryce Jones, *Kingfisher of Hope* (Llandysul, 1993), p. 94.

The fact remained, however, that unless economic circumstances compelled them to work, married women did not generally engage in full-time employment after the war. The 1951 census revealed that only 22.5 per cent of married women in England and Wales were employed and, although the census tables do not provide a breakdown of the situation in local districts, it is certain that the participation rate of married women in the industrial districts of south Wales was much lower.[146] Even if they so desired, the vast majority of wives found it impossible to continue in paid employment, as it became all the more difficult to balance their role in the workplace with the heavy demands of their homes and families. As Paul Addison observed, the role of the housewife was made all the more onerous in the years immediately following the war. The strict rationing of food and many other essential commodities made life extremely difficult, and shopping in particular continued to be a tiring and frustrating business which entailed many hours of standing in queues.[147]

Married women's participation in the workforce was not made any easier by the fact that the limited wartime provisions which had been made to assist working wives and mothers with their domestic responsibilities, such as the introduction of part-time shifts, flexible working hours and child-care facilities, quickly disappeared at the end of the conflict. The vast majority of the 25,156 married women workers who lived in the counties of Glamorgan and Monmouth in 1951 were full-time workers, and it appears that only a handful of local factories worked part-time shifts. Even when part-time work was made available, as at one of the factories on the Hirwaun trading estate in October 1948, such action was usually taken in response to a labour shortage, rather than as a measure to suit the needs of working wives and mothers:

---

[146] *Census of England and Wales, 1951, Occupation Tables*, p. 36. A study of the mining community of Onllwyn in the Dulais valley undertaken during 1949 revealed that very few married women were gainfully employed (only four in Onllwyn and three in the neighbouring settlement of Pant-y-ffordd). Gwyn Evans, 'Onllwyn: a sociological study of a south Wales mining community' (unpublished MA thesis, University of Wales, 1961), pp. 30, 49.

[147] Paul Addison, *Now the War is Over: A Social History of Britain, 1945–51* (London, 1995 edn), p. 29.

Jobs on a 1–6 pm shift are waiting for all available part-time women workers in the Aberdare valley under the age of 40 at one of the largest factories on the Trading Estate which urgently needs female labour. This factory has been putting on hundreds of women workers on a full-time basis for the past couple of weeks, but its requirements are not yet satisfied. At the moment there is an almost complete shortage of women workers in the area. All those available at Aberdare, Mountain Ash and Merthyr have been taken on, and the Rhondda Valley has been scoured by the Employment Exchange . . . So now the factory has decided to establish this five-hour duration afternoon shift for women of this valley under 40 who might be prepared to work part-time and possibly a further part-time shift will also be arranged later.[148]

It is not surprising, therefore, that the vast majority of the married women who remained in employment after the war were either older women whose families had grown up, or young newly-weds who were anxious to provide for their new homes and had not yet started a family. Motherhood remained one of the main barriers to the continued employment of the female worker and, as the oral evidence of several of the women interviewed during the course of this study confirms, the arrival of children heralded the immediate departure of the young, married woman from the workplace.[149] The temporary role attached to the working mother was made explicit at the end of the war, when the wartime nurseries of south Wales closed with what some commentators alleged to be 'an unholy haste'.[150] Working mothers had been drawn into the workforce purely as an emergency measure and, having served their purpose, both the mothers and the institutions which had been provided to assist them with their family responsibilities, became surplus to requirements. From the outset of the war, Ministry of Health officials had emphasized the fact that the 'war nursery', as its name implied, would be provided only as a wartime measure. Writing to Zoë Puxley, assistant secretary in charge of maternity and child welfare at the ministry, in April 1940, one civil servant noted: 'The very fact that a Nursery Centre is neither a nursery school nor a day nursery would stamp them as a purely temporary expedient to deal with war conditions, and would make it easier to get rid of them after the war.'[151]

---

[148] *Aberdare Leader*, 16 October 1948. See also PEP, *Manpower*, p. 61.
[149] Evidence of Respondents 3, 4 and 6.
[150] *Western Mail*, 26 March 1945.
[151] PRO, MH 55/695.

As production demands decreased and growing numbers of working mothers were released from their wartime jobs, the closure of the war nurseries was easily justified by government officials. A survey of Welsh wartime nurseries, undertaken during the early months of 1945 by the chairman of the Welsh Board of Health and Eva Lady Reading, recommended the immediate closure of twenty-eight nurseries, the majority of which were situated in Glamorgan, on the grounds that they were 'redundant so far as the war effort is concerned'.[152] The decision to halve the grant which had been provided by the Welsh Board of Health to maintain the war nurseries, brought about further closures and the responsibility for ensuring future nursery provision was transferred to local education authorities. By March 1945 it was claimed that thirty of the eighty Welsh war nurseries which had been allocated a 100 per cent grant had already closed, while a further twenty-six had been threatened with closure within the month.[153]

Although the provision of child-care assistance to working mothers was no longer deemed necessary, many educationalists and medical experts were keen to build on the good work carried out by the war nurseries and argued in favour of their continuation.[154] Petitions and letters of protest were also sent to the local authorities and newspapers of south Wales, by parents who were keen to express their deep appreciation of the benefits of the wartime nurseries and to appeal for such facilities to be provided after the war.[155] However, the function of the peacetime nursery, as advocated by such individuals, differed greatly from that of the war nursery, which had cared for the children of working mothers only. Unlike its wartime counterpart, the role of the peacetime nursery was seen as complementing that of the home, rather than competing against it. Indeed, many of those who were in favour of extending nursery provision after the war

---

[152] PRO, MH 55/1708.

[153] *Western Mail*, 26 March 1945.

[154] See the detailed report of the proceedings of a conference of local education authorities on 'The future of wartime nurseries', convened at University College, Cardiff, on 24 March 1945, in GRO, Porthcawl UDC minutes, medical officer of health report, April 1945. See also R. M. Galloway, 'The function of nurseries in peace-time', *Journal of the Royal Sanitary Institute*, LXIV, no. 4 (1944), 183–4.

[155] See GRO, Bridgend UDC minutes, 8 March 1945; Maesteg UDC minutes, 13 March 1945; Glamorgan County Council, annual report of the director of education for 1945, 10 April 1945; Caerphilly UDC minutes, 8 May 1945; *Merthyr Express*, 22 January 1944; *Western Mail*, 29 March 1945; *South Wales Echo*, 9, 13 and 27 May 1946.

argued that home and family life would be strengthened as a result.[156] In his annual report for 1942, Dr Greenwood Wilson, the Cardiff medical officer of health, expressed the hope that nursery schools would not only help 'reinforce' the ideal of good parenting but could become 'schools for teaching the art and practice of mothercraft'.[157] Such sentiments were frequently expressed at the end of the war. Speaking at a conference of local education authorities convened by the Nursery School Association of Great Britain (Wales Area) at Cardiff in March 1945, Olive Wheeler, professor of education at University College, Cardiff, and a keen supporter of nursery education, argued strongly in favour of extending nursery provision on these grounds.[158] Nurseries could not only provide a stable and homely social environment for infants and babies from disadvantaged and broken homes, but could also ease tensions and difficulties arising from poor housing conditions by providing respite for their harassed mothers.[159] Speaking in Parliament in March 1945, William Cove, MP for Aberafan, delivered the following impassioned plea in favour of such a scheme on behalf of the miners' wives of south Wales:

> I was born the eldest of 12 children in a terrace house . . . This was in the Rhondda Valley . . . The point I am trying to make is that the bigger the family in the working class home, the greater the necessity for the care of the children between nought and two, and the greater the need, on behalf of the woman and the health of the child, for taking that burden out of the hands of the mother . . . There was never any leisure for the working class

[156] In a letter to Ness Edwards, MP for Caerphilly, dated 12 July 1949, H. V. Enthoven, honorary secretary of the National Society of Childrens' Nurseries, stated that the post-war nurseries should be regarded 'as a family service – an extension of the home, giving care to the child and partial freedom to the mother'. PRO, Lab 26/168. For a fuller examination of this theme, see Riley, 'The free mothers', 99–100.

[157] Cardiff Central Library, *Annual Report of the Medical Officer of Health for Cardiff, 1942*, p. vii.

[158] GRO, Porthcawl UDC minutes, report of the conference on 'The future of wartime nurseries', held at University College, Cardiff, April 1945.

[159] *South Wales Echo*, 24 May 1946; *Western Mail*, 5 and 8 January 1949. In her weekly column 'The feminine point of view', which appeared in the Bridgend-based *Glamorgan Gazette*, 'Eugene' argued that nurseries would be particularly beneficial in this respect: 'Why should young married people be tied to their homes; all work and no play is inclined to encourage frayed nerves, bad tempers and frequent fits of depression. Time and time again the advent of the "stork" has brought such storm clouds – husband accuses wife of neglecting him for the baby, wife retorts that since husband prefers going out to his club she is literally left holding the baby! With the installation of nurseries this problem could partly be solved.' *Glamorgan Gazette*, 27 April 1945.

mother and never any hope of being free from the care of the children . . .
Tens of thousands of mothers in South Wales, of whom I am speaking
more particularly, and in other areas never had a chance of leisure and
decency. There were frayed tempers on the part of the older children and
certainly on the part of the mother. It is a great injustice upon the mother.
It is a very bad thing for the children, particularly in large families with the
young ones coming along, to be a burden on working class mothers . . .
Whatever arguments one may use for and against it, there is in my area a
keen and live demand that the day nursery school should be continued. It
was put there for the war workers but the miners' wives and the miners
now are saying 'Keep this day nursery open.'[160]

While it is clear that the war experience and the passing of the
1944 Education Act gave a new lease of life to the provision of
nursery education in south Wales,[161] it was also the case that the
post-war nursery schools were to serve a very different purpose
from that of the wartime day nurseries and were not regarded as
facilities to enable the mothers of young children to go out to
work.[162] This change was reflected in the service offered at the
nurseries. The opening hours of the nursery schools were generally far shorter than those of the war nurseries and admission was
restricted to children aged between three and five.

The prospect of continuing in full-time employment on these
terms held little attraction for the vast majority of Welsh wives
and mothers. The strain of coping with the heavy demands of
home and work during the war years had proved difficult
enough; the disappearance of initiatives such as child-care assistance gave working mothers little incentive to remain in the

---

[160] *Parliamentary Debates* (Hansard) (5th series), vol. 408, 2438 (9 March 1945).

[161] Details of the wartime nurseries which were taken over by local education
authorities in Glamorgan are provided in Greenaway, 'The impact of the Second World
War on nursery, elementary and secondary education in Glamorgan', p. 66. By July
1946, twenty-three wartime nurseries and eighteen wartime nursery classes had been
taken over by local education authorities in Wales and had been provisionally recognized
by the Welsh Department of the Board of Education as nursery schools and classes
respectively; only one wartime nursery was taken over by a welfare authority (Penarth
UDC) as a day nursery. PP 1945–6 (XX, Cmd. 6938), pp. 32–4.

[162] A circular issued jointly by the Welsh Board of Health and the Ministry of
Education in December 1945 made this point clear: 'The Ministers concerned accept the
view that . . . in the interest of the health and development of the child no less than for the
benefit of his mother . . . the right policy to pursue would be positively to discourage
mothers of children under two from going out to work.' Joint Circular 221/45 Welsh
Board of Health and Circular 75/ Welsh Department of the Ministry of Education,
reproduced in GRO, Glamorgan County Council, annual report of the director of
education for 1945, 20 December 1945.

labour market. One working wife from Cardiff remarked that
women in her situation were 'only too glad to swop the pint and
the pants for the kitchen and all it entails – back to one job – not
two'.[163] The older and middle-aged Welsh women interviewed in
March 1945 by Roma Sanders, a correspondent with the *Western
Mail*, were said to feel that they had 'neglected their homes,
husbands and children long enough' and were ready to return
home.[164] Certainly, for many young women, some of whom had
been estranged from their newly wed husbands or 'sweethearts'
during the conflict, the end of the war heralded a new beginning.
Their personal lives had been put on hold during the conflict and
the desire to settle down after the war to build a home and family
life together was strong.[165] According to 'Eugene', the writer of
the occasional women's column in the *Glamorgan Gazette*, Welsh
women welcomed their release from wartime industries and their
return to 'normality':

> Some of you may have difficulty in settling down to the normal routine of
> life at home again, but if you have [a] few regrets, they will be lost in the
> flood of overwhelming relief that at last your time is your own. No more
> day and night shifts, parades or marching – your energy and attention can
> once more be focused on working for the welfare of home and children.[166]

Attention has already been drawn to the ambiguities inherent
in such commentaries and responses, yet, given the harsh
realities of wartime life, the emphasis placed by many women on
their home and family life in the post-war period was, perhaps,
to be expected. Unless they needed the money, the alternative
prospect of continuing in low-paid, monotonous jobs at local
factories, while juggling home and family responsibilities, was
hardly enticing to the vast majority of women. As a Mass-
Observation inquiry published in 1944 was to note, women who
had been employed in industry during the war were 'more
inclined to long for security and a quiet life than women who

[163] *South Wales Echo*, 11 September 1944.
[164] *Western Mail*, 10 March 1945.
[165] The experience of one young Welsh bride, who was separated from her husband for
three and a half years soon after her marriage in 1943, was all too common. Evidence of
Respondent 3.
[166] *Glamorgan Gazette*, 13 July 1945.

have chosen or been directed into the Services'.[167] This conclusion was echoed in the findings of a detailed report on the post-war aspirations of female factory workers, the majority of whom had stated that they looked forward to 'settling down and making a home after the war'.[168]

The incentives to leave full-time employment and return to the idealized domain of the home were made all the more attractive by the powerful force of propaganda and the promise of a new era in housing and home comforts.[169] Together with concerns regarding post-war employment, the need to address the housing problems of south Wales had featured prominently in wartime discussions on post-war reconstruction.[170] One significant feature of the wartime debate on housing was the emphasis placed on the role which women should play in the formation of future housing policy. For example, at a day school organized by the Women's Section of the Caerphilly Labour Party at Llanbradach in November 1943, a resolution was passed urging the establishment of a women's housing advisory group 'for the purpose of consultation re. the new Housing programme, particularly with regard to the type, fitments and sites of the new houses'.[171] Since women were regarded as the section of the public most vitally affected by housing, it was crucial that their views on future housing needs and designs were conveyed to architects, planners and manufacturers. Writing in July 1943, Elizabeth Andrews expressed the hope that some Welsh women might even consider a career in the building industry and, thus, ensure that new homes – and, more importantly, new kitchens – were built to meet the demands of future housewives:

> We hear continued praise given to the women in the Services and industries and we feel it is well deserved but when peace comes there will be a testing time for women's sphere of work. 'Men build houses, but it's

[167] Mass-Observation, *The Journey Home* (London, 1944), pp. 57–8.
[168] M-O A, FR 2059, 'Will the factory girls want to stay put or go home', p. 2.
[169] See the advertisement 'Electricity improves', *Woman's Journal*, September 1945.
[170] PRO, Inf 1/292.
[171] SWCA, Caerphilly Labour Party Women's Section minutes, 13 November 1943. See also NLW, Idris Cox Papers, 53, 'A brighter future for Abertillery and district: a contribution of the above subject by the Abertillery Communist Party in the sincere hope that it will be earnestly considered by every thinking citizen, *c.*1940–45', p. 8; Pontypridd Public Library, Pontypridd Trades Council and Labour Party minutes, 6 September 1943; *Porth Gazette and Rhondda Leader*, 19 February 1944; *South Wales Echo*, 2 December 1944; *Glamorgan Gazette*, 15 December 1944.

women make homes' is a very true saying. Very little consideration has
been given to equipment inside the home and generally the kitchen is the
worst-planned and darkest room in the house. Here is a chance for women
in the building industry to alter all this, not only in the new houses, but in
modernising existing well-built houses. I hope the women in the WRNS,
WAAFS, ATS and the factories will press forward their claim to be trained
for this great work.[172]

The years immediately following the war witnessed a flurry of
activity in the building trade of south Wales as the Labour
government's housing programme, under the directorship of
Aneurin Bevan, got under way. Between 1945 and 1951, 8,520
houses were built annually in Wales, the vast majority of which
were subsidized 'council' houses and prefabricated dwellings.[173]
Although financial constraints led to a severe curtailment of the
government's ambitious post-war housing scheme after 1947,
there was no doubt that the new accommodation provided vastly
improved living conditions to those who were fortunate enough
to be allocated such homes. The elation of a south Wales housewife who had received news that she had been granted a council
house after the war was captured effectively by the miner and
author, B. L. Coombes:

> After more than ten years of huddling six in a room, and continued
> appeals to every possible source until she had completely lost hope, had
> come this slip of paper which had altered her vision of life for herself and
> the four children. 'Indeed, I feel as if I had been left a big fortune. I'm right
> now for life.' Already she was full of ideas on how to make the most of the
> furniture, so badly knocked about in those cramped quarters, and already
> her friends around there were asking should they come and see her a
> couple of times every week, so that they could enjoy the luxury of a bath in
> a real bathroom.[174]

At Llwynypia, where the first post-war homes in the Rhondda
were built, tenants who moved into the new houses in May 1946
described the occasion as 'a dream come true'.[175] A similar

---

[172] *South Wales Echo*, 3 July 1943.
[173] Davies, *A History of Wales*, pp. 635–6.
[174] Coombes, *Miners Day*, p. 107.
[175] *Porth Gazette and Rhondda Leader*, 4 May 1946. See also the reaction of housewives
who moved into the new council houses and 'prefabs' at Treharris and Wern Isaf,
Dowlais, and the steel houses at Blaenavon in 1947. *Merthyr Express*, 25 January 1947, 12
July 1947; *Free Press of Monmouthshire*, 15 August 1947.

response greeted the official opening of the Pen-y-waun housing estate near Aberdare in January 1947. A local newspaper reporter who visited the fourteen modern brick houses remarked that their design was sure to herald 'a revolutionary change' in the old south Wales way of living. Unlike the old terraced houses of the district in which families 'lived in the kitchen' and reserved the front parlour for special occasions, the new houses provided a small dining recess and scullery to be used for eating and cooking meals only, both of which were 'admirably equipped for domestic work'.[176] The prefabricated aluminium bungalows which were added to the estate at the rate of four a day during the summer of 1947 were equally impressive. The reporter who visited the site commented that 'housewives of all ages were almost in raptures about them . . . The kitchenette is a housewife's dream, no woman could fail to be thrilled with it. It is a model of labour saving ingenuity with plenty of room and light.'[177]

While changes in housing design and the arrival of new labour-saving appliances undoubtedly heralded a 'revolution' in the nature of domestic labour, it was also the case that such developments served to raise expectations regarding standards of housewifery and placed increased pressure on women to buy into the new commercial culture of 'home-making'.[178] The gradual post-war change-over from coal to gas and electricity in the homes of south Wales was of great significance in this respect.[179] Such was the novelty of the all-electric kitchen, complete with refrigerator, electric cooker and water-heater, that women were offered advice, instruction and practical demonstrations on various aspects of the new domestic technology. Seventy housewives who had moved to the new houses on the Pen-y-waun estate were given lessons on the correct method of using electric cookers by the staff of the Aberdare Food Advice Centre.[180] Gas and electricity companies, which were anxious to win new customers, were the main organizers of such classes and

---

[176] *Aberdare Leader*, 11 and 18 January 1947.
[177] Ibid., 30 August 1947.
[178] Roberts, *Women and Families*, pp. 30–3.
[179] See Tibbott and Thomas, *O'r Gwaith i'r Gwely/A Woman's Work*, pp. 39–43.
[180] *Aberdare Leader*, 1 November 1947.

exhibitions.[181] An advertisement by the South Wales Electric Power Company, which featured in the south Wales press in June 1945, appealed directly to the local female war workers whom it clearly regarded as prospective housewives; it promised them a modern, easier-to-run kitchen, equipped with the very latest in domestic appliances:

> If women make up their minds what they want in post-war homes, they'll get it. Industry can equip peace-time kitchens as efficiently as it equipped war-time factories. British manufacturers can make electrical appliances that will wash dishes, scrub floors, peel potatoes, brush shoes – appliances that will be made if the demand is there.[182]

However, such improvements in the living standards of the working-class families of south Wales in the immediate post-war period should not be exaggerated. To those housewives who were struggling to make ends meet in an age of austerity, such commodities were regarded as merely fanciful and unnecessary luxuries.[183] Their greatest concern was the provision of necessities, such as adequate food rations. As elsewhere across Britain, housewives from south Wales voiced a strong protest against the strict post-war rationing of food, and called on the government to take urgent action to ensure that their families were properly fed.[184] In a bid to boost production in the mines, an extra allocation of sugar, fats and consumer goods was granted to coal-mining areas in March 1947; yet this news received an unenthusiastic reception by miners' wives in south Wales.[185] Indeed, their reaction gave some indication of their strong attachment to pre-war standards of housekeeping. Whilst appreciating the additional allowance of sugar and fat, young wives, like Ethel Duggan from Blaen-cwm, regarded the allocation of more fat to

---

[181] A 'Post-war home exhibition', complete with free film shows which promised to demonstrate 'how science is helping the housewife', was held at the Drill Hall, Pontypridd, in April 1946. In October 1946 the Newport Gas Company organized evening cookery classes for 'brides and brides-to-be'. Meanwhile, in the Aman valley in 1949, the Carmarthenshire representative of the South Wales Electricity Consultative Council called for electrical cookery and housework demonstrations to be provided for local housewives. *Porth Gazette and Rhondda Leader*, 30 March 1946; *South Wales Echo*, 2 October 1946; *Western Mail*, 22 June 1949.

[182] *The Rhondda Leader and Gazette*, 30 June 1945.

[183] *Aberdare Leader*, 6 September 1947.

[184] Addison, *Now the War is Over*, p. 29.

[185] *The Rhondda Leader*, 1 and 8 March 1947; *Aberdare Leader*, 8 March 1947.

fish-and-chip shops and more fats and sugar to local confectioners, as both wasteful and insulting. The situation in the Welsh mining valleys, she maintained, was totally unlike that in other parts of Britain, where many women were working and 'appreciated ready-made foodstuffs'. The Rhondda housewife, she declared, would prefer making use of the extra allocation herself.[186]

The nature of the domestic responsibilities and high standards of housewifery upheld in mining households had changed very little as a result of the war.[187] Speaking at a conference organized by the Labour Party at Ystradmynach in September 1946, Ness Edwards, the local MP, observed that miners' wives and daughters were 'not so free as others to engage in factory employment' and, consequently, a lower proportion of women were involved in industrial work in the area than elsewhere.[188] Many houses in the counties of Glamorgan and Monmouth lacked very basic amenities. For example, 28 per cent of households were without exclusive use of a piped water supply (compared with 17 per cent in England and Wales); 28 per cent of households in Glamorgan and 26 per cent of households in Monmouthshire were without exclusive use of a kitchen sink (compared with 13 per cent in England and Wales); 24 per cent of households in Glamorgan and 26 per cent of households in Monmouthshire were without exclusive use of a water closet (compared with 21 per cent in England and Wales); and 19 per cent of households in Glamorgan and Monmouthshire were without exclusive use of a cooking stove (compared with only 7 per cent in England and Wales).[189] The provision of fixed baths in the homes of south Wales was particularly poor: 56 per cent of households in Glamorgan and 59 per cent of households in Monmouthshire were without baths, compared with 45 per cent in England and Wales as a whole. Houses in the mining

---

[186] *The Rhondda Leader*, 8 March 1947.

[187] The only evidence of any changes or 'slippages' in standards or methods of housework was that some women abandoned the laborious ritual of 'pumice-stoning' the flagstones in front of their houses during the war. See the oral testimony of Eirona Richards of Morriston (b. 1928), quoted in Tibbott and Thomas, *O'r Gwaith i'r Gwely/A Woman's Work*, p. 43. It is also unlikely that this practice was as common on the new housing estates to the same extent as outside the uniform rows of terraced houses.

[188] *Rhymney Valley and Merthyr Express*, 7 September 1946.

[189] *Census of England and Wales, 1951, County Report, Glamorganshire*, pp. xxvii–xxviii; *Census of England and Wales, 1951, County Report, Monmouthshire*, pp. xxvi–xxvii.

communities, where washing facilities were most desperately required, fared worst of all, and over 60 per cent of dwellings in the following administrative districts were without fixed baths: Aberdare, Gelligaer, Merthyr Tydfil, Mountain Ash, Ogmore and Garw, Pontypridd, and the Rhondda in Glamorgan; Abertillery, Blaenavon, Nantyglo and Blaina, and Rhymney in Monmouthshire.[190] Given that the majority of the miners of south Wales were still deprived of pithead baths in the late 1940s, this made for difficult conditions in many mining homes.[191] A colliery official from the Glenrhondda pit, Blaen-cwm, estimated that some 85 per cent of the local houses were without bathrooms in 1947 and, consequently, miners bathed in the same room as the children ate their meals and undertook their schoolwork.[192]

This harsh reality was a far cry from the idealized image of post-war home life so often depicted in the literature and advertisements of contemporary magazines.[193] Far from contributing to a revival in family life and domestic happiness, the poor living conditions endured in many post-war homes served to weaken home and family ties. The housing policy pursued by the Labour government failed to live up to its high expectations and, as housing waiting-lists grew, many families found themselves living in cramped or shared accommodation which often lacked basic cooking or washing facilities. Speaking in March 1948, the lord mayor of Cardiff expressed the view that marriages were 'being wrecked weekly, if not daily, by the bad housing conditions in the city'.[194] Similar concerns were voiced in the Rhondda, where it was revealed that a growing number of separation orders were being made each week at the local magistrates' courts as a direct result of the housing shortage. According to Haydn Llewellyn, principal probation officer for the Rhondda, many married couples were 'keeping their wedding vows under the most trying conditions'. He knew of one couple who, along with their two-year-old child, shared two tiny rooms with the husband's elderly

---

[190] Ibid.
[191] Ferdynand Zweig, *Men in the Pits* (London, 1949), p. 125; Evans and Jones, 'A blessing for the miner's wife', 19. For example, in the Aberdare district, where seven pits were working in 1947, no pithead baths had yet been established. *Aberdare Leader*, 29 November 1947.
[192] *Western Mail*, 16 April 1947.
[193] See Cynthia L. White, *The Women's Periodical Press in Britain, 1946–1976* (London, 1977), pp. 10–11.
[194] *Western Mail*, 17 March 1948.

parents. The only living-room measured fifteen feet square, all five slept in a bedroom of the same size, and there was not even any water in the house.[195] Little improvement was recorded in the housing situation in the months that followed. In the opinion of Will Mainwaring, the Rhondda East MP, the people of the Rhondda were among the worst housed in Britain, and in January 1949 he resolved to bring their housing problems to the attention of the minister of health.[196]

It is evident that the relationship between women's domestic situation and their participation in paid employment remained inextricably linked and continued to be a source of considerable tension and conflict in the industrial communities of post-war south Wales.[197] There had been no revolutionary change in attitudes towards women's domestic role and responsibilities, and working women remained preoccupied with the perennial question of how to balance paid employment with the demands of their homes and families. Despite claims that the post-war years witnessed a change in the nature of the marital relationship, there is little evidence to suggest that a significant shift in traditional gender roles and responsibilities occurred in the homes of south Welsh industrial communities.[198] Like the Yorkshire mining community of 'Ashton', which was surveyed by sociologists during the early 1950s, responsibility for domestic chores rested squarely on the shoulders of the female members of the mining households of south Wales.[199] Moreover, recent research, based on the oral evidence of a group of Welsh women (b. c.1915) who would have been in their early thirties during the

[195] Ibid., 21 September 1948.

[196] Ibid., 19 January 1949.

[197] A debate on the motion 'that the employment of women in factories tends to destroy home life' was held at the Glynneath Welfare Hall in March 1949. *Aberdare Leader*, 5 March 1949. The researchers who undertook a sociological study in south-west Wales during the early 1950s also noted that the concept of 'women as workers rather than housekeepers' was one of the main sources of 'conflict' which had resulted from the diversification of the local employment and industrial structure. Brennan et al., *Social Change in South-West Wales*, p. 63.

[198] See Janet Finch and Penny Summerfield, 'Social reconstruction and the emergence of companionate marriage, 1945–59', in David Clark (ed.), *Marriage, Domestic Life and Social Change* (London, 1991), pp. 7–32; Summerfield, 'Women in Britain since 1945', pp. 58–60.

[199] N. Dennis, F. Henriques and C. Slaughter, *Coal is Our Life: An Analysis of a Yorkshire Mining Community* (London, 1956), p. 174. A fictional account of life in a south Wales mining community in the late 1940s offered little indication that any reversal in gender roles had taken place in the domestic sphere. See Menna Gallie, *The Small Mine* (London, 1962), p. 58.

late 1940s, reveals that most women remained 'resistant to the idea of men having a substantial degree of responsibility for housework'.[200] Without the provision of institutional support, such as adequate child-care assistance, the onus of caring for the children of working mothers usually fell to other family members and friends. Social investigators who undertook a study of family and kinship relations in the Swansea area during the early 1960s found that a significant proportion of working wives relied heavily on the support and domestic assistance provided by their mothers.[201]

At the workplace, popular perceptions of female employees as subordinate and marginal workers still held fast. The preoccupation with securing employment for members of the male population – the traditional breadwinners and heads of households – dominated public debate in south Wales during the immediate post-war period, while the work ambitions and aspirations of the female population were considered of secondary importance. Moreover, 'women's work' continued to be characterized as employment of low social and cultural status, which was rewarded accordingly by low wages. Despite the wartime transformation in the scale and nature of female employment in the region, the proportion of females who continued in paid work after the war remained relatively small. As had been the case before 1939, fewer women were employed in Wales in comparison with other parts of Britain.[202] Fewer married women were engaged in full-time employment in Wales compared with elsewhere and, as before the war, the age profile of the Welsh female workforce remained lower than in England and Wales as a whole. Changes in the industrial structure of post-war south Wales may have enabled thousands more women to take up work in their home districts than ever before, but the conception of women's economic and domestic roles as being of low status, and those of low-paid workers and unpaid housewives, remained fundamentally unaltered.

---

[200] Jane Pilcher, 'Who should do the dishes? Three generations of Welsh women talking about men and housework', in Aaron et al. (eds.), Our Sisters' Land, p. 34.

[201] Colin Rosser and Christopher Harris, The Family and Social Change: A Study of Family and Kinship in a South Wales Town (London, 1965), p. 191.

[202] PEP, Manpower, pp. 9, 14–15; C. E. V. Leser, 'Men and women in industry', Economic Journal (1952), 326–44.

CONCLUSION

There is a lump in my throat. It is not caused through sorrow but through pride at being able to state at this moment that I am a Welshwoman. Even the noise of European victory bells has not deadened the praise and tributes paid during the last hours to the women of Wales for their wartime achievements . . . Suffice it to say that for a long time more than 50 per cent of munitions production in Wales was in the hands of Welsh women . . . Wales is proud to think that her womenfolk – the miner's wife and daughter, the farmer's wife, the shopgirl and housewife – contributed to those figures so generously.[1]

In May 1945, as street parties to celebrate VE day got under way in towns and villages across south Wales, the significant contribution which the women of Wales had made towards securing peace in Europe did not go unnoticed. In her tribute to the wartime achievements of Welsh women, Roma Sanders, the *Western Mail*'s 'woman correspondent', drew particular attention to the role of the female munitions workers whose unstinting efforts at the factory benches had been crucial to the success of Britain's military campaign. In wartime south Wales, where tens of thousands of local women had worked 'on munitions' at some of the largest shell-filling factories in Britain, it is not surprising that their active contribution to the propagation of war was awarded special recognition. As this study of their experiences at the war factories of Glamorgan and Monmouthshire has shown, the female munitions workers of south Wales had truly been in the front line of the war effort, performing dangerous work which was vital to the success of Britain's military campaigns.

Future generations may not have been made aware of the hard work and personal sacrifices of the 'forgotten army' of Welsh female munitions workers, but the legacy of the war experience remains for all to see in the factories and light industries which now dominate the industrial landscape of south Wales. Female employees now outnumber males in Wales and are

[1] *Western Mail*, 9 May 1945.

predominant among the labour engaged on assembly-line work at Welsh factories.[2] It was the Second World War which laid the foundations for such dramatic changes in the employment experiences of the Welsh female population. New industrial developments initiated by wartime conditions transformed the industrial structure of the south Wales economy, providing the necessary stimulus for future industrial investment in the region. Of particular significance is the fact that the war firmly established a pattern of female employment constrained by substantial gender divisions. The identification of factory employment as 'women's work', that is, low-paid, low-skilled and of low status, remains one of the central features of female employment in contemporary south Wales.[3]

As the evidence presented in this study has shown, the creation of a new industrial army of female workers did not herald a dramatic shift in traditional gender roles, and the sexual division of labour in the homes of the industrial communities of south Wales remained largely unchallenged. Indeed, historians such as Penny Summerfield and Jane Lewis have argued that one of the legacies of the war was that it 'institutionalized' the double burden shouldered by women at home and at work, proving that it was possible for women to enter paid employment *and* be responsible for their homes and families.[4] The dramatic post-war increase in the number of Welsh women who undertook part-time work, often at the expense of full-time employment, bears witness to the endurance of conventional attitudes towards women's domestic role. Often regarded as a 'solution' to the domestic 'problems' of female workers, allowing women more time to attend to their homes and families, part-time work serves to reinforce attitudes towards female employees as marginal and subordinate workers, whose priorities lie with the affairs of the home, rather than the workplace.[5]

[2] Stephen Drinkwater, 'The Welsh economy: a statistical profile', *Contemporary Wales*, 10 (1997), 225.

[3] See Gwyn A. Williams, 'Women workers in Wales, 1968–82', *Welsh History Review*, 11, no. 4 (1983), 530–48; Victoria Winckler, 'Women and work in contemporary Wales', *Contemporary Wales*, 1 (1987), 53–71; Teresa L. Rees, 'Changing patterns of women's work in Wales: some myths explored', ibid., 2 (1988), 119–30; eadem, 'Women and paid work in Wales', in Aaron et al. (eds.), *Our Sisters' Land*, pp. 89–106; Drinkwater, 'The Welsh economy', 233.

[4] Summerfield, 'Women in Britain since 1945', p. 69; Lewis, *Women in England, 1870–1950*, p. 153.

[5] Winckler, 'Women and work in contemporary Wales', 64.

Attitudes towards women's domestic and economic role may not have been transformed by their participation in wartime employment, but there can be no doubt that the war radically altered many other aspects of women's lives in south Wales. The high wages paid in the munitions factories brought economic salvation to thousands of families in the impoverished industrial communities of Glamorgan and Monmouthshire and gave rise to marked improvements in living and health conditions. On a personal level, women's wartime experiences left an indelible mark on their future outlook and social behaviour. Ultimately, all those who had been involved in wartime employment could not have been left unaffected by their experiences. The harsh reality of life as a munitions worker, who was, after all, conscripted to wartime service often against her will, could hardly be regarded as a step towards female emancipation but, for the majority of women, it had been at the very least a personally 'enriching' and valuable experience which had given them a considerable dose of self-confidence and self-reliance.[6] Even though circumstances prevented many women from achieving their post-war ambitions in the workplace, the new spirit of independence and assertiveness fostered at the war factories was reflected in their elevated expectations of post-war home life[7] and their high hopes for greater equality and opportunity for their daughters.

[6] Price, 'Experiences in World War II', 113. See also M-O A, FR 2149, 'Changes of outlook during the war', August 1944.

[7] A report prepared by Mass-Observation in 1943 concluded: 'although women mostly want home-life again after the war, the signs point to it being a very different, more varied life; a life with the home as basis and background but not as exclusive environment and circumscription.' M-O A, FR 1970, 'Women in pubs', 8 December 1943.

APPENDIX

Female Occupations, Glamorgan and Monmouthshire, 1921, 1931, 1951:[1] Number of females employed in main occupation groups[2] (shown as percentage of total females occupied) in administrative counties, county/municipal boroughs and urban districts
(*Source*: Census Occupation Tables, 1921, 1931, 1951.)

	1921		1931		1951	
	Number	*%*	*Number*	*%*	*Number*	*%*
GLAMORGAN						
Personal service	35090	39.3	38568	43.1	27280	22.0
Commerce and finance	15829	17.7	17283	19.3	20445	16.5
Clerks, typists etc.	7033	7.9	8000	8.9	25354	20.4
Professional occupations	9999	11.2	10535	11.8	13606	11.0
Clothing manufacture	9332	10.5	5400	6.0	8487	6.8
Metal, electrical and textile workers	2896	3.2	940	1.0	5095	4.1
Transport and communications	1422	1.6	1134	1.3	2369	1.9
All other occupations	7626	8.5	7669	8.6	21485	17.3
Total number occupied	89227		89529		124121	
Occupied as % of females in age group	19.6		19.8		25.9	
CARDIFF CB						
Personal service	8389	36.6	11128	40.2	7611	24.1
Commerce and finance	3774	16.5	4769	17.2	4932	15.6
Clerks, typists etc.	2868	12.5	3574	12.9	8689	27.5
Professional occupations	1850	8.1	2268	8.2	2790	8.8
Clothing manufacture	2431	10.6	2117	7.6	1512	4.8
Metal, electrical and textile workers	247	1.1	198	0.7	617	2.0
Transport and communications	459	2.0	389	1.4	818	2.6
All other occupations	2903	12.7	3257	11.8	4614	14.6
Total number occupied	22921		27700		31583	
Occupied as % of females in age group	29.2		30.9		31.6	

	1921		1931		1951	
	Number	*%*	*Number*	*%*	*Number*	*%*
MERTHYR TYDFIL CB						
Personal service	1903	40.4	1777	45.4	1179	19.1
Commerce and finance	1014	21.5	892	22.8	885	14.4
Clerks, typists etc.	218	4.6	198	5.1	790	12.8
Professional occupations	669	14.2	606	15.5	674	10.9
Clothing manufacture	469	10.0	163	4.2	670	10.9
Metal, electrical and textile workers	51	1.1	7	0.2	475	7.7
Transport and communications	49	1.0	39	1.0	65	1.1
All other occupations	340	7.2	231	5.9	1424	23.1
Total number occupied	4713		3913		6162	
Occupied as % of females in age group	16.4		15.3		25.2	
SWANSEA CB						
Personal service	5525	38.4	6519	43.2	4178	23.8
Commerce and finance	2530	17.6	3207	21.2	3175	18.1
Clerks, typists etc.	1213	8.4	1281	8.5	3156	18.0
Professional occupations	1457	10.1	1420	9.4	1853	10.6
Clothing manufacture	1440	10.0	967	6.4	1280	7.3
Metal, electrical and textile workers	885	6.2	241	1.6	682	3.9
Transport and communications	459	3.2	206	1.4	351	2.0
All other occupations	865	6.0	1262	8.4	2850	16.3
Total number occupied	14374		15103		17525	
Occupied as % of females in age group	23.5		23.5		26.8	
ABERDARE UD						
Personal service	1112	39.7	1089	44.1	695	19.4
Commerce and finance	566	20.2	573	23.2	660	18.4
Clerks, typists etc.	138	4.9	158	6.4	564	15.8
Professional occupations	385	13.7	370	15.0	464	13.0
Clothing manufacture	344	12.3	135	5.5	67	1.9
Metal, electrical and textile workers	24	0.9	3	0.1	245	6.8
Transport and communications	33	1.2	29	1.2	50	1.4
All other occupations	200	7.1	113	4.6	835	23.3
Total number occupied	2802		2470		3580	
Occupied as % of females in age group	14.2		13.8		21.7	

	1921		1931		1951	
	Number	*%*	*Number*	*%*	*Number*	*%*
BRIDGEND UD						
Personal service	401	41.4	529	47.7	362	24.5
Commerce and finance	178	18.4	252	22.7	246	16.6
Clerks, typists etc.	74	7.6	82	7.4	291	19.7
Professional occupations	116	12.0	161	14.5	307	20.8
Clothing manufacture	90	9.3	45	4.1	66	4.5
Metal, electrical and textile workers	2	0.2	-	-	9	0.6
Transport and communications	14	1.4	10	0.9	42	2.8
All other occupations	93	9.6	30	2.7	155	10.5
Total number occupied	968		1109		1478	
Occupied as % of females in age group	26.9		27.7		26.4	
MAESTEG UD						
Personal service	528	39.6	440	42.3	327	18.1
Commerce and finance	334	25.1	272	26.1	406	22.5
Clerks, typists etc.	34	2.6	39	3.7	229	12.7
Professional occupations	176	13.2	197	18.9	191	10.6
Clothing manufacture	160	12.0	59	5.7	188	10.4
Metal, electrical and textile workers	5	0.4	1	0.1	36	2.0
Transport and communications	12	0.9	8	0.8	24	1.3
All other occupations	83	6.2	25	2.4	404	22.4
Total number occupied	1332		1041		1805	
Occupied as % of females in age group	13.6		12.1		21.0	
MOUNTAIN ASH UD						
Personal service	749	40.7	656	43.3	492	16.5
Commerce and finance	382	20.8	337	22.2	485	16.3
Clerks, typists etc.	86	4.7	93	6.1	526	17.6
Professional occupations	307	16.7	324	21.4	328	11.0
Clothing manufacture	197	10.7	49	3.2	220	7.4
Metal, electrical and textile workers	2	0.1	1	0.1	210	7.0
Transport and communications	20	1.1	22	1.5	27	0.9
All other occupations	97	5.3	34	2.2	694	23.3
Total number occupied	1840		1516		2982	
Occupied as % of females in age group	12.5		11.8		24.4	

	1921		1931		1951	
	Number	*%*	*Number*	*%*	*Number*	*%*
NEATH MB						
Personal service	573	35.8	968	37.7	718	20.2
Commerce and finance	288	18.0	543	21.2	690	19.4
Clerks, typists etc.	91	5.7	157	6.1	528	14.8
Professional occupations	123	7.7	237	9.2	404	11.3
Clothing manufacture	134	8.4	125	4.9	120	3.4
Metal, electrical and textile workers	242	15.1	80	3.1	419	11.8
Transport and communications	19	1.2	29	1.1	44	1.2
All other occupations	130	8.1	426	16.6	640	18.0
Total number occupied	1600		2565		3563	
Occupied as % of females in age group	22.4		20.3		26.8	
OGMORE AND GARW UD						
Personal service	466	39.1	408	43.2	383	23.3
Commerce and finance	265	22.2	212	22.5	347	21.1
Clerks, typists etc.	41	3.4	43	4.6	213	12.9
Professional occupations	176	14.8	192	20.3	195	11.8
Clothing manufacture	160	13.4	46	4.9	107	6.5
Metal, electrical and textile workers	1	0.1	-	-	41	2.5
Transport and communications	4	0.3	15	1.6	25	1.5
All other occupations	80	6.7	28	3.0	336	20.4
Total number occupied	1193		944		1647	
Occupied as % of females in age group	12.0		10.8		19.4	
PONTYPRIDD UD						
Personal service	1100	37.4	1065	41.1	803	18.6
Commerce and finance	651	22.1	622	24.0	678	15.7
Clerks, typists etc.	183	6.2	189	7.3	914	21.2
Professional occupations	342	11.6	368	14.2	393	9.1
Clothing manufacture	278	9.4	124	4.8	360	8.3
Metal, electrical and textile workers	23	0.8	7	0.3	255	5.9
Transport and communications	58	2.0	20	0.8	45	1.0
All other occupations	308	10.5	198	7.6	866	20.1
Total number occupied	2943		2593		4314	
Occupied as % of females in age group	17.9		17.3		28.1	

	1921		**1931**		**1951**	
	Number	*%*	*Number*	*%*	*Number*	*%*

RHONDDA UD

Personal service	2748	40.2	2361	43.0	1698	16.3
Commerce and finance	1528	22.4	1189	21.7	1495	14.4
Clerks, typists etc.	299	4.4	308	5.6	1689	16.2
Professional occupations	1043	15.3	1151	21.0	1232	11.8
Clothing manufacture	849	12.4	266	4.9	1438	13.8
Metal, electrical and textile workers	10	0.1	11	0.2	511	4.9
Transport and communications	89	1.3	44	0.8	78	0.7
All other occupations	265	3.9	154	2.8	2271	21.8
Total number occupied	6831		5484		10412	
Occupied as % of females in age group	12.5		11.4		23.5	

MONMOUTHSHIRE

Personal service	12307	43.4	12981	46.8	9442	23.7
Commerce and finance	5177	18.3	5485	19.8	6868	17.2
Clerks, typists etc.	1721	6.1	1896	6.8	7177	18.0
Professional occupations	3373	11.9	3735	13.5	4642	11.6
Clothing manufacture	2220	7.8	1008	3.6	2123	5.3
Metal, electrical and textile workers	403	1.4	176	0.6	1522	3.8
Transport and communications	384	1.4	335	1.2	946	2.4
All other occupations	2782	9.8	2115	7.6	7167	18.0
Total number occupied	28367		27731		39887	
Occupied as % of females in age group	17.7		17.9		24.3	

NEWPORT CB

Personal service	3597	40.8	4188	46.1	2896	23.8
Commerce and finance	1542	17.5	1786	19.7	2162	17.7
Clerks, typists etc.	794	9.0	791	8.7	2705	22.2
Professional occupations	795	9.0	809	8.9	1183	9.7
Clothing manufacture	768	8.7	423	4.7	585	4.8
Metal, electrical and textile workers	62	0.7	45	0.5	579	4.8
Transport and communications	180	2.0	99	1.1	393	3.2
All other occupations	1085	12.3	938	10.3	1683	13.8
Total number occupied	8823		9079		12186	
Occupied as % of females in age group	25.0		26.2		28.9	

	1921		**1931**		**1951**	
	Number	*%*	*Number*	*%*	*Number*	*%*

ABERTILLERY UD

Personal service	622	40.9	536	43.9	440	21.2
Commerce and finance	401	26.4	346	28.3	485	23.3
Clerks, typists etc.	64	4.2	51	4.2	269	12.9
Professional occupations	188	12.4	192	15.7	225	10.8
Clothing manufacture	117	7.7	29	2.4	63	3.0
Metal, electrical and textile workers	36	2.4	4	0.3	64	3.1
Transport and communications	11	0.7	12	1.0	36	1.7
All other occupations	82	5.4	51	4.2	498	23.9
Total number occupied	1521		1221		2080	
Occupied as % of females in age group	11.9		11.6		20.1	

BLAENAVON UD

Personal service	244	44.0	229	49.7	162	22.3
Commerce and finance	149	26.8	116	25.2	149	20.6
Clerks, typists etc.	28	5.0	17	3.7	109	15.0
Professional occupations	74	13.3	75	16.3	62	8.6
Clothing manufacture	40	7.2	12	2.6	19	2.6
Metal, electrical and textile workers	1	0.2	-	-	29	4.0
Transport and communications	5	0.9	1	0.2	13	1.8
All other occupations	14	2.5	11	2.4	182	25.1
Total number occupied	555		461		725	
Occupied as % of females in age group	12.7		12.1		19.4	

EBBW VALE UD

Personal service	687	43.1	579	44.0	537	25.4
Commerce and finance	350	22.0	352	26.7	477	22.6
Clerks, typists etc.	88	5.5	86	6.5	378	17.9
Professional occupations	249	15.6	215	16.3	275	13.0
Clothing manufacture	95	6.0	37	2.8	179	8.5
Metal, electrical and textile workers	5	0.3	3	0.2	36	1.7
Transport and communications	15	0.9	16	1.2	24	1.1
All other occupations	104	6.5	28	2.1	206	9.8
Total number occupied	1593		1316		2112	
Occupied as % of females in age group	13.4		12.5		19.2	

	1921		1931		1951	
	Number	*%*	*Number*	*%*	*Number*	*%*
NANTYGLO AND BLAINA UD						
Personal service	228	37.1	192	39.9	156	18.0
Commerce and finance	148	24.1	97	20.2	143	16.5
Clerks, typists etc.	23	3.7	25	5.2	125	14.4
Professional occupations	103	16.8	127	26.4	144	16.6
Clothing manufacture	76	12.4	22	4.6	108	12.5
Metal, electrical and textile workers	-	-	-	-	24	2.8
Transport and communications	5	0.8	10	2.1	5	0.6
All other occupations	31	5.0	8	1.7	162	18.7
Total number occupied	614		481		867	
Occupied as % of females in age group	11.1		10.7		20.1	
PONTYPOOL UD						
Personal service	255	45.1	215	45.6	923	22.3
Commerce and finance	127	22.5	129	27.3	618	14.9
Clerks, typists etc.	17	3.0	20	4.2	707	17.1
Professional occupations	53	9.4	51	10.8	544	13.1
Clothing manufacture	33	5.8	11	2.3	65	1.6
Metal, electrical and textile workers	20	3.5	-	-	162	3.9
Transport and communications	8	1.4	4	0.9	90	2.2
All other occupations	52	9.2	42	8.9	1035	25.0
Total number occupied	565		472		4144	
Occupied as % of females in age group	22.7		19.8		24.9	
TREDEGAR UD						
Personal service	549	45.2	444	44.4	398	24.4
Commerce and finance	219	18.0	232	23.2	316	19.4
Clerks, typists etc.	47	3.9	51	5.1	197	12.1
Professional occupations	177	14.6	197	19.7	228	14.0
Clothing manufacture	121	10.0	40	4.0	222	13.6
Metal, electrical and textile workers	4	0.3	-	-	13	0.8
Transport and communications	10	0.8	11	1.1	20	1.2
All other occupations	87	7.2	25	2.5	238	14.6
Total number occupied	1214		1000		1632	
Occupied as % of females in age group	14.4		12.9		21.1	

[1] 1921: 12 years and over; 1931: 14 years and over; 1951: 15 years and over.
[2] Some changes occurred in the classification of occupation groups between 1921 and 1951. In order to ensure a degree of compatibility between the numbers occupied in each group, full account was taken of the exact occupations included in each group. For example, in the 1951 Census

Occupation Tables, workers involved in the occupations classified as 'Metal, electrical and textile workers' were drawn from only two occupational groups, namely, Group VI (Workers in metal manufacture, engineering) and Group VII (Textile workers). In both the 1921 and 1931 Census Occupation Tables, however, these workers were included in the following five occupational groups: Group VII (Metal workers), Group VIII (Workers in precious metals and electro plate), Group IX (Electrical apparatus makers and fitters), Group X (Makers of watches, clocks and scientific instruments) and Group XII (Textile workers).

BIBLIOGRAPHY

1. Archival sources
2. Oral evidence
3. Official publications and reports
4. Newspapers and journals
5. Contemporary works: Books and articles
6. Secondary works: Books and articles
7. Theses and dissertations
8. Broadcasts

1. Archival sources

(a) Aberdare Library, Aberdare
W. W. Price Collection, LH5/19, *Rules and Regulations of the Royal Ordnance Factories*
(London, 1937), issued to Mary A. Evans on 5 February 1941

(b) Cardiff Central Library, Cardiff
Annual Reports of the Cardiff Medical Officer of Health
City of Cardiff Education Committee Annual Reports

(c) Glamorgan Record Office, Cardiff
Sir J. Frederick Rees Papers
Industrial Development Council of Wales and Monmouthshire Papers
Aberdare Education Committee minutes
Aberdare UDC minutes
Bridgend UDC minutes
Caerphilly UDC minutes
Cardiff RDC minutes
City of Cardiff licensing sessions minutes and reports
Gelligaer UDC minutes
Glamorgan County Council, annual reports of the director of education
Glamorgan Quarter Sessions minutes
Maesteg UDC minutes
Mountain Ash Education Committee minutes
Ogmore and Garw UDC minutes
Penybont RDC minutes
Pontypridd Education Committee minutes
Pontypridd UDC minutes
Porthcawl UDC minutes
Rhondda UDC minutes
Logbook of the Cwmaman and the Hirwaun wartime nurseries, 1943–4

(d) Gwent Record Office, Cwmbran
Records of the Blaenavon Co. Ltd
Abertillery UDC minutes
Tredegar UDC minutes

(e) Mass-Observation Archive, University of Sussex
File Reports
  533   Women and the war effort, December 1940
1151   The demand for day nurseries, 11 March 1942
1163   Women in industry, 19 March 1942
1196   Blaina investigation, 2 April 1942
1498   Blaina: a study of a coal mining town, November 1942
1611   Social change – women in public houses, 23 March 1943
1635   Women in public houses, 30 March 1943
1970   Women in pubs, 8 December 1943
2059   Will the factory girls want to stay put or go home?, 8 March 1944
2149   Changes of outlook during the war, August 1944

Topic Collections
   1   Sexual behaviour, Box 1, File G
   2   Reconstruction, Box 3, File E
  19   Day nurseries, Box 1, File D
  64   Coal mining, Box 1, Files A–D
  85   Drinking habits, Box 8, Files A–C

Directive Replies
2678, May 1943, April 1944
3137, April 1944
3419, April 1944
3450, May 1943, April 1944
3527, April 1944
3528, April 1944

Diary
5460

(f) Merthyr Tydfil Town Public Library
Merthyr Tydfil CB minutes
Merthyr Tydfil Education Committee minutes

(g) Modern Records Centre, University of Warwick, MSS
292/79C/56: Annual returns of the Cynon Valley Trades Council
292/79M/29: Annual returns of the Mid Glamorgan Trades Council
292/79R/12: Annual returns of the Rhymney and Abertysswg Trades and Labour
    Council
292/79R/13: Annual returns of the Rhymney Valley Industrial Committee of the
    (previously) Caerphilly Divisional Labour Party

(h) National Library of Wales, Aberystwyth
BBC (Wales) Archive
Idris Cox Papers
James Griffiths Papers
Jack Jones MSS
Thomas Jones Papers
Labour Party of Wales Archive
Plaid Cymru Archives
Undeb Cymru Fydd Papers

MS 15450C: minute book of Cardiff and District Citizens' Union, South Wales and Monmouthshire Vigilance Association

MS 16594D: minute book of the Pontardawe branch of 'Undeb Dirwestol Merched y De' (the South Wales Women's Temperance Union), 1937–54

MS 22413E: Idris Davies radio scripts, 'A holiday at home: in a Welsh mining valley', *c*.1941

MSS N23071E and N23072–3D: Parachutes and Petticoats archive

Minor Deposit A1994/81: records and minutes of the National Union of General and Municipal Workers, South Western Division, 1937–46

Minor Deposit 1992: Deian R. Hopkin Papers, minute book of the Llanelly Trades Council and Divisional Labour Party, 1940–6

Minor Deposit 1995/62: minute book of Rhondda West Divisional Labour Party Executive Committee, 1942–9

(i) Pontypridd Public Library
Pontypridd Trades Council and Labour Party minutes

(j) Public Record Office, London
Inf 1/264: Home Intelligence Reports on opinion and morale, 1940–1

Inf 1/292: Home Intelligence Reports on opinion and morale, 1941–4

Lab 8/378: Questions of rate of wages and recruitment of women in the munitions industries and their retention in these industries

Lab10/365–9: Wales Office, chief conciliation and industrial relations officer, weekly reports, 1939–43

Lab 10/446: Wales Office, chief conciliation and industrial relations officer, weekly reports, 1944

Lab 10/555: Wales Office, chief conciliation and industrial relations officer, weekly reports, 1945

Lab 12/82: Wales Division, district controller's monthly reports on labour supply position, November 1939–August 1941

Lab 12/137: Official Committee on the Machinery of Government, war cabinet memorandum on administrative arrangements in Wales

Lab 26/4: Enquiry into absence from work. Reports prepared by the Central Statistical Office, 1943–4, August 1945

Lab 26/57: Provision for the care of children of married women in industry, wartime nurseries, general policy, 1940

Lab 26/58: Provision for the care of children of married women in industry, wartime nurseries, general policy, 1940–2

Lab 26/60: Shop hours for war workers

Lab 26/61: Shopping difficulties, 1941–3

Lab 26/90: Transport difficulties for workers in Wales Division

Lab 26/91: Transport difficulties at ROFs. Referred to the controller general of transportation, Ministry of Supply

Lab 26/131: Industrial efficiency and absenteeism. Enquiry into absence from work, 1942–3

Lab 26/132: Enquiry into absence from work. Papers submitted to the Factory and Welfare Advisory Board, 1945

Lab 26/133: Provision for the care of children of married women in industry, wartime nurseries, general policy, 1943–4

Lab 26/168: Provision for the care of children of married women in industry, 1946

Lab 43/1: Deputation from Welsh MPs to discuss unemployment situation in south Wales, 1946

MH 55/695: Arrangements for the provision of wartime nurseries, 1940

MH 55/884: Children of war workers, 1941–2
MH 55/1708: Nurseries for children of war workers, closure and disposal of premises, 1945–7

(k) South Wales Coalfield Archive, University of Wales Swansea
Aberdare Trades and Labour Council minutes
Ammanford, Llandybïe and District Trades and Labour Council minutes
Caerphilly Labour Party, Women's Section minutes
Caerphilly Labour Party, Gelligaer Area Committee minutes
Caerphilly Trades and Labour Council minutes
Mineworkers' Federation of Great Britain minutes
New Tredegar Trades and Labour Council minutes
South Wales Miners' Federation Executive Committee minutes

(l) West Glamorgan Record Office, Swansea
Glyncorrwg Urban District Council minutes
Swansea County Borough minutes

2. ORAL EVIDENCE

(a) Interviews
Respondent 1 (b. 1919, Pyle, Glamorgan)
Respondent 2 (b. 1919, Pyle, Glamorgan)
Respondent 3 (b. 1923, Pen-coed, Glamorgan)
Respondent 4 (b. 1922, Aberkenfig, Glamorgan)
Respondent 5 (b. 1923, North Cornelly, Glamorgan)
Respondent 6 (b. 1926, Maesteg, Glamorgan)
Respondent 7 (b. 1922, Bettws, Bridgend, Glamorgan)
Respondent 8 (b. 1924, Bettws, Bridgend, Glamorgan)
Respondent 9 (b. 1923, Wyndham, Ogmore Vale, Glamorgan)
Respondent 10 (b. 1912, Wyndham, Ogmore Vale, Glamorgan)
Respondent 11 (b. 1917, Aberaman, Glamorgan)
Respondent 12 (b. 1913, Garth, Maesteg, Glamorgan)
Respondent 13 (b. 1912, Nantyffyllon, Glamorgan)
Respondent 14 (b. 1923, Maesteg, Glamorgan)
Respondent 15 (b. 1920, Nantyffyllon, Glamorgan)
Respondent 16 (b. 1918, Llangynwyd, Glamorgan)
Respondent 17 (b. 1919, Barry, Glamorgan)
Respondent 18 (b. 1917, Devon)
Respondent 19 (b. 1920, Treherbert, Glamorgan)
Respondent 20 (b. 1924, Treherbert, Glamorgan)
Respondent 21 (b. 1918, Treherbert, Glamorgan)
Respondent 22 (b. 1924, Treherbert, Glamorgan)

(b) Recorded interviews held at the South Wales Miners' Library, Swansea
Tape 88 (Reg Fine, Maerdy)
Tape 148 (Nancy Davies, Seven Sisters)

(c) Broadcasts
BBC Radio Wales, 'The girls who made the thing-ummy-bobs', 7 November 1989

3. OFFICIAL PUBLICATIONS AND REPORTS

(a) Census of England and Wales, County Reports and Occupation Tables, 1921, 1931, 1951

(b) Parliamentary Debates (Hansard) (5th series), 1935–46

(c) British Parliamentary Papers

1929–30, XVII, Cmd. 3508, A Study of the Factors which have Operated in the Past and those which are Operating now to Determine the Distribution of Women in Industry, December 1929

1933–4, XIII, Cmd. 4728, Ministry of Labour, Reports of Investigations into the Industrial Conditions in Certain Depressed Areas. Vol. III, South Wales and Monmouthshire, 2 July 1934

1934–5, X, Cmd. 4957, First Report of the Commissioner for the Special Areas (England and Wales), July 1935

1935–6, XIV, Cmd. 5039, Report of the Royal Commission on Merthyr Tydfil, November 1935

1936–7, XI, Cmd. 5423, Ministry of Health, Report on Maternal Mortality in Wales, April 1937

1939–40, IV, Cmd. 6182, Report on Hours of Employment of Women and Young Persons in Factories during the first five months of the War, March 1940

1940–1, III, Seventeenth Report from the Select Committee on National Expenditure, 'Labour problems in filling factories', 10 July 1941

1940–1, III, Twenty-first Report from the Select Committee on National Expenditure, 'Output of labour', 6 August 1941

1940–1, VIII, Cmd. 6310, Memorandum by the Ministry of Labour and National Service on Welfare Work outside the Factory, June 1940 to August 1941, September 1941

1941–2, III, Seventh Report from the Select Committee on National Expenditure, 'Supply of labour', 26 March 1942

1941–2, III, Eleventh Report from the Select Committee on National Expenditure, 'Royal Ordnance Factories', 16 July 1942

1941–2, IV, Cmd. 6340, Ministry of Health, Summary Report for the period 1 April 1939–31 March 1941, February 1942

1941–2, IV, Cmd. 6384, Report of the Committee on Amenities and Welfare Conditions in the Three Women's Services, August 1942

1942–3, III, Third Report from the Select Committee on National Expenditure, 'Health and welfare of women in war factories', 17 December 1942

1942–3, VI, Cmd. 6404, Social Insurance and Allied Services, Report by Sir William Beveridge, November 1942

1944–5, V, Cmd. 6650, Report on Post-war Organisation of Private Domestic Employment, June 1945

1945–6, X, Cmd. 6886, Marriage Bar in the Civil Service, Report of the Civil Service National Whitley Council Committee, August 1946

1945–6, XI, Cmd. 6937, Report of the Royal Commission on Equal Pay 1944–6, October 1946

1945–6, XX, Cmd. 6938, Wales and Monmouthshire, A Summary of Government Action, 1 August 1945–31 July 1946, October 1946

1945–6, XIV, Report of His Majesty's Inspectors of Constabulary for the year ended 29th September 1945

1946–7, XIX, Cmd. 7046, Economic Survey for 1947, February 1947

1947–8, XVI, Cmd. 7267, Wales and Monmouthshire, Report of Government Action for the year ended 30 June 1947, November 1947

1948, II, Cmd. 7532, Wales and Monmouthshire, Report of Government Action for the year ended 30 June 1948, October 1948

1948, II, Cmd. 7540, Board of Trade, Distribution of Industry, October 1948

(d) Central Office of Information Surveys

'Women at work: the attitudes of working women towards post-war employment and some related problems. An inquiry made for the office of the minister of reconstruction' by Geoffrey Thomas (June 1944)

'Women and industry: an inquiry into the problem of recruiting women to industry carried out for the Ministry of Labour and National Service' by Geoffrey Thomas (1948)

4. NEWSPAPERS AND JOURNALS

Aberdare Leader
Baner ac Amserau Cymru
British Medical Journal
Caerphilly Journal
Cambria
Y Cymro
Y Darian
Y Ddraig Goch
Y Drysorfa
Economic Journal
The Economist
Yr Efrydydd
Empire News and Sunday Chronicle
Free Press of Monmouthshire
Free Press and Rhondda Leader
Glamorgan Advertiser
Glamorgan County Times
Glamorgan Free Press and Rhondda Leader
Glamorgan Gazette
Y Gymraes
Journal of the Royal Sanitary Institute
The Listener
Manchester School of Economic and Social Studies
Merthyr Express
Ministry of Labour Gazette
National Geographic Magazine
Neath Guardian
New Statesman
The Porth Gazette and Rhondda Leader
The Rhondda Clarion
Rhondda Fach Gazette
The Rhondda Gazette
The Rhondda Leader
The Rhondda Leader and Gazette
Rhymney Valley and Merthyr Express
Sociological Review
South Wales Argus
South Wales Echo
South Wales Evening Post

The Times
Transactions of the Honourable Society of Cymmrodorion
The Welsh Nationalist
The Welsh Outlook
The Welsh Review
Western Mail
Woman's Journal

5. CONTEMPORARY WORKS

(a) Books and Pamphlets

Annual Report of the Aberdare Medical Officer of Health, 1928 (Aberdare, 1929).
Annual Reports of the Ogmore and Garw Medical Officer of Health (Cardiff, 1930–45).
Annual Reports of the Rhondda Medical Officer of Health (Ferndale, 1930–45).
Annual Reports of the South Wales Temperance and Band of Hope Union/Undeb Cymdeithasau Dirwestol a Gobeithluoedd Deheudir Cymru (Cardiff, 1939–45).
Annual Reports of the South Wales Women's Temperance Union (Undeb Dirwestol Merched Deheudir Cymru) (Rhymni and Treforys, 1939–45).
Adroddiad Blynyddol Jerusalem M.C., Ton (Pentre, 1941).
Andrews, Elizabeth, *A Woman's Work is Never Done* (Ystrad Rhondda, 1956).
Anthony, Sylvia, *Women's Place in Industry and Home* (London, 1932).
Belshaw, D. G. R., *The Changing Economic Geography of Merthyr Tydfil* (Merthyr Tydfil, 1955).
Bevin, Ernest, *The Job to be Done* (Kingswood, 1942).
Board of Education, Pamphlet no. 86, *Educational Problems of the South Wales Coalfield* (London, 1931).
Idem, *Curriculum and Examinations in Secondary Schools: Report of the Committee of the Secondary School Examinations Council appointed by the President of the Board of Education in 1941* (London, 1943).
Board of Trade, *An Industrial Survey of South Wales* (London, 1932).
Booth, Egert P., *Women at War: Engineering* (London, 1943).
Bowlby, John, *Forty-Four Juvenile Thieves: Their Characters and Home Life* (London, 1946).
Idem, *Maternal Care and Maternal Health* (Geneva, 1951).
Brennan, T., Cooney, E. W., and Pollins, H., *Social Change in South-West Wales* (London, 1954).
Communist Party of Mid-Glamorgan, *When War Jobs Finish: Contributions by the Communist Party of Mid-Glamorgan* (Abertridwr, 1944).
Coombes, B. L., *These Poor Hands: The Autobiography of a Miner Working in South Wales* (London, 1939).
Idem, *Those Clouded Hills* (London, 1944).
Idem, *Miners Day* (London, 1945).
Court, W. H. B., *Coal* (London, 1951).
Crawshay-Williams, Eliot, *No One Wants Poetry* (Newtown, 1938).
Davies, D. J., *The Tredegar Workmen's Hall, 1861–1951: Ninety Years of Endeavour* (Cardiff, 1951).
Davies, D. J., and Davies, Noëlle, *Wales . . . The Land of our Children? A Survey of Welsh Population Problems* (Caernarfon, 1942).
Davies, Margaret Llewellyn (ed.), *Life as We Have Known It*, 1st edn 1931 (London, 1977).
Dennis, N., Henriques, F., and Slaughter, C., *Coal is Our Life: An Analysis of a Yorkshire Mining Community* (London, 1956).
Douie, Vera, *Daughters of Britain: An Account of the Work of British Women during the Second World War* (London, 1949).

Edwards, Wil Jon, *From the Valley I Came* (London, 1956).

Executive Committee of the Conference for the Protection of Welsh Culture, *Evacuation Schemes and Service of Youth* (Denbigh, 1940).

Ferguson, Sheila, and Fitzgerald, Hilde, *Studies in the Social Services* (London, 1954).

Ginzberg, Eli, *A World Without Work: The Story of the Welsh Miners* (New Jersey, 1991) (originally published in 1942 as *Grass on the Slag Heaps*).

Goldsmith, Margaret, *Women at War* (London, 1943).

Gollan, John, *Youth in British Industry: A Survey of Labour Conditions To-day* (London, 1937).

Gwyther, Cyril E., *The Valley Shall Be Exalted: Light Shines in the Rhondda* (London, 1949).

Hancock, W. K., and Gowing, M. M., *British War Economy* (London, 1949).

Hanley, James, *Grey Children: A Study in Humbug and Misery in South Wales* (London, 1937).

Hannington, Wal, *Industrial History in Wartime* (London, 1940).

Harris, E. M., *Married Women in Industry*, Institute of Personnel Management Occasional Papers no. 4 (London, 1954).

Haslett, Caroline, *Munitions Girl: A Handbook for the Women of the Industrial Army* (London, 1942).

Hay, Ian, *R.O.F.: The Story of the Royal Ordnance Factories, 1939–1948* (London, 1949).

Hooks, J. M. [United States Department of Labor, Bulletin of the Women's Bureau], *British Policies and Methods in Employing Women in Wartime* (Washington, 1944).

Hopcyn, Idris, *Hanes Eglwys yr Annibynwyr Cymraeg, Wheeler Street, Birmingham, 1860–1960* (Maesteg, n.d.).

Hornby, William, *Factories and Plant* (London, 1958).

Hunt, Walter William, *To Guard My People: An Account of the Origin and History of the Swansea Police* (Swansea, 1957).

Inman, P., *Labour in the Munitions Industries* (London, 1957).

International Labour Office, *Transference of Labour in Great Britain* (Montreal, 1942).

Idem, *The War and Women's Employment: The Experience of the United Kingdom and the United States* (Montreal, 1946).

Jennings, Hilda, *Brynmawr: A Study of a Distressed Area* (London, 1934).

Jephcott, A. P., *Girls Growing Up* (London, 1942).

Jones, E. Wyn, *Yr Afiechydon Gwenerol a Dirwest: Rhai Agweddau Meddygol* (Liverpool, 1943).

Jones, Gwyn, *Times Like These* (London, 1936).

Jones, Jack, *Me and Mine* (London, 1946).

Jones, T. Trefor, *Iechyd yng Nghymru* (Liverpool, 1946).

Jones, Thomas, *A Diary with Letters, 1931–1950* (Oxford, 1954).

Katin, Zelma, *'Clippie': The Autobiography of a War Time Conductress* (London, 1944).

Labour Party, *South Wales: Report of Labour Party's Commission of Enquiry into the Distressed Areas* (London, 1937).

Labour Research Department, *Women in War Jobs* (London, 1942).

Idem, *A Complete Guide to the Call Up of Women* (London, [c.1943]).

Laird, Sydney M., *Venereal Disease in Britain* (Harmondsworth, 1943).

Lewis, E. D., *The Rhondda Valleys* (London, 1959).

Marquand, H. A., *South Wales Needs a Plan* (London, 1936).

Mass-Observation, *People in Production: An Enquiry into British War Production* (London, 1942).

Idem, *War Factory*, 1st edn 1943 (London, 1987).

Idem, *The Journey Home* (London, 1944).

Massey, Philip, *Industrial South Wales: A Social and Political Survey* (London, 1940).

Meara, Gwynne, *Unemployment in Merthyr Tydfil: A Survey made at the request of the Merthyr Settlement* (Newtown, [c.1933]).

Idem, *Juvenile Unemployment in South Wales* (Cardiff, 1936).

Ministry of Health, *Reports on Public Health and Medical Subjects*, no. 86, E. Lewis-Faning, 'A study of the trend of mortality rates in urban communities of England and Wales, with special reference to "Depressed Areas"' (London, 1938).

Ministry of Information, *British Women at War* (London, 1944).

Ministry of Labour, *Annual Reports on the Work of (Local) Advisory Committees for Juvenile Employment* (London, 1926–38).

Idem, *Local Unemployment Index* (London, 1931–9).

Morton, H. V., *In Search of Wales* (London, 1932).

National Industrial Development Council of Wales and Monmouthshire, *Wales and Monmouthshire: An Illustrated Review of the Industries and Tourist Attractions of the Principality* (Cardiff, 1948/9).

Newsom, John, *The Education of Girls* (London, 1948).

Office of the Minister of Reconstruction, *Welsh Reconstruction Advisory Council – First Interim Report* (London, 1944).

Padley, Richard, and Cole, Margaret (eds.), *Evacuation Survey: A Report to the Fabian Society* (London, 1940).

Parker, H. M. D., *Manpower: A Study of War-Time Policy and Administration* (London, 1957).

The People's Convention, 'What a war factory is really like', *Women Want 'Square Deal'* (1941).

The Pilgrim Trust, *Interim Reports of Unemployment Inquiry*, nos. III–IV (London, 1937).

Idem, *Men Without Work* (Cambridge, 1938).

Plaid Genedlaethol Cymru, *Gorfodaeth Filwrol ar Ferched Cymru* (Caernarfon, 1945).

Political and Economic Planning [PEP], Broadsheet no. 94, *The Problem of South Wales*, 9 March 1937.

Idem, *Report on the Location of Industry* (London, 1939).

Idem, *Manpower: A Series of Studies of the Composition and Distribution of Britain's Labour-Force* (London, 1951).

Postan, M. M., *British War Production* (London, 1952).

Priestley, J. B., *British Women Go to War* (London, 1943).

Rooff, Madeline, *Youth and Leisure: A Survey of Girls' Organisations in England and Wales* (Edinburgh,1935).

Royal Commission on Licensing (England and Wales), *Minutes of Evidence, 16th Public Session, 21 January 1930* (London, 1930).

Salway, C. C., *Refugees and Industry* (London, 1942).

Samuel, Wynne, *Transference Must Stop* (Caernarfon, 1943).

Scott, George Ryley, *Sex Problems and Dangers in War-Time: A Book of Practical Advice for Men and Women on the Fighting and Home Fronts* (London, 1940).

Scott, Peggy, *British Women in War* (London, 1940).

Second Industrial Survey of South Wales (3 vols., Cardiff, 1937).

The Second Interim Report of the General Committee on Women's Training and Employment for the period ending 31st December 1922 (London, 1923).

South Wales and Monmouthshire Council of Social Service, *3rd Annual Report, 1936–37: Life in South Wales Today* (Cardiff, 1937).

Spring-Rice, Margery, *Working Class Wives: Their Health and Conditions* (Harmondsworth, 1939).

Summerskill, Dr Edith, *Women Fall In: A Guide to Women's Work in War-Time* (London, 1941).

Trades Union Congress, *National Women's Advisory Council Minutes, 1939–45* (Harvester Microfilms).

Idem, *Workmen's Compensation and Factories Committee Minutes, 1940–43* (Harvester Microfilms).

The War Effort at the Curran Works, Cardiff (Cardiff, 1945).

Watkins, Percy, *Educational Settlements in South Wales and Monmouthshire* (Cardiff, 1940).

Williams, D. J., *Storïau'r Tir Du* (Aberystwyth, 1949).

Williams, Gertrude, *The Price of Social Security* (London, 1944).

Eadem, *Women and Work* (London, 1945).

Williams-Ellis, Amabel, *Women in War Factories* (London, 1943).

Wilson, Harold, *New Deal for Coal* (London, 1945).

Wyatt, S., et al., *A Study of Certified Sickness Absence among Women in Industry*, MRC Industrial Health Research Board Report no. 86 (London, 1945).

Idem, *A Study of Women on War Work in Four Factories*, MRC Industrial Health Research Board Report no. 88 (London, 1945).

Zweig, Ferdynand, *Men in the Pits* (London, 1949).

(b) Articles and Essays

Beacham, A., 'The future of the South Wales Coalfield', *The Welsh Review*, V, no. 2 (1946), 138–44.

Coombe-Tennant JP, Mrs, 'The adolescent and the home', *The Welsh Outlook*, XV, no. 9 (1928), 278–9.

Daniel, Goronwy H., 'Labour migration and age-composition', *Sociological Review*, XXXI, no. 3 (1939), 281–308.

Davies, W. Morgan, 'Pride of race', in Davies Aberpennar (ed.), *'Look You': A Miscellany Concerning Wales* (Caernarfon, 1948), pp. 5–8.

Dunning, J. H., 'Employment for women in the Development Areas 1939/51', *Manchester School of Economic and Social Studies*, XXI, no. 3 (1953), 271–7.

Galloway, R. M., 'The function of nurseries in peace-time', *Journal of the Royal Sanitary Institute*, LXIV, no. 4 (1944), 183–4.

Hutchinson, Isobel Wylie, 'Wales in wartime', *National Geographic Magazine*, LXXXV (1944), 751–68.

James, E., 'Women at work in twentieth century Britain', *Manchester School of Economic and Social Studies*, XXX (1960), 283–99.

Jones, Eirene Lloyd, 'The work of the Central Committee on Women's Training', in Welsh School of Social Service (ed.), *Wales and the New Leisure* (Llandysul, 1935), pp. 22–3.

Jones, Gwenan, 'Benywaeth – gwir a gau', *Yr Efrydydd*, II, no. 3 (1942), 14–18.

Eadem, 'Purdeb – gwir a gau', *Yr Efrydydd*, IX, no. 5 (1944), 13–18.

Jones, W. Idris, 'The future pattern of Welsh industry', *The Welsh Review*, V, no. 3 (1946), 208–16.

Leser, C. E. V., 'Men and women in industry', *Economic Journal*, LXII (1952), 326–44.

Massey, Philip, 'Portrait of a mining town', *Fact*, no. 8 (1937), 7–78.

Morgan, Dennis H., 'The changing face of south Wales', *Wales*, VII, no. 27 (1947), 364–75.

Owen, E. C., 'Domestic Training Schemes for unemployed women and girls', *Cambria*, no. 3 (1930), 38.

Portal, Lord, 'The industrial future of south Wales', *Transactions of the Honourable Society of Cymmrodorion* (1938), 19–32.

Simon, Shena D., 'Married women and munition making', *Industrial Welfare and Personnel Management*, XXII (1940), 356–7.

Williams, Idris, 'The sleepers awake', in Davies Aberpennar (ed.), *'Look You': A Miscellany Concerning Wales* (Caernarfon, 1948), pp. 14–17.

Wright, Ada L., 'Clubs and centres for women', in Welsh School of Social Service (ed.), *Wales and the New Leisure* (Llandysul, 1935), pp. 54–5.

6. SECONDARY WORKS

(a) Books and Pamphlets

Aaron, Jane et al. (eds.), *Our Sisters' Land: The Changing Identities of Women in Wales* (Cardiff, 1994).

Addison, Paul, *Now the War is Over: A Social History of Britain, 1945–51* (London, 1995 edn).

Arnot, R. Page, *The Miners in Crisis and War* (London, 1961).

Beddoe, Deirdre, *Back to Home and Duty: Women between the Wars, 1918–1939* (London, 1989).

Eadem, *Out of the Shadows: A History of Women in Twentieth-Century Wales* (Cardiff, 2000).

Berry, David, *Wales and Cinema: The First Hundred Years* (Cardiff, 1994).

Boston, Sarah, *Women Workers and the Trade Union Movement* (London, 1980).

Bourke, Joanna, *Working-Class Cultures in Britain, 1890–1960: Gender, Class and Ethnicity* (London, 1994).

Braybon, Gail, and Summerfield, Penny, *Out of the Cage: Women's Experiences in Two World Wars* (London, 1987).

Calder, Angus, *The People's War: Britain, 1939–1945* (London, 1992 edn).

Cartwell, J. D., *Images of War: British Posters, 1939–45* (London, 1989).

Cooke, Miriam, and Woollacott, Angela (eds.), *Gendering War Talk* (Princeton, 1993).

Costello, John, *Love, Sex and War: Changing Values, 1939–45* (London, 1985).

Damousi, Joy, and Lake, Marilyn (eds.), *Gender and War: Australians at War in the Twentieth Century* (Cambridge, 1995).

Davies, Andrew, *Leisure, Gender and Poverty: Working-Class Culture in Salford and Manchester, 1900–1939* (Buckingham, 1992).

Davies, John, *A History of Wales* (London, 1993).

Davies, Mark (ed.), *The Valleys Autobiography: A People's History of the Garw, Llynfi and Ogmore Valleys* (Blaengarw, 1992).

Davies, Rhys, *Print of a Hare's Foot* (London, 1969).

Francis, Hywel, and Smith, David, *The Fed: A History of the South Wales Miners in the Twentieth Century* (London, 1980).

Gallie, Menna, *The Small Mine* (London, 1962).

Gardiner, Juliet, *'Over Here': The G.I.'s in Wartime Britain* (London, 1992).

Garside, W. R., *The Measurement of Unemployment: Methods and Sources in Great Britain, 1850–1979* (Oxford, 1980).

Gittins, Diana, *Fair Sex: Family Size and Structure, 1900–39* (London, 1982).

Glucksmann, Miriam, *Women Assemble: Women Workers and the New Industries in Inter-War Britain* (London, 1990).

Grenfell-Hill, Jeffrey (ed.), *Growing Up in Wales: Collected Memories of Childhood in Wales, 1895–1939* (Llandysul, 1996).

Griffiths, Winifred, *One Woman's Story* (Rhondda, 1979).

Hartley, Jenny, *Millions Like Us: British Women's Fiction of the Second World War* (London, 1997).

Haste, Cate, *Rules of Desire: Sex in Britain, World War I to the Present* (London, 1992).

Hayes, Nick, and Hill, Jeff (eds.), *'Millions Like Us'? British Culture in the Second World War* (Liverpool, 1999).

Higonnet, Margaret Randolph et al. (eds.), *Behind the Lines: Gender and the Two World Wars* (New Haven, 1987).

Humphrys, Graham, *Industrial Britain – South Wales* (Newton Abbot, 1972).

John, Angela V. (ed.), *Our Mothers' Land: Chapters in Welsh Women's History, 1830–1939* (Cardiff, 1991).

Jones, Bill, and Thomas, Beth, *Teyrnas y Glo: Golwg Hanesyddol ar Fywyd ym Meysydd Glo Cymru / Coal's Domain: Historical Glimpses of Life in the Welsh Coalfields* (Cardiff, 1993).

Jones, David J. V., *Crime and Policing in the Twentieth Century: The South Wales Experience* (Cardiff, 1996).

Jones, Maggie Pryce, *Kingfisher of Hope* (Llandysul, 1993).

Jones, R. Gerallt, *A Bid for Unity: The Story of Undeb Cymru Fydd, 1941–1966* (Aberystwyth, 1971).

Jones, R. Merfyn, *Cymru 2000: Hanes Cymru yn yr Ugeinfed Ganrif* (Caerdydd, 1999).

Klein, Yvonne M. (ed.), *Beyond the Home Front: Women's Autobiographical Writing of the Two World Wars* (Basingstoke, 1997).

Lee, Jennie, *This Great Journey: A Volume of Autobiography, 1904–45* (London, 1963).

Lewis, Jane, *Women in England, 1870–1950: Sexual Divisions and Social Change* (Hemel Hempstead, 1984).

Eadem, *Women in Britain since 1945: Women, Family, Work and the State in the Post-War Years* (Oxford, 1992).

Lieven, Michael, *Senghennydd. The Universal Pit Village, 1890–1930* (Llandysul, 1994).

Liverpool City Council, *Liverpool Women at War: An Anthology of Personal Memories* (Liverpool, 1991).

Llwyd, Alan, and Edwards, Elwyn (eds.), *Gwaedd y Lleiddiad* (Llandybïe, 1995).

Longmate, Norman, *How We Lived Then: A History of Everyday Life during the Second World War* (London, 1971).

Marwick, Arthur, *War and Social Change in the Twentieth Century: A Comparative Study of Britain, France, Germany, Russia and the United States* (London, 1974).

Minns, Raynes, *Bombers and Mash: The Domestic Front, 1939–45* (London, 1980).

Morgan, Kenneth O., *Rebirth of a Nation: Wales, 1880–1980* (Oxford, 1982 edn).

Mullins, Samuel, and Griffiths, Gareth, *Cap and Apron: An Oral History of Domestic Service in the Shires, 1880–1950* (Leicestershire Museums, 1986).

Naylor, Barrie, *Quakers in the Rhondda, 1926–1986* (Brockweir, Chepstow, 1986).

Nicholson, Mavis, *What Did You Do in the War, Mummy? Women in World War II* (London, 1995).

Pahl, R. E. (ed.), *On Work: Historical, Comparative and Theoretical Approaches* (Oxford, 1988).

Pierson, Ruth Roach, *'They're Still Women After All': The Second World War and Canadian Womanhood* (Toronto, 1986).

Pritchard, Katie Olwen, *Y Glas a'r Coch (Darlith Flynyddol Llyfrgell Penygroes, 1980/81)* (Cyngor Sir Gwynedd, 1981).

Reynolds, David, *Rich Relations: The American Occupation of Britain, 1942–1945* (London, 1995).

Roberts, Elizabeth, *A Woman's Place: An Oral History of Working-Class Women, 1890–1940* (Oxford, 1995 edn).

Eadem, *Women and Families: An Oral History, 1940–1970* (Oxford, 1995).

Rosser, Colin, and Harris, Christopher, *The Family and Social Change: A Study of Family and Kinship in a South Wales Town* (London, 1965).

Samuel, Raphael, and Thompson, Paul (eds.), *The Myths We Live By* (London, 1990).

Schweitzer Pam et al. (eds.), *What Did you Do in the War, Mum?* (London, 1985).

Sheridan, Dorothy (ed.), *Wartime Women: A Mass-Observation Anthology* (London, 1990).

Smith, Dai, *Wales! Wales?* (London, 1984).

Smith, Harold L. (ed.), *Britain in the Second World War* (Manchester, 1996).

Soldon, Norbert C., *Women in British Trade Unions, 1874–1976* (Dublin, 1978).

Summerfield, Penny, *Women Workers in the Second World War: Production and Patriarchy in Conflict* (London, 1989 edn).

Eadem, *'My Dress for an Army Uniform': Gender Instabilities in the Two World Wars* (Leicester, 1997).

Eadem, *Reconstructing Women's Wartime Lives: Discourse and Subjectivity in Oral Histories of the Second World War* (Manchester, 1998).

Swain, Fay, *Wales and the Second World War: Women* (Bridgend, 1989).

Tapper, Philip, and Hawthorne, Susan, *Wales and the Second World War* (Bridgend, 1991).

Thomas, Brinley (ed.), *The Welsh Economy: Studies in Expansion* (Cardiff, 1962).

Tibbott, S. Minwel, and Thomas, Beth, *O'r Gwaith i'r Gwely: Cadw Tŷ, 1890–1960/A Woman's Work: Housework, 1890–1960* (Cardiff, 1994).

Treanor, Dei et al. (eds.), *Green, Black and Back: The Story of Blaenllechau* (Treorchy, 1994).

Undeb Cymru Fydd, *Undeb Cymru Fydd, 1939–1960* (Aberystwyth, 1960).

Verrill-Rhys, Leigh, and Beddoe, Deirdre (eds.), *Parachutes and Petticoats: Welsh Women Writing on the Second World War* (Dinas Powys, 1992).

Webb, Rachael Ann, *Sirens Over the Valley* (Port Talbot, 1988).

White, Carol, and Williams, Sian Rhiannon (eds.), *Struggle or Starve: Women's Lives in the South Wales Valleys between the Two World Wars* (Dinas Powys, 1998).

White, Cynthia L., *The Women's Periodical Press in Britain, 1946–1976* (London, 1977).

Wightman, Clare, *More than Munitions: Women, Work and the Engineering Industries, 1900–1950* (London, 1999).

Williams, Chris, *Democratic Rhondda: Politics and Society, 1885–1951* (Cardiff, 1996).

Williams, D. Glyn (Foreword and Commentaries), *Old Bridgend in Photographs* (Barry, 1978).

Williams, Gwyn A., *When Was Wales? A History of the Welsh* (Harmondsworth, 1985).

Williams, J. Ronald, and Williams, Gwyneth, *History of Caersalem, Dowlais, Welsh Baptist Church* (Llandysul, 1967).

Williams, John, *Digest of Welsh Historical Statistics* (2 vols., Cardiff, 1985).

Wise, Nancy Baker, *A Mouthful of Rivets: Women at Work in World War II* (San Francisco, 1994).

Woollacott, Angela, *On Her Their Lives Depend: Munitions Workers in the Great War* (London, 1994).

(b) Articles and Essays

Allen, Margaret, 'The domestic ideal and the mobilization of womanpower in World War II', *Women's Studies International Forum*, 6, no. 4 (1983), 401–12.

Baber, Colin, and Dessant, Jeffrey, 'Modern Glamorgan: economic development after 1945', in A. H. John and Glanmor Williams (eds.), *Glamorgan County History, Volume V. Industrial Glamorgan, 1700–1970* (Cardiff, 1980), pp. 581–658.

Baber, Colin, and Thomas, Dennis, 'The Glamorgan economy, 1914–45', in A. H. John and Glanmor Williams (eds.), *Glamorgan County History, Volume V. Industrial Glamorgan, 1700–1970* (Cardiff, 1980), pp. 519–79.

Beddoe, Deirdre, 'Images of Welsh women', in Tony Curtis (ed.), *Wales: The Imagined Nation* (Bridgend, 1986), pp. 227–38.

Eadem, 'Women between the wars', in Trevor Herbert and Gareth Elwyn Jones (eds.), *Wales between the Wars* (Cardiff, 1988), pp. 128–60.

Eadem, 'Munitionettes, maids and mams: women in Wales, 1914–1939', in Angela V. John (ed.), *Our Mothers' Land: Chapters in Welsh Women's History, 1830–1939* (Cardiff, 1991), pp. 189–209.

Bianchi, Diana, 'The creation of a myth: the Welsh Mam', *Radical Wales*, no. 17 (1988), 11–13.

Broomfield, Stuart, 'The apprentice boys' strikes of the Second World War', *Llafur*, 3, no. 2 (1981), 53–67.

Burge, Alun, 'A "subtle danger"? The voluntary sector and coalfield society in south Wales, 1926–1939', *Llafur*, 7, nos. 3 and 4 (1998–9), 127–41.

Carruthers, Susan L., ' "Manning the factories": propaganda and policy on the employment of women, 1939–1947', *History*, 75, no. 244 (1990), 232–56.

Chandler, Andy, 'The Black Death on wheels: unemployment and migration – the experience of inter-war south Wales', *Papers in Modern Welsh History 1* [1982], 1–15.

Crofts, William, 'The Attlee government's pursuit of women', *History Today* (1986), 29–35.

Crook, Rosemary, ' "Tidy women": women in the Rhondda between the wars', *Oral History*, 10, no. 12 (1982), 40–6.

Davies, Gareth Alban, 'The fur coat', in Meic Stephens (ed.), *A Rhondda Anthology* (Bridgend, 1993), pp. 150–7.

Drinkwater, Stephen, 'The Welsh economy: a statistical profile', *Contemporary Wales*, 10 (1997), 219–41.

Elliott, Jane, 'The Welsh Mam', in Rob Humphreys and Anna-Marie Taylor (eds.), *Opening up 'The Keep' by Gwyn Thomas* (Swansea, 1996), pp. 41–4.

England, J. W., 'The Merthyr of the twentieth century: a postscript', in Glanmor Williams (ed.), *Merthyr Politics: The Making of a Working-Class Tradition* (Cardiff, 1966), pp. 82–101.

Evans, Neil, and Jones, Dot, ' "A blessing for the miner's wife": the campaign for pithead baths in the South Wales Coalfield, 1908–1950', *Llafur*, 6, no. 3 (1994), 5–28.

Idem, ' "To help forward the great work of humanity": women in the Labour Party', in Duncan Tanner et al. (eds.), *The Labour Party in Wales, 1900–2000* (Cardiff, 2000), pp. 215–40.

Ferguson, Neal A., 'Women's work: employment opportunities and economic roles, 1918–1939', *Albion*, 7, no. 1 (1975), 55–68.

Finch, Janet, and Summerfield, Penny, 'Social reconstruction and the emergence of companionate marriage,1945–59', in David Clark (ed.), *Marriage, Domestic Life and Social Change* (London, 1991), pp. 7–32.

Glaser, Anthony, 'Jewish refugees and Jewish refugee industries', in Ursula R. Q. Henriques (ed.), *The Jews of South Wales: Historical Studies* (Cardiff, 1993), pp. 177–205.

Glucksmann, Miriam, 'In a class of their own? Women workers in the new industries in inter-war Britain', *Feminist Review*, no. 24 (1986), 7–37.

Goode, Graham, and Delamont, Sara, 'Opportunity denied: the voices of the lost grammar school girls of the inter-war years', in Sandra Betts (ed.), *Our Daughters' Land: Past and Present* (Cardiff, 1996), pp. 103–24.

Harper, Sue, 'The years of total war: propaganda and entertainment', in Christine Gledhill and Gillian Swanson (eds.), *Nationalising Femininity: Culture, Sexuality and British Cinema in the Second World War* (Manchester, 1996), pp. 193–212.

Hill, Bridget, 'Women, work and the census: a problem for historians of women', *History Workshop Journal*, no. 35 (1993), 78–94.

Ineson, Antonia, and Thom, Deborah, 'T.N.T. poisoning and the employment of women workers in the First World War', in Paul Weindling (ed.), *The Social History of Occupational Health* (Beckenham, 1985), pp. 89–107.

John, Angela V., 'A miner struggle? Women's protests in Welsh mining history', *Llafur*, 4, no. 1 (1984), 72–90.

Jones, Dot, 'Serfdom and slavery: women's work in Wales, 1890–1930', in Deian R. Hopkin and Gregory S. Kealey (eds.), *Class, Community and the Labour Movement: Wales and Canada, 1850–1930* (Aberystwyth, 1989), pp. 86–100.

Eadem, 'Counting the cost of coal: women's lives in the Rhondda, 1881–1911', in Angela V. John (ed.), *Our Mothers' Land: Chapters in Welsh Women's History, 1830–1939* (Cardiff, 1991), pp. 109–33.

Jones, Jack, 'Women in adversity', in Patrick Hannan (ed.), *Wales on the Wireless: A Broadcasting Anthology* (Llandysul, 1988), p. 103.

Kirkham, Pat, 'Beauty and duty: keeping up the (home) front', in eadem and David Thoms (eds.), *War Culture: Social Change and Changing Experience in World War Two Britain* (London, 1995), pp. 13–28.

Eadem, 'Fashioning the feminine: dress, appearance and femininity in wartime Britain', in Christine Gledhill and Gillian Swanson (eds.), *Nationalising Femininity: Culture, Sexuality and British Cinema in the Second World War* (Manchester, 1996), pp. 152–74.

Lant, Antonia, 'Prologue: mobile femininity', in Christine Gledhill and Gillian Swanson (eds.), *Nationalising Femininity: Culture, Sexuality and British Cinema in the Second World War* (Manchester, 1996), pp. 13–32.

Levine, Philippa, ' "Walking the streets in a way no decent woman should": women police in World War I', *Journal of Modern History*, 66, no. 1 (1994), 34–78.

Lewis, Jane, 'In search of a real equality: women between the wars', in Frank Gloversmith (ed.), *Class, Culture and Social Change: A New View of the 1930s* (Brighton, 1980), pp. 208–39.

Lieven, Michael, 'Senghenydd and the historiography of the South Wales Coalfield', *Morgannwg*, XLIII (1999), 8–35.

Macey, Bridget, 'Social dynamics of oral history making: women's experiences of wartime', *Oral History*, 19, no. 2 (1991), 42–8.

Michel, Sonya, 'American women and the discourse of the democratic family in World War II', in Margaret Randolph Higonnet et al. (eds.), *Behind the Lines: Gender and the Two World Wars* (New Haven, 1987), pp. 154–67.

Montgomerie, Deborah, 'Reassessing Rosie: World War II, New Zealand women and the iconography of femininity', *Gender and History*, 8, no. 1 (1996), 108–32.

Morgan, Kenneth O., 'Post-war reconstruction in Wales, 1918 and 1945', in Jay Winter (ed.), *The Working Class in Modern British History: Essays in Honour of Henry Pelling* (Cambridge, 1983), pp. 82–98.

Oram, Alison M., 'Serving two masters? The introduction of a marriage bar in teaching in the 1920s', in London Feminist History Group (ed.), *The Sexual Dynamics of History* (London, 1983), pp. 134–48.

Pierson, Ruth Roach, 'Beautiful soul or just warrior: gender and war', *Gender and History*, 1, no. 1 (1989), 77–86.

Eadem, 'Embattled femininity: Canadian womanhood and the Second World War', in T. G. Fraser and Keith Jeffery (eds.), *Men, Women and War* (Dublin, 1993), pp. 195–210.

Pilcher, Jane, 'Who should do the dishes? Three generations of Welsh women talking about men and housework', in Jane Aaron et al. (eds.), *Our Sisters' Land: The Changing Identities of Women in Wales* (Cardiff, 1994), pp. 31–47.

Price, Hilda H., 'Experiences in World War II', *Llafur*, 6, no. 1 (1992), 110–13.

Rees, Teresa L., 'Changing patterns of women's work in Wales: some myths explored', *Contemporary Wales*, 2 (1988), 119–30.

Eadem, 'Women and paid work in Wales', in Jane Aaron et al. (eds.), *Our Sisters' Land: The Changing Identities of Women in Wales* (Cardiff, 1994), pp. 89–106.

Eadem, 'Women in post-war Wales', in Trevor Herbert and Gareth Elwyn Jones (eds.), *Post-War Wales* (Cardiff, 1995), pp. 78–106.

Ridgwell, Stephen, 'South Wales and the cinema in the 1930s', *Welsh History Review*, 17, no. 4 (1995), 590–615.

Riley, Denise, 'War in the nursery', *Feminist Review*, 2 (1979), 82–108.

Eadem, ' "The free mothers": pronatalism and working women in industry at the end of the last war in Britain', *History Workshop Journal*, 11 (1981), 58–118.

Roberts, Brian, 'A mining town in wartime: the fears for the future', *Llafur*, 6, no. 1 (1992), 82–95.

Idem, 'The "budgie train": women and wartime munitions work in a mining valley', *Llafur*, 7, nos. 3 and 4 (1998–9), 143–52.

Rose, Sonya O., 'Girls and GIs: race, sex, and diplomacy in Second World War Britain', *The International History Review*, XIX, no. 1 (1997), 146–60.

Scott, Joan W., 'Rewriting history', in Margaret Randolph Higonnet, Jane Jenson, Sonya Michel and Margaret Collins Weitz (eds.), *Behind the Lines: Gender and the Two World Wars* (New Haven, 1987), pp. 21–30.

Sheridan, Dorothy, 'Ambivalent memories: women and the 1939–45 war in Britain', *Oral History*, 18, no. 1 (1990), 32–40.

Smith, David, 'The future of coalfield history in south Wales', *Morgannwg*, XIX (1975), 57–70.

Smith, Harold (see also Smith, Harold L.), 'The problem of "equal pay for equal work" in Great Britain during World War II', *Journal of Modern History*, 53, no. 4 (1981), 652–72.

Smith, Harold L., 'The womanpower problem in Britain during the Second World War', *Historical Journal*, 27, no. 4 (1984), 925–45.

Idem, 'The effect of the war on the status of women', in idem (ed.), *War and Social Change: British Society in the Second World War* (Manchester, 1986), pp. 208–29.

Stead, Peter, 'The people as stars: feature films as national expression', in Philip M. Taylor (ed.), *Britain and the Cinema in the Second World War* (London, 1988), pp. 62–83.

Street, Ernest, 'Royal Ordnance Factory, Glascoed', *Gwent Local History*, no. 60 (1986), 15–18.

Summerfield, Penelope (see also Summerfield, Penny), 'Women, work and welfare: a study of child care and shopping in Britain in the Second World War', *Journal of Social History*, 17, no. 2 (1983), 249–69.

Summerfield, Penny, 'Women, war and social change: women in Britain in World War II', in Arthur Marwick (ed.), *Total War and Social Change* (London, 1988), pp. 95–118.

Eadem, 'Approaches to women and social change in the Second World War', in Brian Brivati and Harriet Jones (eds.), *What Difference Did the War Make?* (London, 1993), pp. 63–79.

Eadem, 'Women in Britain since 1945: companionate marriage and the double burden', in James Obelkevich and Peter Catterall (eds.), *Understanding Post-war British society* (London, 1994), pp. 58–72.

Eadem, ' "The girl that makes the thing that drills the hole that holds the spring . . .": discourses of women and work in the Second World War', in Christine Gledhill and Gillian Swanson (eds.), *Nationalising Femininity: Culture, Sexuality and British Cinema in the Second World War* (Manchester, 1996), pp. 35–52.

Eadem, 'Gender and war in the twentieth century', *The International History Review*, XIX, no. 1 (1997), 3–15.

Summerfield, Penny, and Crockett, Nicole, ' "You weren't taught that with the welding": lessons in sexuality in the Second World War', *Women's History Review*, 1, no. 3 (1992), 435–54.

Taylor, Pam, 'Daughters and mothers – maids and mistresses: domestic service between the wars', in John Clarke et al. (eds.), *Working-Class Culture: Studies in History and Theory* (London, 1979), pp. 121–39.

Thane, Pat, 'Towards equal opportunities? Women in Britain since 1945', in Terry Gourvish and Alan O'Day (eds.), *Britain since 1945* (London, 1991), pp. 183–208.

Eadem, 'Women since 1945', in Paul Johnson (ed.), *Twentieth-Century Britain: Economic, Social and Cultural Change* (New York, 1994), pp. 392–410.

Thomas, Beth, 'Accounting for language shift in a south Wales mining community', *Cardiff Working Papers in Welsh Linguistics*, no. 5 (1987), 55–100.

Thomas, D. A., 'War and the economy: the south Wales experience', in Colin Baber and L. J. Williams (eds.), *Modern South Wales: Essays in Economic History* (Cardiff, 1986), pp. 251–77.

Williams, Gwyn A., 'Women workers in Wales, 1968–82', *Welsh History Review*, 11, no. 4 (1983), 530–48.

Williams, L. J., and Jones, Dot, 'Women at work in nineteenth century Wales', *Llafur*, 3, no. 3 (1982), 20–32.

Williams, Mari A., 'Yr ymgyrch i "achub y mamau" yng nghymoedd diwydiannol de Cymru, 1918–1939', in Geraint H. Jenkins (ed.), *Cof Cenedl XI: Ysgrifau ar Hanes Cymru* (Llandysul, 1996), pp. 117–46.

Eadem, ' "In the wars": Wales 1914–1945', in Gareth Elwyn Jones and Dai Smith (eds.), *The People of Wales* (Llandysul, 1999), pp. 188–98.

Eadem, 'Aspects of women's working lives in the mining communities of south Wales, c.1891–1939', *Folk Life*, 38 (2000), 56–70.

Winckler, Victoria, 'Women and work in contemporary Wales', *Contemporary Wales*, 1 (1987), 53–71.

Winter, J. M., 'The demographic consequences of the war', in Harold L. Smith (ed.), *War and Social Change: British Society in the Second World War* (Manchester, 1986), pp. 151–78.

Woollacott, Angela, ' "Khaki fever" and its control: gender, class, age and sexual morality on the British homefront in the First World War', *Journal of Contemporary History*, 29, no. 2 (1994), 325–47.

7. UNPUBLISHED THESES

Allen, Margaret, 'Woman's place and World War Two' (MA thesis, University of Essex, 1979).

Armbruster, G. H., 'The social determination of ideologies: being a study of a Welsh mining community' (Ph.D thesis, University of London, 1940).

Broomfield, Stuart R., 'South Wales in the Second World War: the coal industry and its community' (Ph.D. thesis, University of Wales, 1979).

Castree, J. R., 'An economic investigation of industrial estates in Wales' (MA thesis, University of Wales, 1966).

Chandler, Andrew J., 'The re-making of a working class: migration from the South Wales Coalfield to the new industry areas of the Midlands c.1920–1940' (Ph.D. thesis, University of Wales, 1988).

Crook, Rosemary, 'Women in the Rhondda valley between the wars' (MA thesis, University of Leeds, 1980).

Davies, Walter Haydn, 'The influence of recent changes in the social environment on the outlook and habits of individuals, with special reference to mining communities in south Wales' (MA thesis, University of Wales, 1933).

Evans, Gwyn, 'Onllwyn: a sociological study of a south Wales mining community' (MA thesis, University of Wales, 1961).

Gier, Jaclyn J., 'Miners' wives: gender, culture and society in the south Wales coalfields, 1919–1939' (Ph.D. thesis, Northwestern University (US), 1993).

Greenaway, David W., 'The impact of the Second World War on nursery, elementary and secondary education in Glamorgan' (M.Ed. thesis, University of Wales, 1985).

Keane, J. M., 'The impact of unemployment: a study of the social effects of un-employment in a working-class district of Cardiff in the depression years, 1930–1935' (M.Sc. (Econ.) thesis, University of Wales, 1983).

Scadden, Rosemary, ' "Be good sweet maid, and let who will be clever": a study of Welsh girls in domestic service during the inter-war period' (M.Sc. (Econ.) thesis, University of Wales, 1996).

Summerfield, Penny, 'Women workers in the Second World War: a study of the interplay in official policy between the need to mobilise women for war and conventional expectations about their roles at work and at home in the period 1939–45' (D.Phil. thesis, University of Sussex, 1982).

Thomas, Dennis A., 'Recovery in the Special Areas and the effects of the Second World War, with particular reference to south Wales' (M.Sc.Econ. thesis, University of Wales, 1973).

INDEX

UNIVERSITY OF WALES, NEWPORT

LIBRARY
AND
INFORMATION
SERVICES
CAERLEON